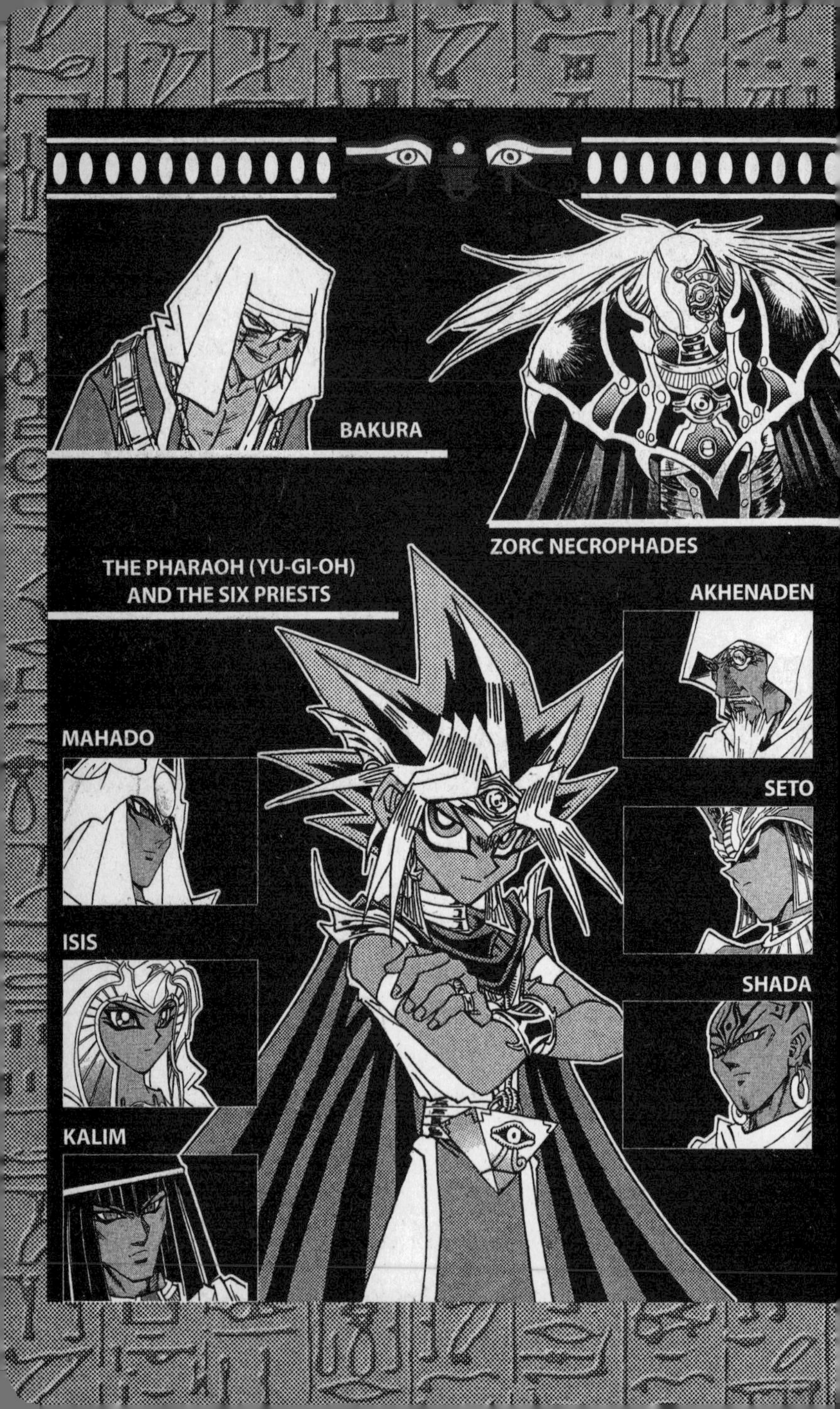
BAKURA
ZORC NECROPHADES
THE PHARAOH (YU-GI-OH)
AND THE SIX PRIESTS
AKHENADEN
MAHADO
SETO
ISIS
SHADA
KALIM

# Yu-Gi-Oh! Millennium World

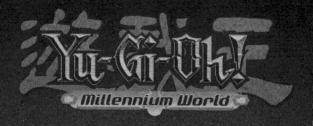

## Vol. 4

CONTENTS

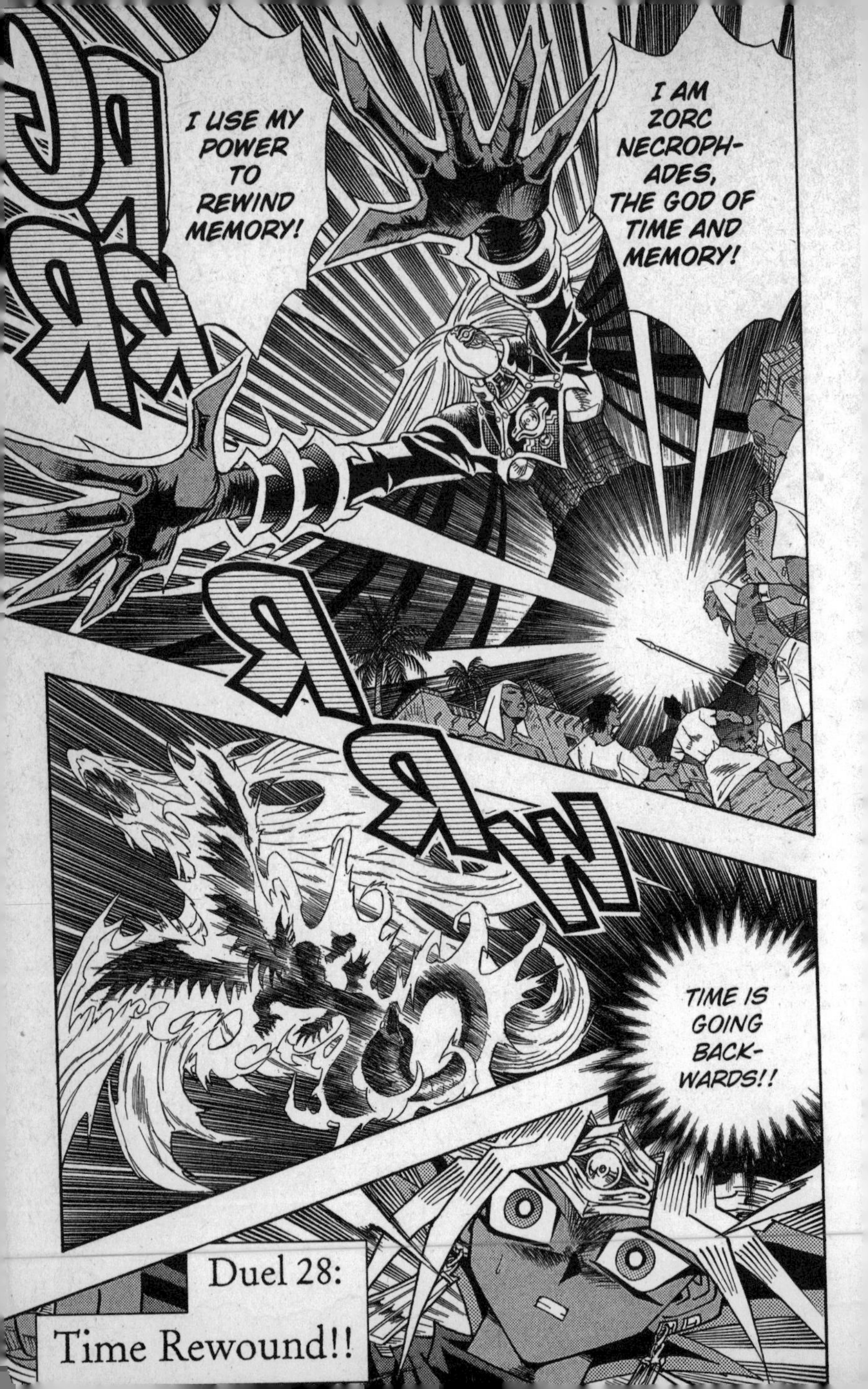
I AM ZORC NECROPH-ADES, THE GOD OF TIME AND MEMORY!
I USE MY POWER TO REWIND MEMORY!
GGRR
RRW
TIME IS GOING BACK-WARDS!!
Duel 28: Time Rewound!!

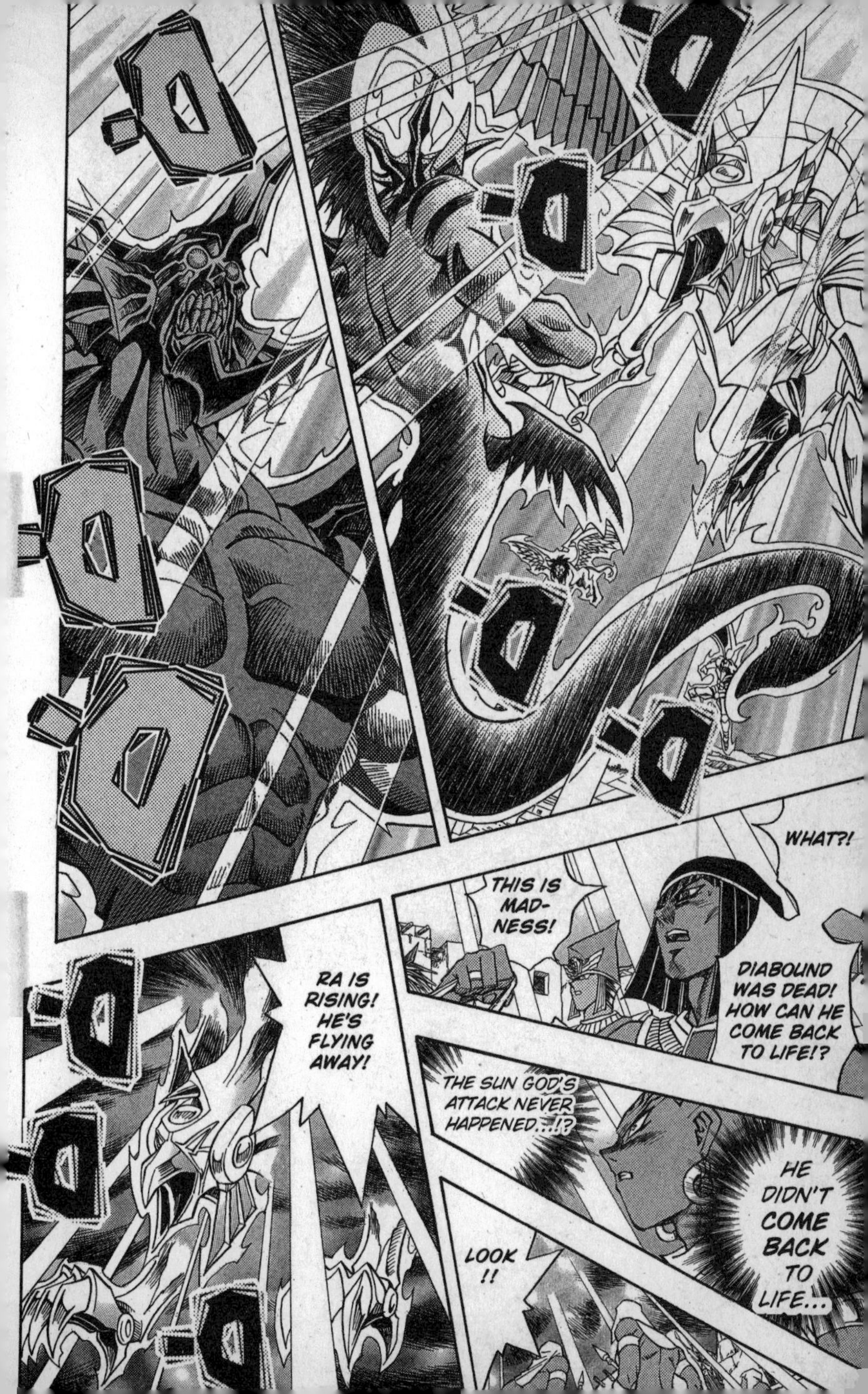
WHAT?!
THIS IS MAD-NESS!
DIABOUND WAS DEAD! HOW CAN HE COME BACK TO LIFE!?
THE SUN GOD'S ATTACK NEVER HAPPENED...!?
HE DIDN'T COME BACK TO LIFE...
LOOK !!
RA IS RISING! HE'S FLYING AWAY!

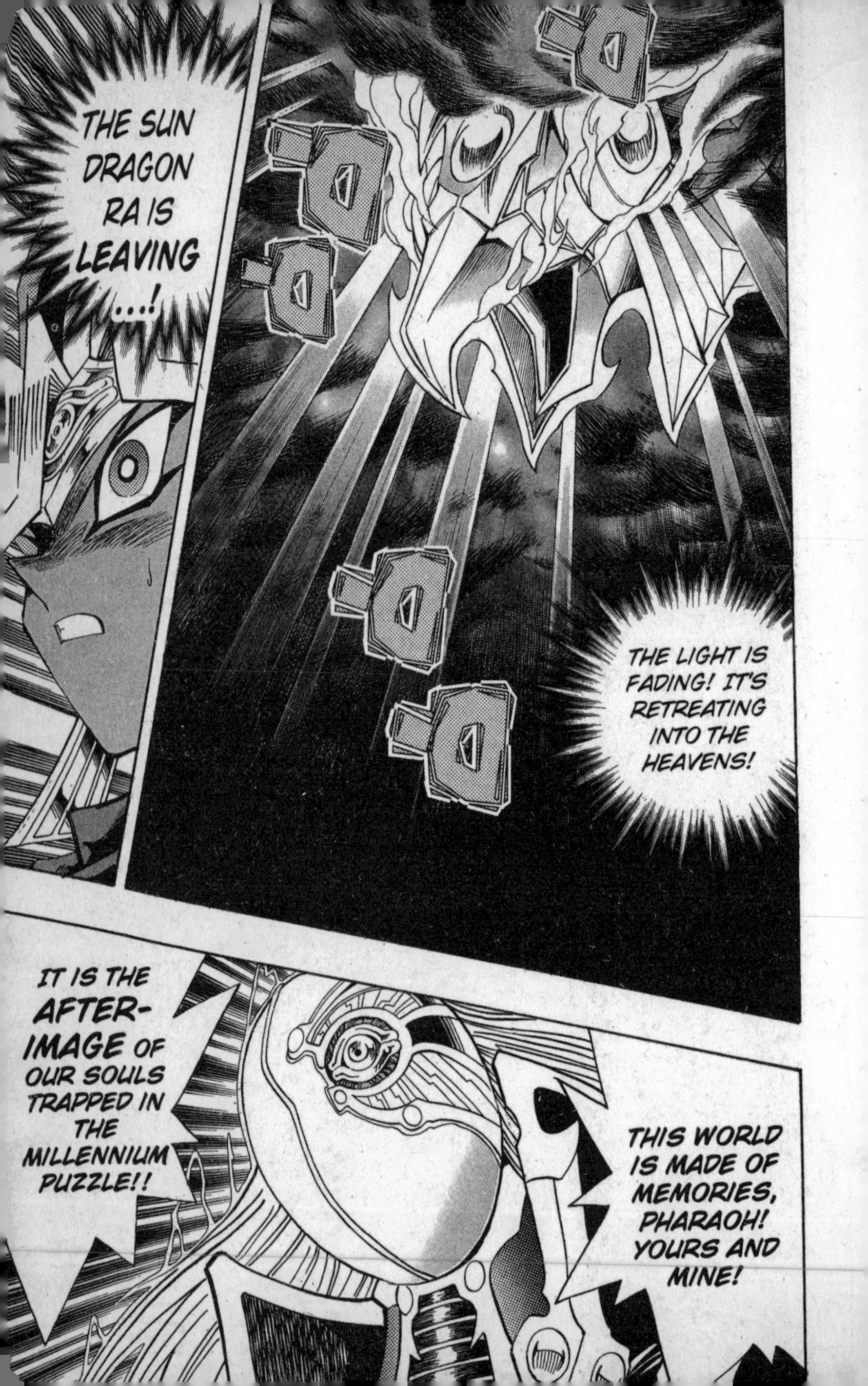
THE LIGHT IS FADING! IT'S RETREATING INTO THE HEAVENS!
THE SUN DRAGON RA IS LEAVING ...!
THIS WORLD IS MADE OF MEMORIES, PHARAOH! YOURS AND MINE!
IT IS THE AFTER-IMAGE OF OUR SOULS TRAPPED IN THE MILLENNIUM PUZZLE!!

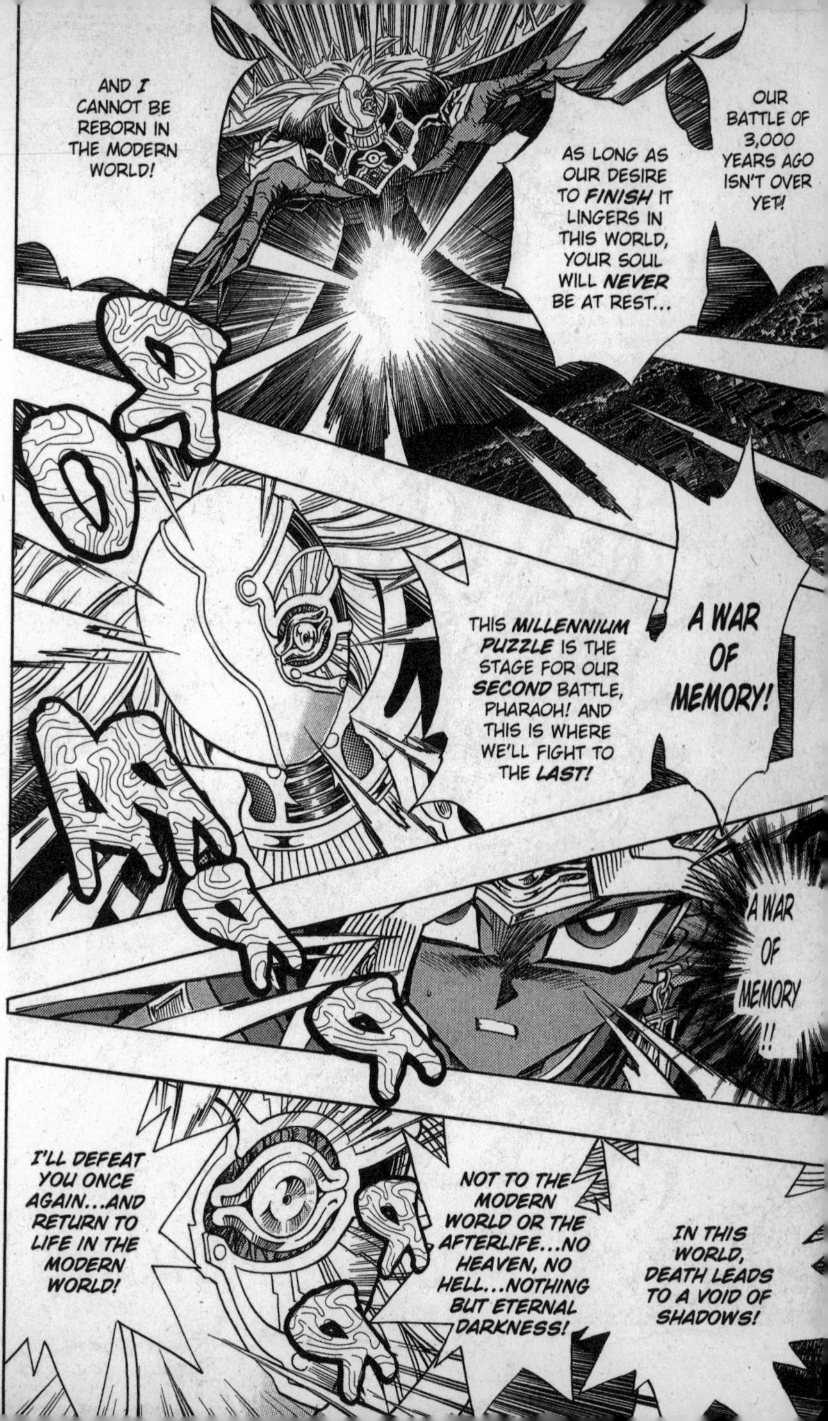
OUR BATTLE OF 3,000 YEARS AGO ISN'T OVER YET!
AS LONG AS OUR DESIRE TO ***FINISH*** IT LINGERS IN THIS WORLD, YOUR SOUL WILL ***NEVER*** BE AT REST...
AND *I* CANNOT BE REBORN IN THE MODERN WORLD!
A WAR OF MEMORY!
THIS ***MILLENNIUM PUZZLE*** IS THE STAGE FOR OUR ***SECOND*** BATTLE, PHARAOH! AND THIS IS WHERE WE'LL FIGHT TO THE ***LAST!***
A WAR OF MEMORY!!
IN THIS WORLD, DEATH LEADS TO A VOID OF SHADOWS!
NOT TO THE MODERN WORLD OR THE AFTERLIFE...NO HEAVEN, NO HELL...NOTHING BUT ETERNAL DARKNESS!
I'LL DEFEAT YOU ONCE AGAIN...AND RETURN TO LIFE IN THE MODERN WORLD!

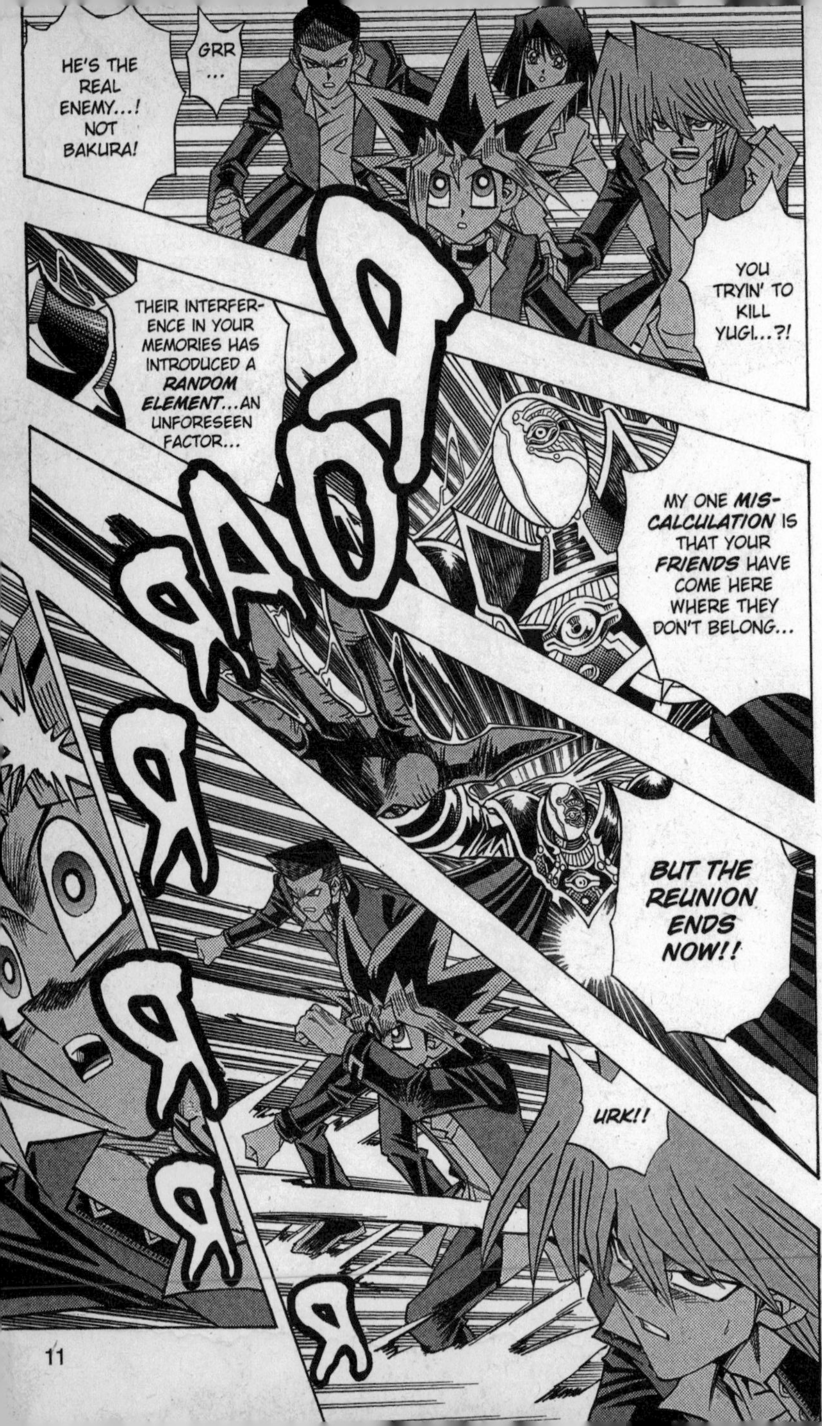
YOU TRYIN' TO KILL YUGI...?!
GRR ...
HE'S THE REAL ENEMY...! NOT BAKURA!
MY ONE **MIS-CALCULATION** IS THAT YOUR **FRIENDS** HAVE COME HERE WHERE THEY DON'T BELONG...
THEIR INTERFERENCE IN YOUR MEMORIES HAS INTRODUCED A ***RANDOM ELEMENT***...AN UNFORESEEN FACTOR...
ROAR
RRRR
***BUT THE REUNION ENDS NOW!!***
*URK!!*

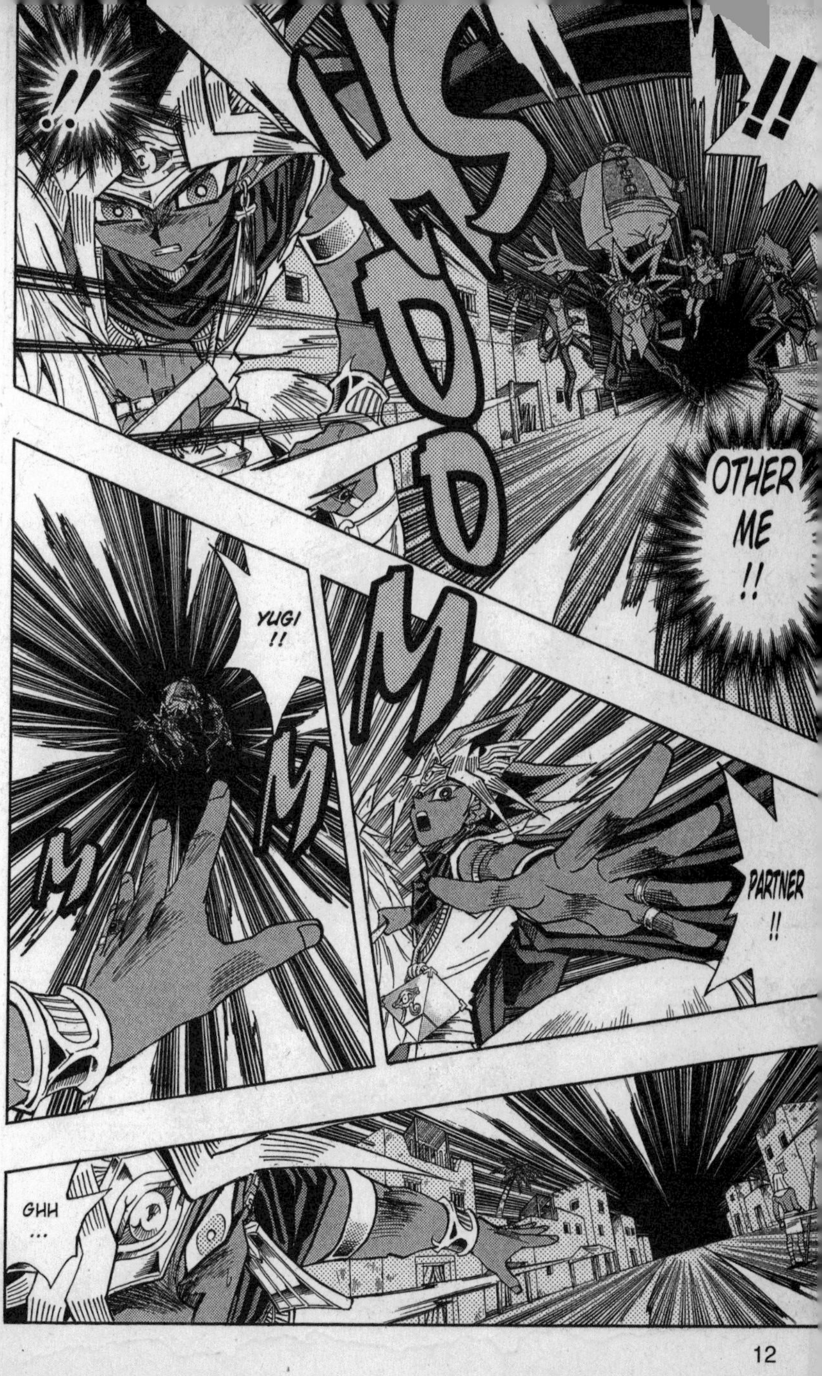
OTHER ME !!
!!
PARTNER !!
YUGI !!
GHH ...

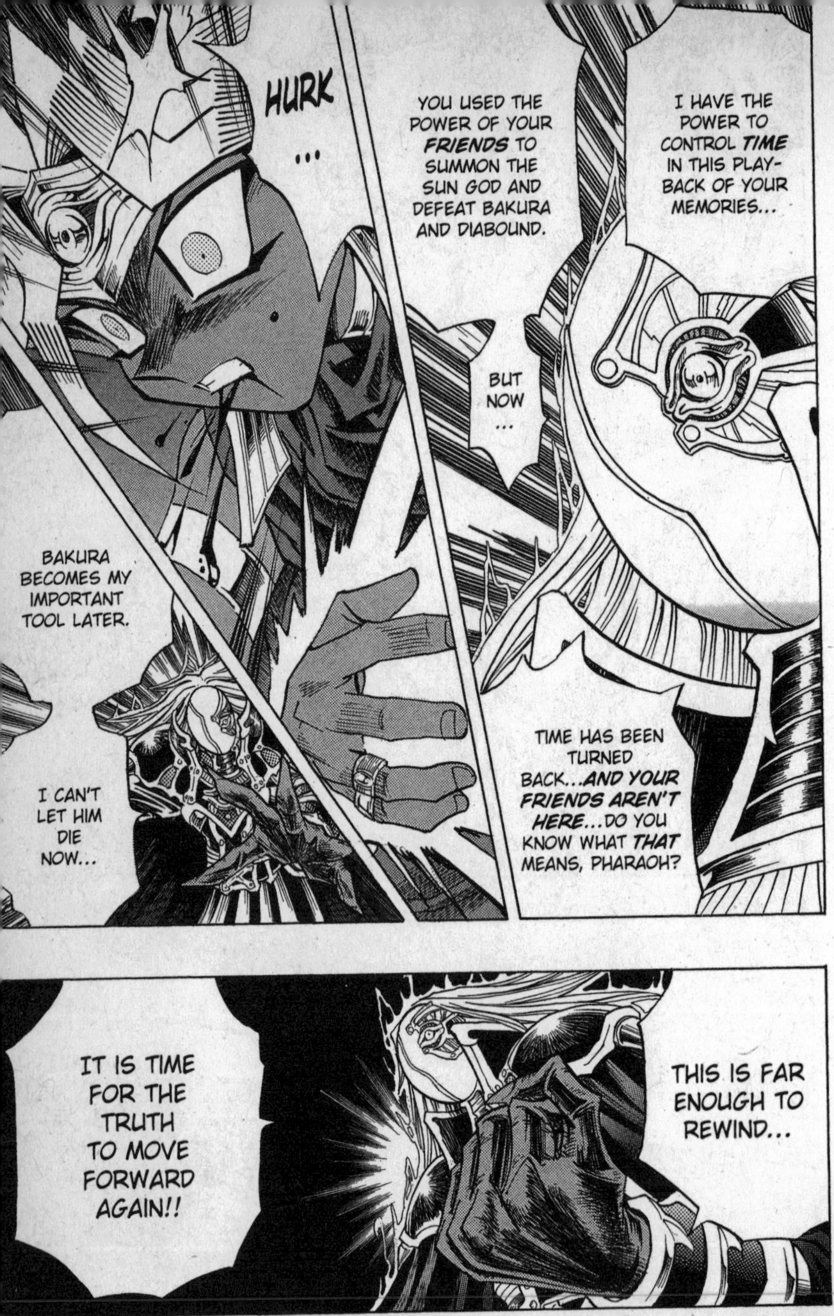
I HAVE THE POWER TO CONTROL *TIME* IN THIS PLAY-BACK OF YOUR MEMORIES...
YOU USED THE POWER OF YOUR *FRIENDS* TO SUMMON THE SUN GOD AND DEFEAT BAKURA AND DIABOUND.
BUT NOW ...
TIME HAS BEEN TURNED BACK...*AND YOUR FRIENDS AREN'T HERE*...DO YOU KNOW WHAT *THAT* MEANS, PHARAOH?
HURK
...
BAKURA BECOMES MY IMPORTANT TOOL LATER.
I CAN'T LET HIM DIE NOW...
THIS IS FAR ENOUGH TO REWIND...
IT IS TIME FOR THE TRUTH TO MOVE FORWARD AGAIN!!

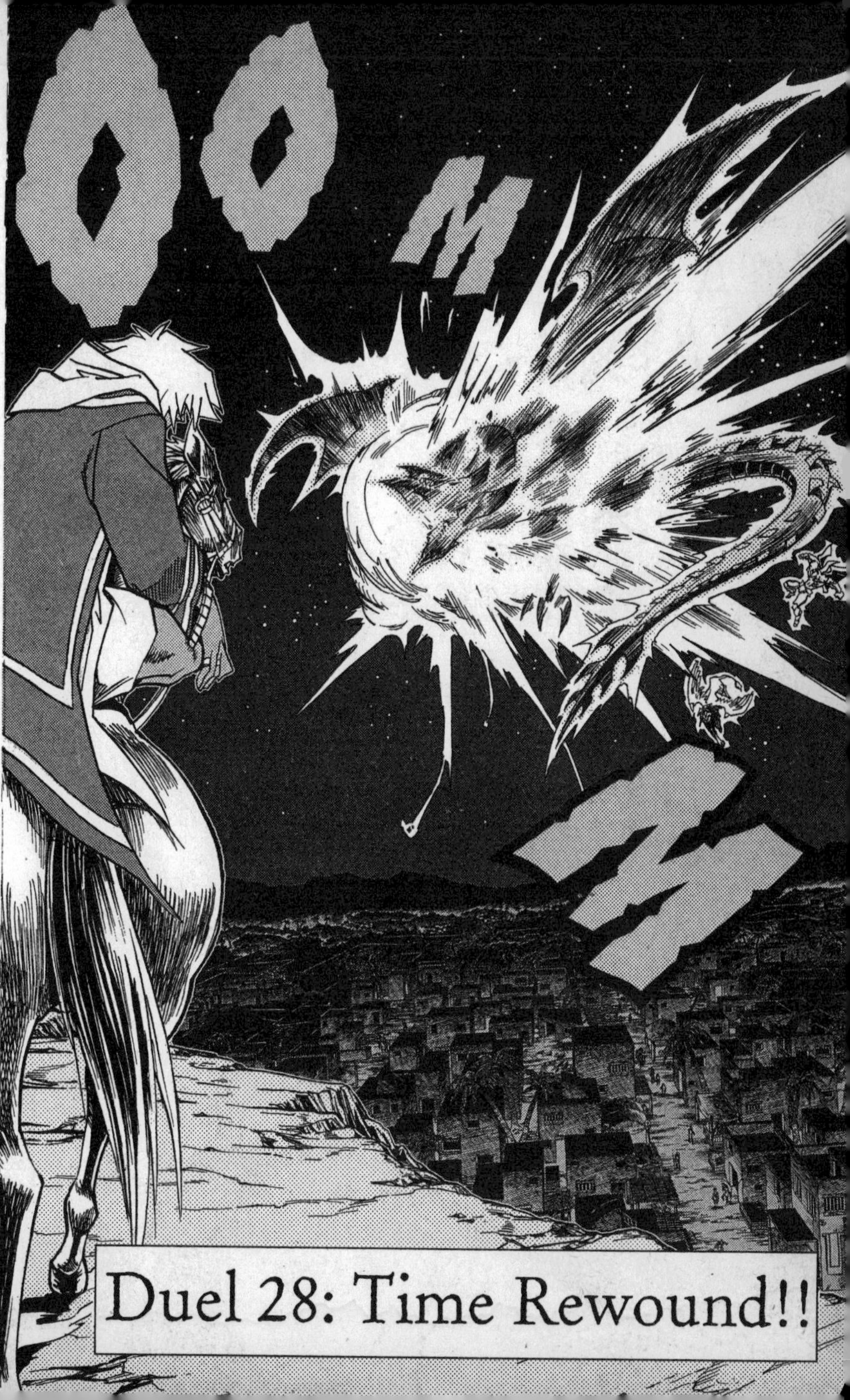
OOM
M
Duel 28: Time Rewound!!

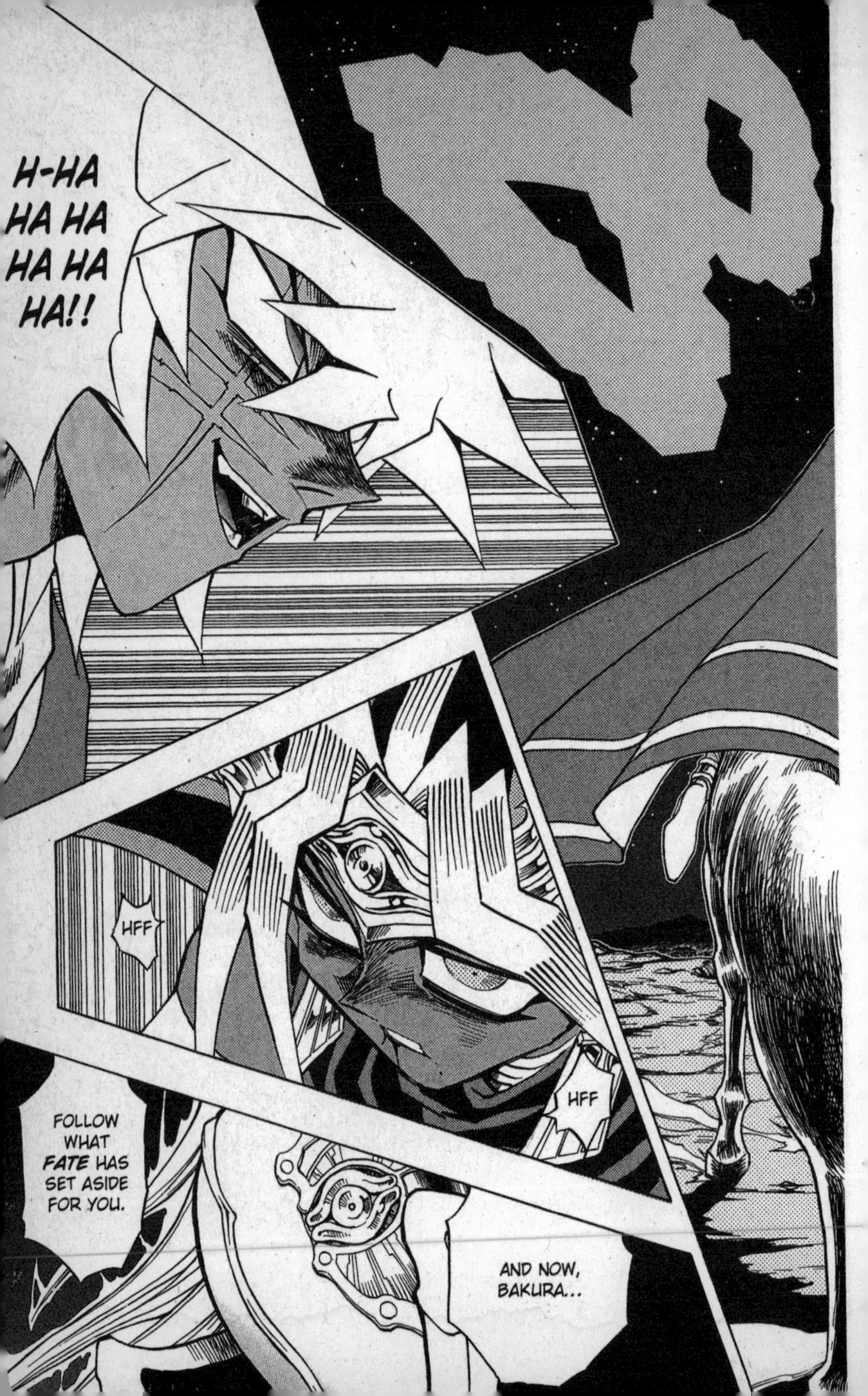
H-HA HA HA HA HA HA!!
HFF
HFF
AND NOW, BAKURA...
FOLLOW WHAT FATE HAS SET ASIDE FOR YOU.

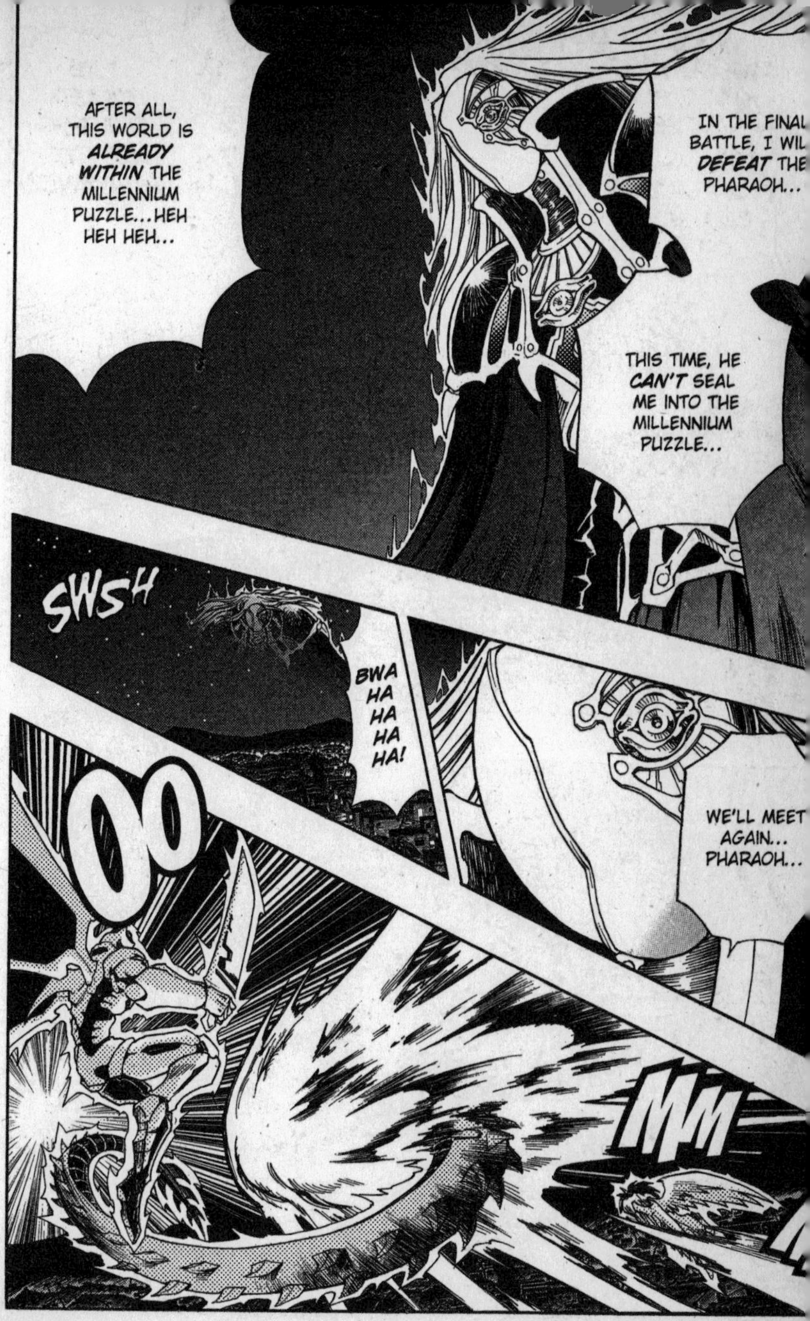
IN THE FINAL BATTLE, I WIL DEFEAT THE PHARAOH...
THIS TIME, HE CAN'T SEAL ME INTO THE MILLENNIUM PUZZLE...
AFTER ALL, THIS WORLD IS ALREADY WITHIN THE MILLENNIUM PUZZLE...HEH HEH HEH...
WE'LL MEET AGAIN... PHARAOH...
BWA HA HA HA HA!
SWSH
OO
MM

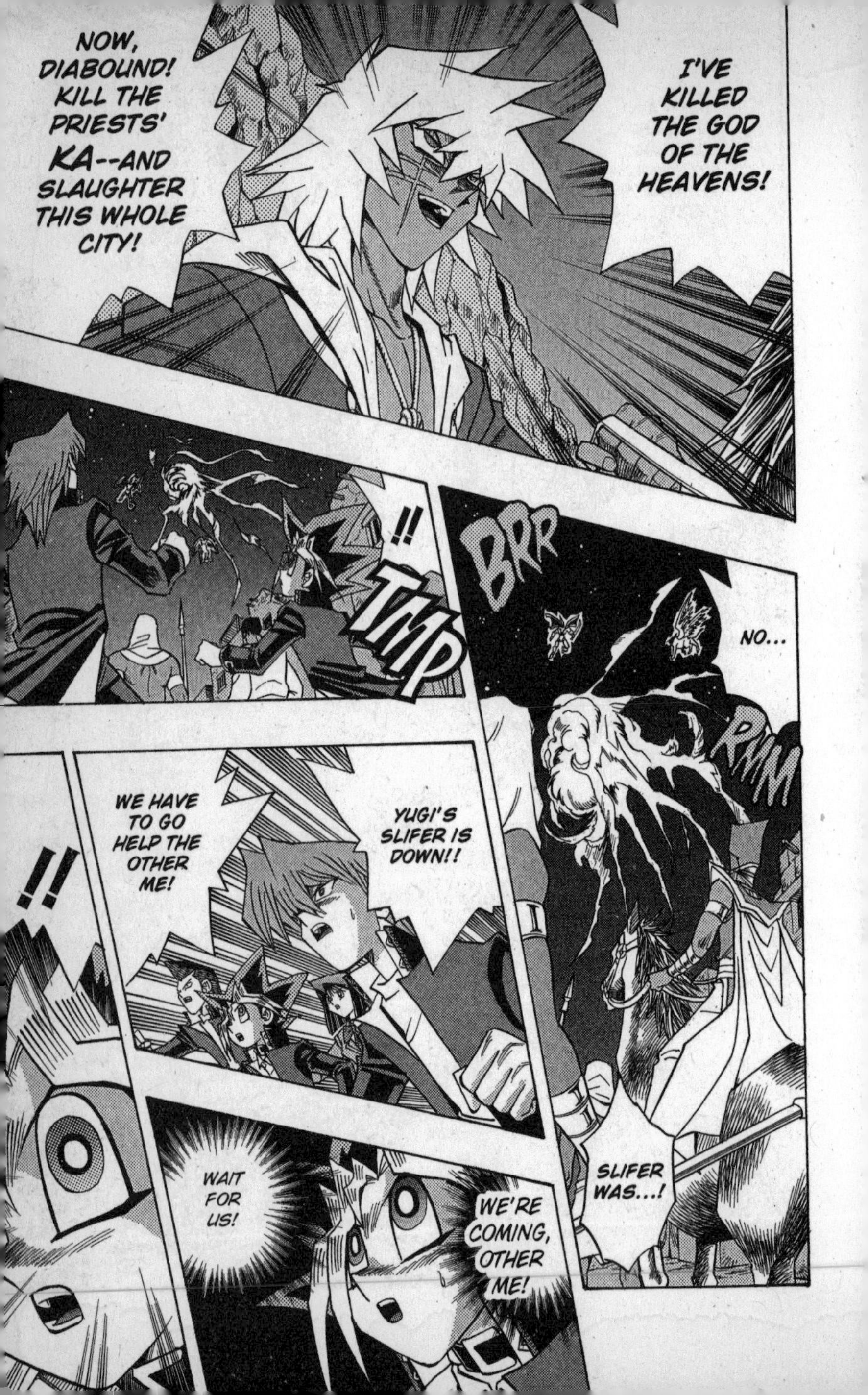
I'VE KILLED THE GOD OF THE HEAVENS!
NOW, DIABOUND! KILL THE PRIESTS' KA--AND SLAUGHTER THIS WHOLE CITY!
BRR
NO...
RMM
SLIFER WAS...!
!!
TMP
YUGI'S SLIFER IS DOWN!!
WE HAVE TO GO HELP THE OTHER ME!
!!
WE'RE COMING, OTHER ME!
WAIT FOR US!

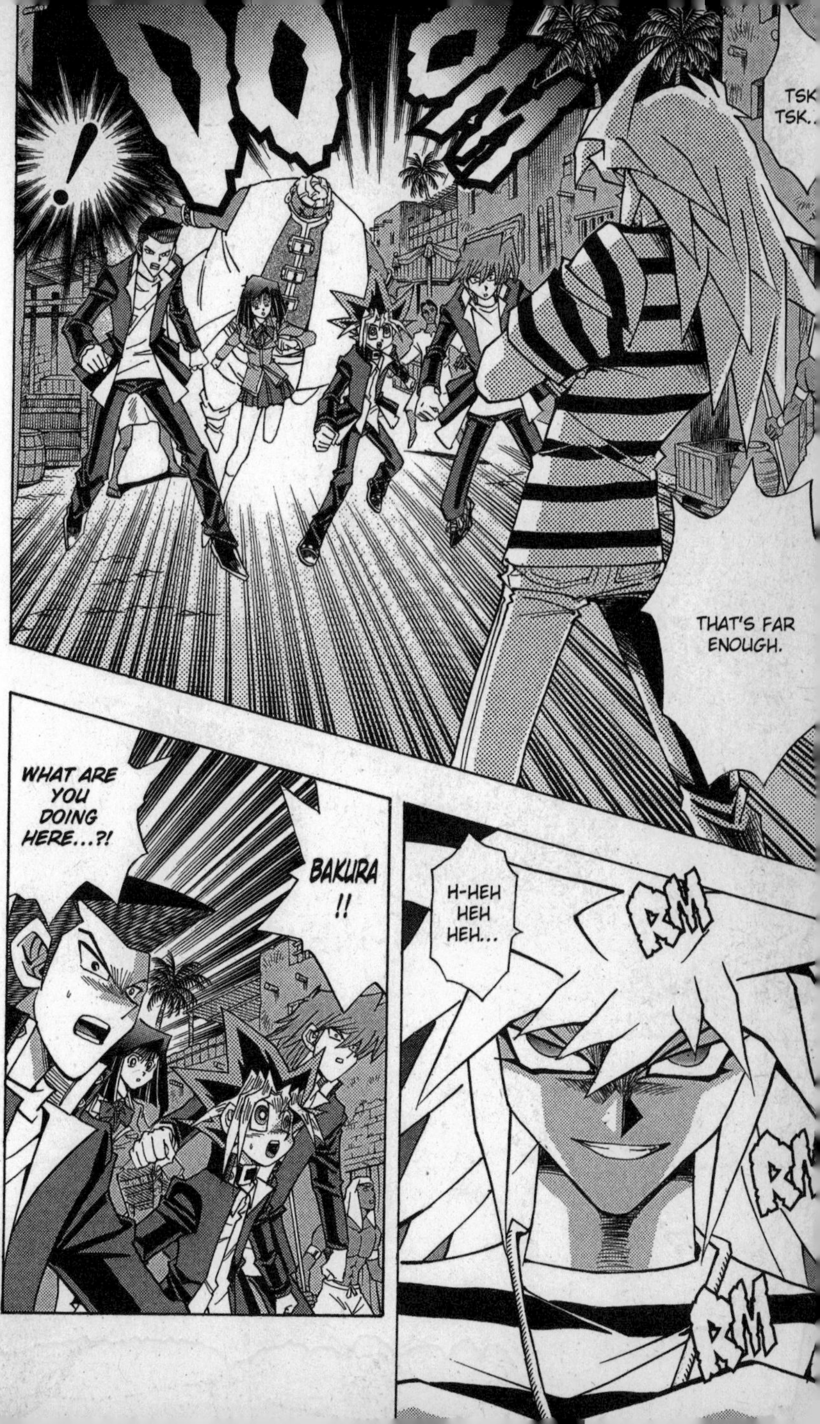
TSK TSK...
THAT'S FAR ENOUGH.
H-HEH HEH HEH...
RM
RM
RM
WHAT ARE YOU DOING HERE...?!
BAKURA !!

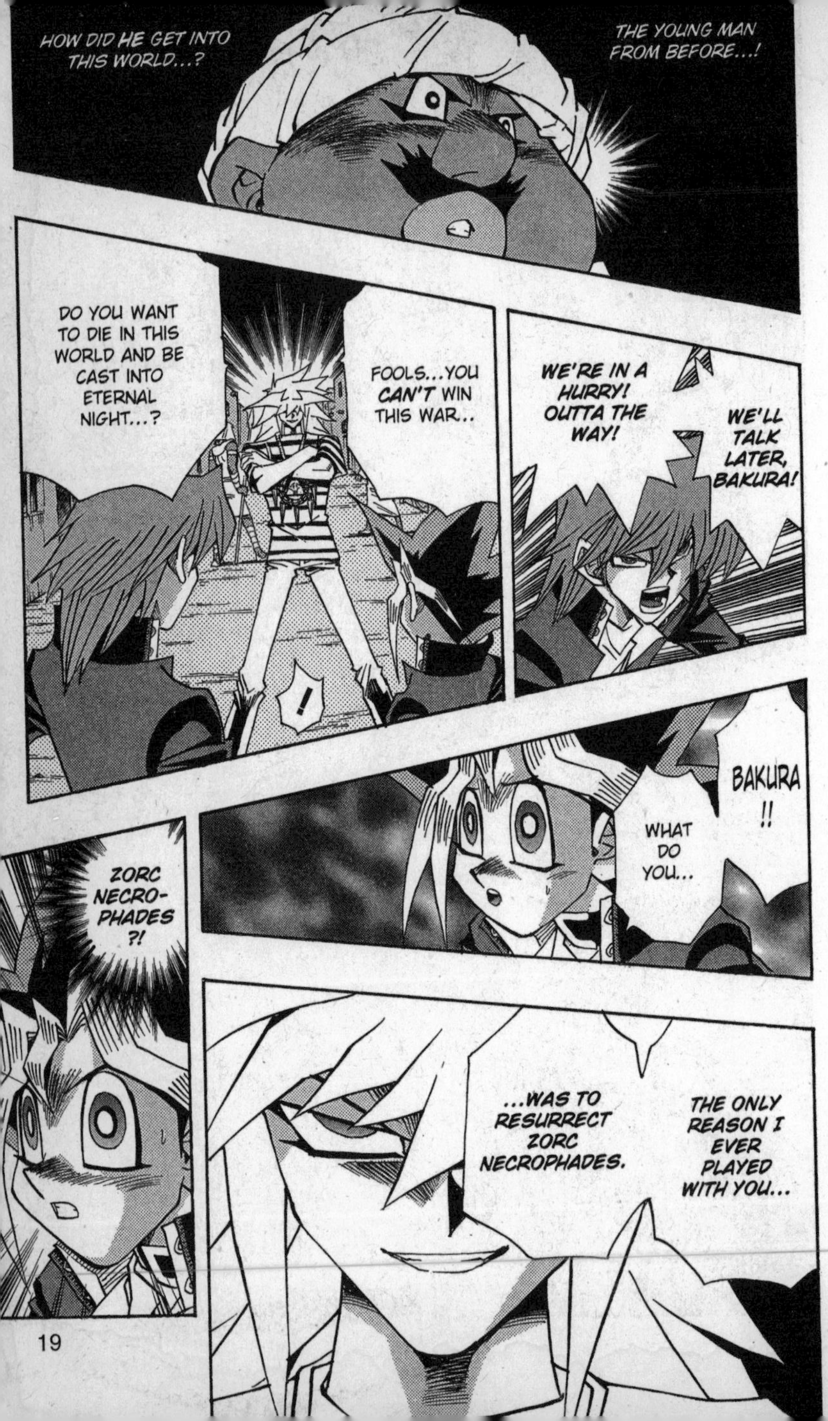
THE YOUNG MAN FROM BEFORE...!
HOW DID HE GET INTO THIS WORLD...?
WE'RE IN A HURRY! OUTTA THE WAY!
WE'LL TALK LATER, BAKURA!
FOOLS...YOU CAN'T WIN THIS WAR..
DO YOU WANT TO DIE IN THIS WORLD AND BE CAST INTO ETERNAL NIGHT...?
!
BAKURA !!
WHAT DO YOU...
ZORC NECROPHADES ?!
THE ONLY REASON I EVER PLAYED WITH YOU...
...WAS TO RESURRECT ZORC NECROPHADES.

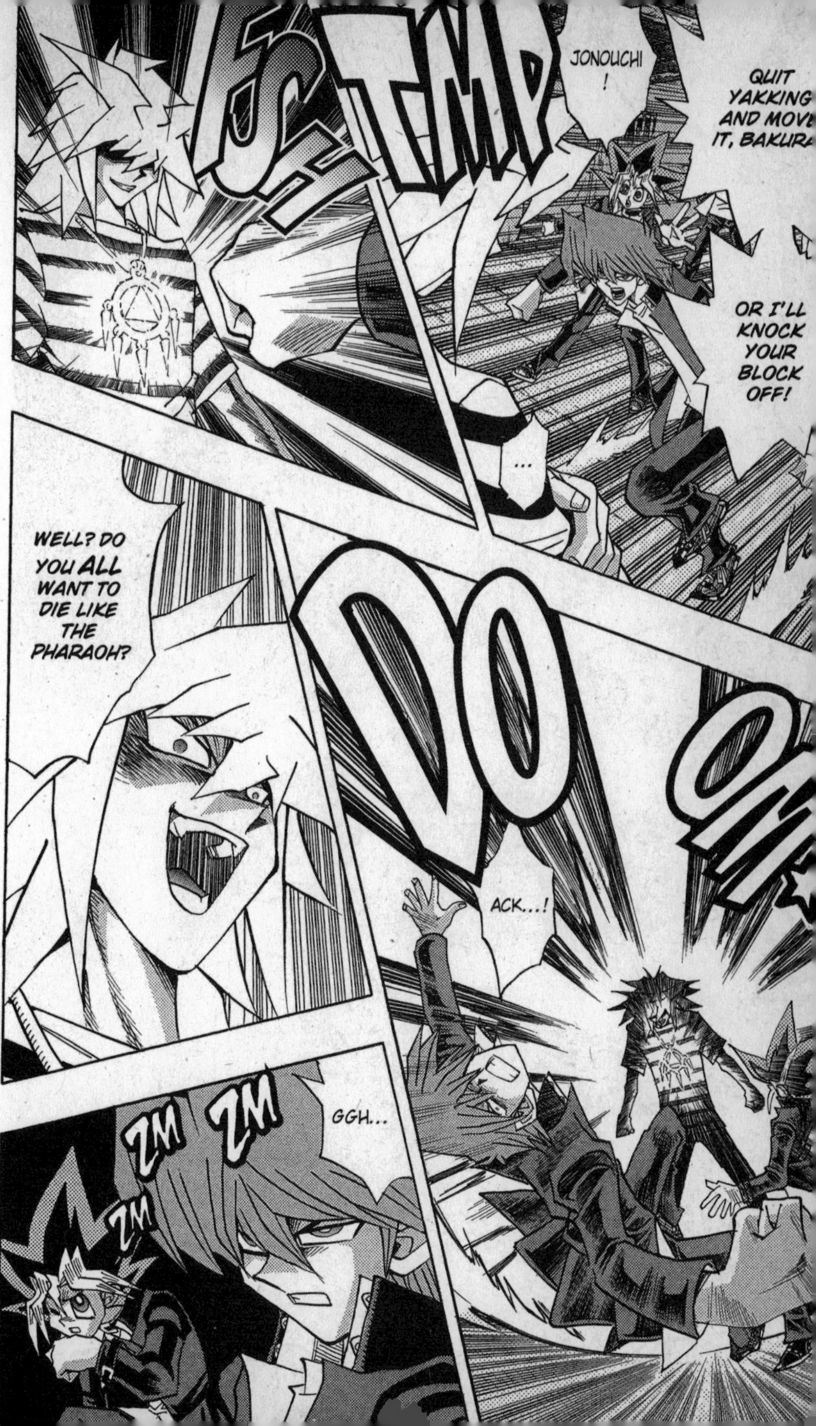
JONOUCHI!
QUIT YAKKING AND MOVE IT, BAKURA
OR I'LL KNOCK YOUR BLOCK OFF!
...
DO
ACK...!
WELL? DO YOU ALL WANT TO DIE LIKE THE PHARAOH?
GGH...
ZM ZM
ZM

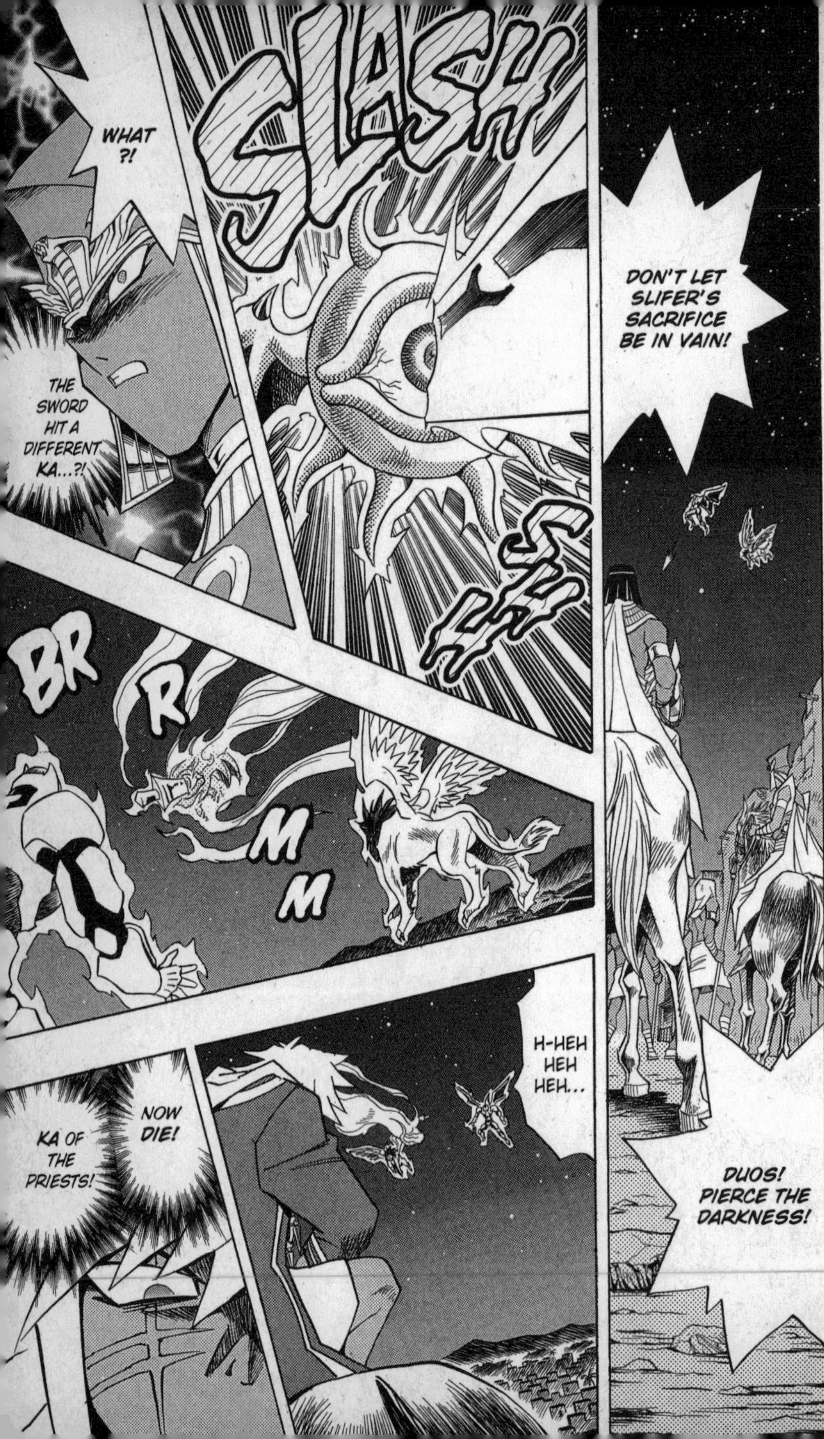
DON'T LET SLIFER'S SACRIFICE BE IN VAIN!
DUOS! PIERCE THE DARKNESS!
SLASH!
WHAT ?!
THE SWORD HIT A DIFFERENT KA...?!
BR R M M
H-HEH HEH HEH...
NOW DIE!
KA OF THE PRIESTS!

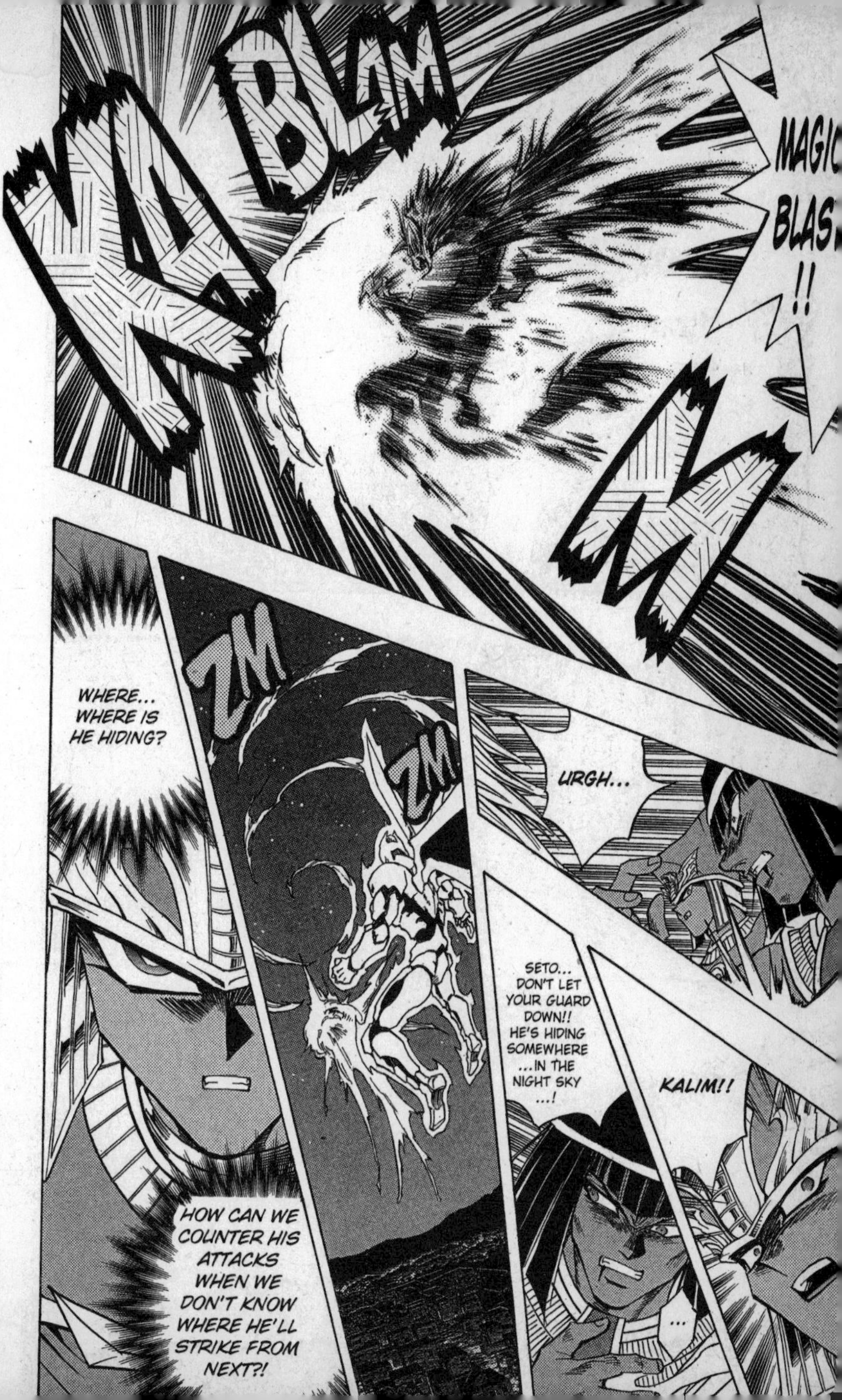
MAGIC BLAS
!!
KA-BLAM
GM
URGH...
KALIM!!
...
SETO... DON'T LET YOUR GUARD DOWN!! HE'S HIDING SOMEWHERE ...IN THE NIGHT SKY ...!
ZM
ZM
WHERE... WHERE IS HE HIDING?
HOW CAN WE COUNTER HIS ATTACKS WHEN WE DON'T KNOW WHERE HE'LL STRIKE FROM NEXT?!

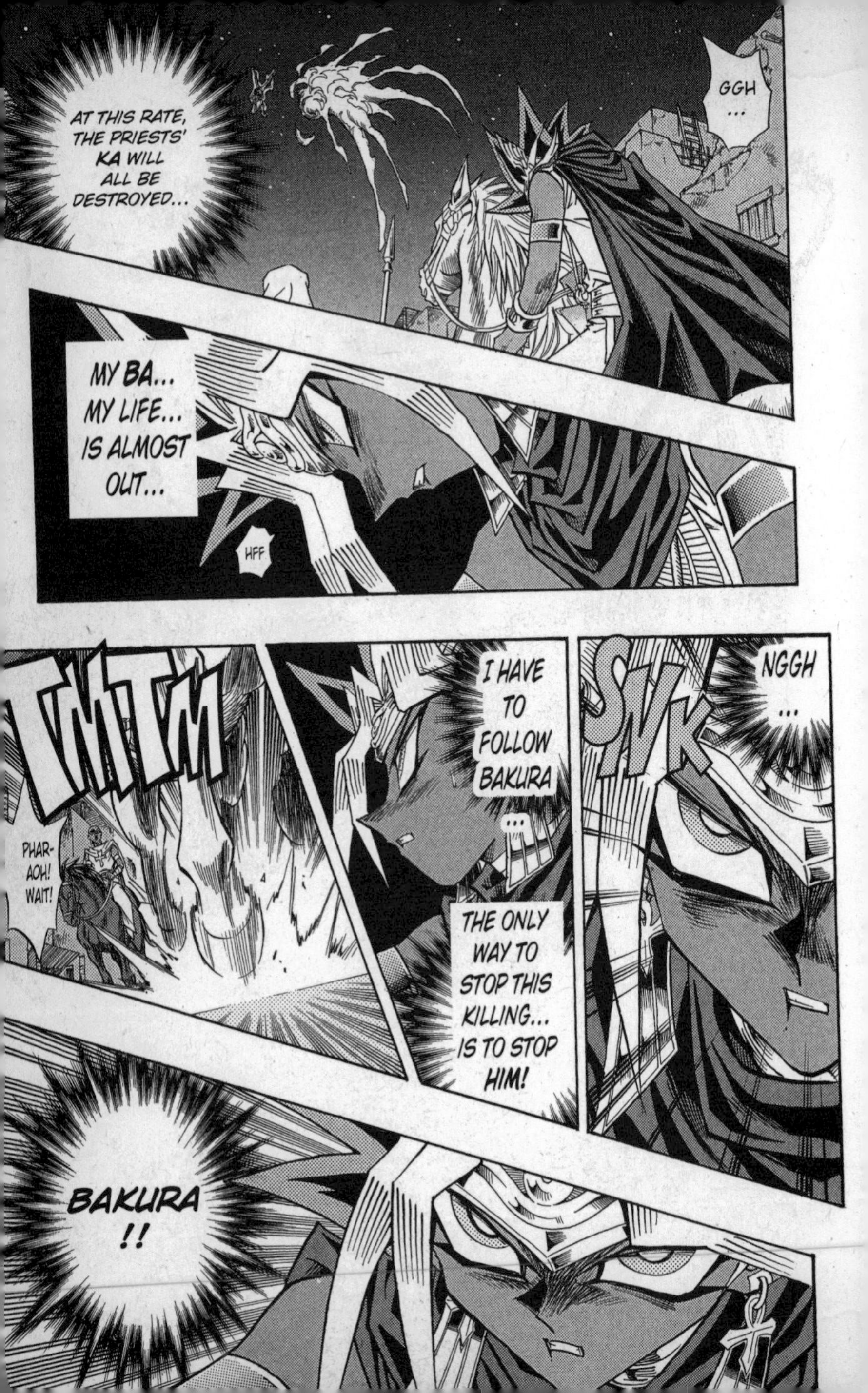
GGH ...
AT THIS RATE, THE PRIESTS' KA WILL ALL BE DESTROYED...
MY BA... MY LIFE... IS ALMOST OUT...
HFF
NGGH ...
I HAVE TO FOLLOW BAKURA ...
THE ONLY WAY TO STOP THIS KILLING... IS TO STOP HIM!
PHAR-AOH! WAIT!
BAKURA !!

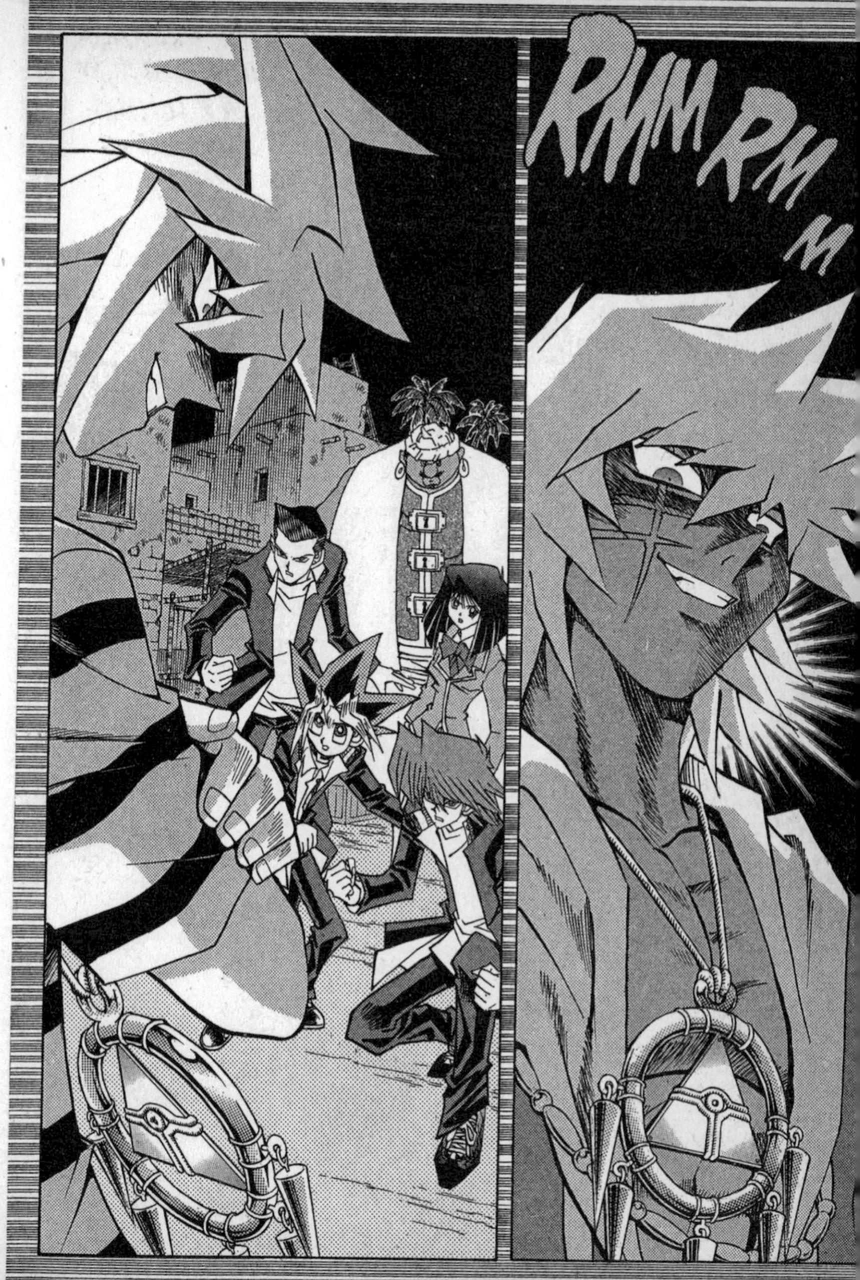
RMM RM M

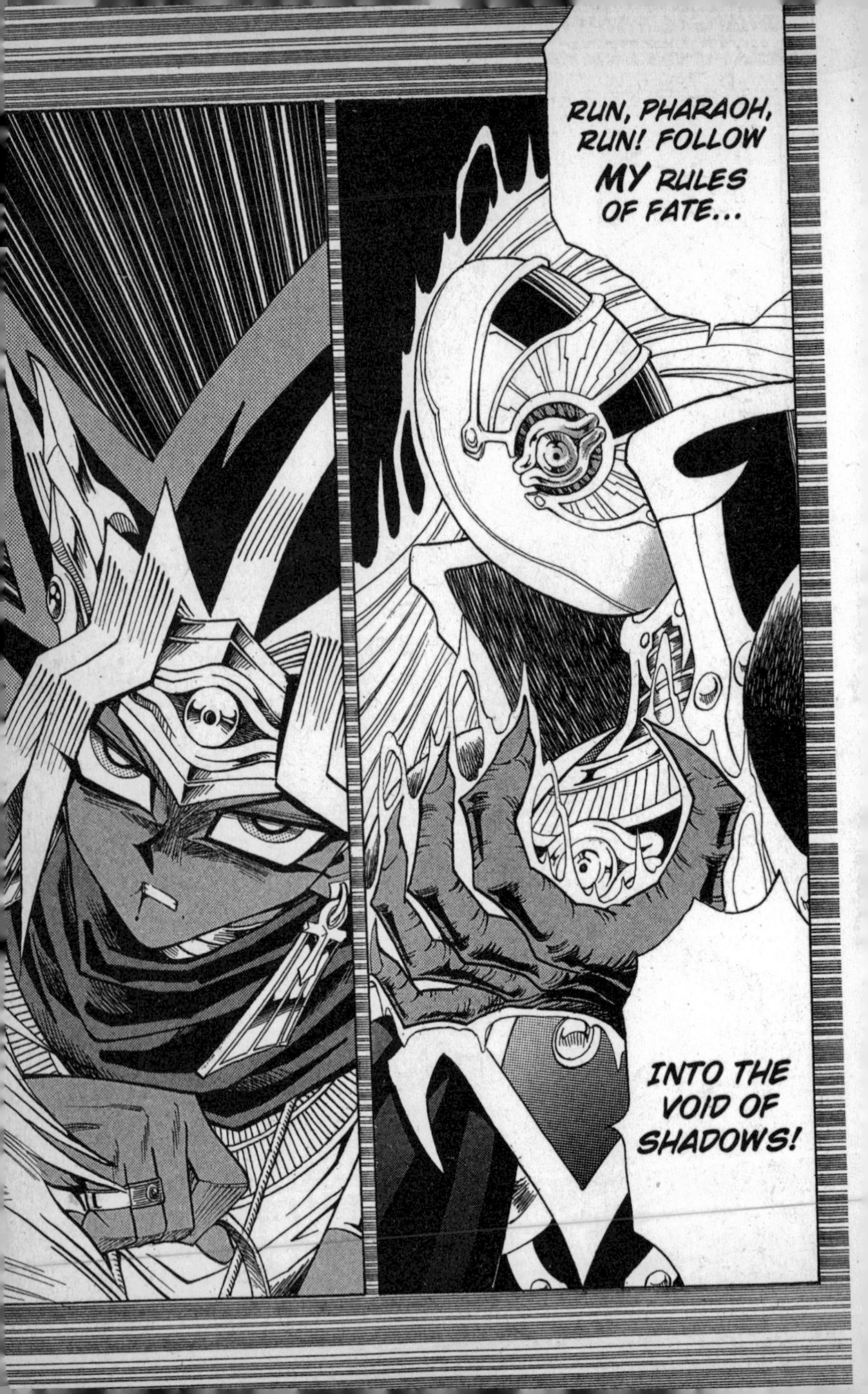
RUN, PHARAOH, RUN! FOLLOW MY RULES OF FATE...
INTO THE VOID OF SHADOWS!

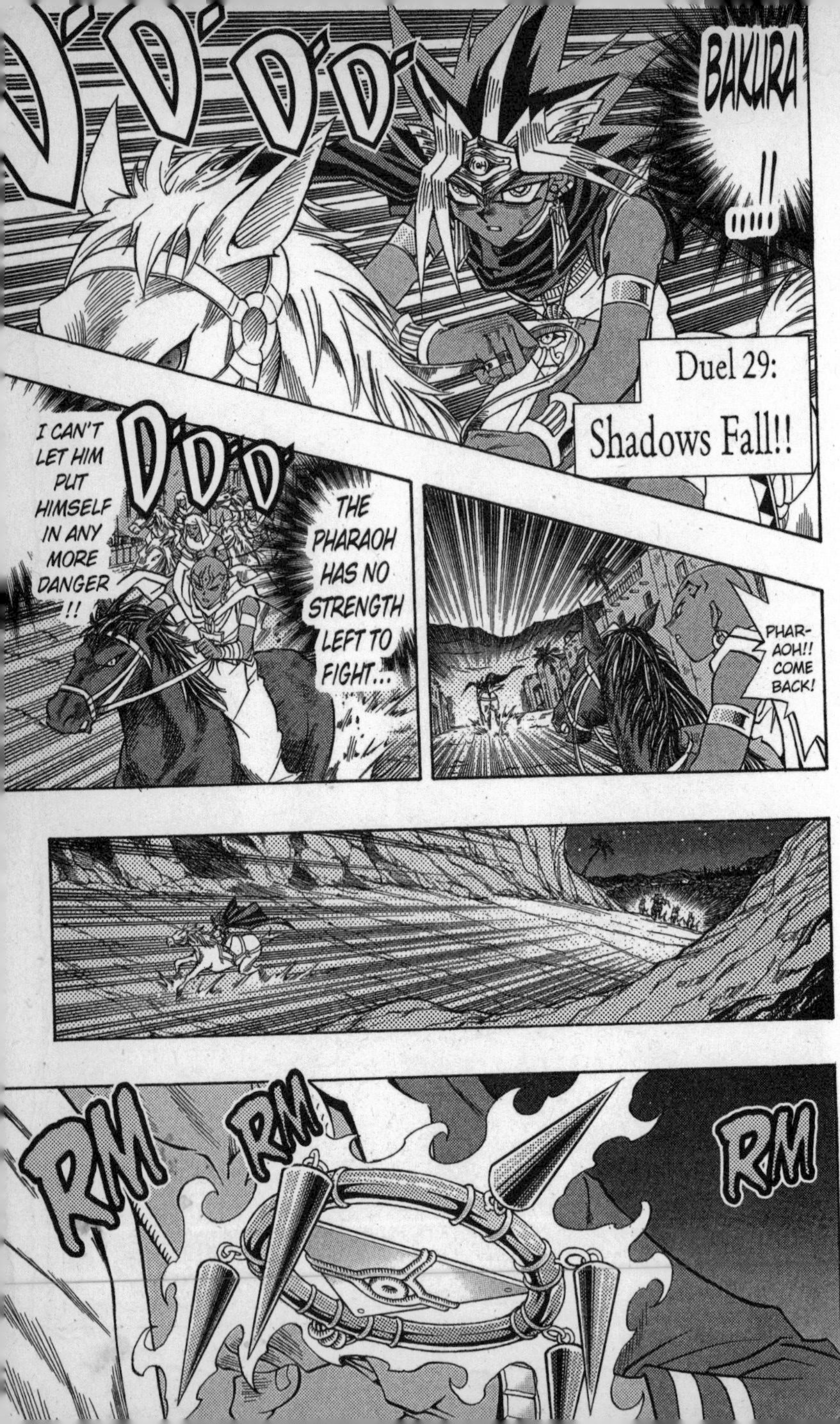
D D D D D D
BAKURA ......!!
Duel 29:
Shadows Fall!!
PHARAOH!! COME BACK!
D D D
THE PHARAOH HAS NO STRENGTH LEFT TO FIGHT...
I CAN'T LET HIM PUT HIMSELF IN ANY MORE DANGER!!
RM
RM RM

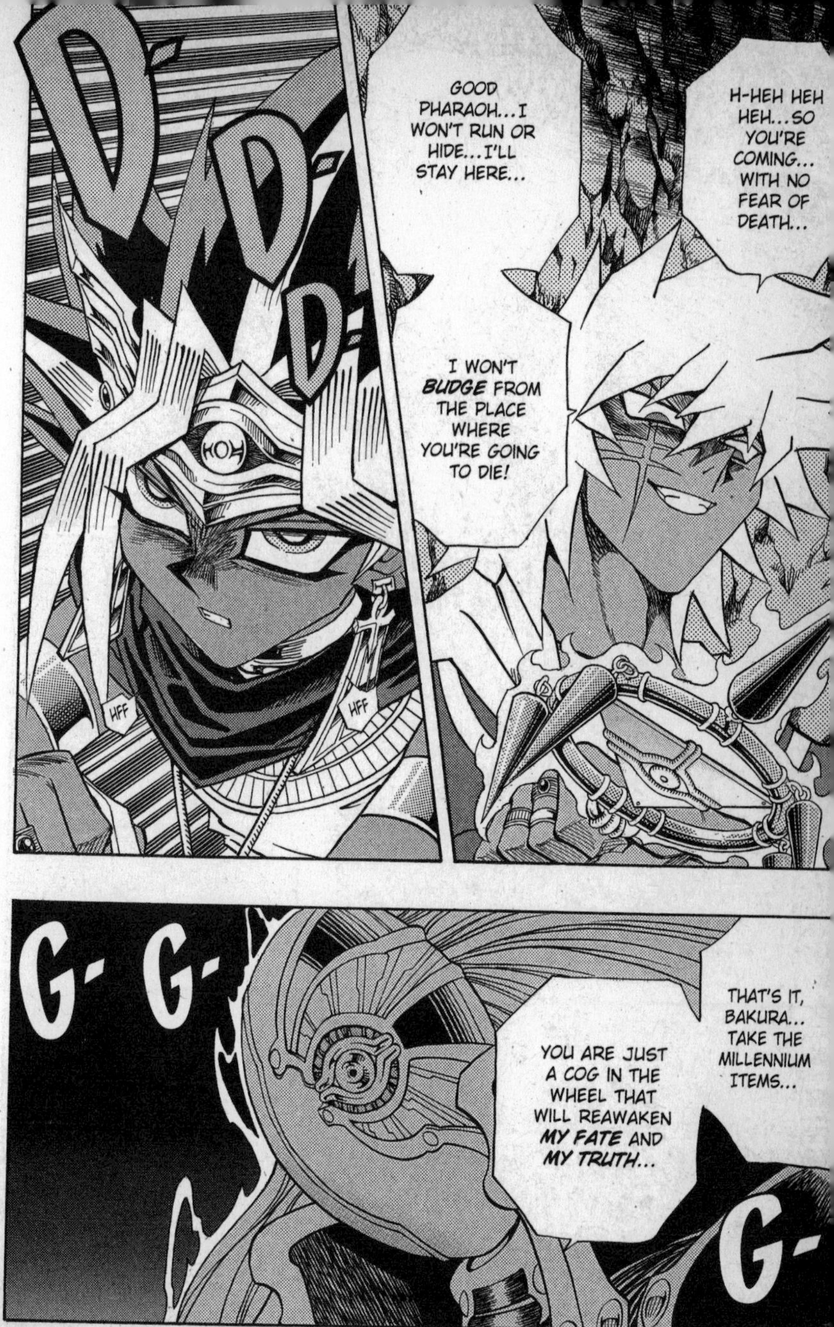
H-HEH HEH HEH...SO YOU'RE COMING... WITH NO FEAR OF DEATH...
GOOD PHARAOH...I WON'T RUN OR HIDE...I'LL STAY HERE...
I WON'T *BUDGE* FROM THE PLACE WHERE YOU'RE GOING TO DIE!
D D D
HFF
HFF
THAT'S IT, BAKURA... TAKE THE MILLENNIUM ITEMS...
YOU ARE JUST A COG IN THE WHEEL THAT WILL REAWAKEN *MY FATE* AND *MY TRUTH*...
G- G- G-

# Duel 29:
# Shadows Fall!!

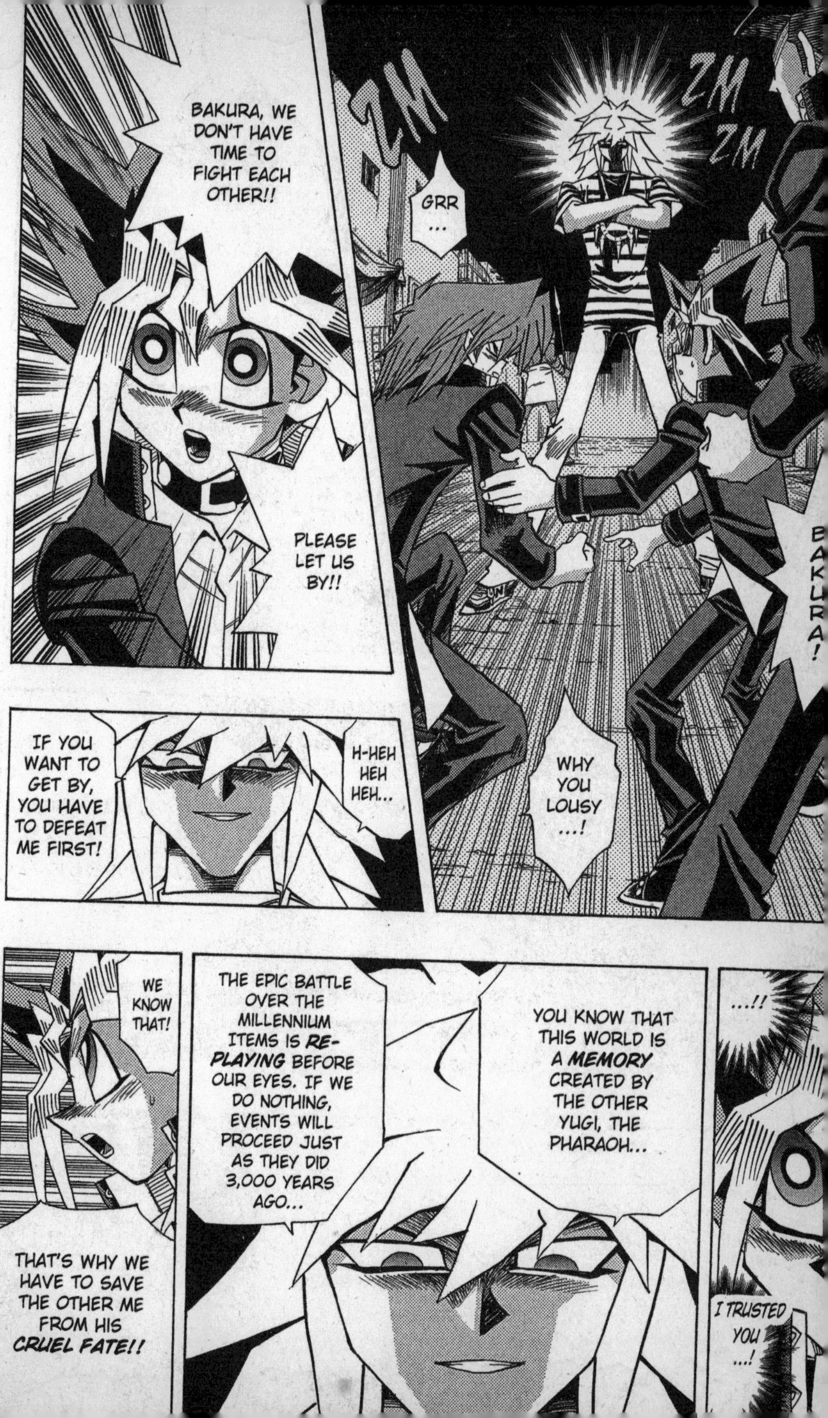
ZM ZM
ZM
ZM
GRR ...
BAKURA!
WHY YOU LOUSY ...!
BAKURA, WE DON'T HAVE TIME TO FIGHT EACH OTHER!!
PLEASE LET US BY!!
H-HEH HEH HEH...
IF YOU WANT TO GET BY, YOU HAVE TO DEFEAT ME FIRST!
...!!
I TRUSTED YOU ...!
YOU KNOW THAT THIS WORLD IS A *MEMORY* CREATED BY THE OTHER YUGI, THE PHARAOH...
THE EPIC BATTLE OVER THE MILLENNIUM ITEMS IS *RE-PLAYING* BEFORE OUR EYES. IF WE DO NOTHING, EVENTS WILL PROCEED JUST AS THEY DID 3,000 YEARS AGO...
WE KNOW THAT!
THAT'S WHY WE HAVE TO SAVE THE OTHER ME FROM HIS *CRUEL FATE!!*

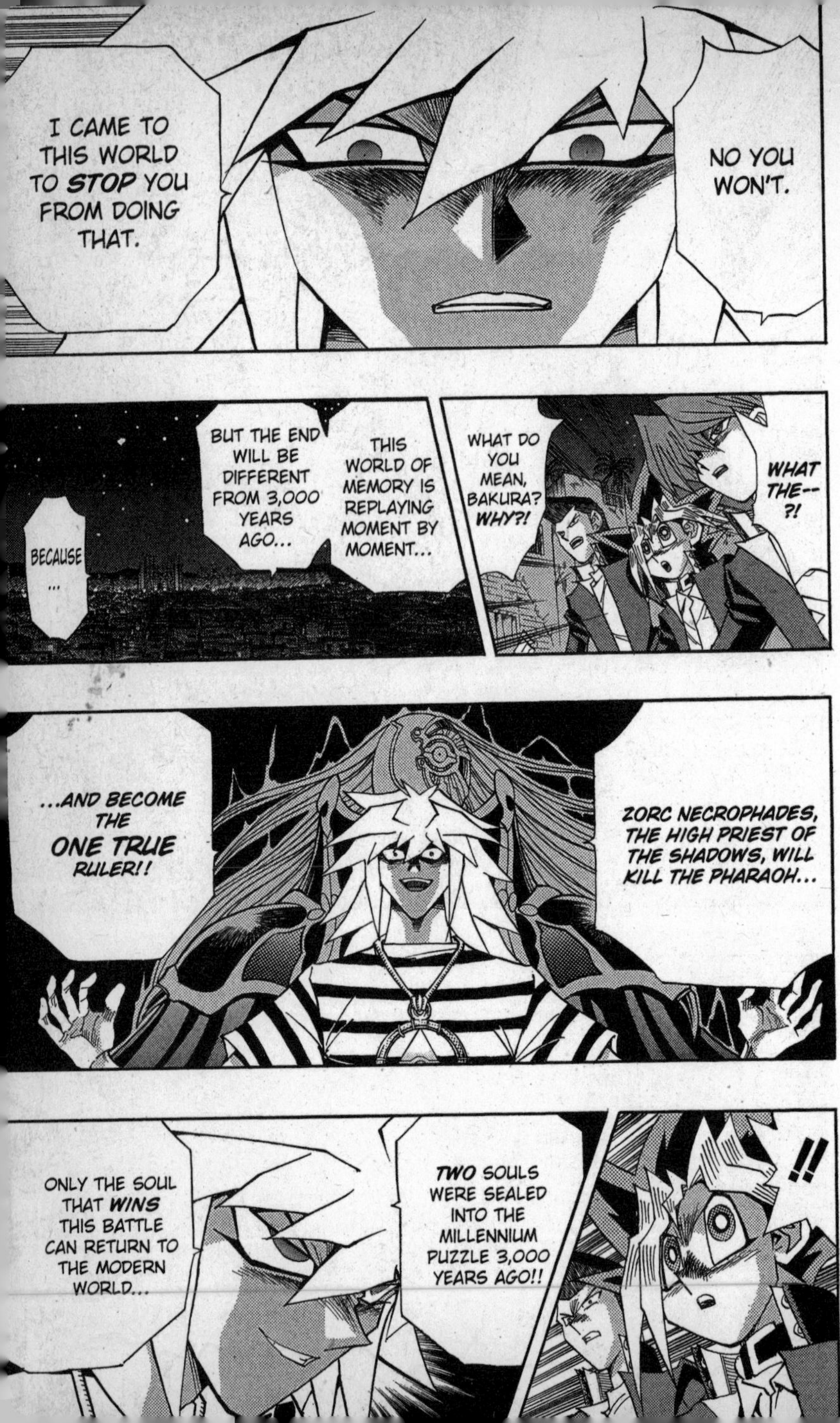
NO YOU WON'T.
I CAME TO THIS WORLD TO STOP YOU FROM DOING THAT.
WHAT THE--?!
WHAT DO YOU MEAN, BAKURA? WHY?!
THIS WORLD OF MEMORY IS REPLAYING MOMENT BY MOMENT...
BUT THE END WILL BE DIFFERENT FROM 3,000 YEARS AGO...
BECAUSE ...
ZORC NECROPHADES, THE HIGH PRIEST OF THE SHADOWS, WILL KILL THE PHARAOH...
...AND BECOME THE ONE TRUE RULER!!
!!
TWO SOULS WERE SEALED INTO THE MILLENNIUM PUZZLE 3,000 YEARS AGO!!
ONLY THE SOUL THAT WINS THIS BATTLE CAN RETURN TO THE MODERN WORLD...

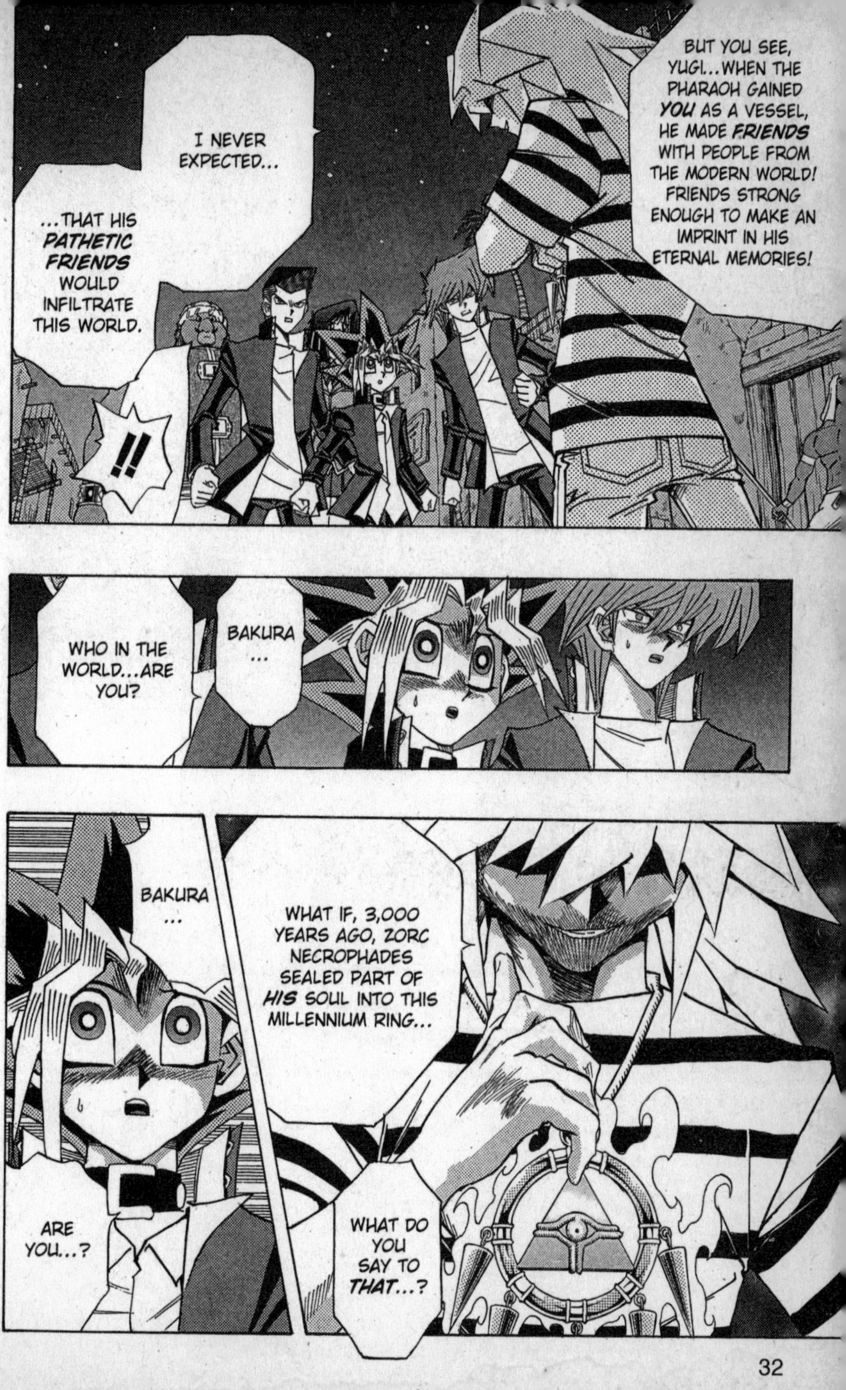
BUT YOU SEE, YUGI...WHEN THE PHARAOH GAINED *YOU* AS A VESSEL, HE MADE *FRIENDS* WITH PEOPLE FROM THE MODERN WORLD! FRIENDS STRONG ENOUGH TO MAKE AN IMPRINT IN HIS ETERNAL MEMORIES!
I NEVER EXPECTED...
...THAT HIS *PATHETIC FRIENDS* WOULD INFILTRATE THIS WORLD.
!!
BAKURA ...
WHO IN THE WORLD...ARE YOU?
WHAT IF, 3,000 YEARS AGO, ZORC NECROPHADES SEALED PART OF *HIS* SOUL INTO THIS MILLENNIUM RING...
WHAT DO YOU SAY TO *THAT*...?
BAKURA ...
ARE YOU...?

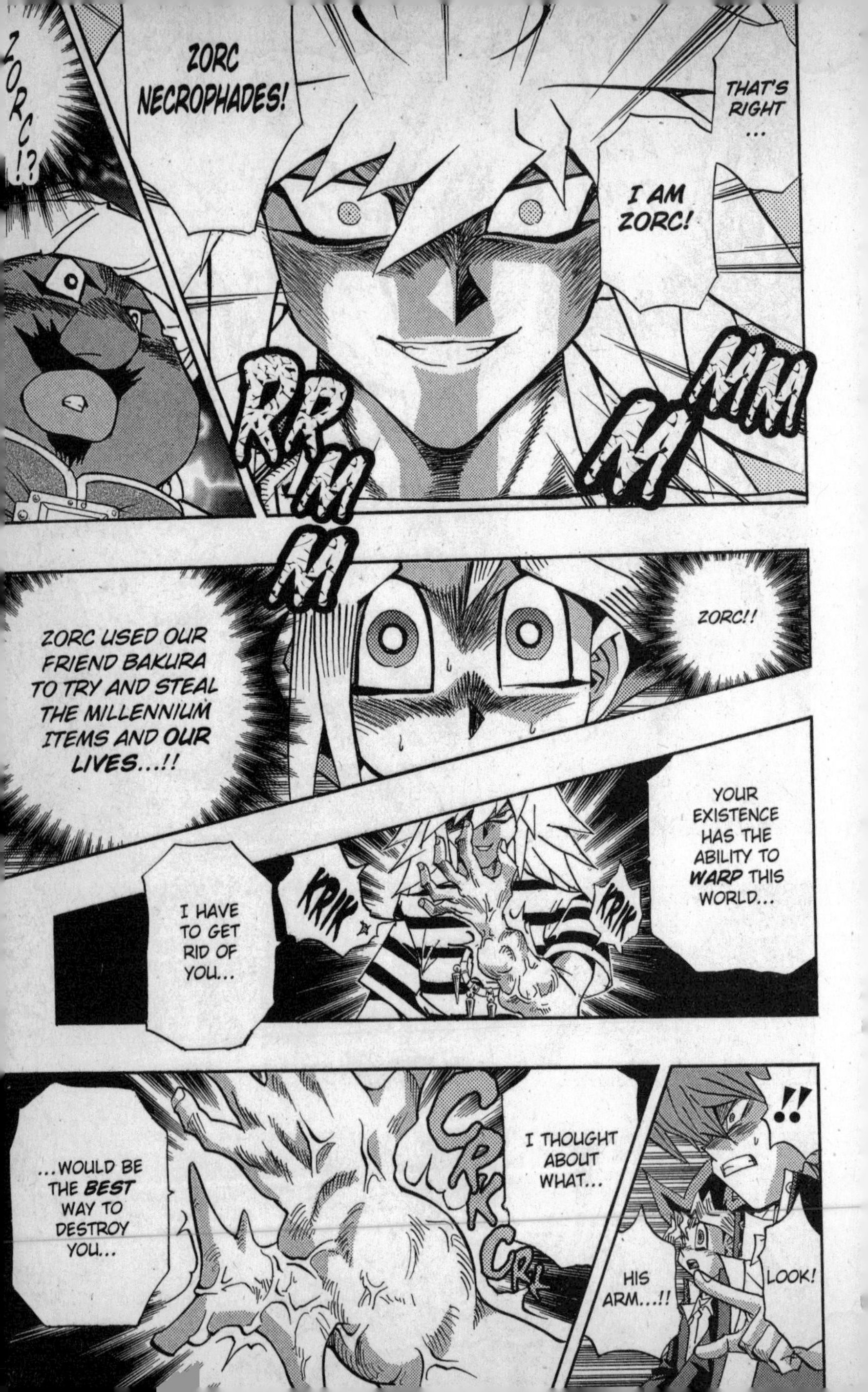
ZORC NECROPHADES!
THAT'S RIGHT...
I AM ZORC!
RRMMM
MMMM
ZORC!?
ZORC!!
ZORC USED OUR FRIEND BAKURA TO TRY AND STEAL THE MILLENNIUM ITEMS AND OUR LIVES...!!
YOUR EXISTENCE HAS THE ABILITY TO WARP THIS WORLD...
KRIK
KRIK
I HAVE TO GET RID OF YOU...
!!
LOOK!
HIS ARM...!!
I THOUGHT ABOUT WHAT...
CRK
CRK
...WOULD BE THE BEST WAY TO DESTROY YOU...

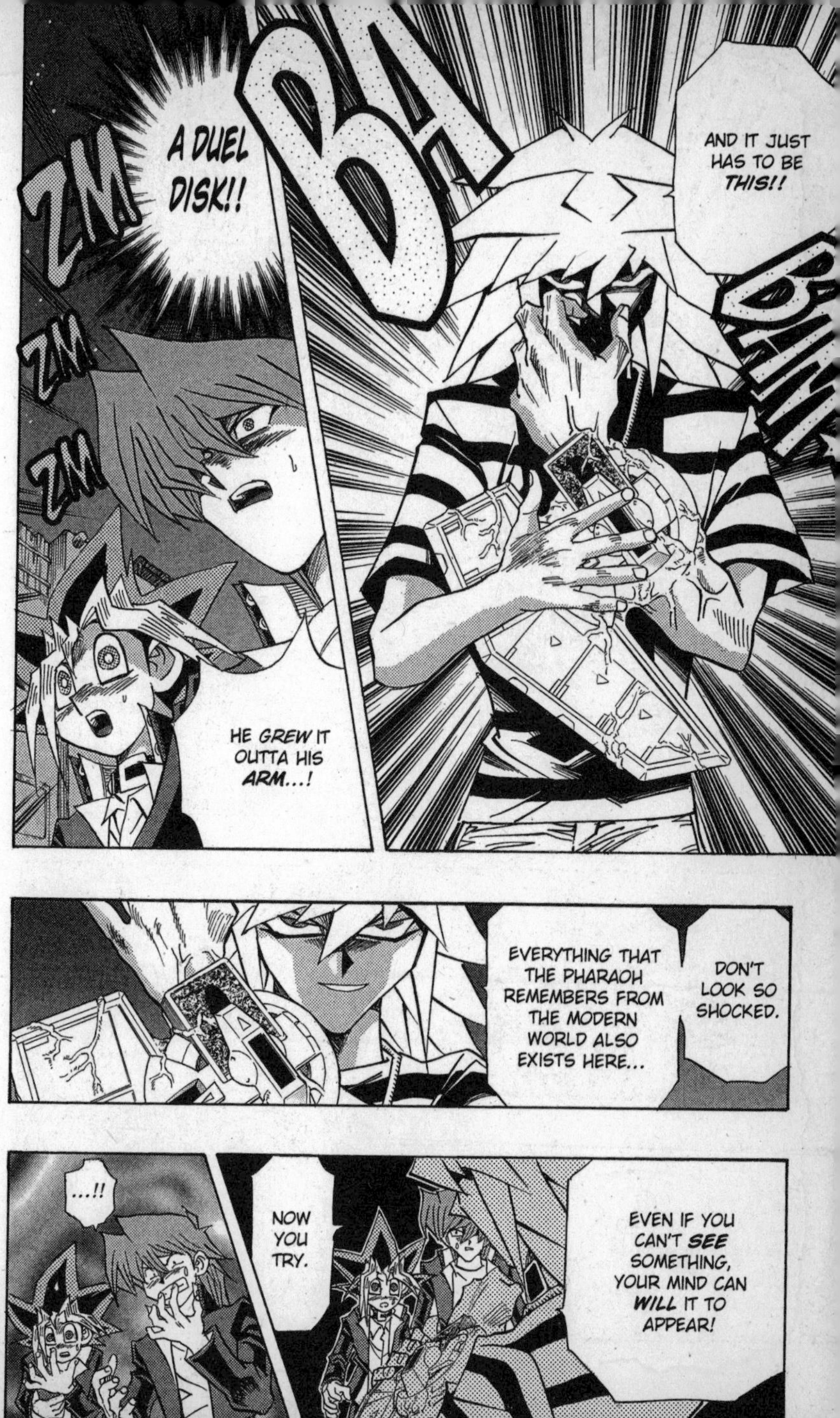
AND IT JUST HAS TO BE *THIS!!*
BA
A DUEL DISK!!
ZM
ZM
ZM
HE *GREW* IT OUTTA HIS *ARM*...!
DON'T LOOK SO SHOCKED.
EVERYTHING THAT THE PHARAOH REMEMBERS FROM THE MODERN WORLD ALSO EXISTS HERE...
EVEN IF YOU CAN'T *SEE* SOMETHING, YOUR MIND CAN *WILL* IT TO APPEAR!
NOW YOU TRY.
...!!

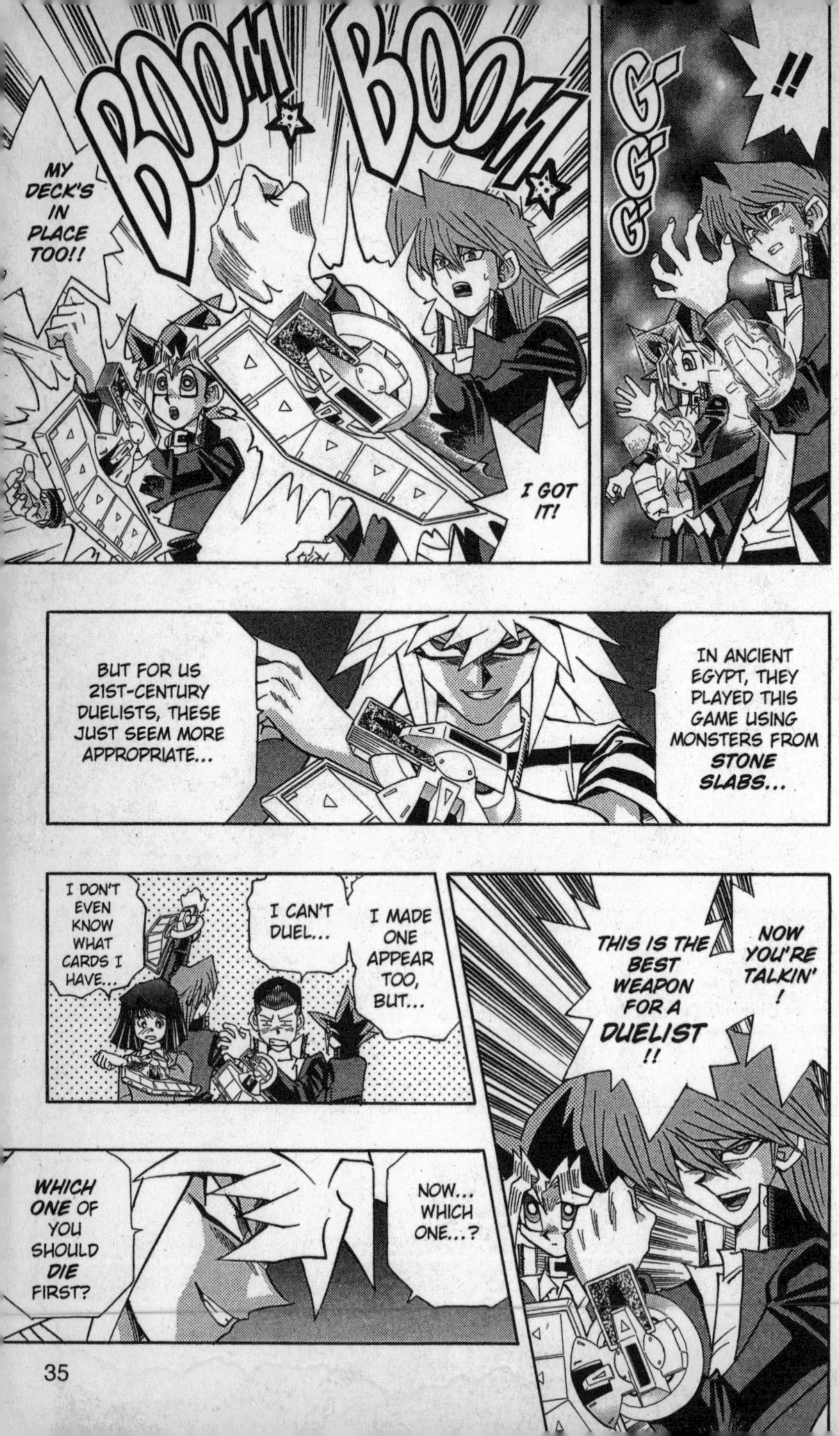
G-G-G-
!!
BOOM! BOOM!
I GOT IT!
MY DECK'S IN PLACE TOO!!
IN ANCIENT EGYPT, THEY PLAYED THIS GAME USING MONSTERS FROM STONE SLABS...
BUT FOR US 21ST-CENTURY DUELISTS, THESE JUST SEEM MORE APPROPRIATE...
NOW YOU'RE TALKIN'!
THIS IS THE BEST WEAPON FOR A DUELIST!!
I MADE ONE APPEAR TOO, BUT...
I CAN'T DUEL...
I DON'T EVEN KNOW WHAT CARDS I HAVE...
NOW... WHICH ONE...?
WHICH ONE OF YOU SHOULD DIE FIRST?

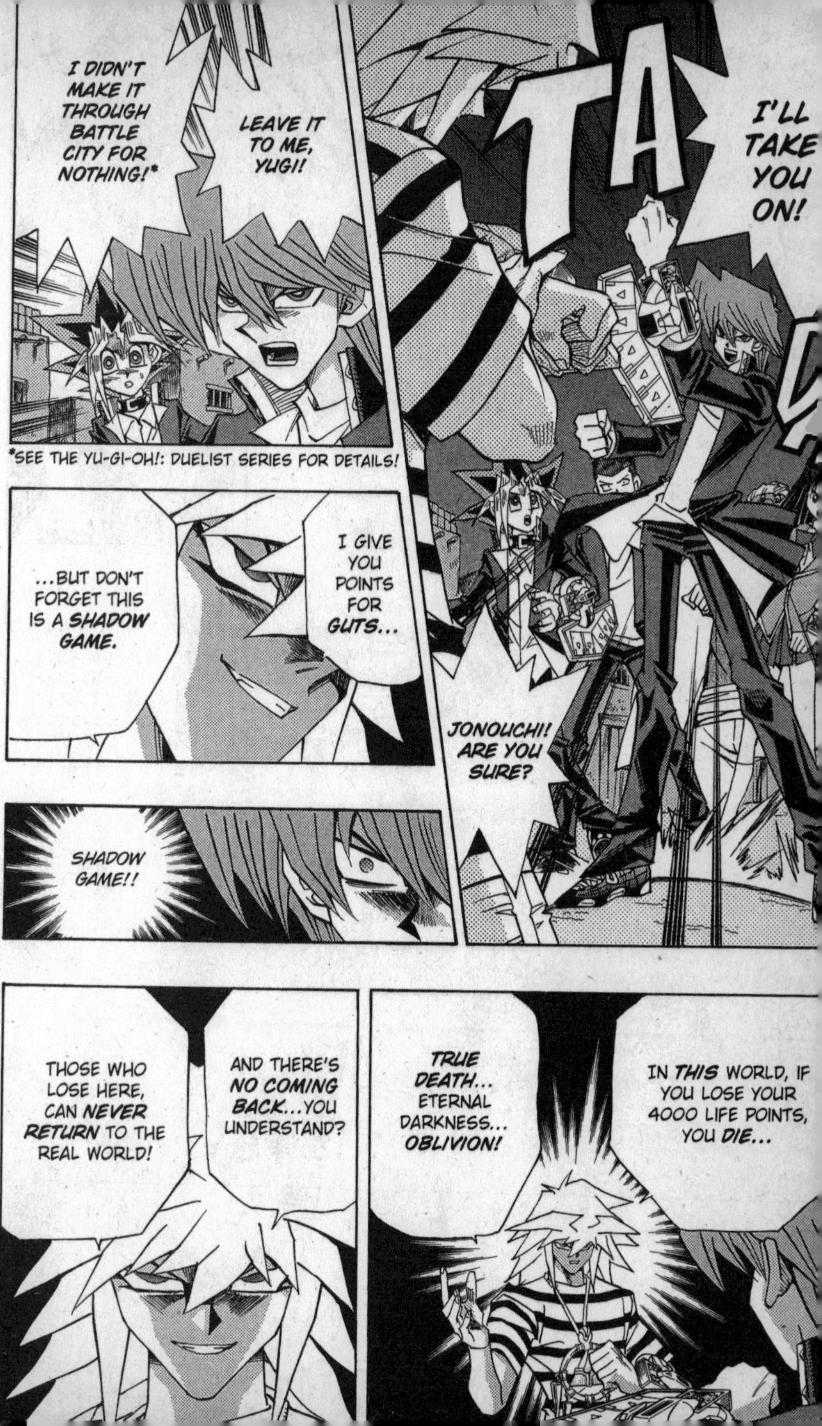
TA
I'LL TAKE YOU ON!
JONOUCHI! ARE YOU SURE?
LEAVE IT TO ME, YUGI!
I DIDN'T MAKE IT THROUGH BATTLE CITY FOR NOTHING!*
I GIVE YOU POINTS FOR GUTS...
...BUT DON'T FORGET THIS IS A SHADOW GAME.
SHADOW GAME!!
IN THIS WORLD, IF YOU LOSE YOUR 4000 LIFE POINTS, YOU DIE...
TRUE DEATH... ETERNAL DARKNESS... OBLIVION!
AND THERE'S NO COMING BACK...YOU UNDERSTAND?
THOSE WHO LOSE HERE, CAN NEVER RETURN TO THE REAL WORLD!

*SEE THE YU-GI-OH!: DUELIST SERIES FOR DETAILS!

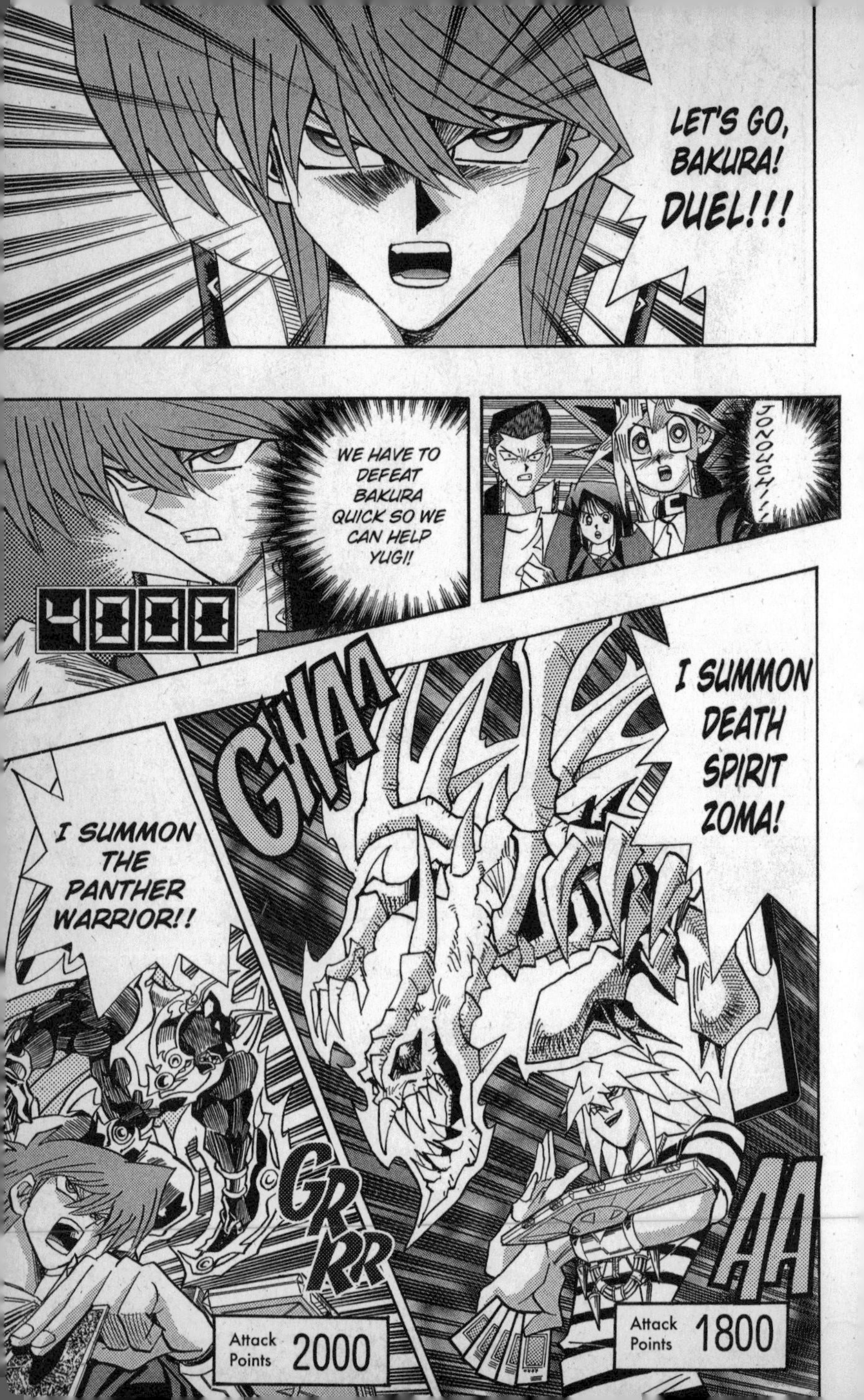
LET'S GO, BAKURA! DUEL!!!
JONOUCHI!!
WE HAVE TO DEFEAT BAKURA QUICK SO WE CAN HELP YUGI!!
4000
I SUMMON DEATH SPIRIT ZOMA!
GHAA
AA
Attack Points 1800
I SUMMON THE PANTHER WARRIOR!!
GRRR
Attack Points 2000

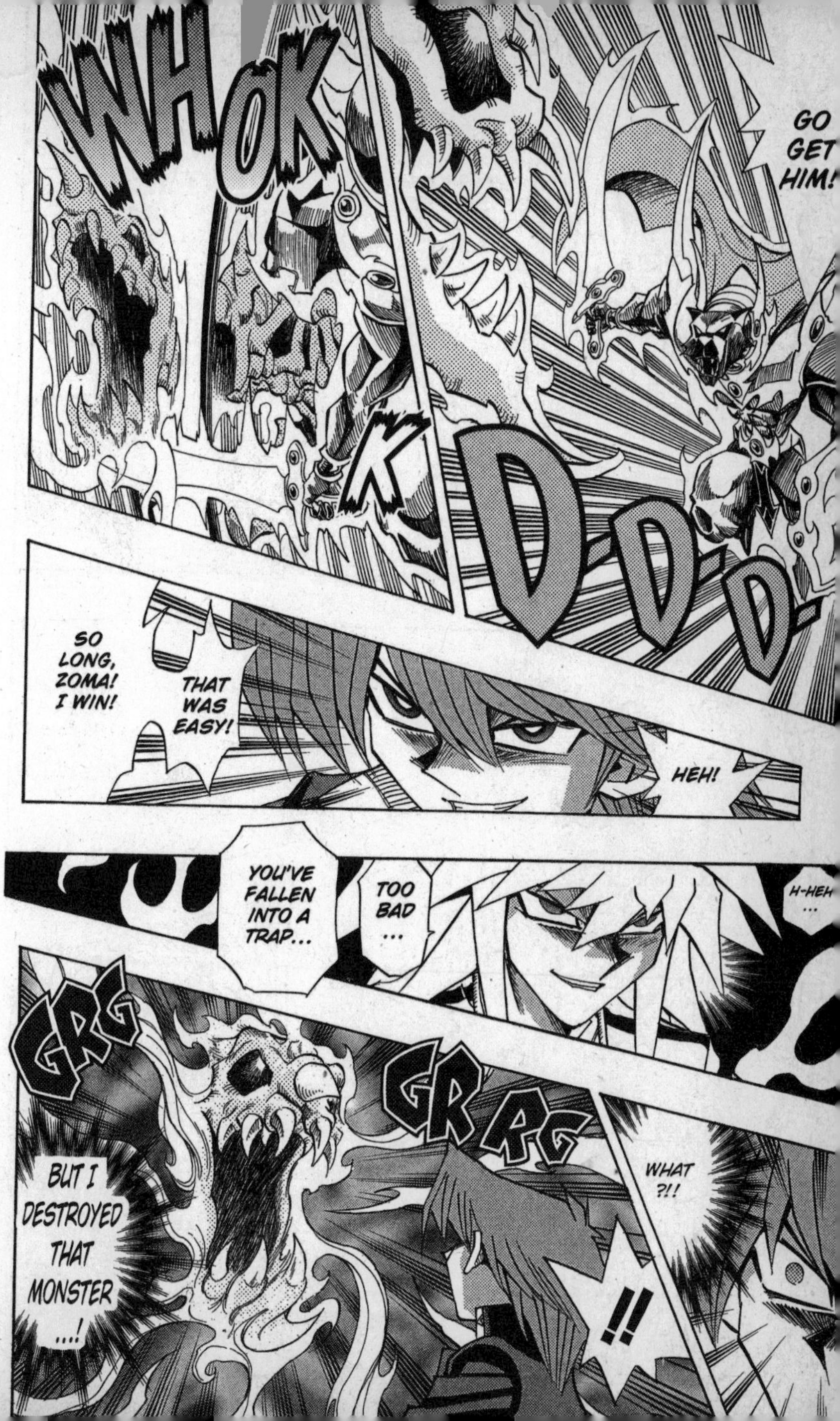
GO GET HIM!
WHOK
K
D-D-D-
HEH!
THAT WAS EASY!
SO LONG, ZOMA! I WIN!
H-HEH...
TOO BAD...
YOU'VE FALLEN INTO A TRAP...
WHAT?!!
!!
GRRG
GRG
BUT I DESTROYED THAT MONSTER...!

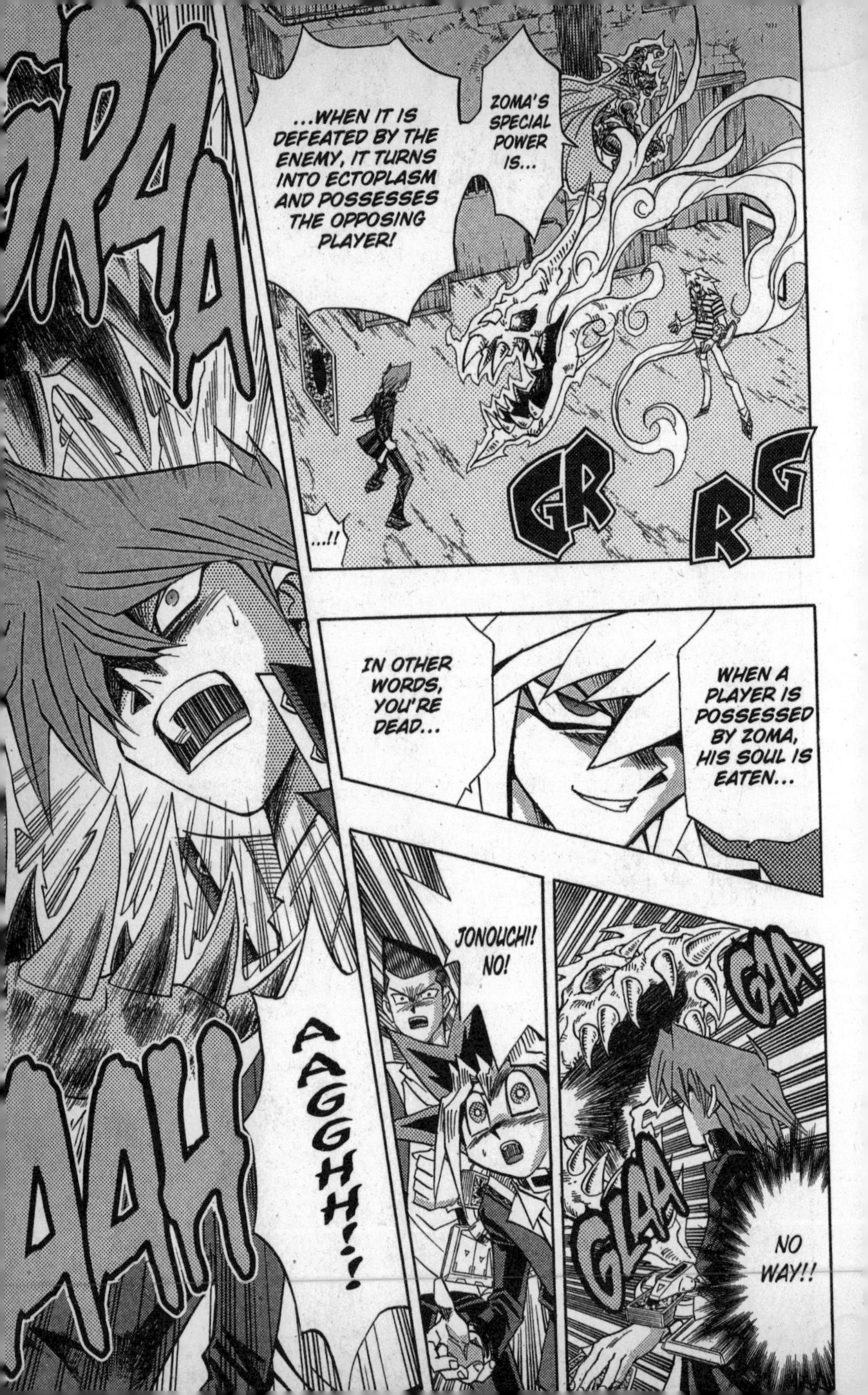
ZOMA'S SPECIAL POWER IS...
...WHEN IT IS DEFEATED BY THE ENEMY, IT TURNS INTO ECTOPLASM AND POSSESSES THE OPPOSING PLAYER!
GR RG
...!!
WHEN A PLAYER IS POSSESSED BY ZOMA, HIS SOUL IS EATEN...
IN OTHER WORDS, YOU'RE DEAD...
GAA
GAA
NO WAY!!
JONOUCHI! NO!
AAGGHH!!

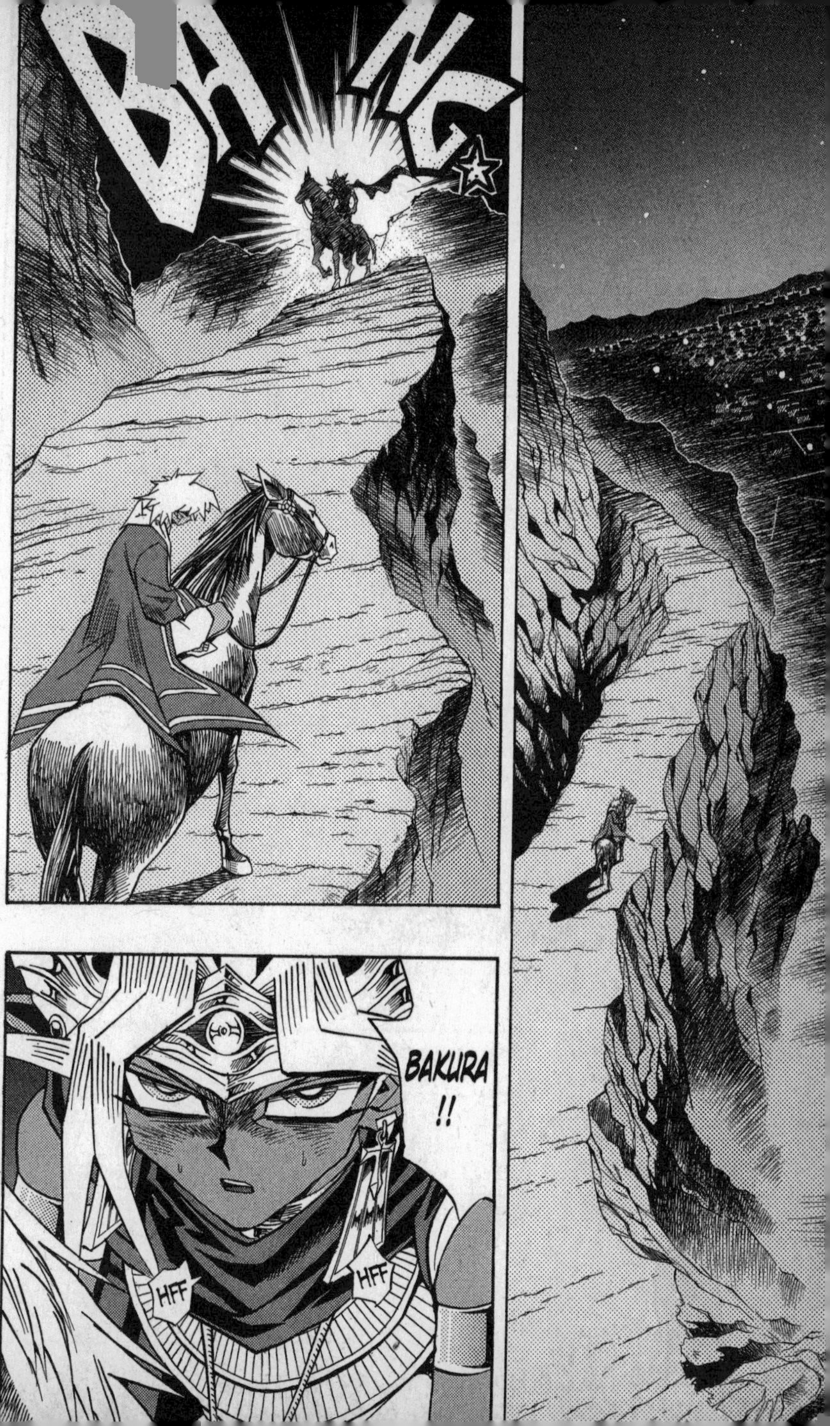
BANG
BAKURA !!
HFF
HFF

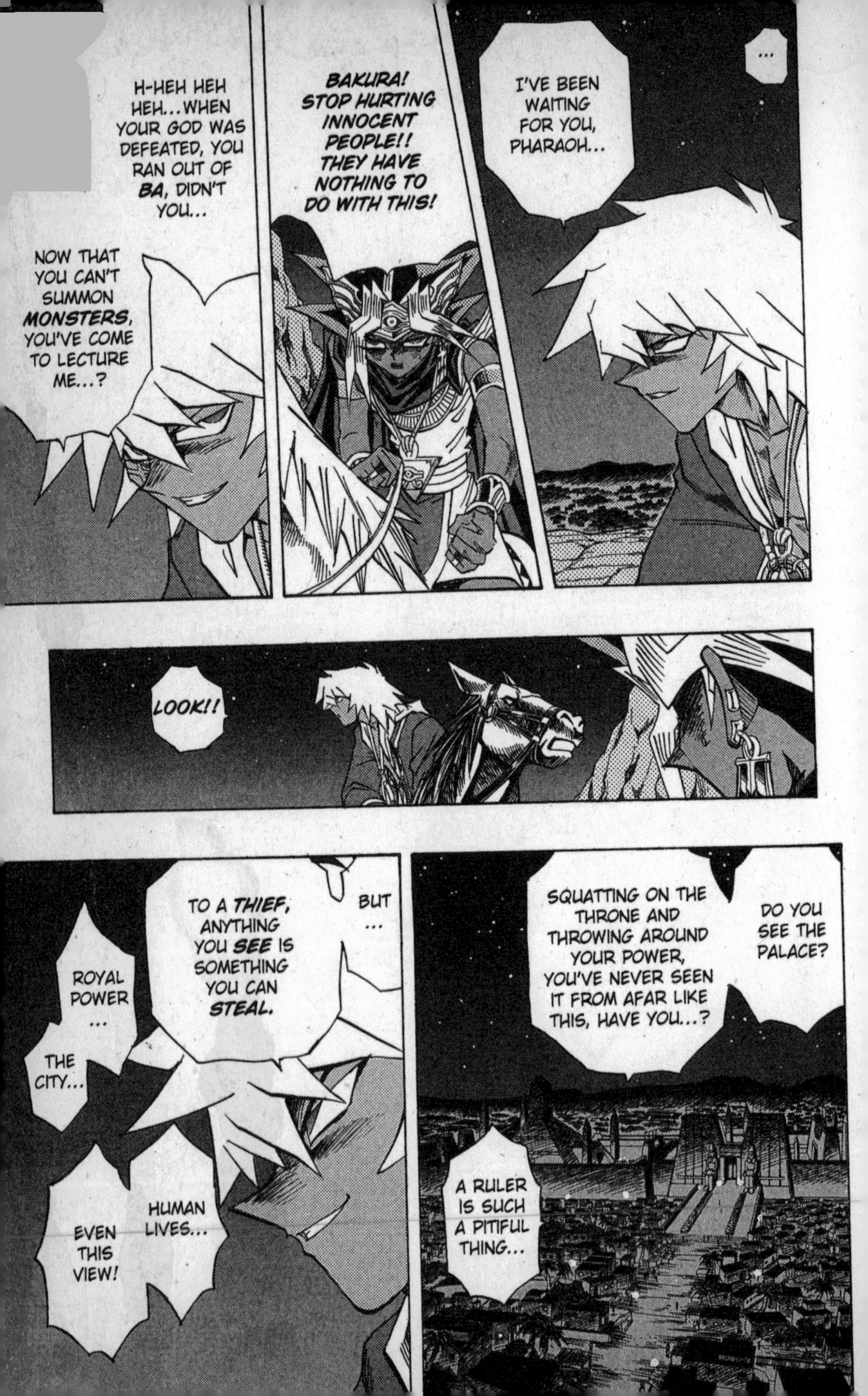
...
I'VE BEEN WAITING FOR YOU, PHARAOH...
BAKURA! STOP HURTING INNOCENT PEOPLE!! THEY HAVE NOTHING TO DO WITH THIS!
H-HEH HEH HEH...WHEN YOUR GOD WAS DEFEATED, YOU RAN OUT OF BA, DIDN'T YOU...
NOW THAT YOU CAN'T SUMMON MONSTERS, YOU'VE COME TO LECTURE ME...?
LOOK!!
DO YOU SEE THE PALACE?
SQUATTING ON THE THRONE AND THROWING AROUND YOUR POWER, YOU'VE NEVER SEEN IT FROM AFAR LIKE THIS, HAVE YOU...?
A RULER IS SUCH A PITIFUL THING...
BUT...
TO A THIEF, ANYTHING YOU SEE IS SOMETHING YOU CAN STEAL.
ROYAL POWER...
THE CITY...
HUMAN LIVES...
EVEN THIS VIEW!

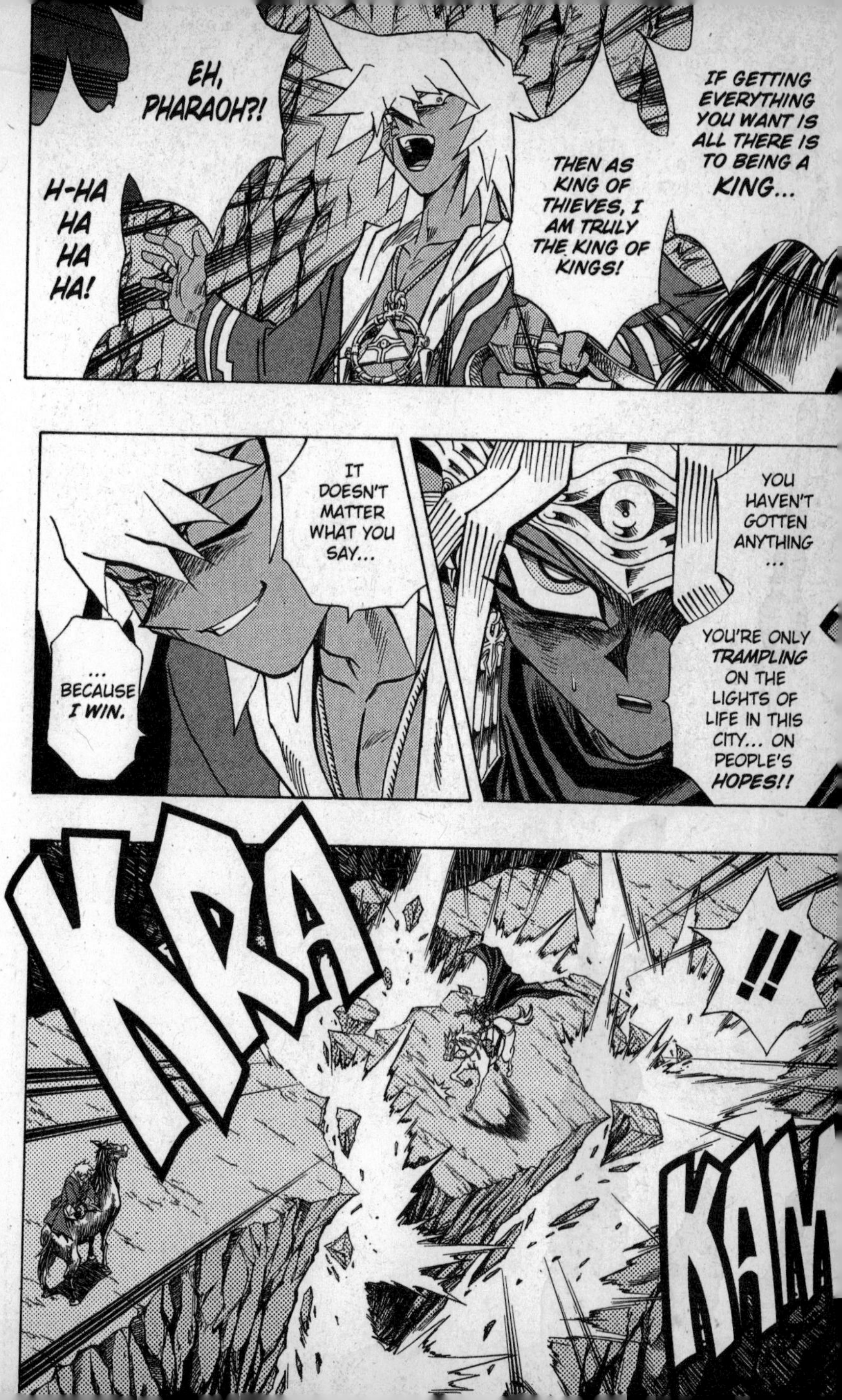
IF GETTING EVERYTHING YOU WANT IS ALL THERE IS TO BEING A KING...
THEN AS KING OF THIEVES, I AM TRULY THE KING OF KINGS!
EH, PHARAOH?!
H-HA HA HA HA!
YOU HAVEN'T GOTTEN ANYTHING...
YOU'RE ONLY TRAMPLING ON THE LIGHTS OF LIFE IN THIS CITY... ON PEOPLE'S HOPES!!
IT DOESN'T MATTER WHAT YOU SAY...
...BECAUSE I WIN.
!!
KRA
KAM

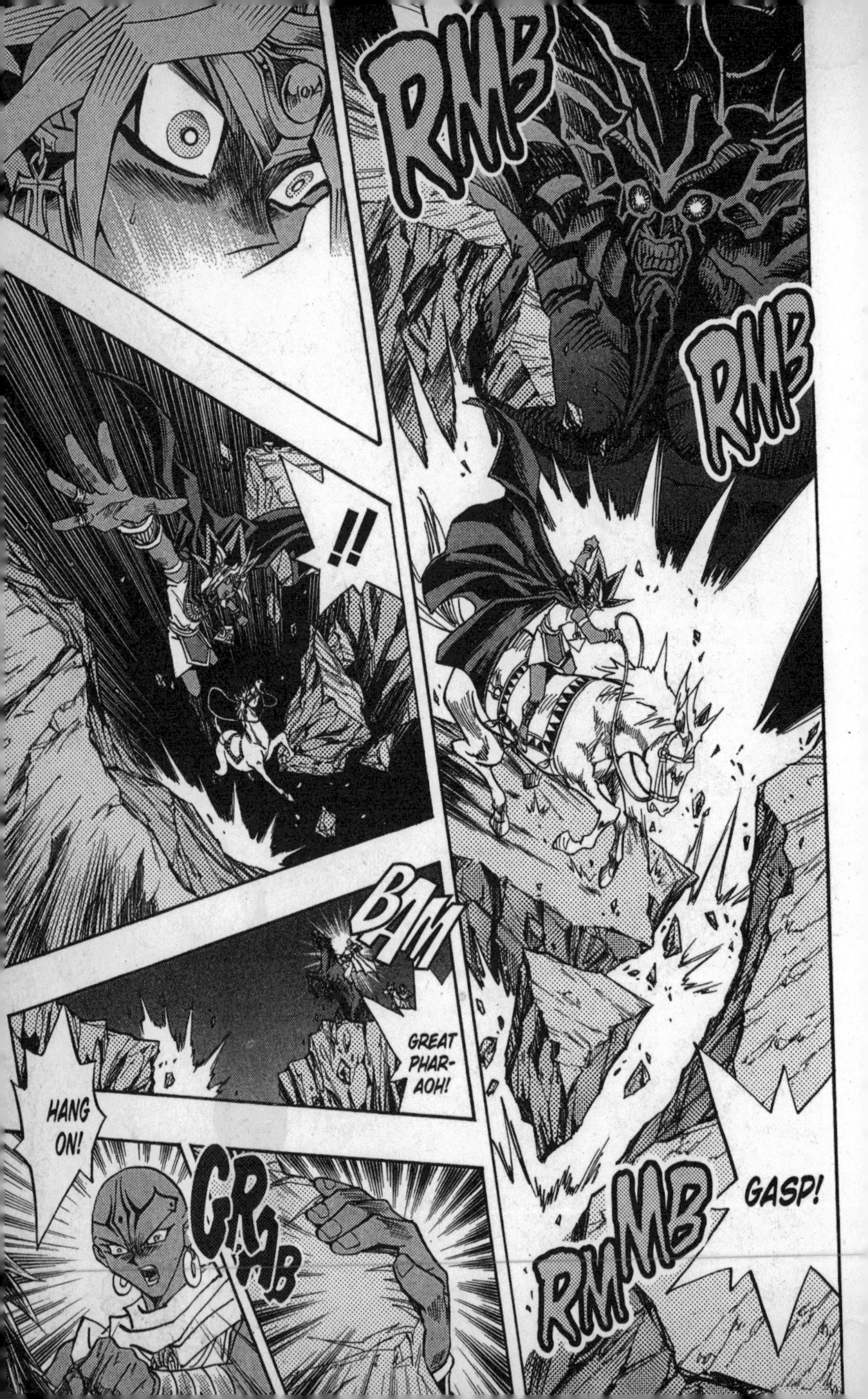
RMB
RMB
GASP!
RMMB
!!
BAM
GREAT PHAR-AOH!
HANG ON!
GRAB

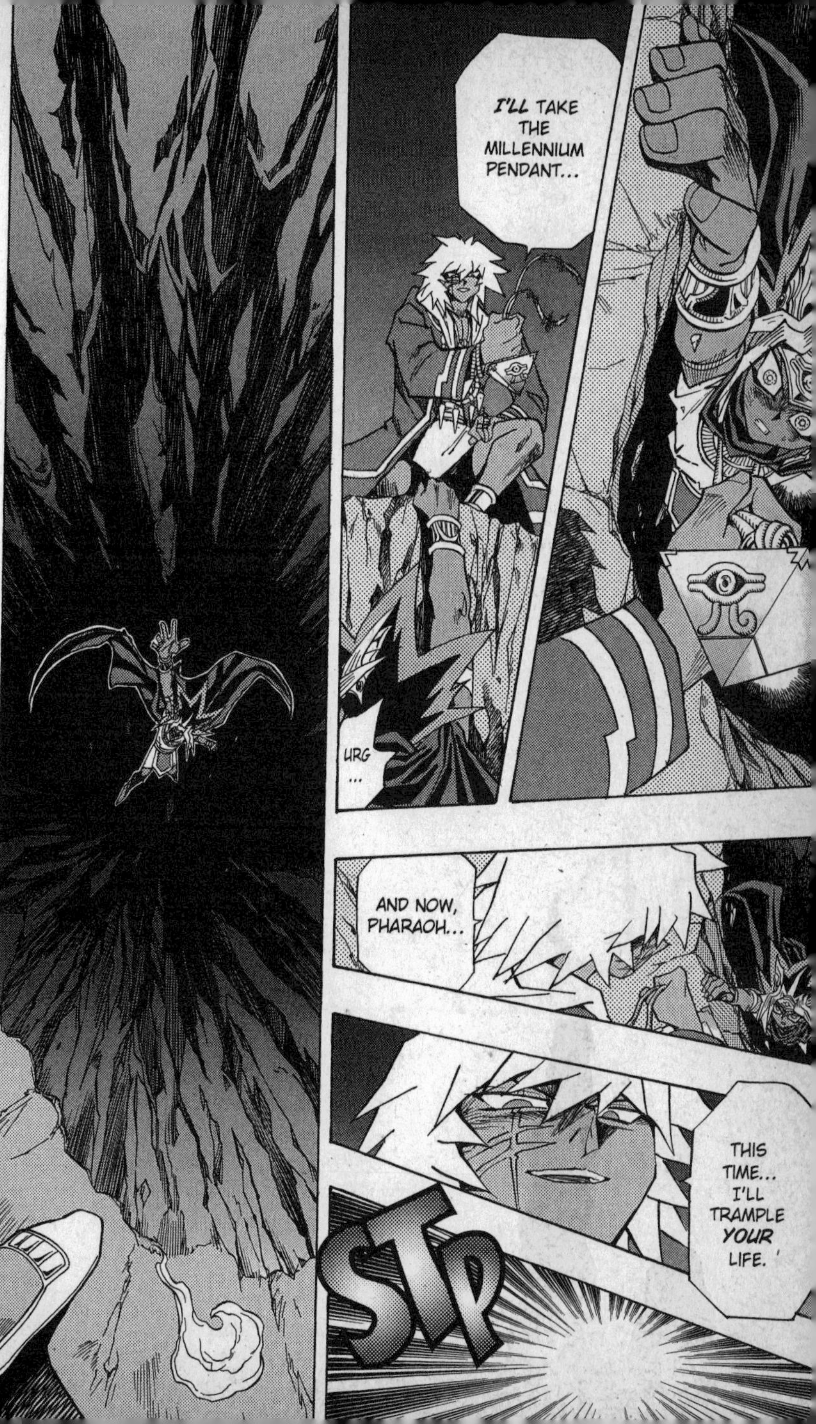

I'LL TAKE THE MILLENNIUM PENDANT...
URG ...
AND NOW, PHARAOH...
THIS TIME... I'LL TRAMPLE YOUR LIFE.
STP

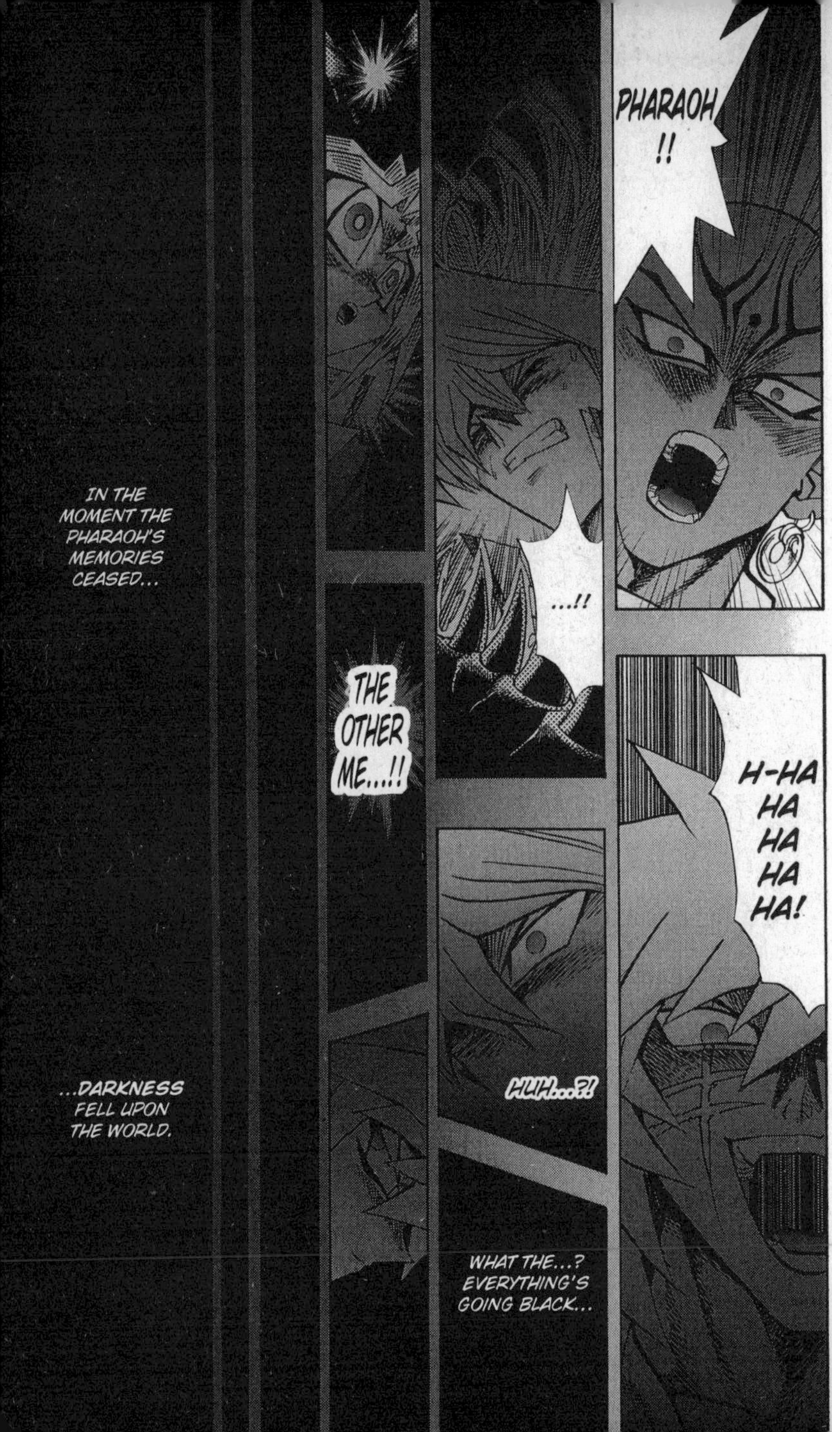
PHARAOH!!
H-HA HA HA HA HA!
...!!
HUH...?!
WHAT THE...? EVERYTHING'S GOING BLACK...
THE OTHER ME...!!
IN THE MOMENT THE PHARAOH'S MEMORIES CEASED...
...DARKNESS FELL UPON THE WORLD.

# Duel 30: The Birth of the Millennium Items!!

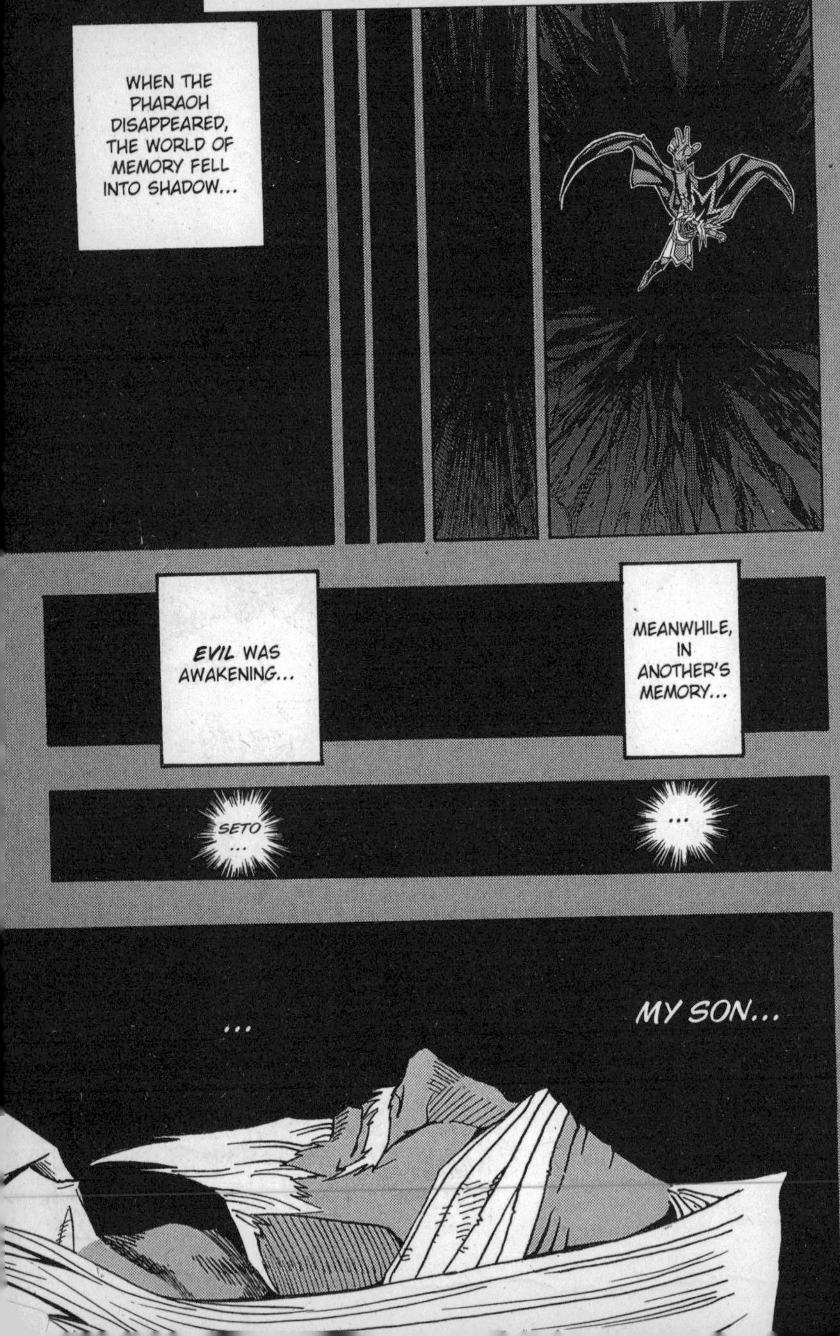
WHEN THE PHARAOH DISAPPEARED, THE WORLD OF MEMORY FELL INTO SHADOW...
MEANWHILE, IN ANOTHER'S MEMORY...
EVIL WAS AWAKENING...
...
SETO ...
MY SON...
...

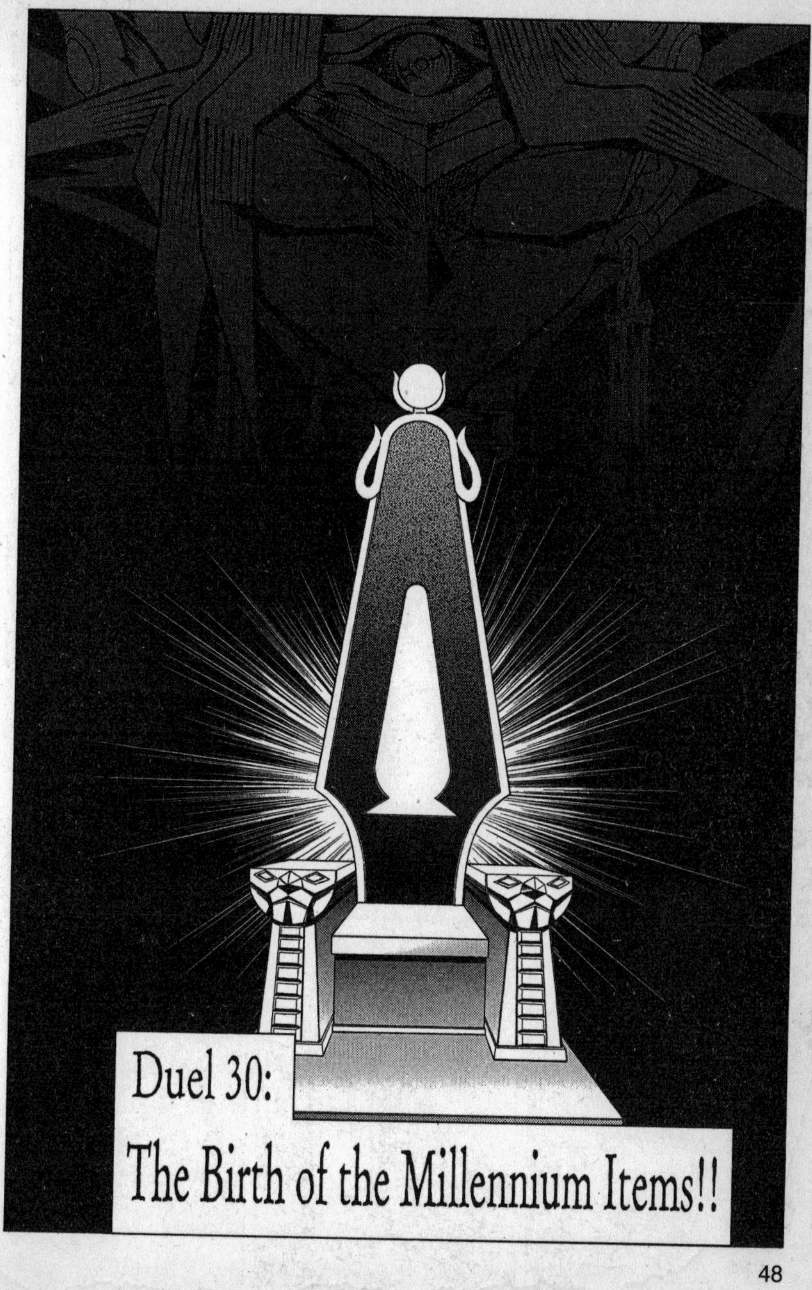

# Duel 30: The Birth of the Millennium Items!!

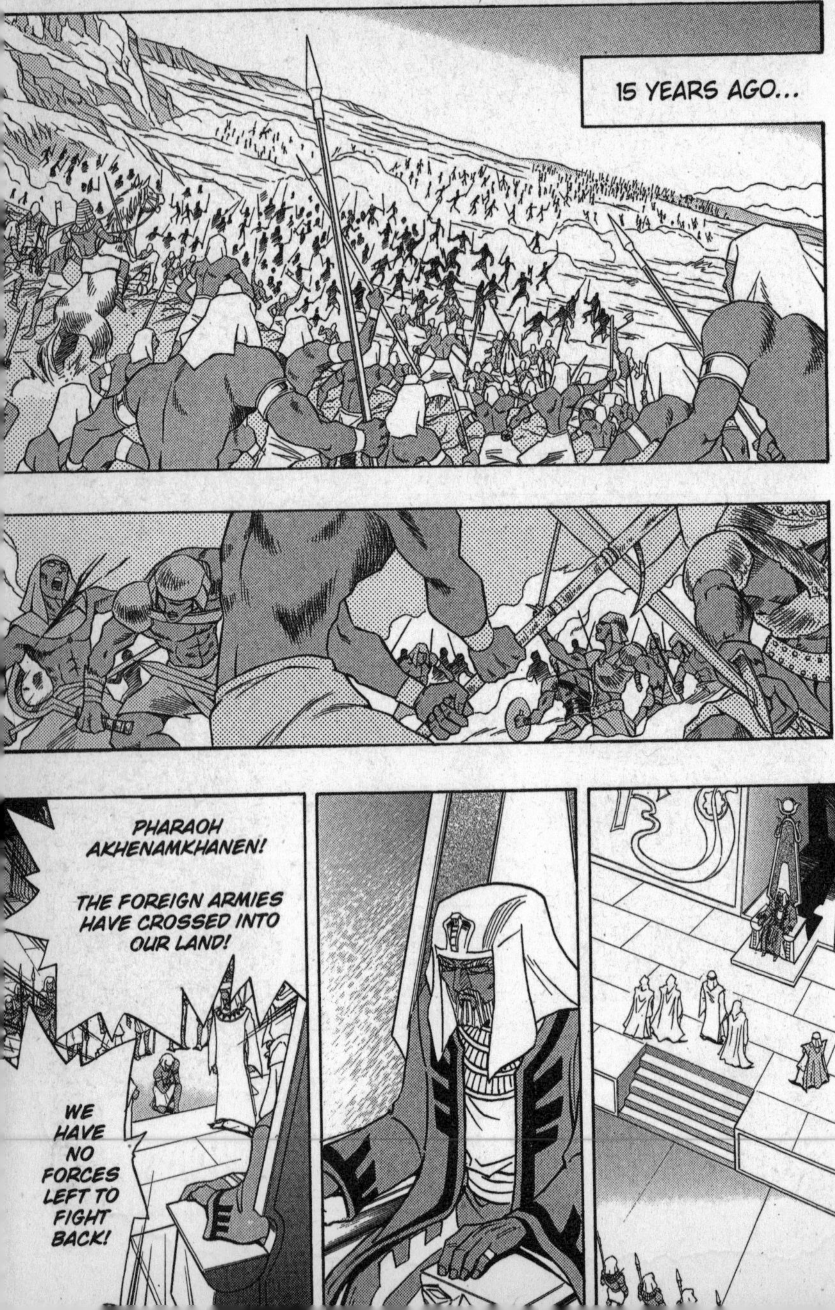
15 YEARS AGO...
PHARAOH AKHENAMKHANEN!
THE FOREIGN ARMIES HAVE CROSSED INTO OUR LAND!
WE HAVE NO FORCES LEFT TO FIGHT BACK!

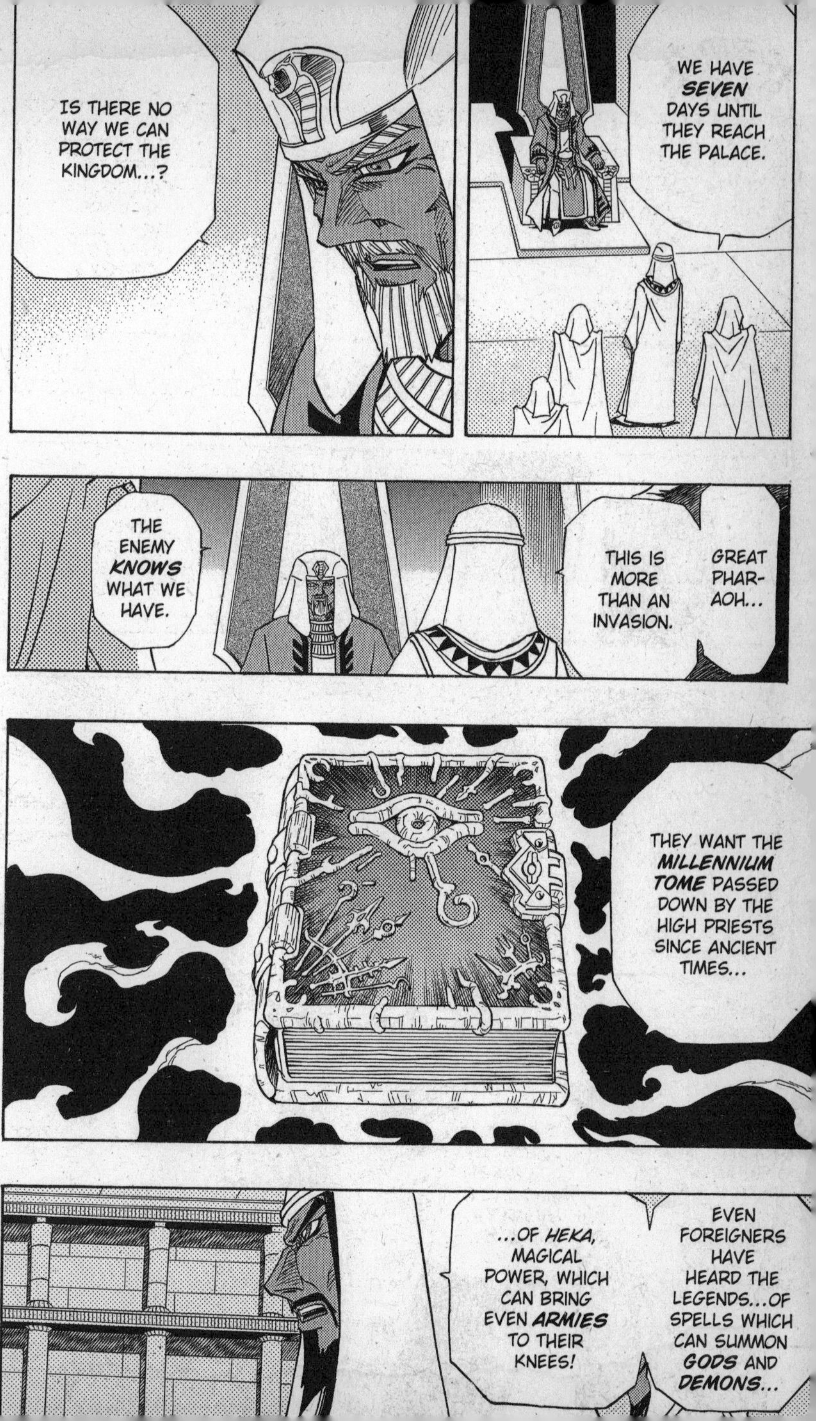
WE HAVE SEVEN DAYS UNTIL THEY REACH THE PALACE.
IS THERE NO WAY WE CAN PROTECT THE KINGDOM...?
GREAT PHARAOH...
THIS IS MORE THAN AN INVASION.
THE ENEMY KNOWS WHAT WE HAVE.
THEY WANT THE MILLENNIUM TOME PASSED DOWN BY THE HIGH PRIESTS SINCE ANCIENT TIMES...
EVEN FOREIGNERS HAVE HEARD THE LEGENDS...OF SPELLS WHICH CAN SUMMON GODS AND DEMONS...
...OF HEKA, MAGICAL POWER, WHICH CAN BRING EVEN ARMIES TO THEIR KNEES!

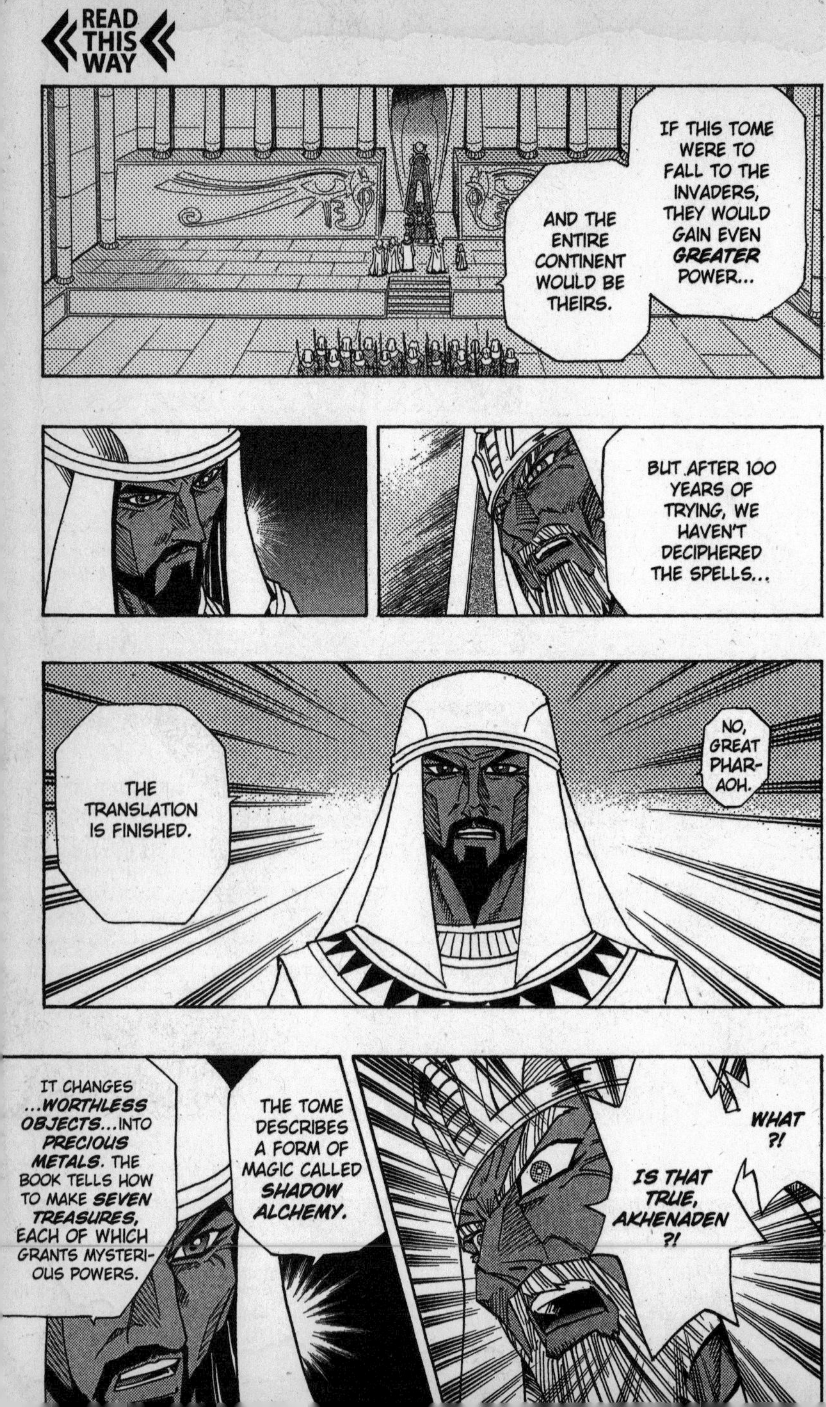
READ THIS WAY
IF THIS TOME WERE TO FALL TO THE INVADERS, THEY WOULD GAIN EVEN GREATER POWER...
AND THE ENTIRE CONTINENT WOULD BE THEIRS.
BUT AFTER 100 YEARS OF TRYING, WE HAVEN'T DECIPHERED THE SPELLS...
NO, GREAT PHAR-AOH.
THE TRANSLATION IS FINISHED.
WHAT ?!
IS THAT TRUE, AKHENADEN ?!
THE TOME DESCRIBES A FORM OF MAGIC CALLED SHADOW ALCHEMY.
IT CHANGES ...WORTHLESS OBJECTS...INTO PRECIOUS METALS. THE BOOK TELLS HOW TO MAKE SEVEN TREASURES, EACH OF WHICH GRANTS MYSTERI-OUS POWERS.

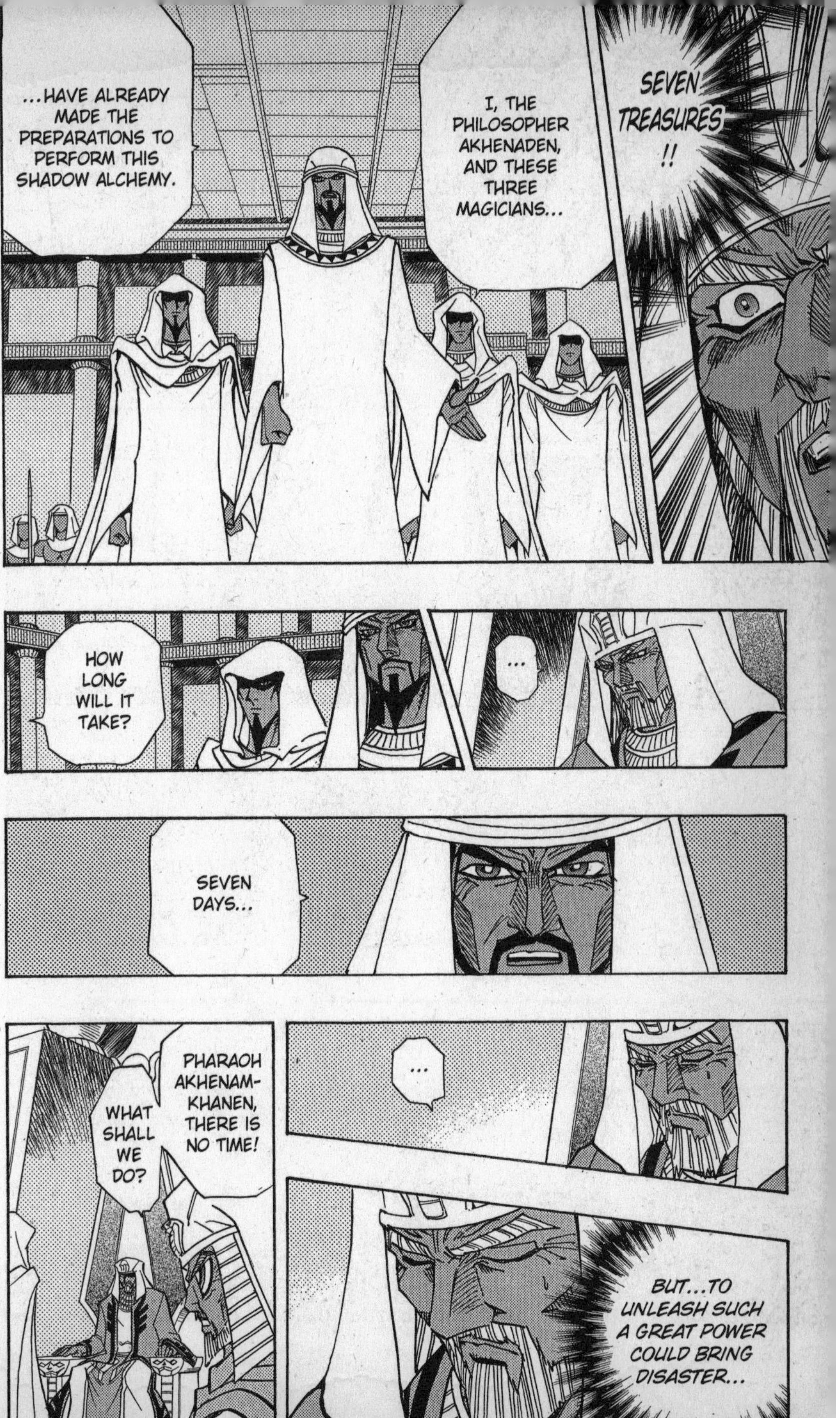
SEVEN TREASURES !!
I, THE PHILOSOPHER AKHENADEN, AND THESE THREE MAGICIANS...
...HAVE ALREADY MADE THE PREPARATIONS TO PERFORM THIS SHADOW ALCHEMY.
...
HOW LONG WILL IT TAKE?
SEVEN DAYS...
...
BUT...TO UNLEASH SUCH A GREAT POWER COULD BRING DISASTER...
PHARAOH AKHENAMKHANEN, THERE IS NO TIME!
WHAT SHALL WE DO?

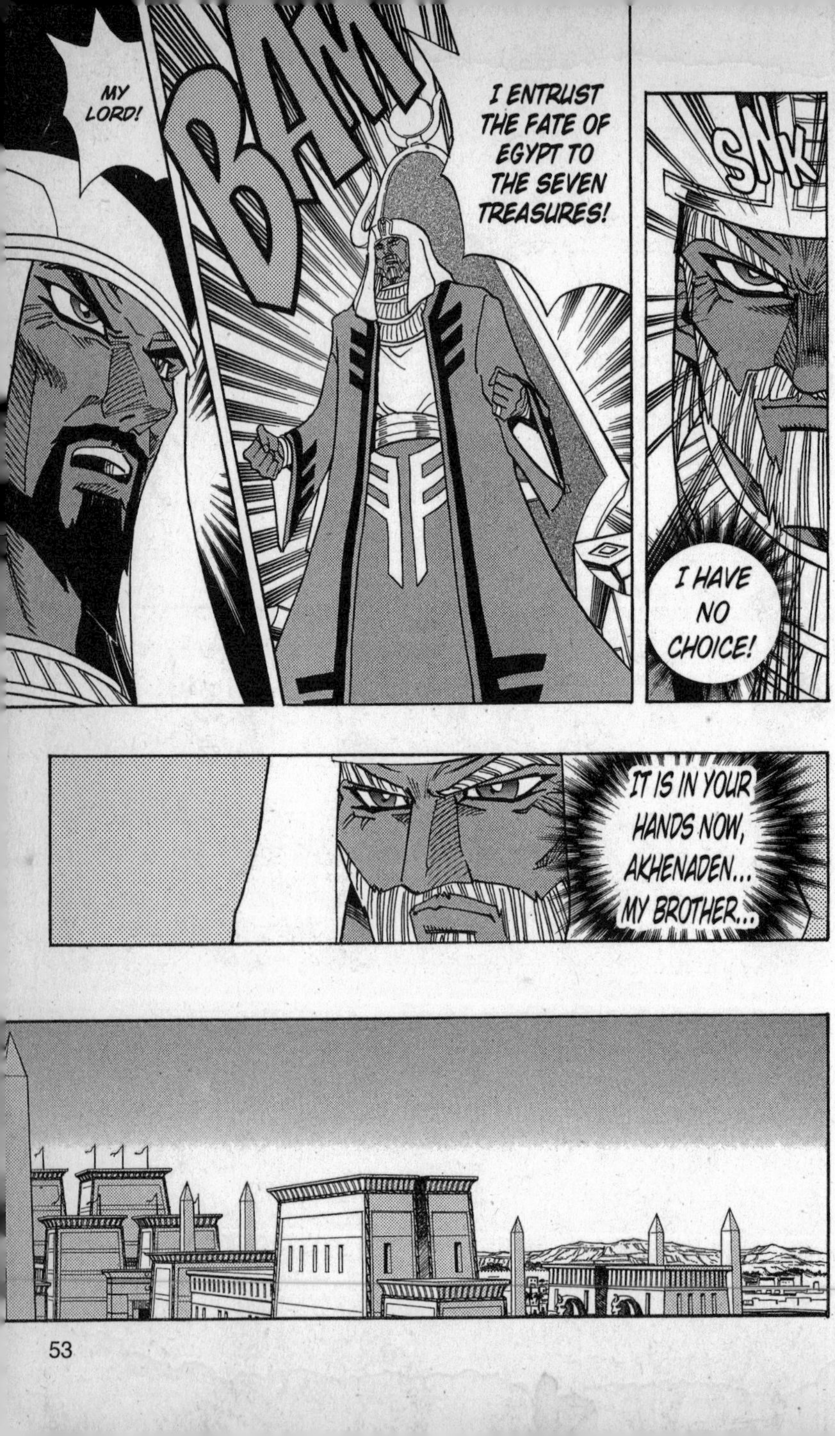
SNK
I HAVE NO CHOICE!
I ENTRUST THE FATE OF EGYPT TO THE SEVEN TREASURES!
BAM
MY LORD!
IT IS IN YOUR HANDS NOW, AKHENADEN... MY BROTHER...

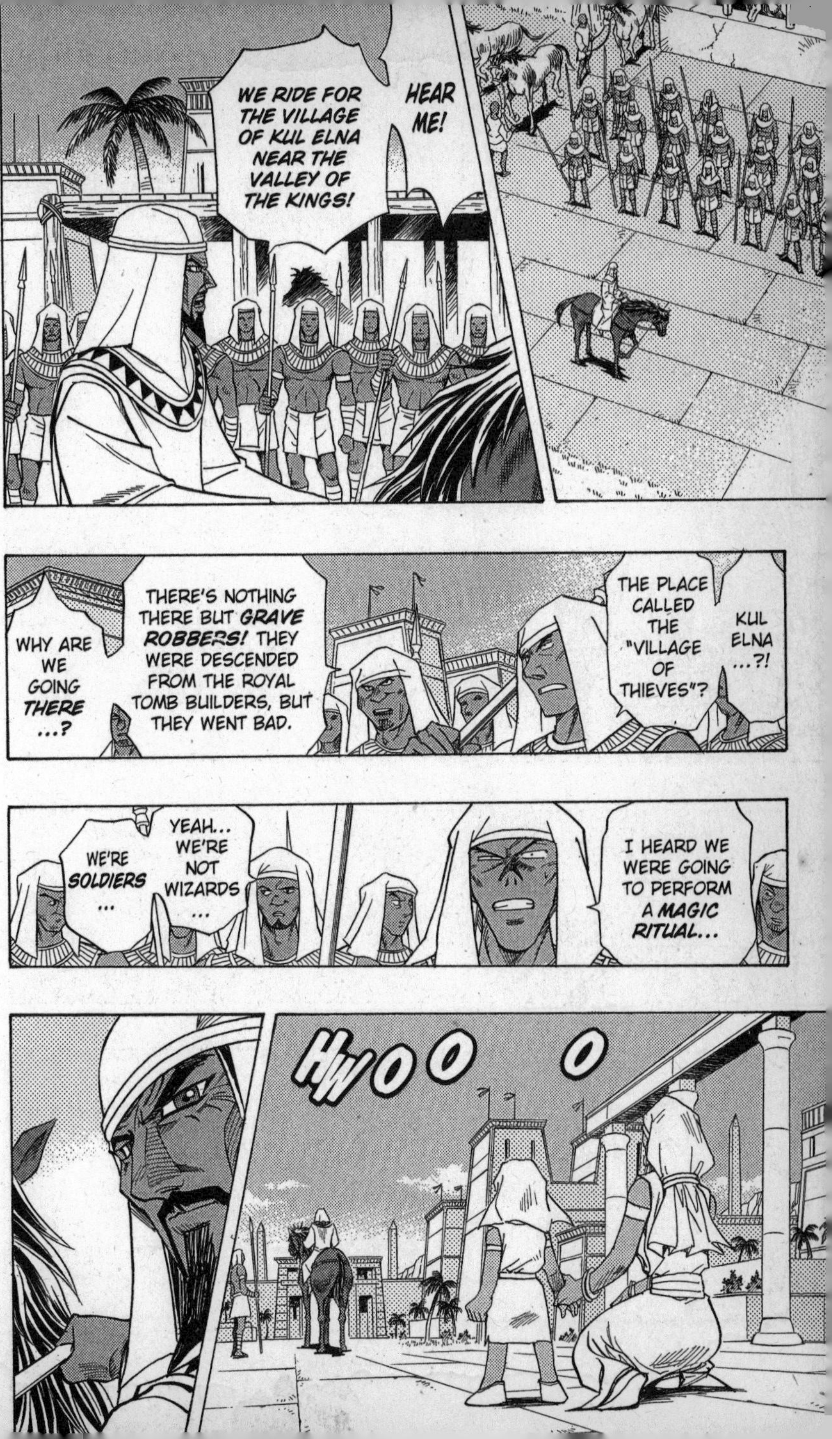
HEAR ME!
WE RIDE FOR THE VILLAGE OF KUL ELNA NEAR THE VALLEY OF THE KINGS!
KUL ELNA ...?!
THE PLACE CALLED THE "VILLAGE OF THIEVES"?
THERE'S NOTHING THERE BUT GRAVE ROBBERS! THEY WERE DESCENDED FROM THE ROYAL TOMB BUILDERS, BUT THEY WENT BAD.
WHY ARE WE GOING THERE ...?
I HEARD WE WERE GOING TO PERFORM A MAGIC RITUAL...
YEAH... WE'RE NOT WIZARDS ...
WE'RE SOLDIERS ...
HWOO O

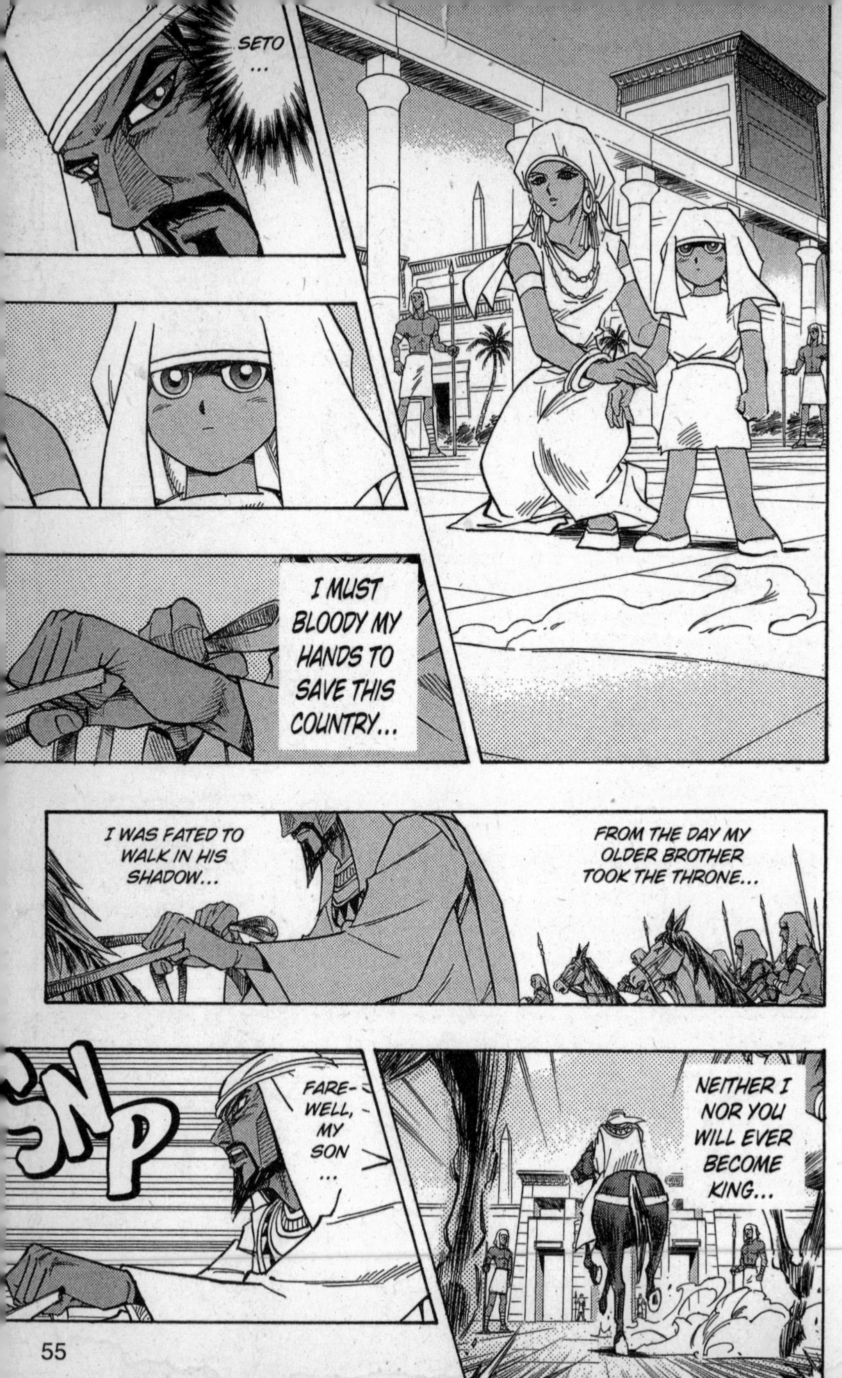
SETO ...
I MUST BLOODY MY HANDS TO SAVE THIS COUNTRY...
FROM THE DAY MY OLDER BROTHER TOOK THE THRONE...
I WAS FATED TO WALK IN HIS SHADOW...
NEITHER I NOR YOU WILL EVER BECOME KING...
SNP
FARE-WELL, MY SON ...

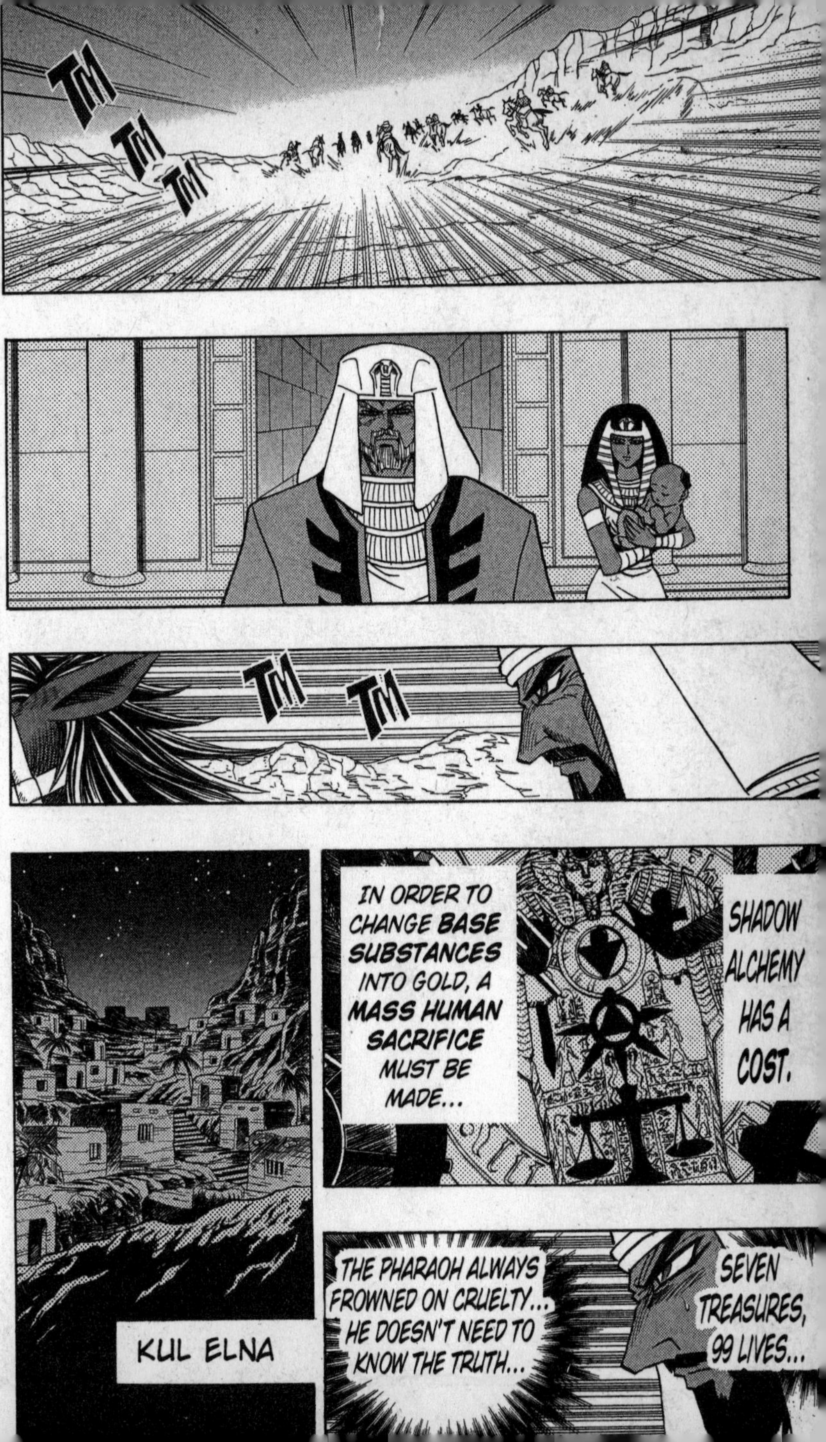
TM
TM
TM
TM
TM
SHADOW ALCHEMY HAS A COST.
IN ORDER TO CHANGE **BASE SUBSTANCES** INTO GOLD, A **MASS HUMAN SACRIFICE** MUST BE MADE...
SEVEN TREASURES, 99 LIVES...
THE PHARAOH ALWAYS FROWNED ON CRUELTY... HE DOESN'T NEED TO KNOW THE TRUTH...
KUL ELNA

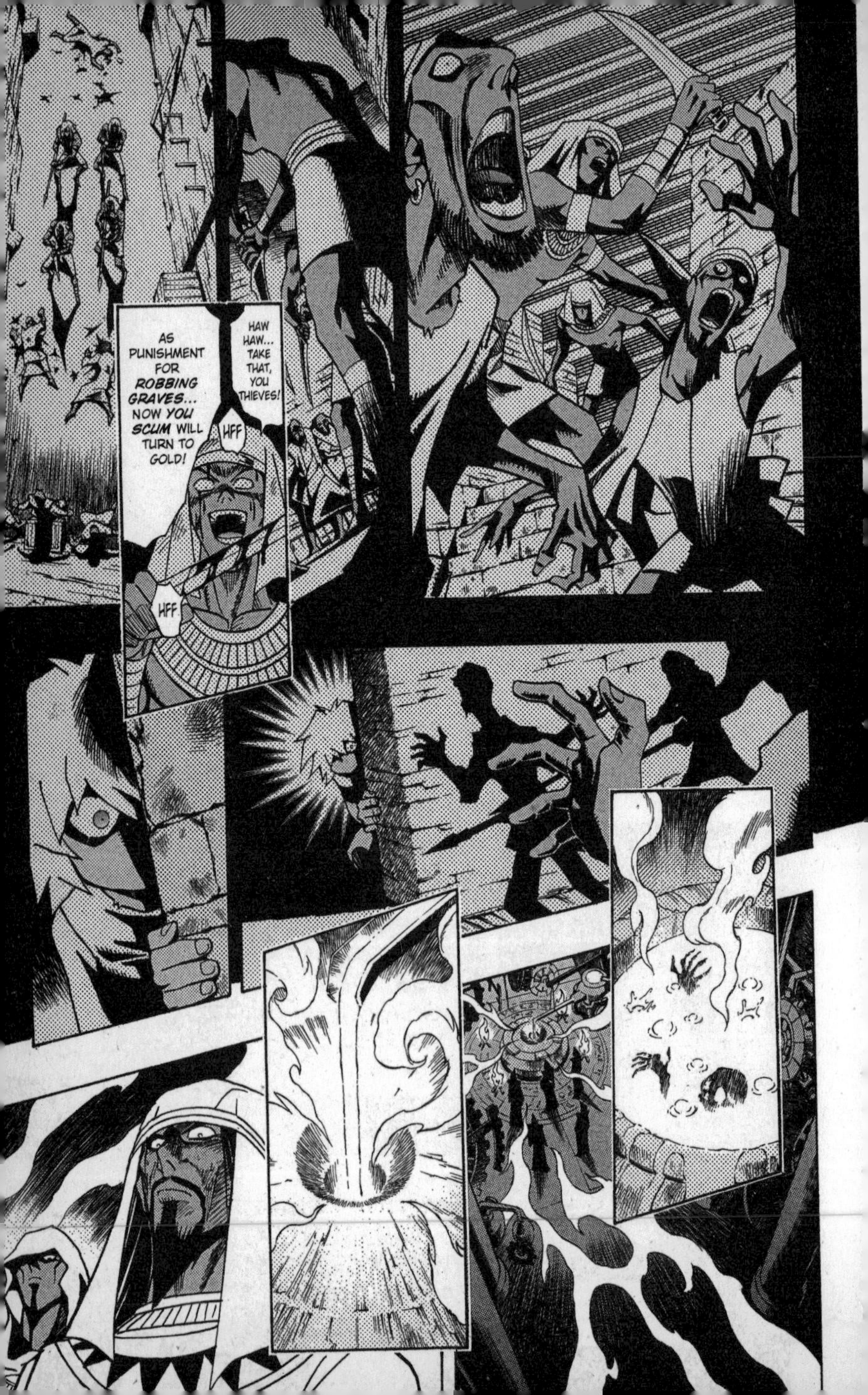
HAW HAW... TAKE THAT, YOU THIEVES!
AS PUNISHMENT FOR *ROBBING GRAVES...* NOW *YOU SCUM* WILL TURN TO GOLD!
HFF
HFF

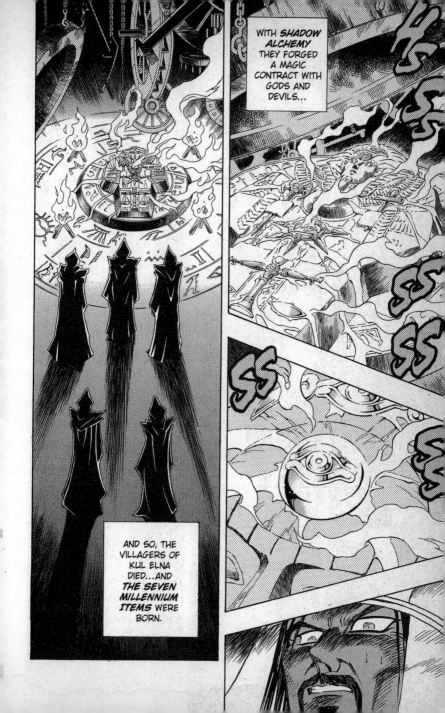

WITH *SHADOW ALCHEMY* THEY FORGED A MAGIC CONTRACT WITH GODS AND DEVILS...

AND SO, THE VILLAGERS OF KUL ELNA DIED...AND *THE SEVEN MILLENNIUM ITEMS* WERE BORN.

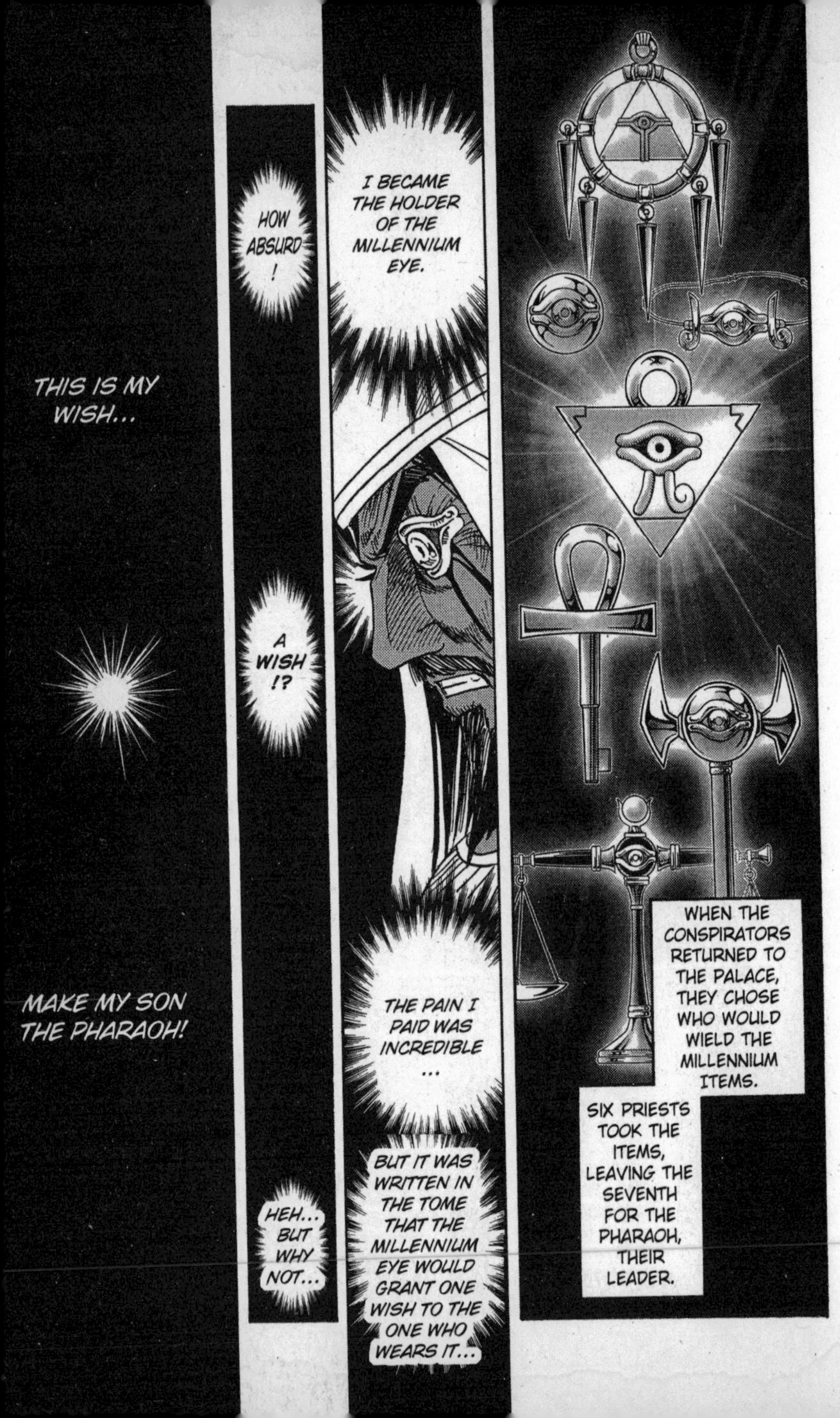

WHEN THE CONSPIRATORS RETURNED TO THE PALACE, THEY CHOSE WHO WOULD WIELD THE MILLENNIUM ITEMS.
SIX PRIESTS TOOK THE ITEMS, LEAVING THE SEVENTH FOR THE PHARAOH, THEIR LEADER.
I BECAME THE HOLDER OF THE MILLENNIUM EYE.
THE PAIN I PAID WAS INCREDIBLE ...
BUT IT WAS WRITTEN IN THE TOME THAT THE MILLENNIUM EYE WOULD GRANT ONE WISH TO THE ONE WHO WEARS IT...
HOW ABSURD !
A WISH !?
HEH... BUT WHY NOT...
THIS IS MY WISH...
MAKE MY SON THE PHARAOH!

SEVEN DAYS LATER

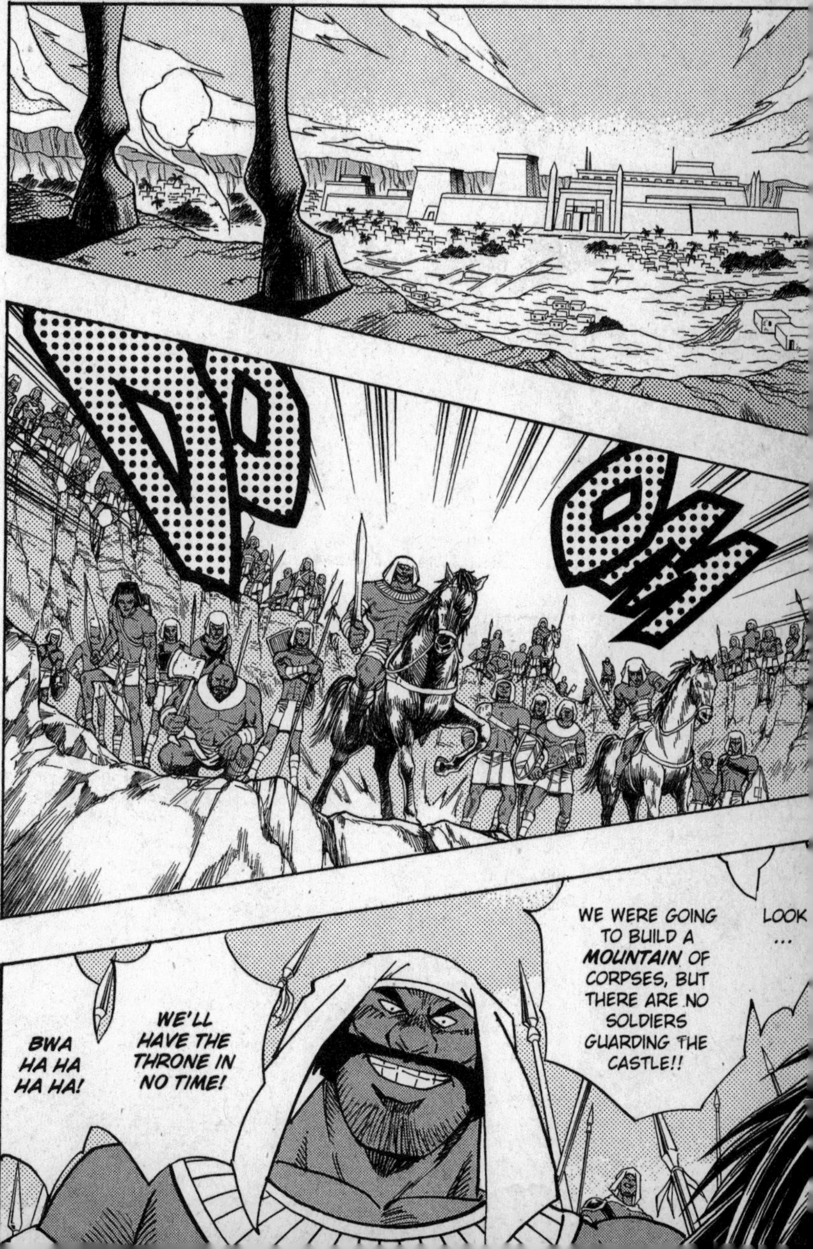
DOOM
LOOK...
WE WERE GOING TO BUILD A *MOUNTAIN* OF CORPSES, BUT THERE ARE NO SOLDIERS GUARDING THE CASTLE!!
WE'LL HAVE THE THRONE IN NO TIME!
BWA HA HA HA HA!

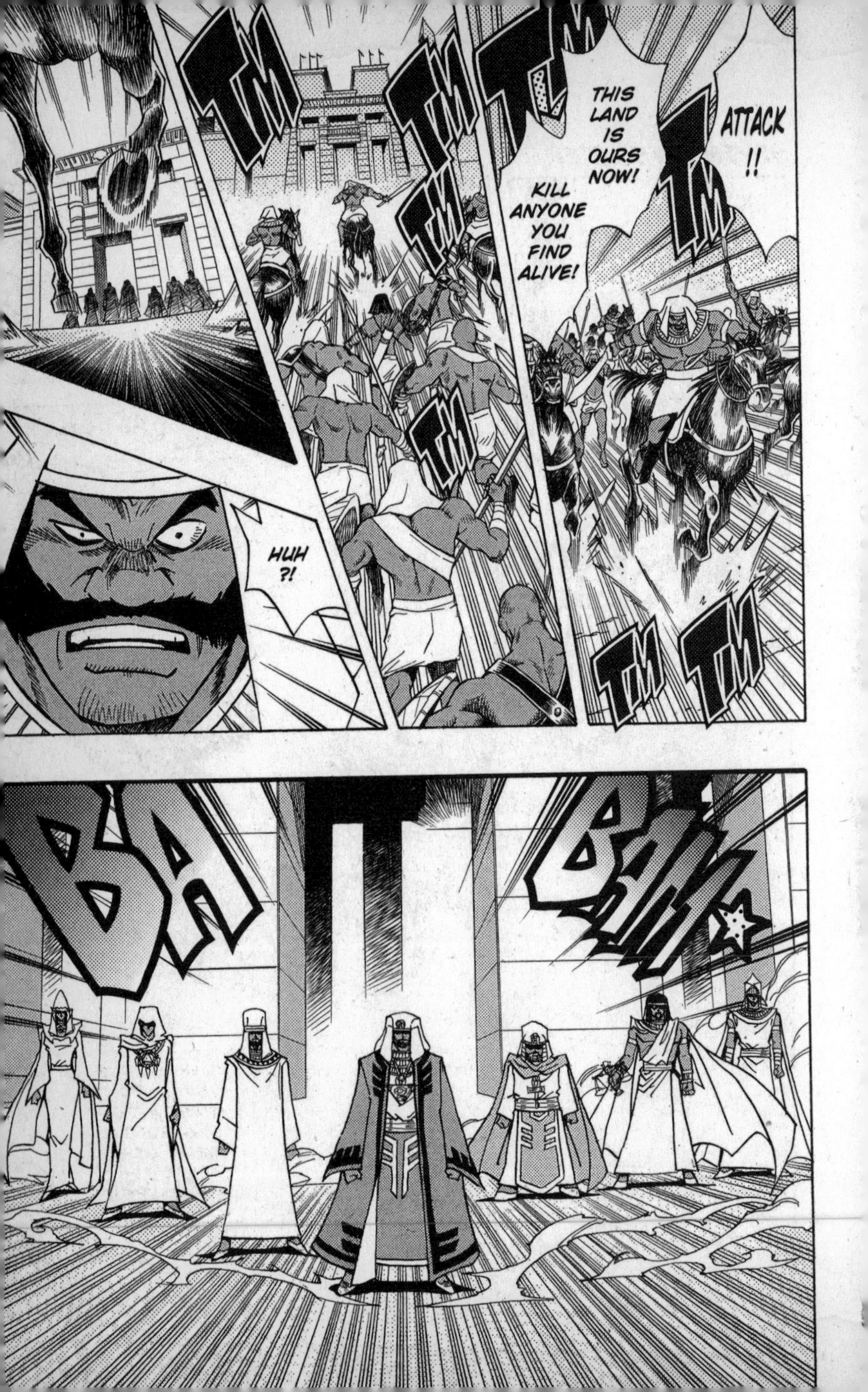
ATTACK !!
THIS LAND IS OURS NOW!
KILL ANYONE YOU FIND ALIVE!
TM TM
HUH ?!

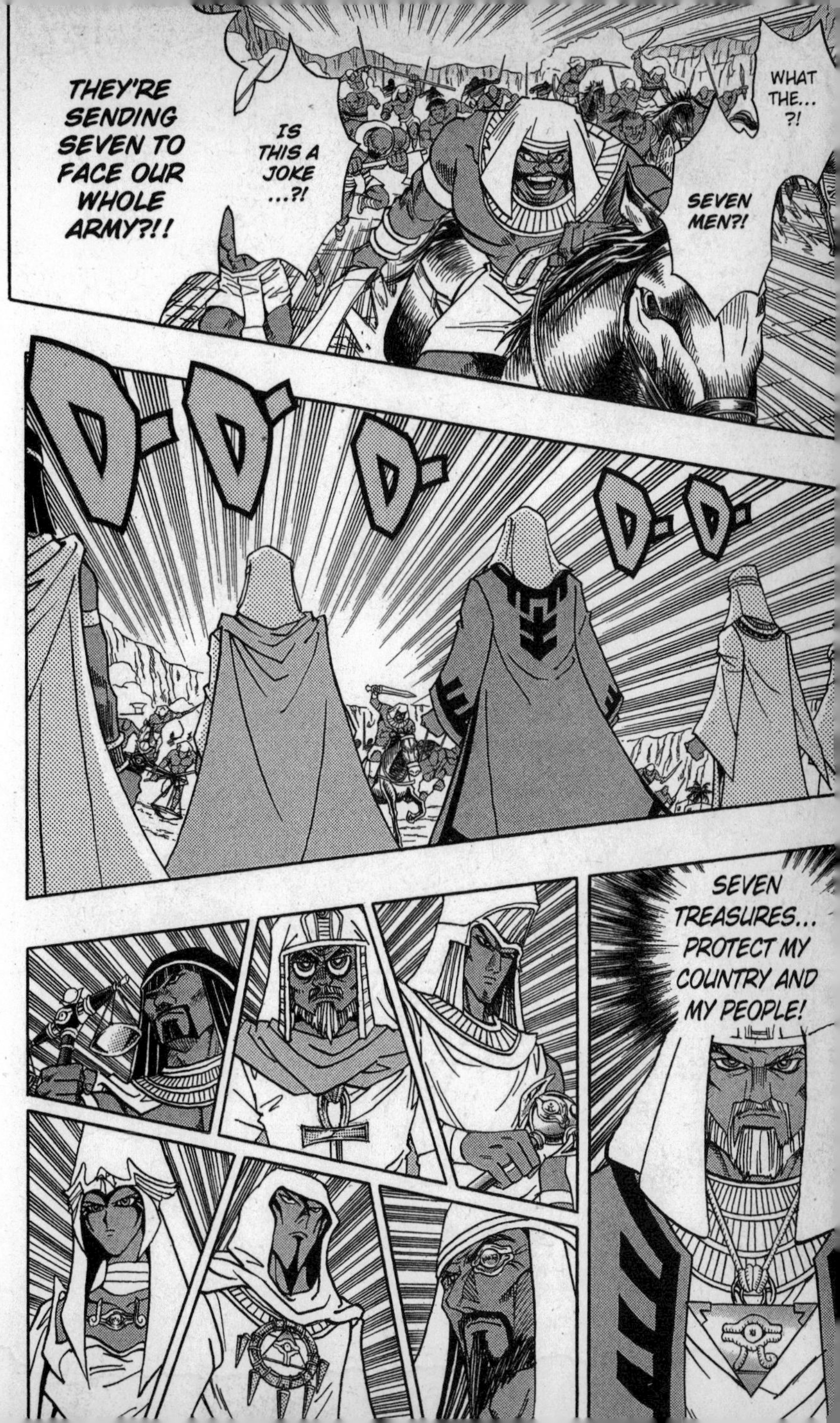
WHAT THE... ?!
SEVEN MEN?!
IS THIS A JOKE ...?!
THEY'RE SENDING SEVEN TO FACE OUR WHOLE ARMY?!!
D-D- D- D-D-
SEVEN TREASURES... PROTECT MY COUNTRY AND MY PEOPLE!

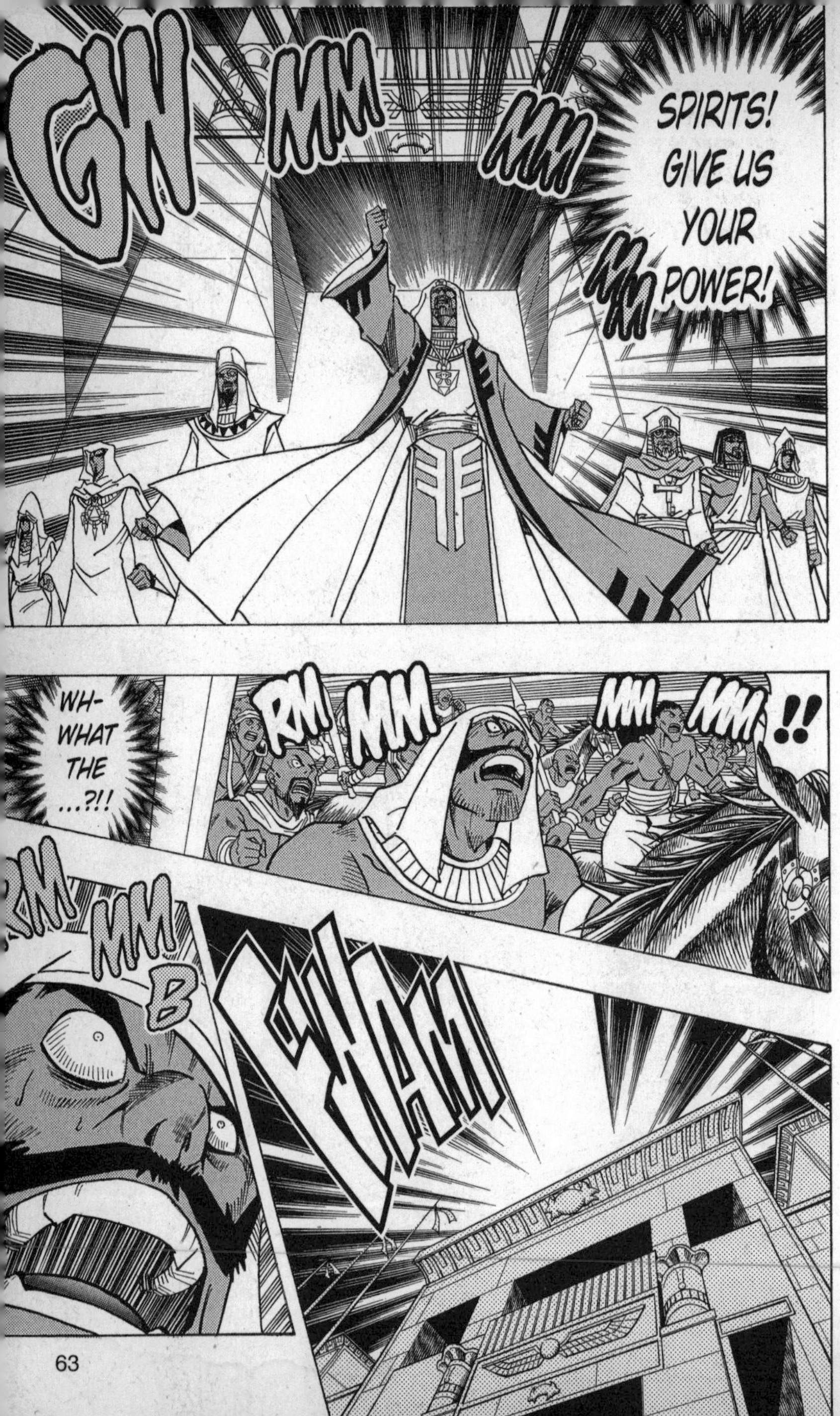
SPIRITS! GIVE US YOUR POWER!
GH MM MM MMM
RM MM MM MM!!
WH-WHAT THE ...?!!
RM MM B

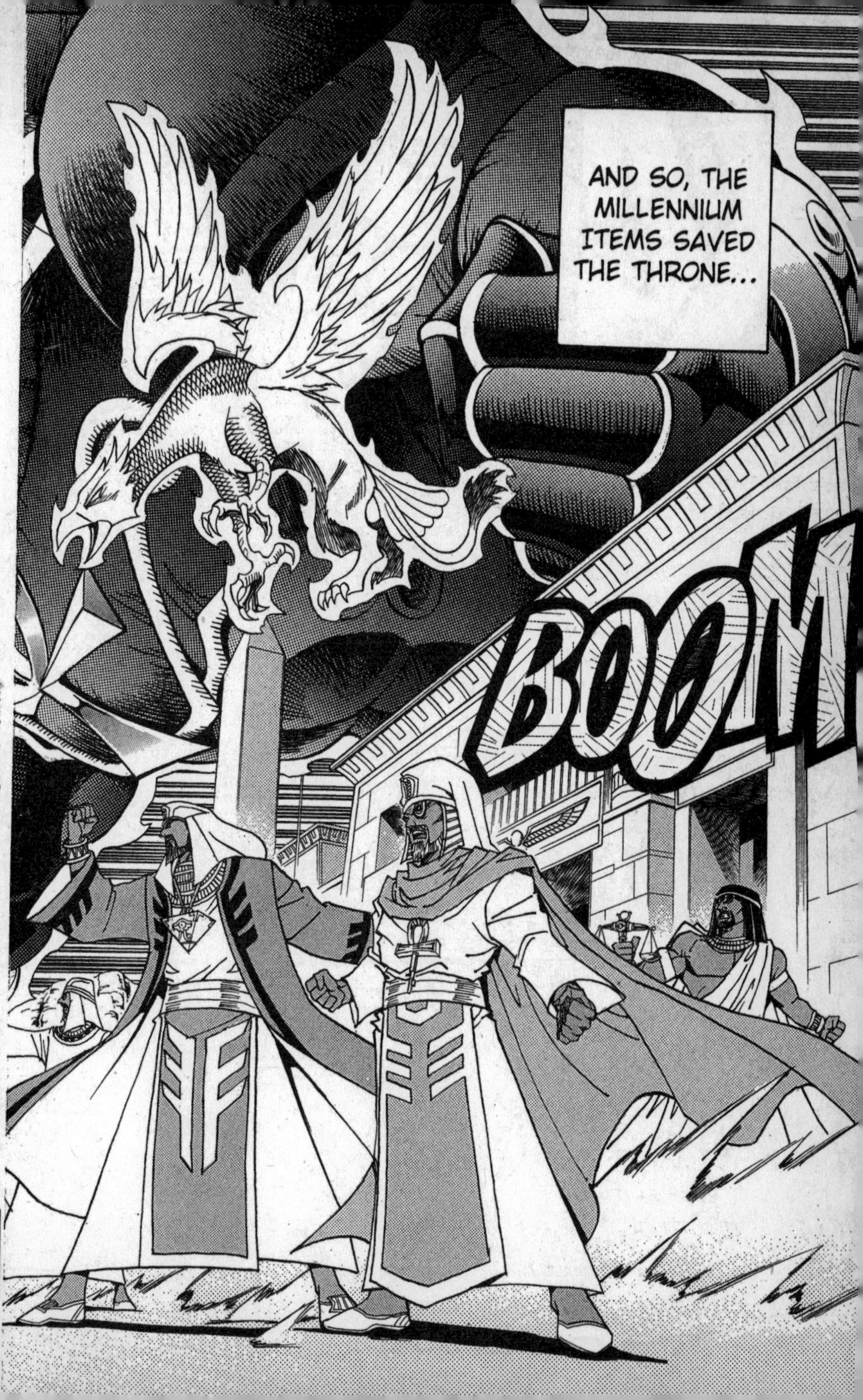
AND SO, THE MILLENNIUM ITEMS SAVED THE THRONE...
BOOM

# Duel 31: Ripples in the Shadows

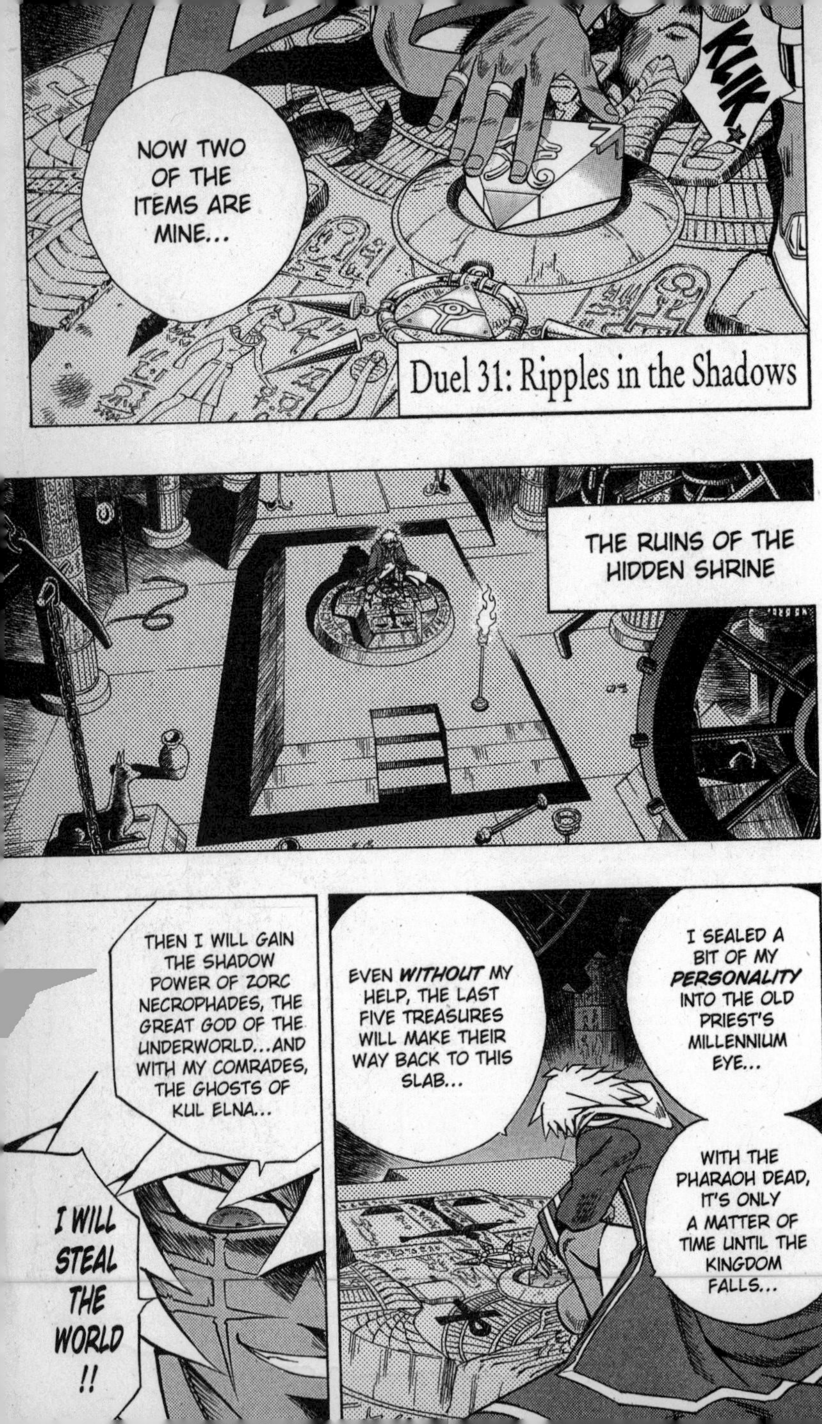
KLIK
NOW TWO OF THE ITEMS ARE MINE...
THE RUINS OF THE HIDDEN SHRINE
I SEALED A BIT OF MY *PERSONALITY* INTO THE OLD PRIEST'S MILLENNIUM EYE...
WITH THE PHARAOH DEAD, IT'S ONLY A MATTER OF TIME UNTIL THE KINGDOM FALLS...
EVEN *WITHOUT* MY HELP, THE LAST FIVE TREASURES WILL MAKE THEIR WAY BACK TO THIS SLAB...
THEN I WILL GAIN THE SHADOW POWER OF ZORC NECROPHADES, THE GREAT GOD OF THE UNDERWORLD...AND WITH MY COMRADES, THE GHOSTS OF KUL ELNA...
I WILL STEAL THE WORLD!!

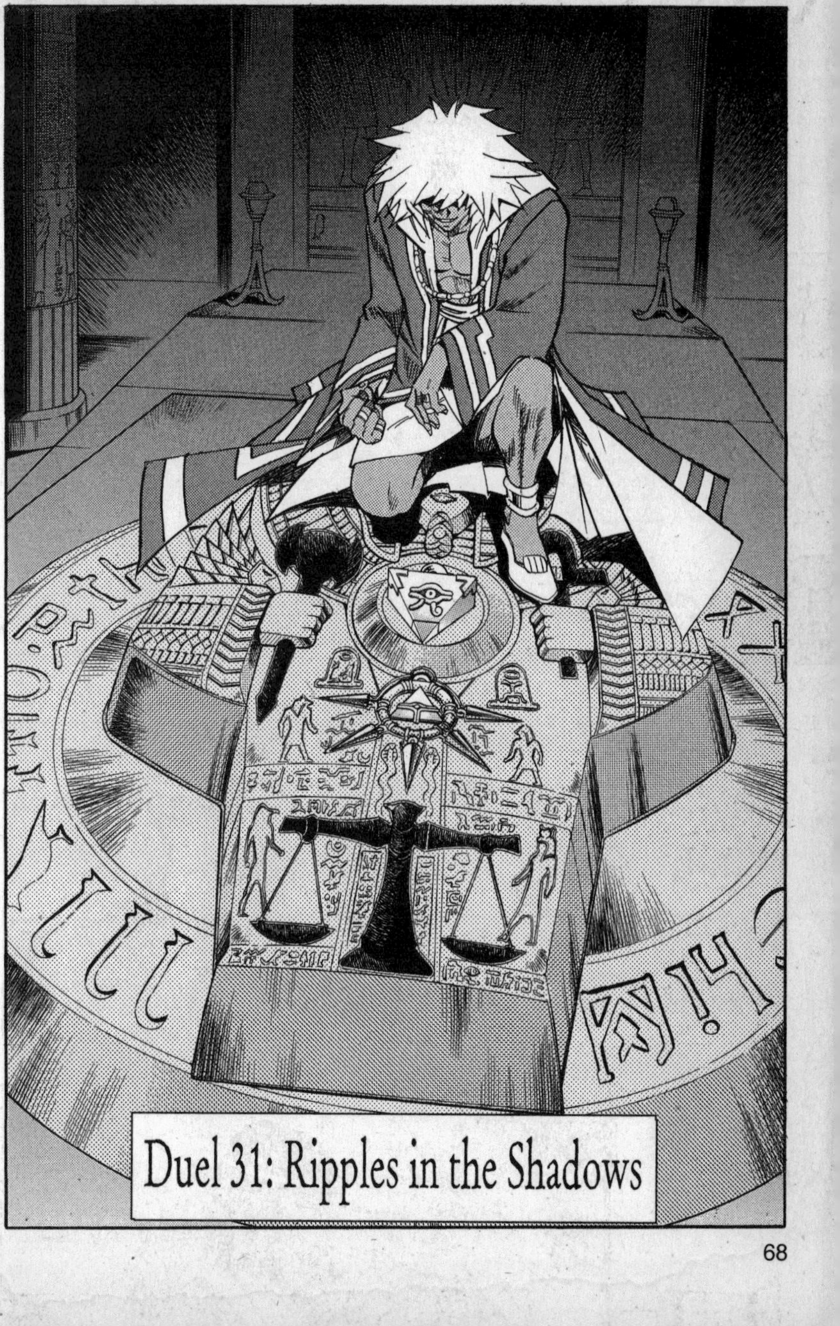
Duel 31: Ripples in the Shadows

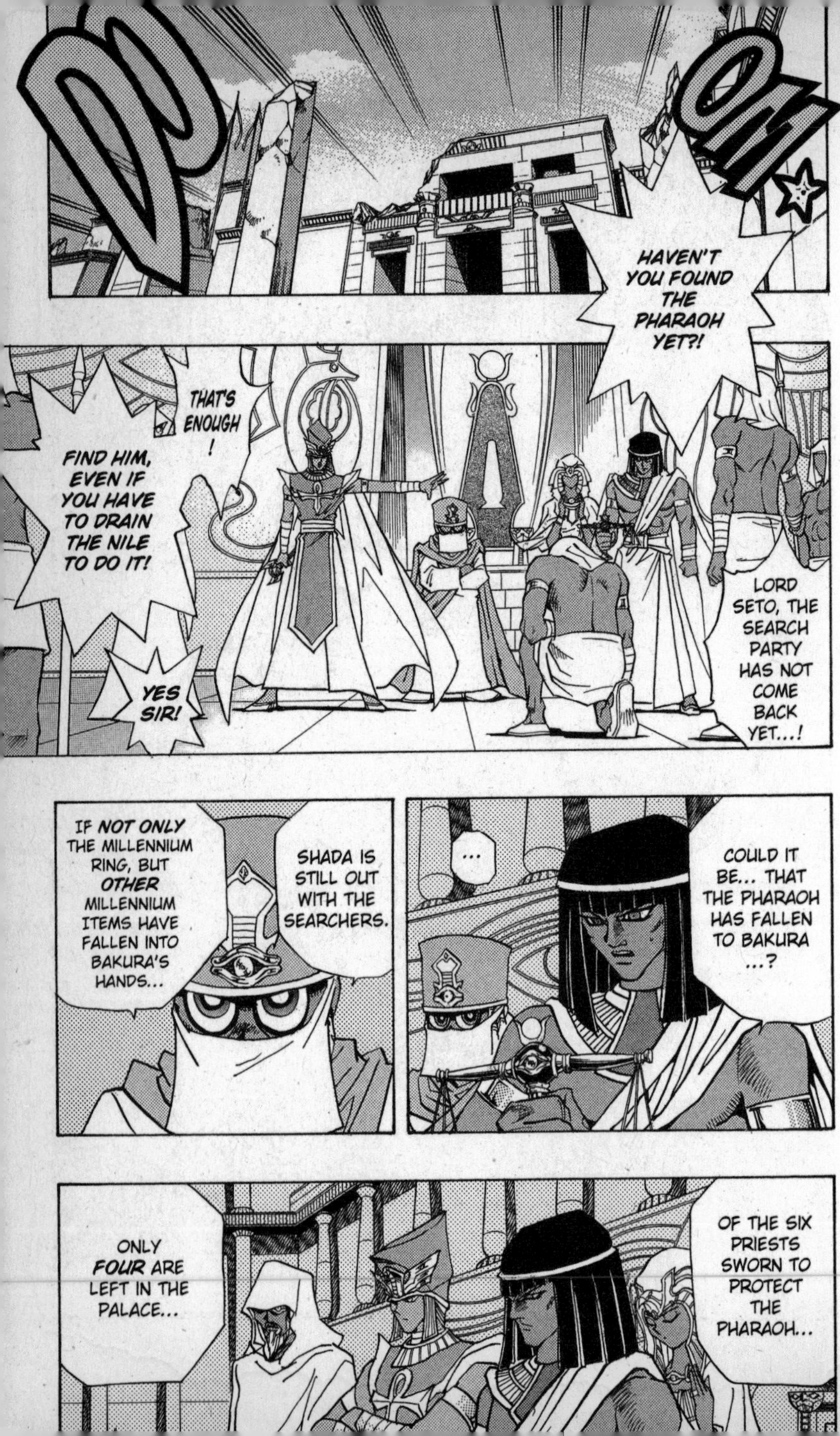
HAVEN'T YOU FOUND THE PHARAOH YET?!
LORD SETO, THE SEARCH PARTY HAS NOT COME BACK YET...!
THAT'S ENOUGH!
FIND HIM, EVEN IF YOU HAVE TO DRAIN THE NILE TO DO IT!
YES SIR!
COULD IT BE... THAT THE PHARAOH HAS FALLEN TO BAKURA...?
...
SHADA IS STILL OUT WITH THE SEARCHERS.
IF NOT ONLY THE MILLENNIUM RING, BUT OTHER MILLENNIUM ITEMS HAVE FALLEN INTO BAKURA'S HANDS...
OF THE SIX PRIESTS SWORN TO PROTECT THE PHARAOH...
ONLY FOUR ARE LEFT IN THE PALACE...

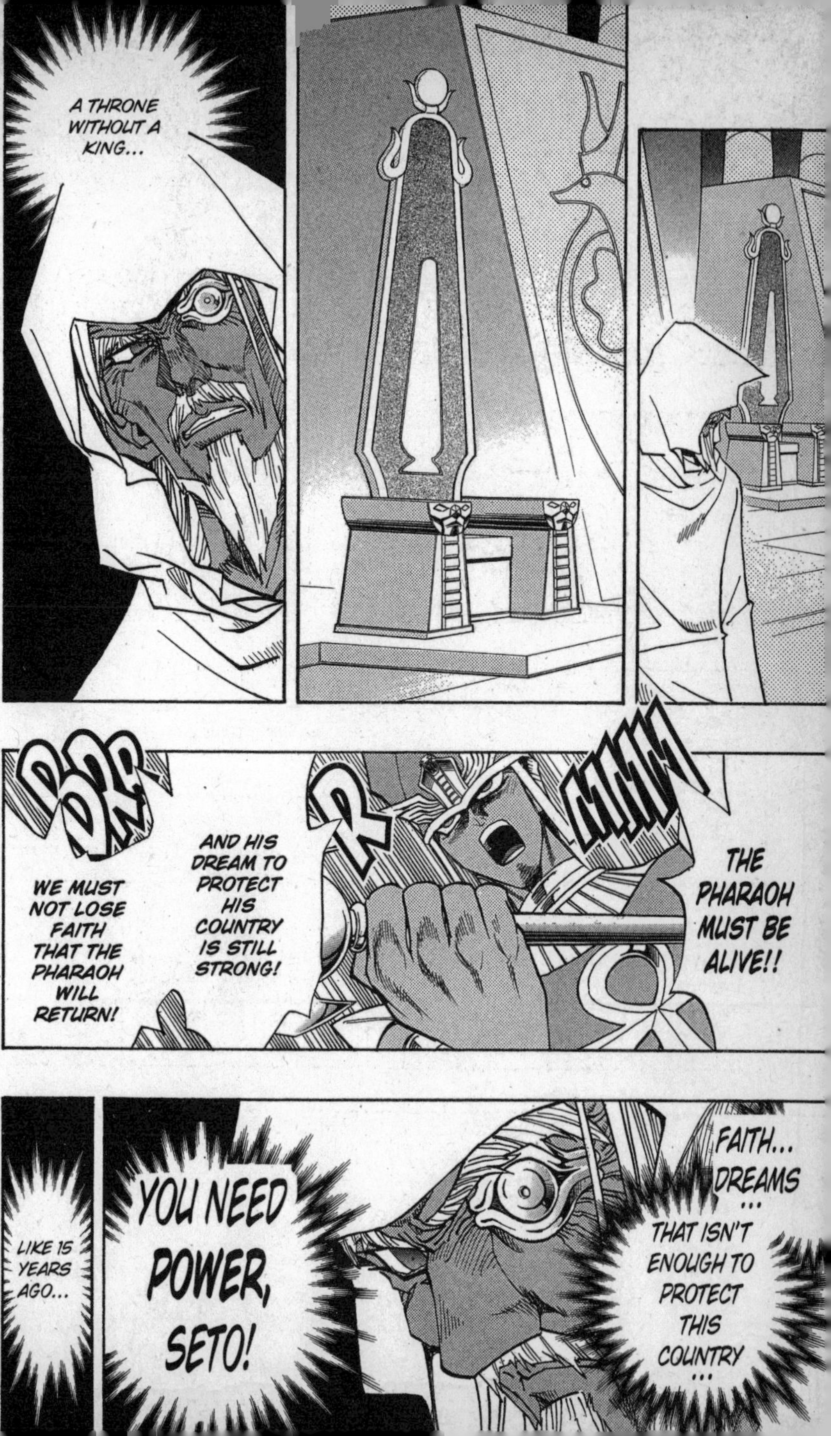

A THRONE WITHOUT A KING...
THE PHARAOH MUST BE ALIVE!!
AND HIS DREAM TO PROTECT HIS COUNTRY IS STILL STRONG!
WE MUST NOT LOSE FAITH THAT THE PHARAOH WILL RETURN!
FAITH... DREAMS...
THAT ISN'T ENOUGH TO PROTECT THIS COUNTRY...
YOU NEED POWER, SETO!
LIKE 15 YEARS AGO...

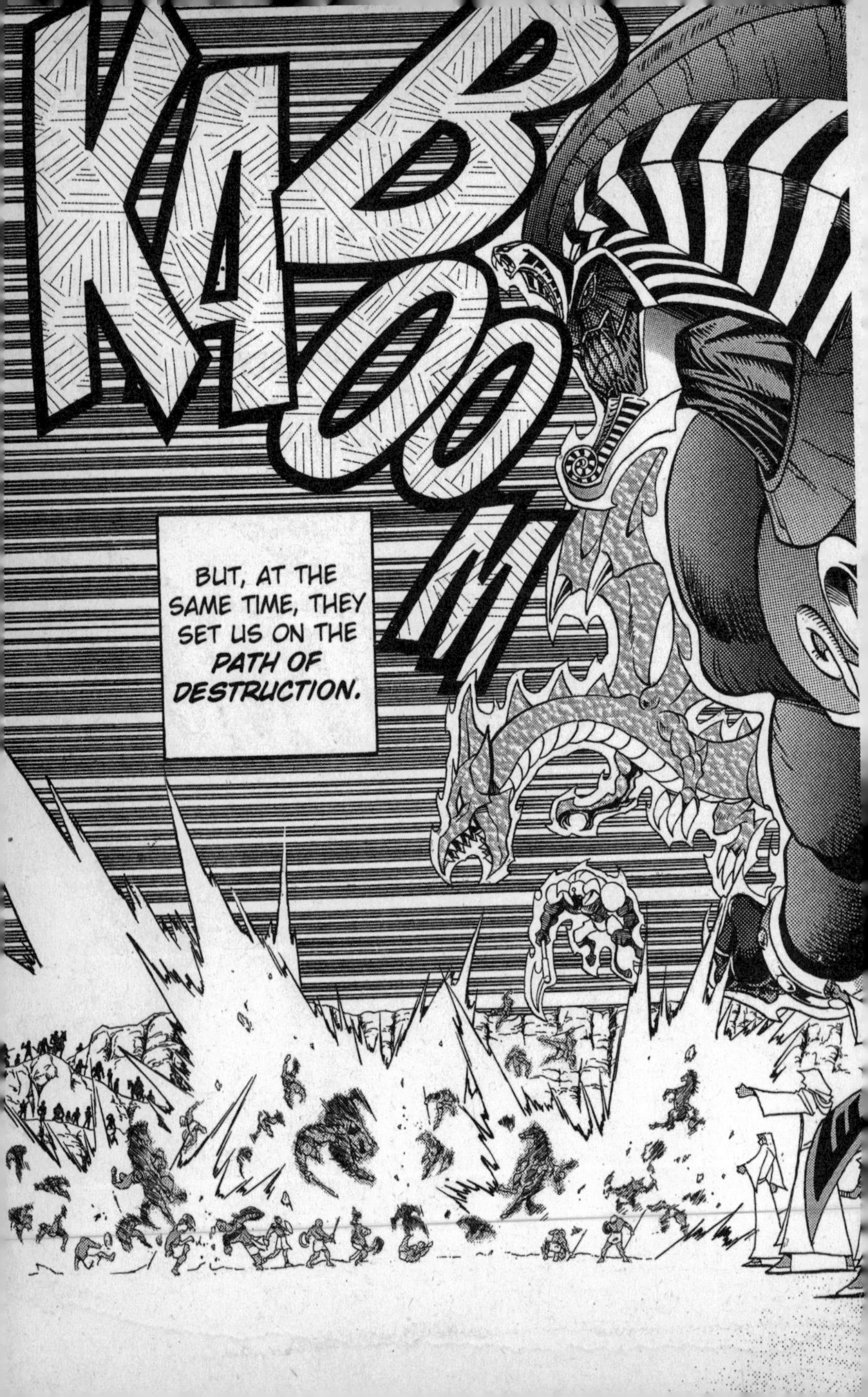
KABOOM
BUT, AT THE SAME TIME, THEY SET US ON THE *PATH OF DESTRUCTION.*

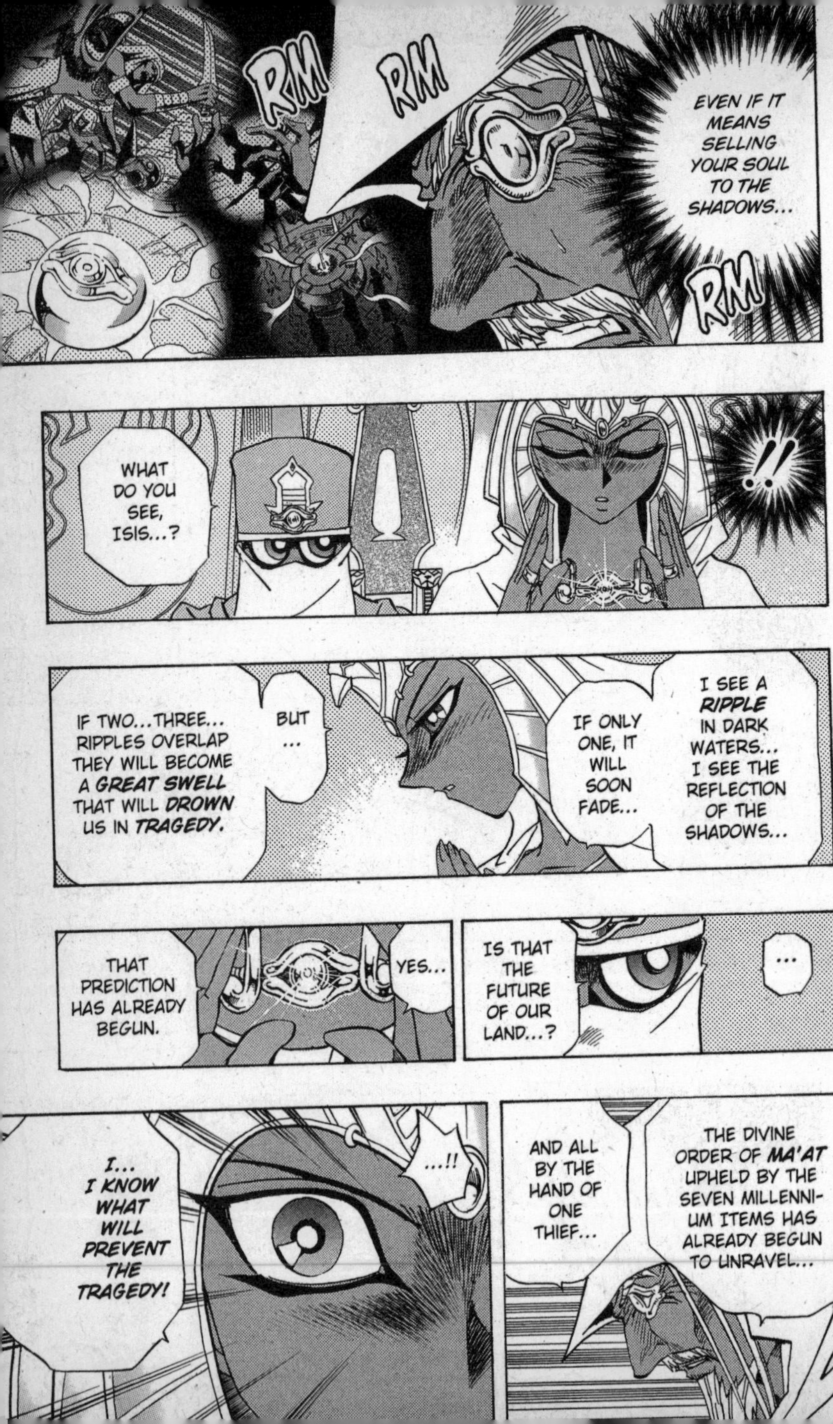
EVEN IF IT MEANS SELLING YOUR SOUL TO THE SHADOWS...
RM
RM
RM
!!
WHAT DO YOU SEE, ISIS...?
I SEE A RIPPLE IN DARK WATERS... I SEE THE REFLECTION OF THE SHADOWS...
IF ONLY ONE, IT WILL SOON FADE...
BUT...
IF TWO...THREE... RIPPLES OVERLAP THEY WILL BECOME A GREAT SWELL THAT WILL DROWN US IN TRAGEDY.
...
IS THAT THE FUTURE OF OUR LAND...?
YES...
THAT PREDICTION HAS ALREADY BEGUN.
THE DIVINE ORDER OF MA'AT UPHELD BY THE SEVEN MILLENNIUM ITEMS HAS ALREADY BEGUN TO UNRAVEL...
AND ALL BY THE HAND OF ONE THIEF...
...!!
I... I KNOW WHAT WILL PREVENT THE TRAGEDY!

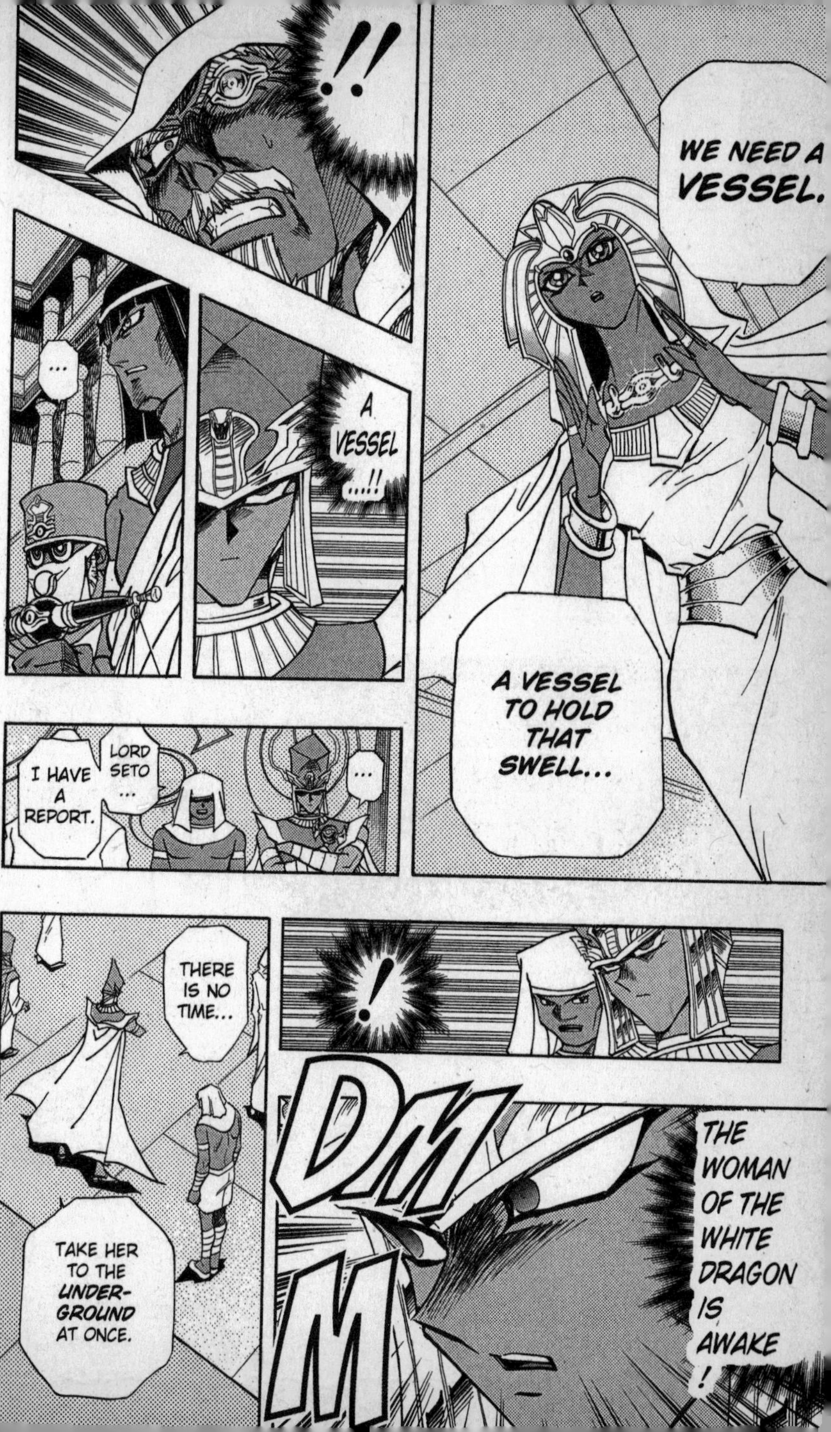
WE NEED A VESSEL.
A VESSEL TO HOLD THAT SWELL...
!!
A VESSEL ...!!
...
...
LORD SETO ...
I HAVE A REPORT.
!
DMM
THE WOMAN OF THE WHITE DRAGON IS AWAKE!
THERE IS NO TIME...
TAKE HER TO THE UNDER-GROUND AT ONCE.

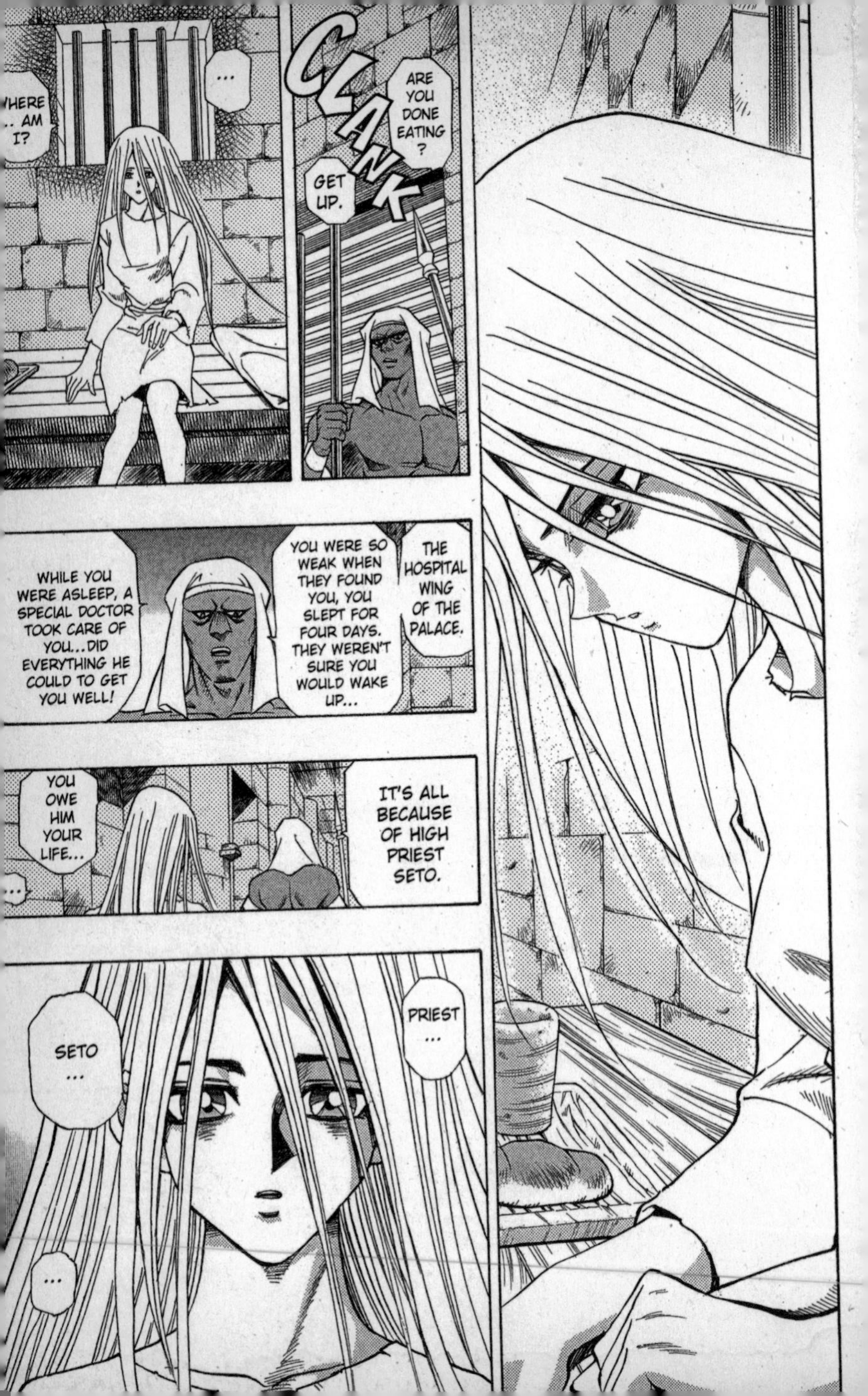
CLANK
ARE YOU DONE EATING?
GET UP.
...
HERE .. AM I?
THE HOSPITAL WING OF THE PALACE.
YOU WERE SO WEAK WHEN THEY FOUND YOU, YOU SLEPT FOR FOUR DAYS. THEY WEREN'T SURE YOU WOULD WAKE UP...
WHILE YOU WERE ASLEEP, A SPECIAL DOCTOR TOOK CARE OF YOU...DID EVERYTHING HE COULD TO GET YOU WELL!
IT'S ALL BECAUSE OF HIGH PRIEST SETO.
YOU OWE HIM YOUR LIFE...
...
PRIEST...
SETO...
...

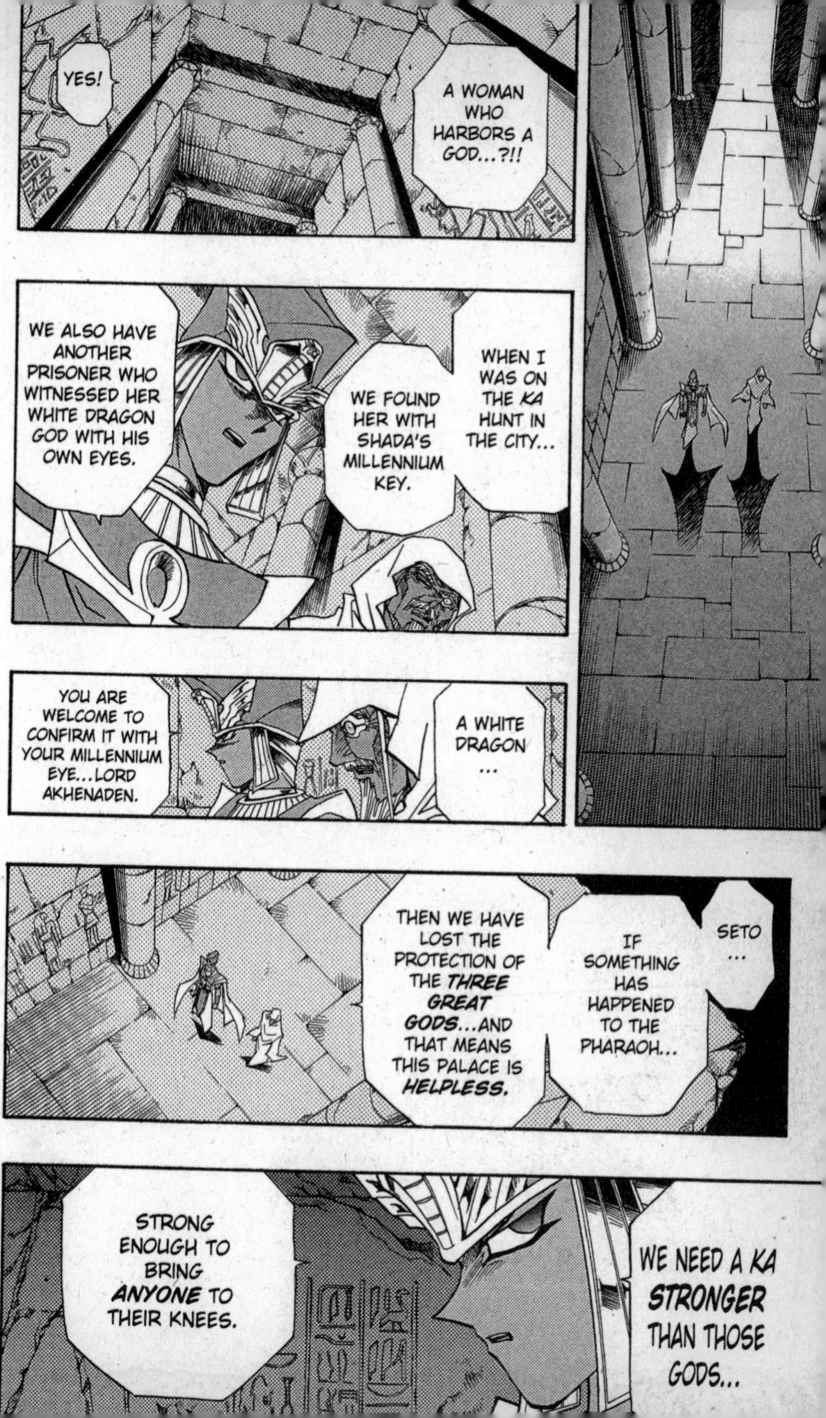
A WOMAN WHO HARBORS A GOD...?!!
YES!
WHEN I WAS ON THE KA HUNT IN THE CITY...
WE FOUND HER WITH SHADA'S MILLENNIUM KEY.
WE ALSO HAVE ANOTHER PRISONER WHO WITNESSED HER WHITE DRAGON GOD WITH HIS OWN EYES.
A WHITE DRAGON ...
YOU ARE WELCOME TO CONFIRM IT WITH YOUR MILLENNIUM EYE...LORD AKHENADEN.
SETO ...
IF SOMETHING HAS HAPPENED TO THE PHARAOH...
THEN WE HAVE LOST THE PROTECTION OF THE THREE GREAT GODS...AND THAT MEANS THIS PALACE IS HELPLESS.
WE NEED A KA STRONGER THAN THOSE GODS...
STRONG ENOUGH TO BRING ANYONE TO THEIR KNEES.

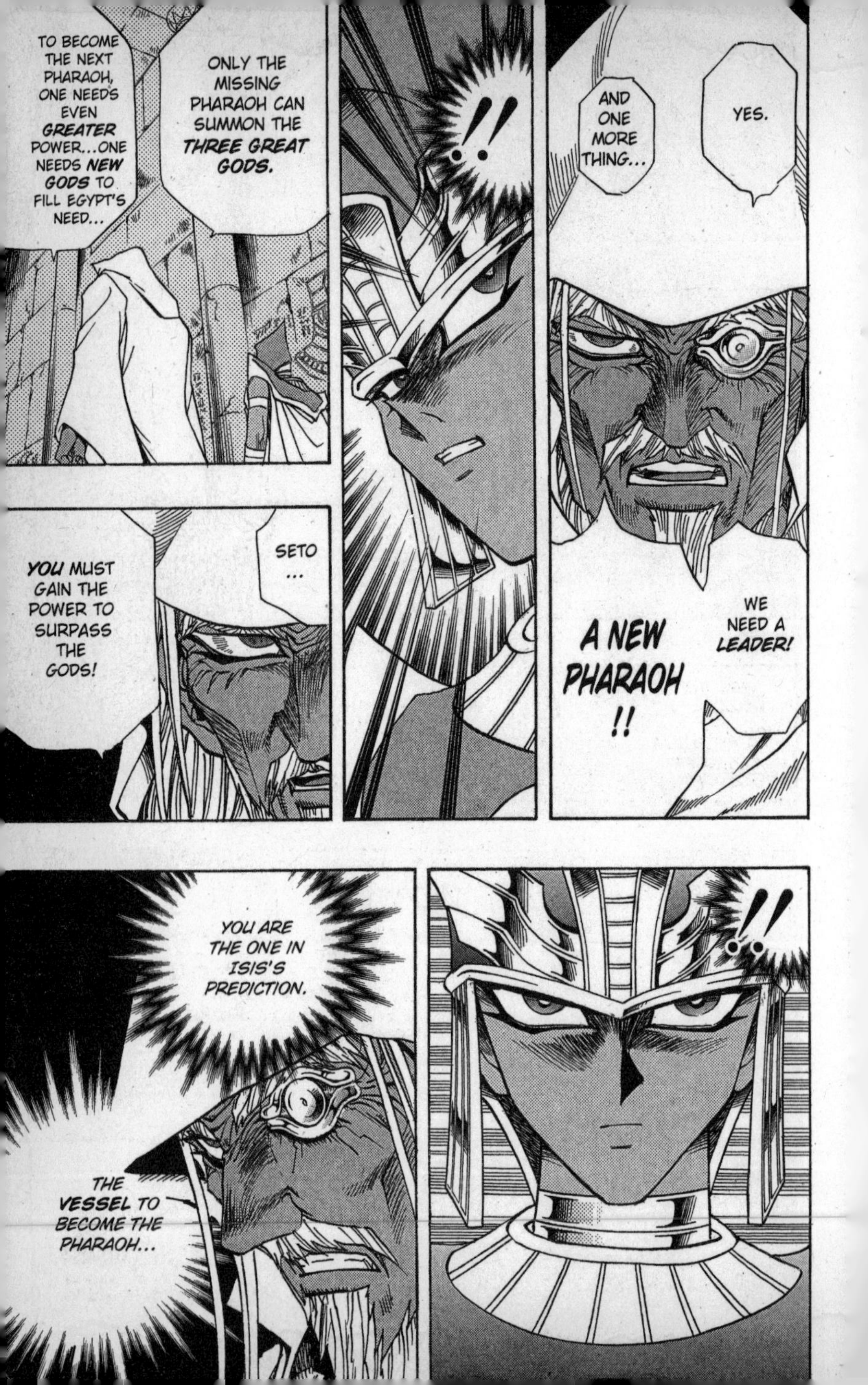
YES.
AND ONE MORE THING...
WE NEED A LEADER!
A NEW PHARAOH !!
!!
ONLY THE MISSING PHARAOH CAN SUMMON THE THREE GREAT GODS.
TO BECOME THE NEXT PHARAOH, ONE NEED'S EVEN GREATER POWER...ONE NEEDS NEW GODS TO FILL EGYPT'S NEED...
SETO...
YOU MUST GAIN THE POWER TO SURPASS THE GODS!
!!
YOU ARE THE ONE IN ISIS'S PREDICTION.
THE VESSEL TO BECOME THE PHARAOH...

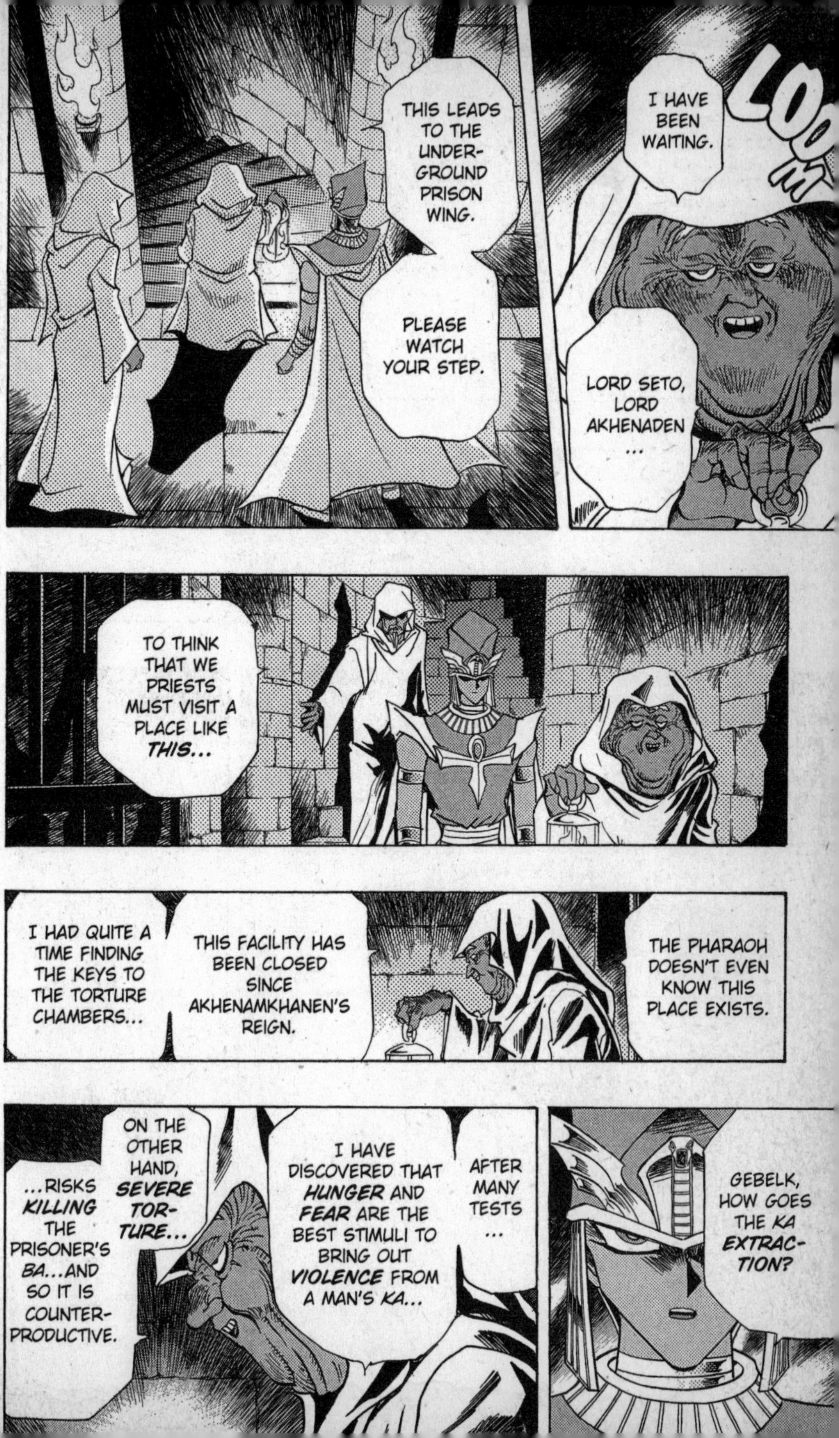
LOOM
I HAVE BEEN WAITING.
LORD SETO, LORD AKHENADEN ...
THIS LEADS TO THE UNDER-GROUND PRISON WING.
PLEASE WATCH YOUR STEP.
TO THINK THAT WE PRIESTS MUST VISIT A PLACE LIKE *THIS...*
THE PHARAOH DOESN'T EVEN KNOW THIS PLACE EXISTS.
THIS FACILITY HAS BEEN CLOSED SINCE AKHENAMKHANEN'S REIGN.
I HAD QUITE A TIME FINDING THE KEYS TO THE TORTURE CHAMBERS...
GEBELK, HOW GOES THE *KA* ***EXTRACTION?***
AFTER MANY TESTS ...
I HAVE DISCOVERED THAT ***HUNGER*** AND ***FEAR*** ARE THE BEST STIMULI TO BRING OUT ***VIOLENCE*** FROM A MAN'S *KA*...
ON THE OTHER HAND, ***SEVERE TORTURE...***
...RISKS ***KILLING*** THE PRISONER'S *BA*...AND SO IT IS COUNTER-PRODUCTIVE.

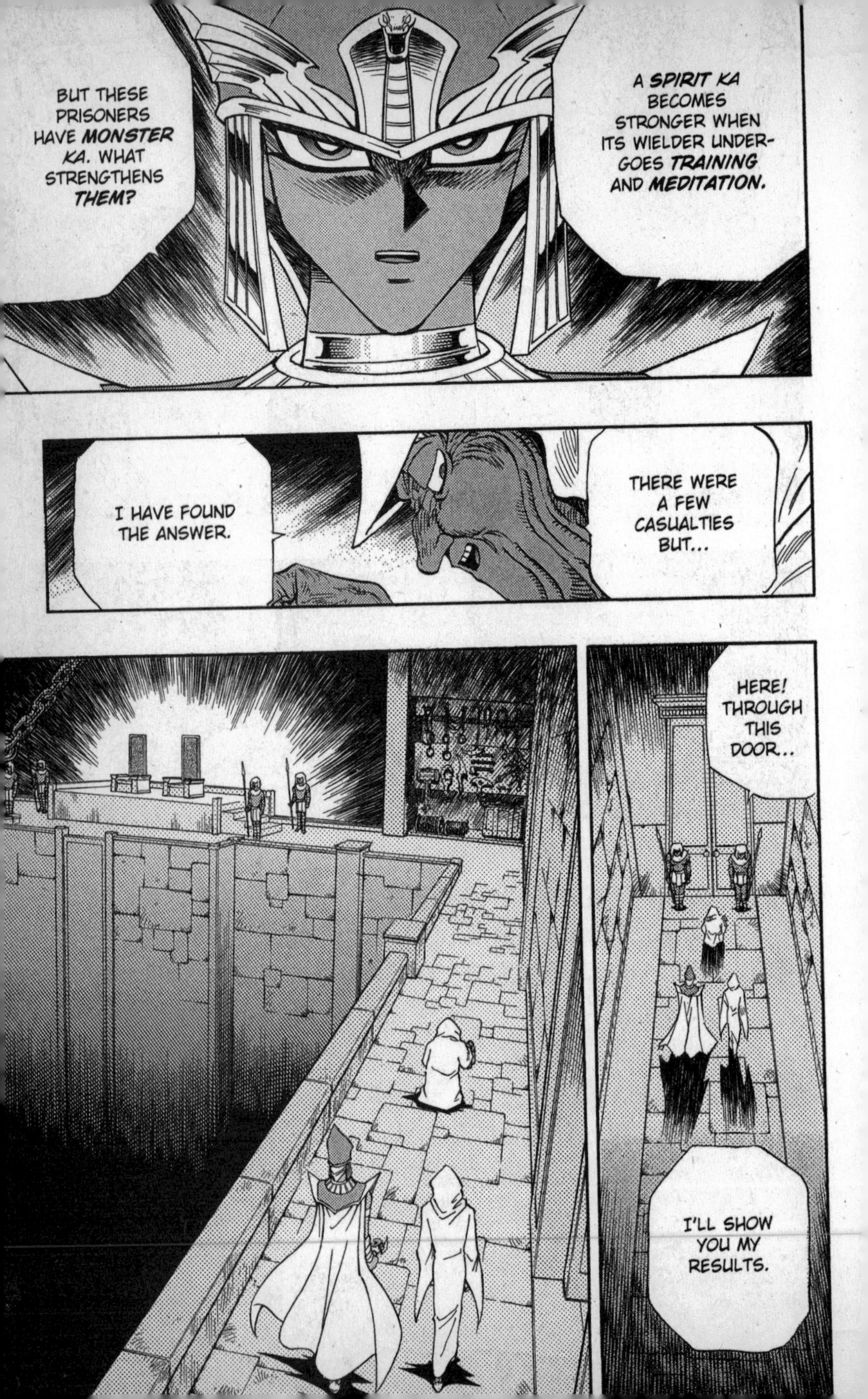
A SPIRIT KA BECOMES STRONGER WHEN ITS WIELDER UNDERGOES TRAINING AND MEDITATION.
BUT THESE PRISONERS HAVE MONSTER KA. WHAT STRENGTHENS THEM?
THERE WERE A FEW CASUALTIES BUT...
I HAVE FOUND THE ANSWER.
HERE! THROUGH THIS DOOR...
I'LL SHOW YOU MY RESULTS.

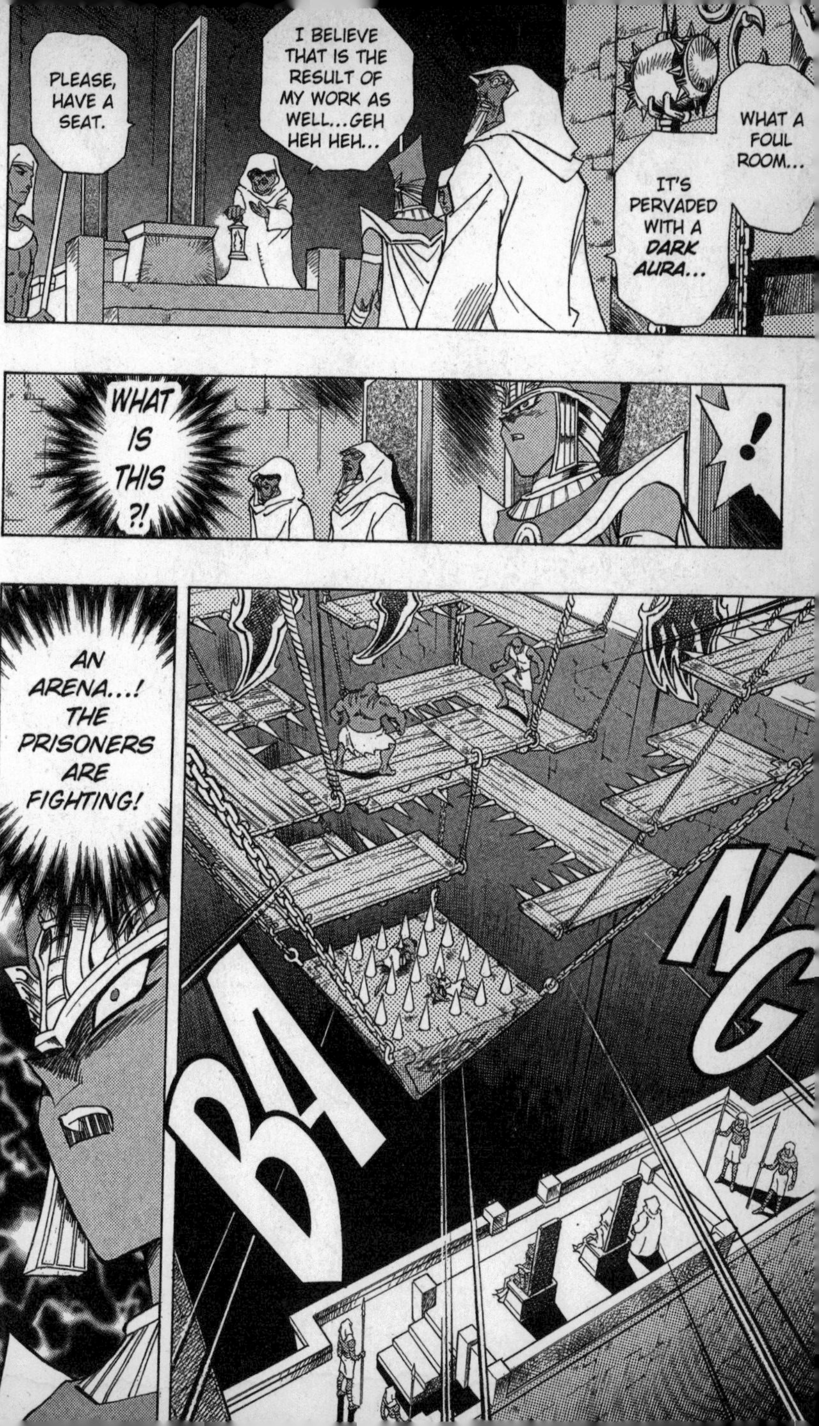
WHAT A FOUL ROOM...
IT'S PERVADED WITH A DARK AURA...
I BELIEVE THAT IS THE RESULT OF MY WORK AS WELL...GEH HEH HEH...
PLEASE, HAVE A SEAT.
!
WHAT IS THIS?!
BANG
AN ARENA...! THE PRISONERS ARE FIGHTING!

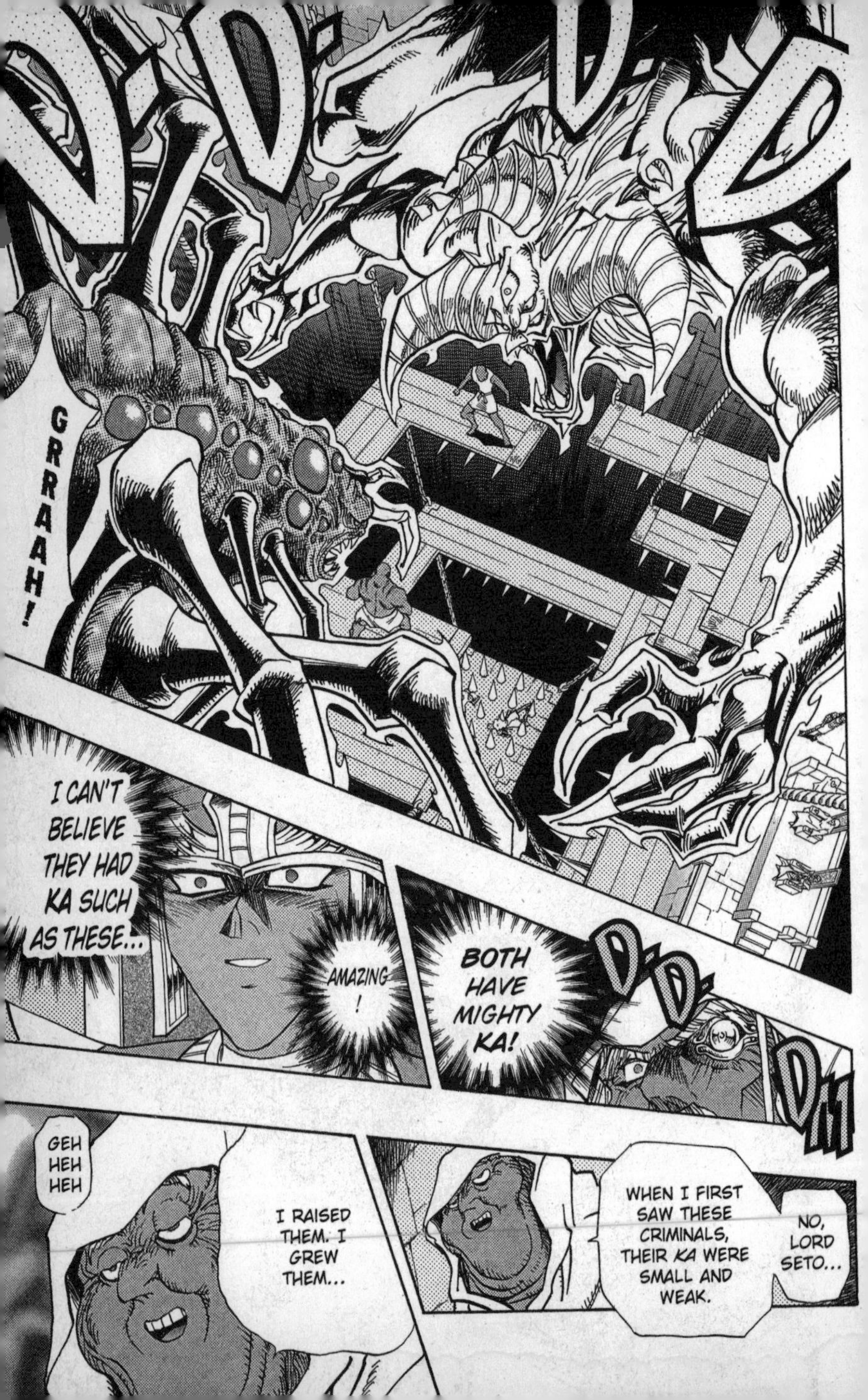
GRRAAH!
BOTH HAVE MIGHTY KA!
I CAN'T BELIEVE THEY HAD KA SUCH AS THESE...
AMAZING!
NO, LORD SETO...
WHEN I FIRST SAW THESE CRIMINALS, THEIR KA WERE SMALL AND WEAK.
GEH HEH HEH
I RAISED THEM. I GREW THEM...

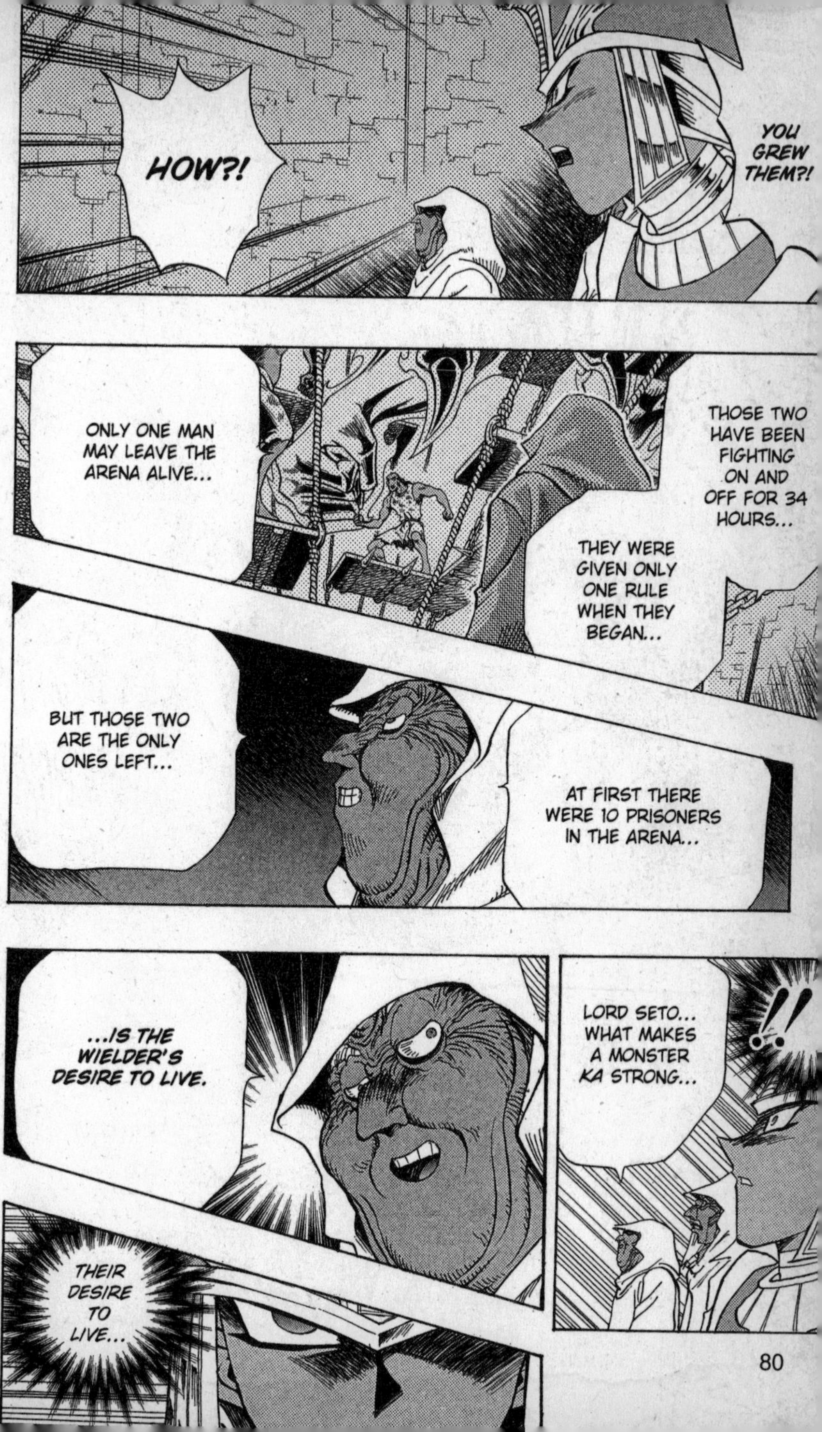
YOU GREW THEM?!
HOW?!
THOSE TWO HAVE BEEN FIGHTING ON AND OFF FOR 34 HOURS...
THEY WERE GIVEN ONLY ONE RULE WHEN THEY BEGAN...
ONLY ONE MAN MAY LEAVE THE ARENA ALIVE...
AT FIRST THERE WERE 10 PRISONERS IN THE ARENA...
BUT THOSE TWO ARE THE ONLY ONES LEFT...
!!
LORD SETO... WHAT MAKES A MONSTER KA STRONG...
...IS THE WIELDER'S DESIRE TO LIVE.
THEIR DESIRE TO LIVE...

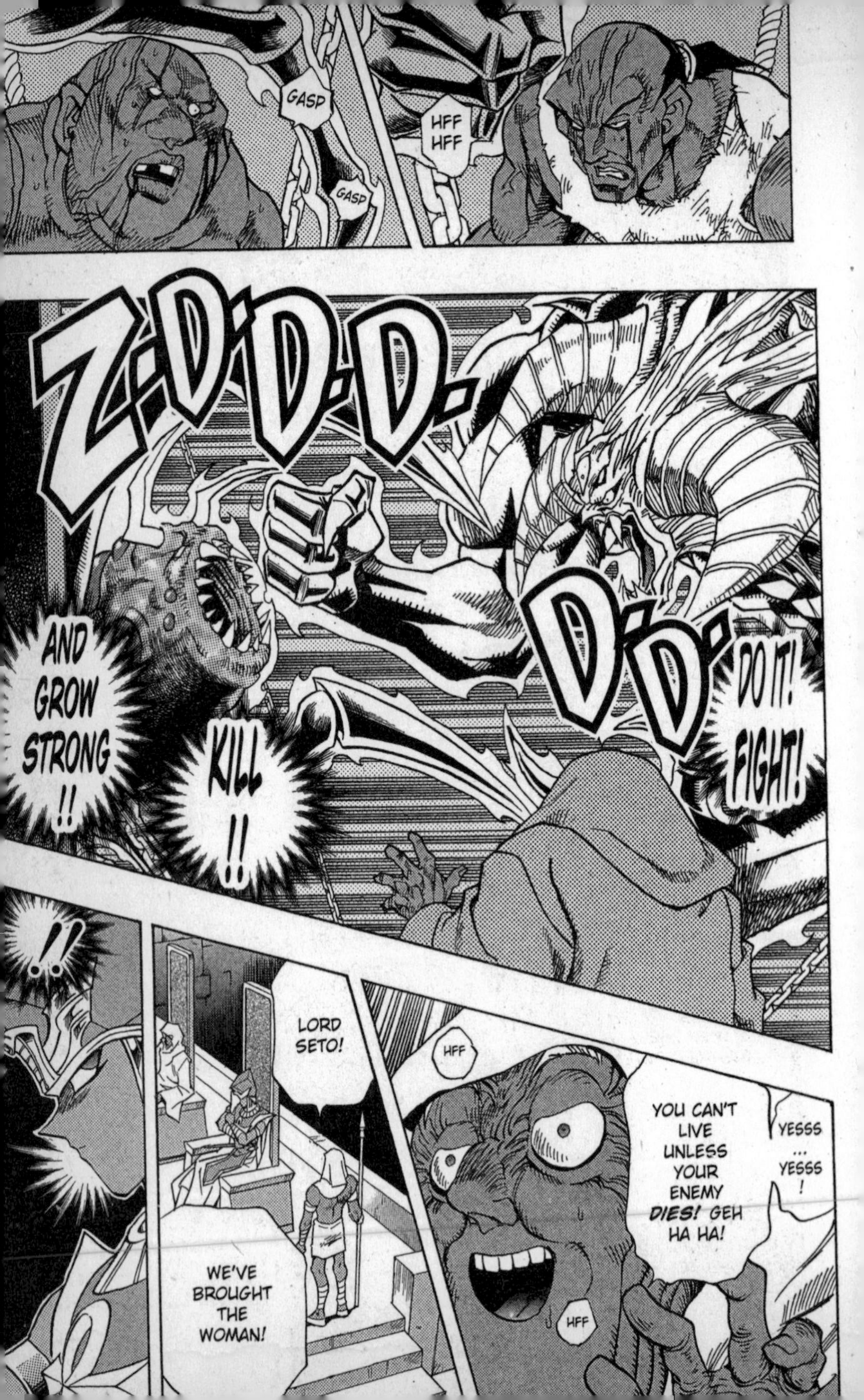

HFF HFF
GASP
GASP
Z.D.D.D.
D.D.
DO IT! FIGHT!
KILL !!
AND GROW STRONG !!
YESSS ... YESSS !
YOU CAN'T LIVE UNLESS YOUR ENEMY DIES! GEH HA HA!
HFF
HFF
LORD SETO!
WE'VE BROUGHT THE WOMAN!
!!

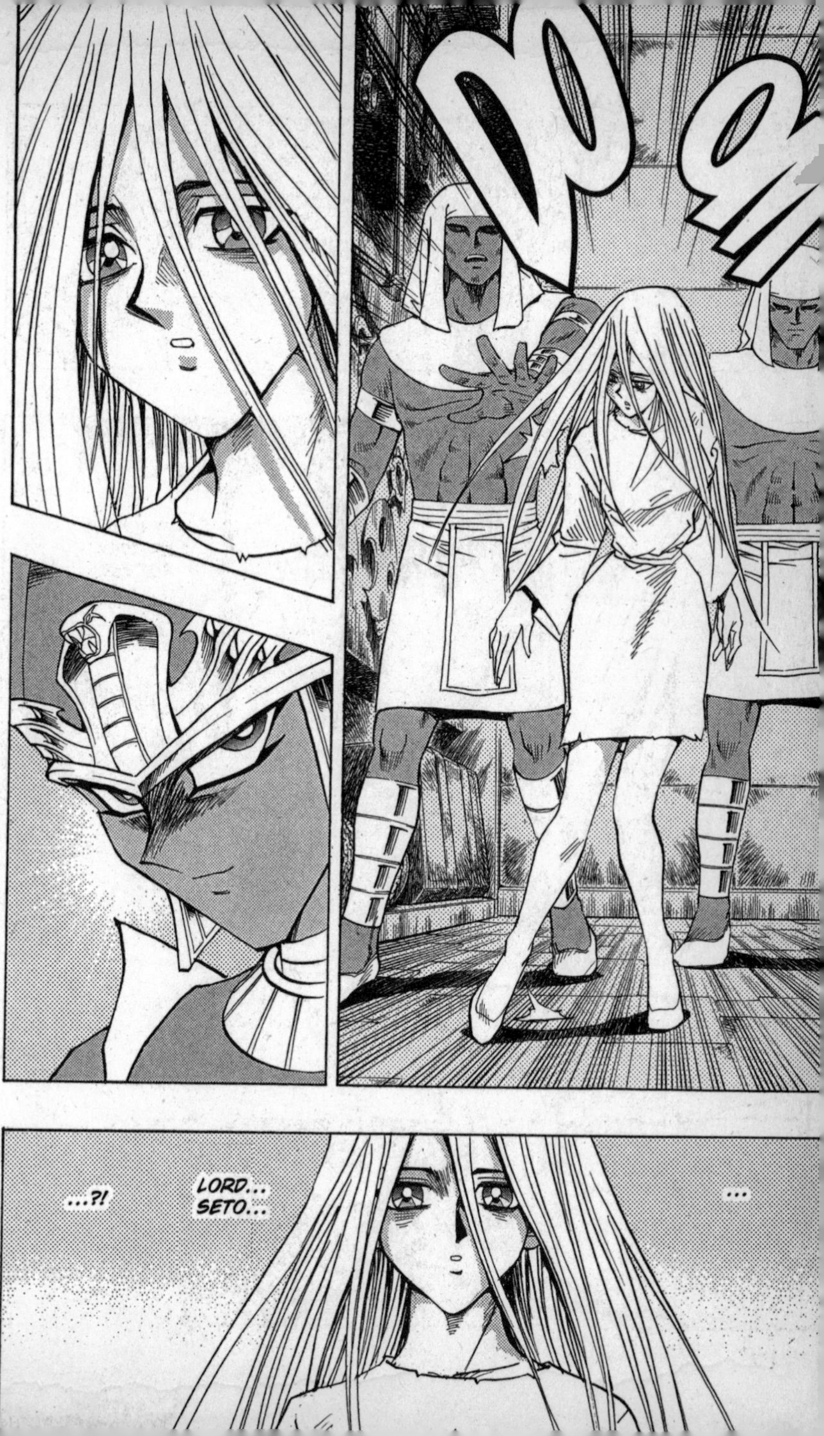
...
LORD...
SETO...
...?!

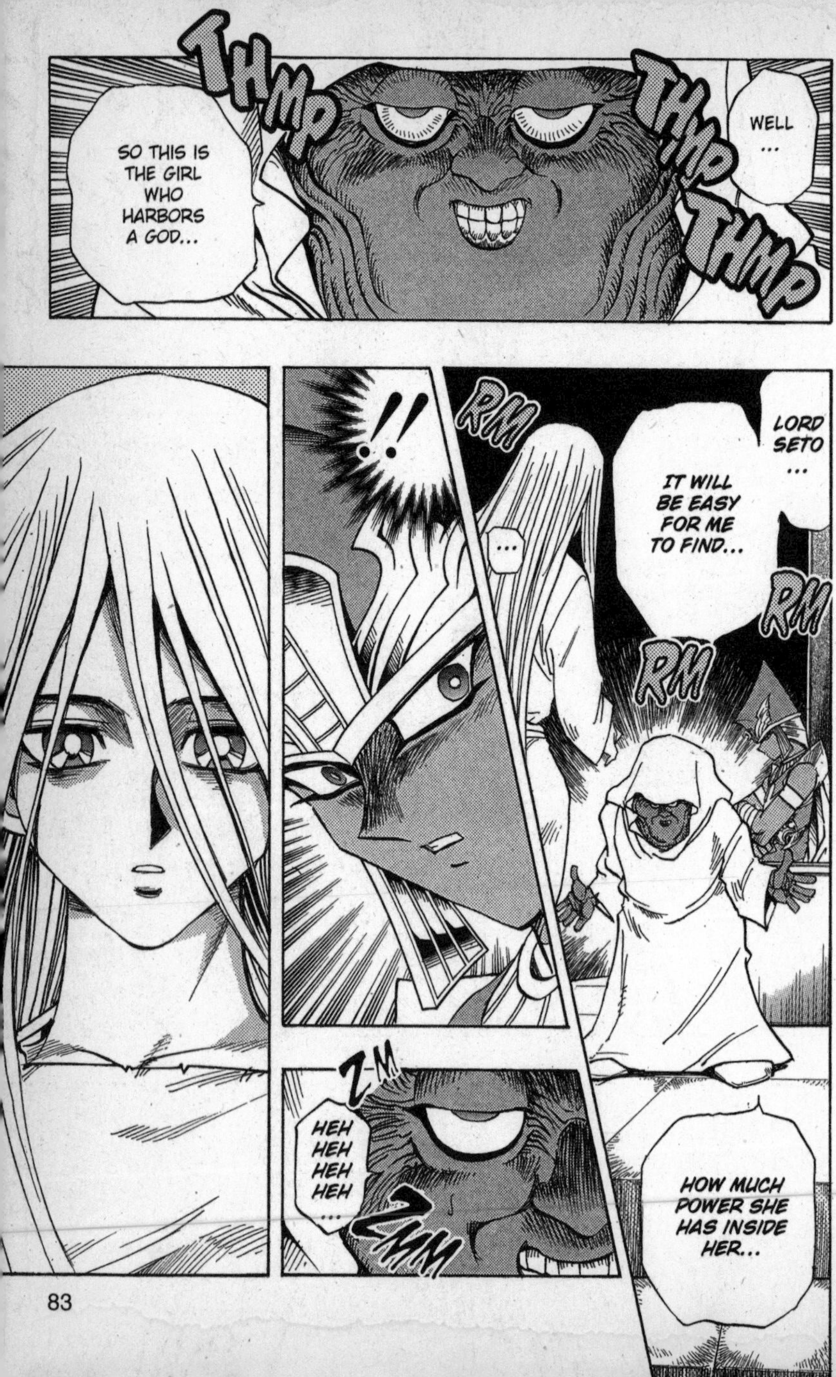
WELL...
THMP
THMP THMP
THMP
SO THIS IS THE GIRL WHO HARBORS A GOD...
LORD SETO...
IT WILL BE EASY FOR ME TO FIND...
RM
RM
RM
...
HOW MUCH POWER SHE HAS INSIDE HER...
!!
ZM
HEH HEH HEH HEH...
ZMM

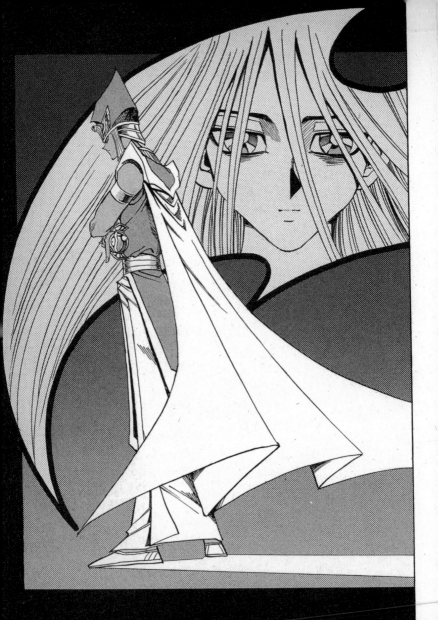

# Duel 32:
# The White Dragon Awakes!

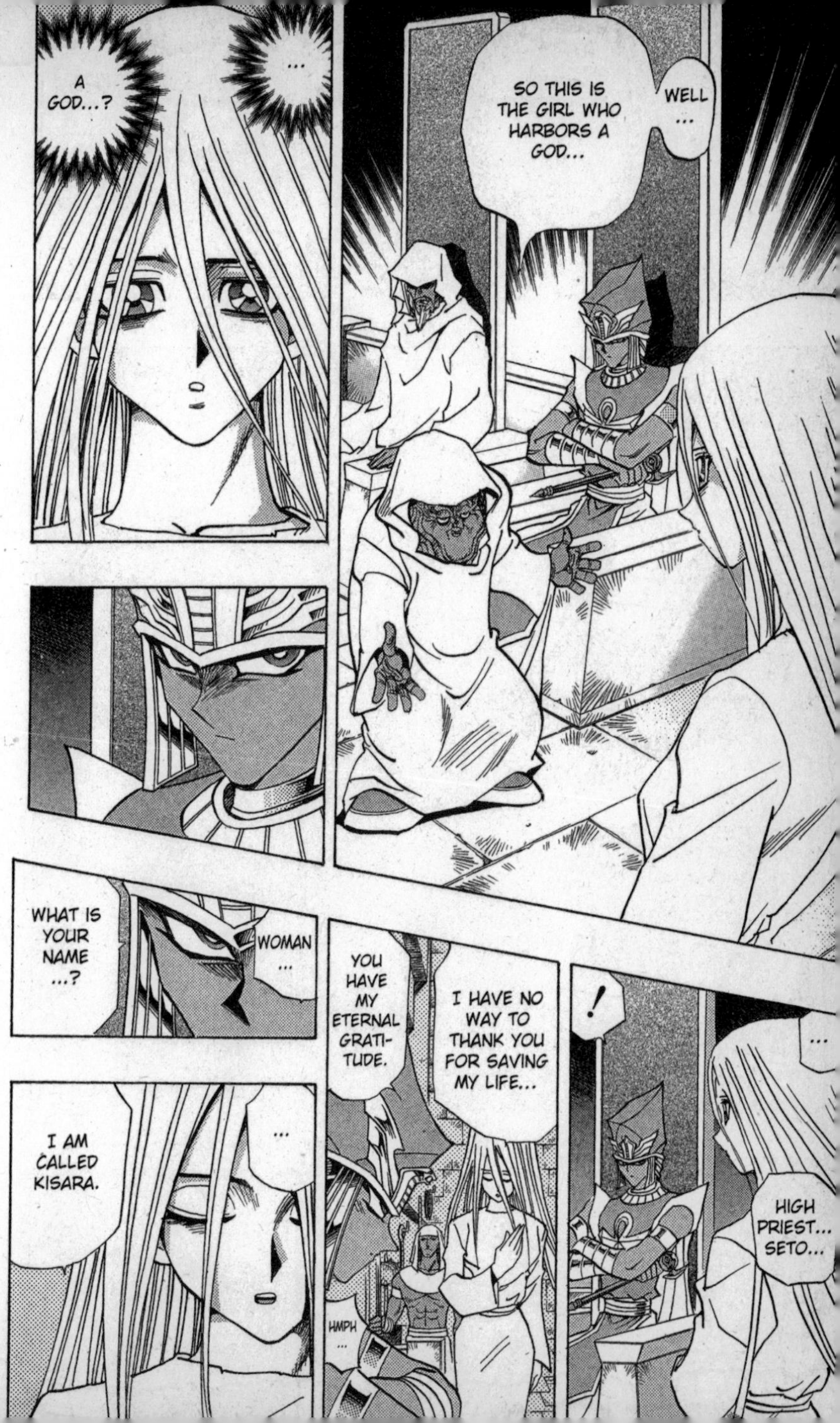
WELL...
SO THIS IS THE GIRL WHO HARBORS A GOD...
...
A GOD...?
...
!
HIGH PRIEST... SETO...
I HAVE NO WAY TO THANK YOU FOR SAVING MY LIFE...
YOU HAVE MY ETERNAL GRATITUDE.
HMPH...
WOMAN...
WHAT IS YOUR NAME...?
...
I AM CALLED KISARA.

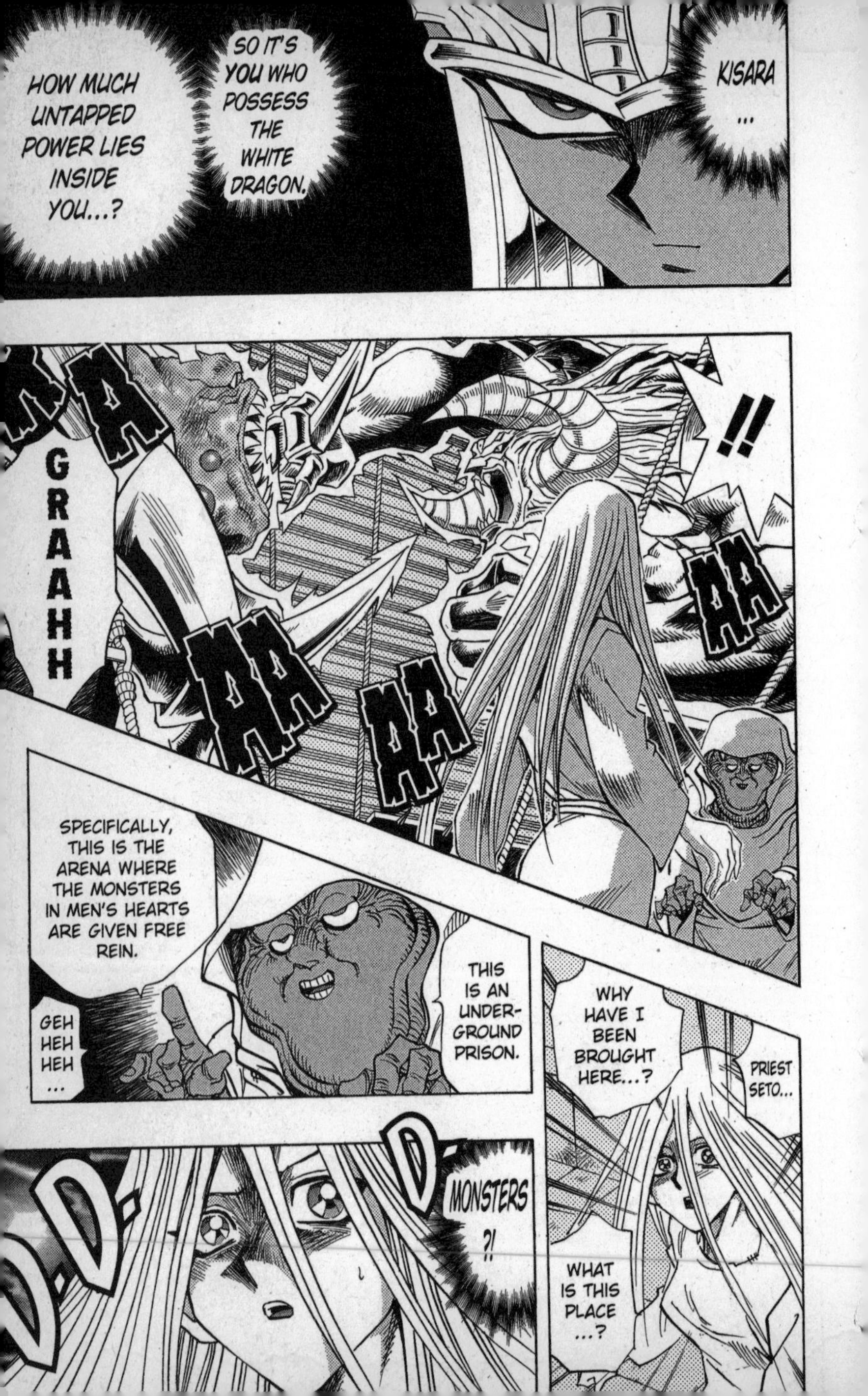
KISARA ...
SO IT'S YOU WHO POSSESS THE WHITE DRAGON.
HOW MUCH UNTAPPED POWER LIES INSIDE YOU...?
!!
AA
AA
AA
AA
GRAAHH
PRIEST SETO...
WHY HAVE I BEEN BROUGHT HERE...?
WHAT IS THIS PLACE ...?
THIS IS AN UNDERGROUND PRISON.
SPECIFICALLY, THIS IS THE ARENA WHERE THE MONSTERS IN MEN'S HEARTS ARE GIVEN FREE REIN.
GEH HEH HEH ...
D-
MONSTERS ?!
D-D-

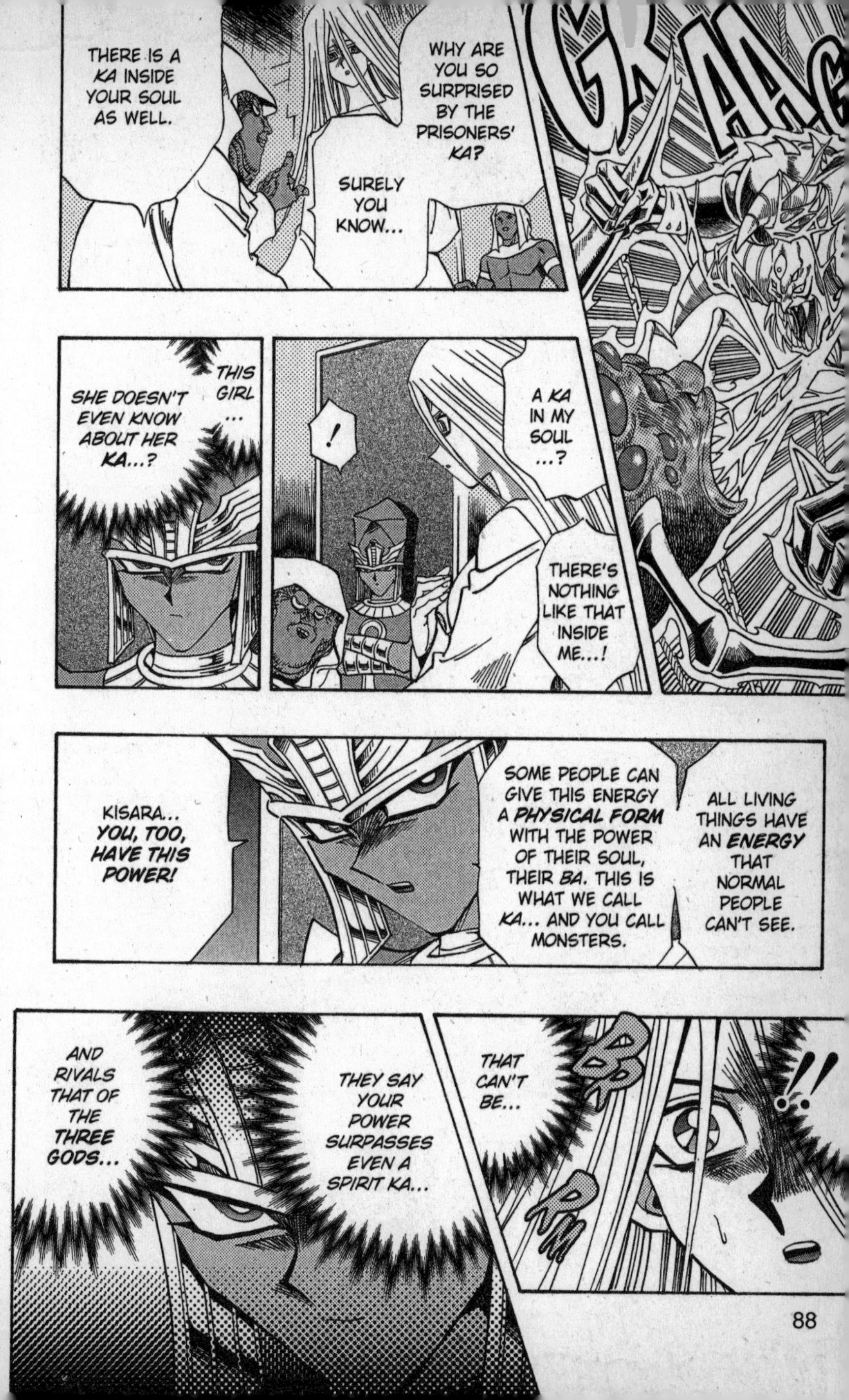
WHY ARE YOU SO SURPRISED BY THE PRISONERS' KA?
SURELY YOU KNOW...
THERE IS A KA INSIDE YOUR SOUL AS WELL.
A KA IN MY SOUL ...?
!
THERE'S NOTHING LIKE THAT INSIDE ME...!
THIS GIRL ...
SHE DOESN'T EVEN KNOW ABOUT HER KA...?
ALL LIVING THINGS HAVE AN ENERGY THAT NORMAL PEOPLE CAN'T SEE.
SOME PEOPLE CAN GIVE THIS ENERGY A PHYSICAL FORM WITH THE POWER OF THEIR SOUL, THEIR BA. THIS IS WHAT WE CALL KA... AND YOU CALL MONSTERS.
KISARA... YOU, TOO, HAVE THIS POWER!
!!
THAT CAN'T BE...
THEY SAY YOUR POWER SURPASSES EVEN A SPIRIT KA...
AND RIVALS THAT OF THE THREE GODS...

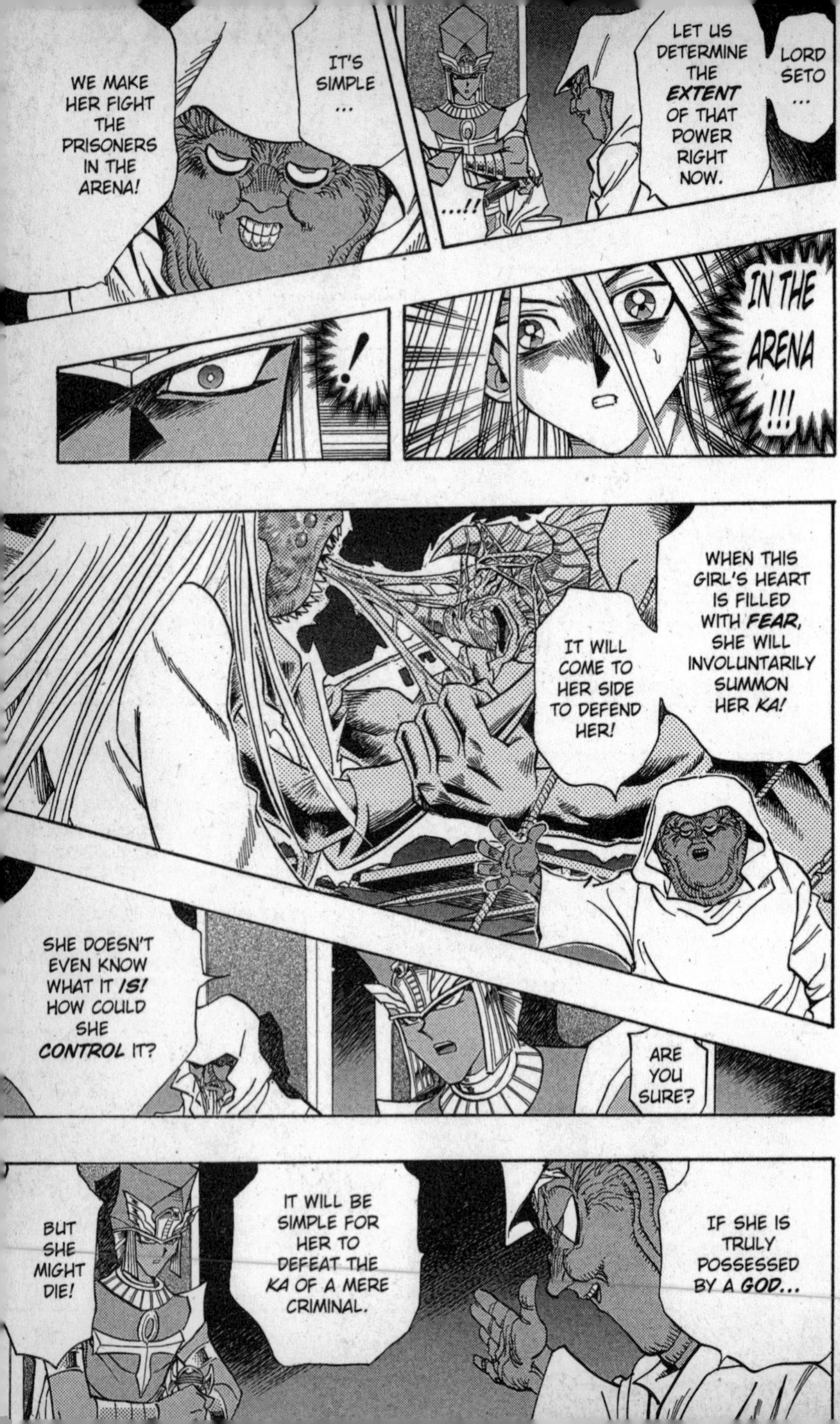
LORD SETO ...
LET US DETERMINE THE EXTENT OF THAT POWER RIGHT NOW.
IT'S SIMPLE ...
...!!
WE MAKE HER FIGHT THE PRISONERS IN THE ARENA!
IN THE ARENA !!!
!
WHEN THIS GIRL'S HEART IS FILLED WITH FEAR, SHE WILL INVOLUNTARILY SUMMON HER KA!
IT WILL COME TO HER SIDE TO DEFEND HER!
ARE YOU SURE?
SHE DOESN'T EVEN KNOW WHAT IT IS! HOW COULD SHE CONTROL IT?
IF SHE IS TRULY POSSESSED BY A GOD...
IT WILL BE SIMPLE FOR HER TO DEFEAT THE KA OF A MERE CRIMINAL.
BUT SHE MIGHT DIE!

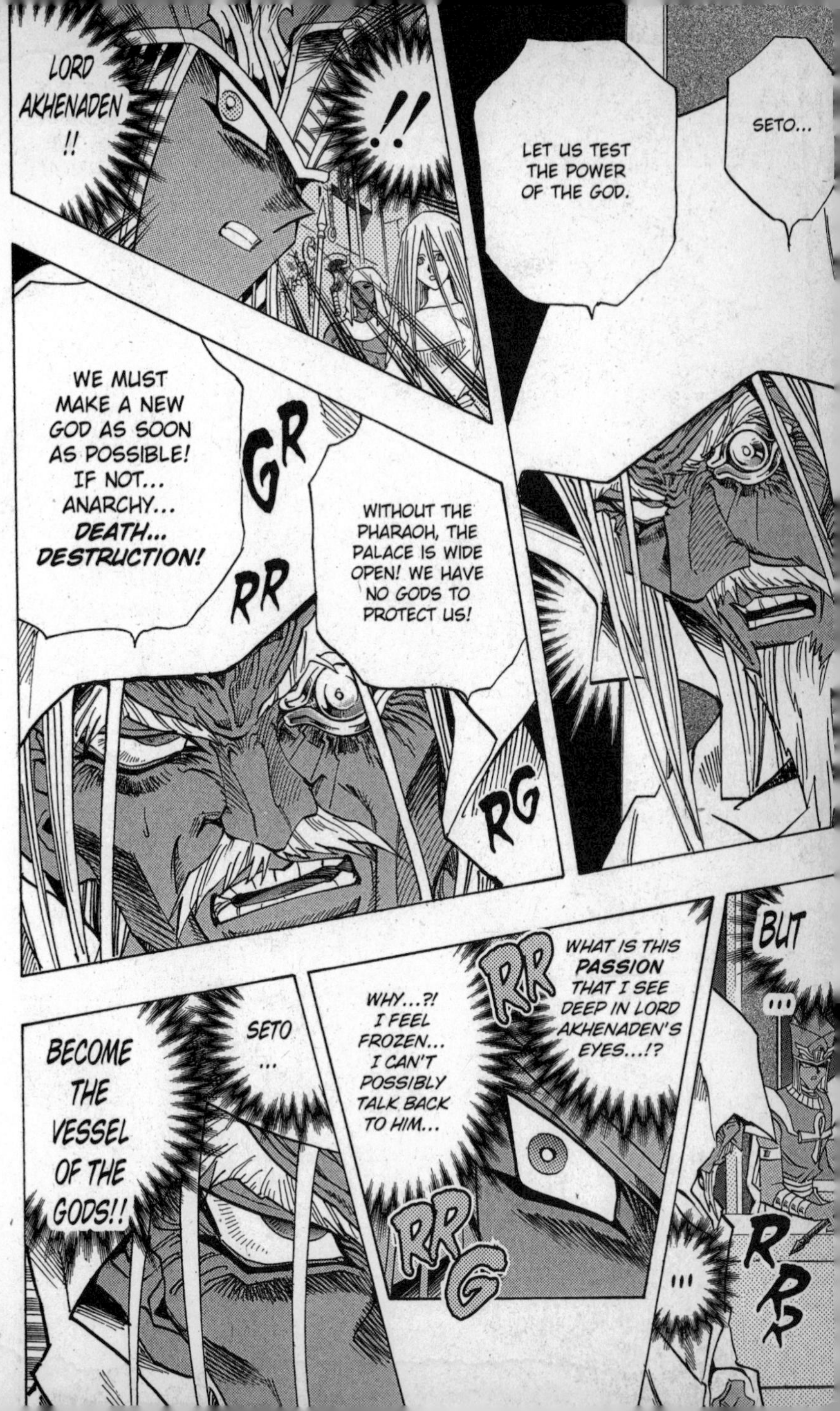
SETO...
LET US TEST THE POWER OF THE GOD.
!!
LORD AKHENADEN!!
WITHOUT THE PHARAOH, THE PALACE IS WIDE OPEN! WE HAVE NO GODS TO PROTECT US!
GR
RR
RG
WE MUST MAKE A NEW GOD AS SOON AS POSSIBLE! IF NOT... ANARCHY... DEATH... DESTRUCTION!
BUT ...
R R R
...
WHAT IS THIS PASSION THAT I SEE DEEP IN LORD AKHENADEN'S EYES...!?
RR
WHY...?! I FEEL FROZEN... I CAN'T POSSIBLY TALK BACK TO HIM...
RRG
SETO ...
BECOME THE VESSEL OF THE GODS!!

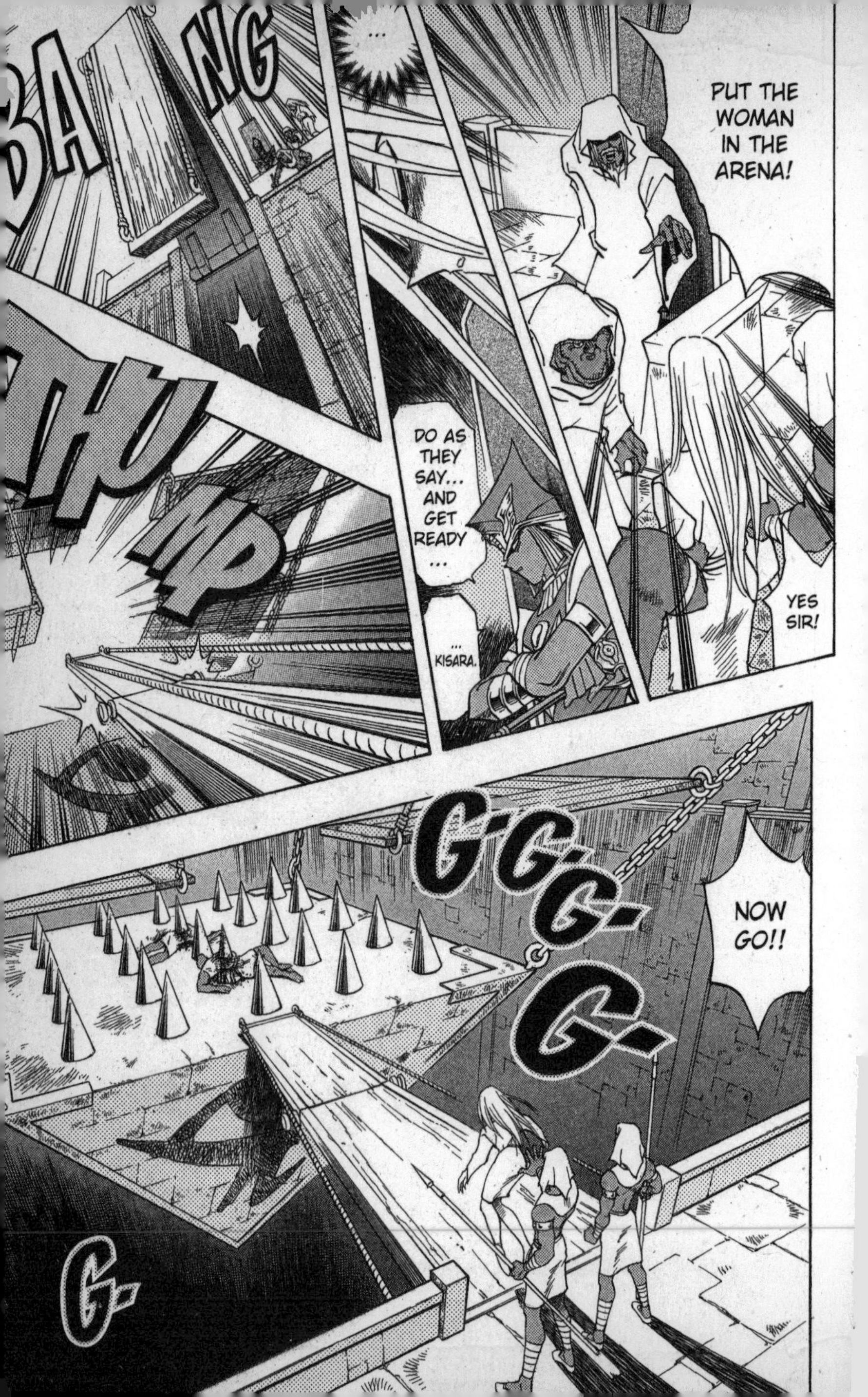
PUT THE WOMAN IN THE ARENA!
YES SIR!
DO AS THEY SAY... AND GET READY...
... KISARA.
...
BANG
THUMP
NOW GO!!
G-G-G-G-
G-

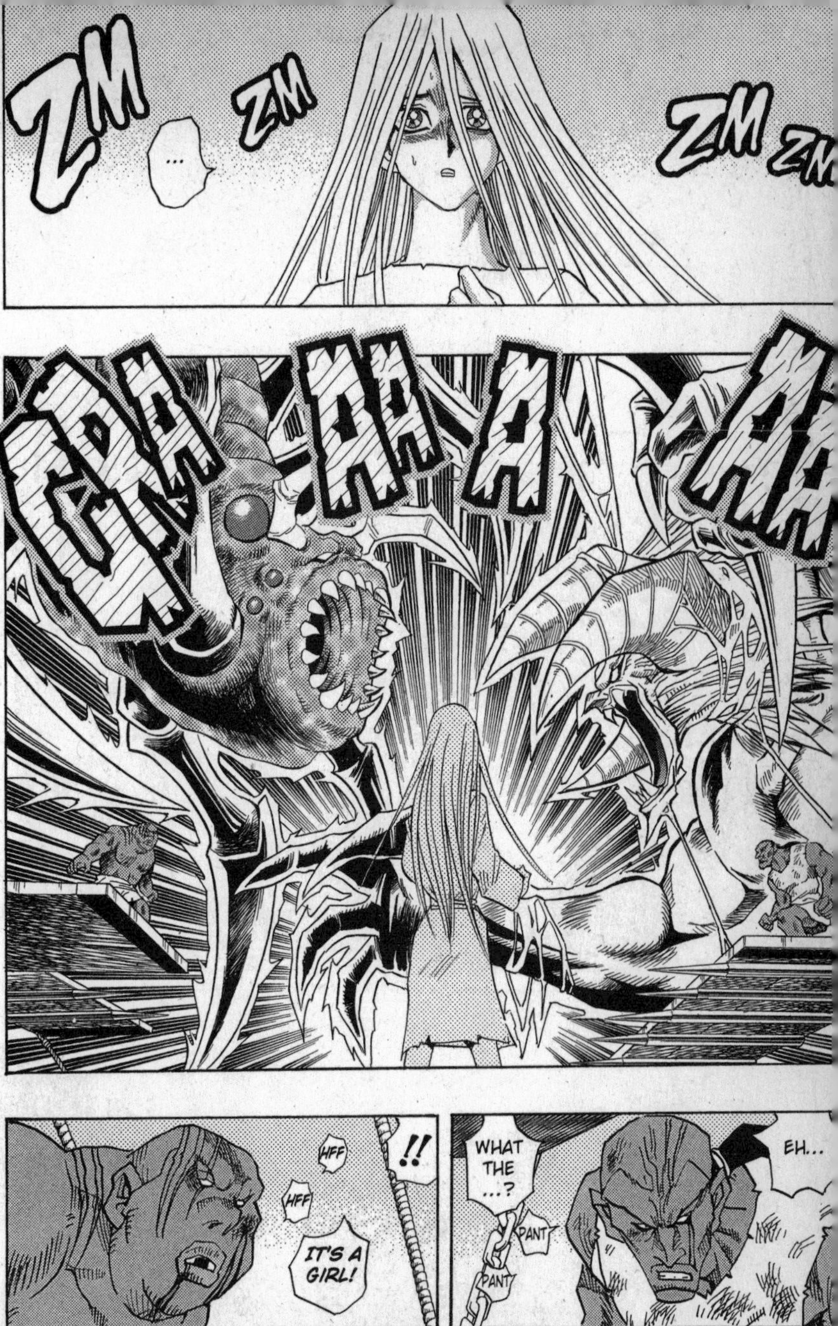
ZM
ZM
...
ZM
GRA-AA-A-AA
EH...
WHAT THE ...?
PANT
PANT
!!
HFF
HFF
IT'S A GIRL!

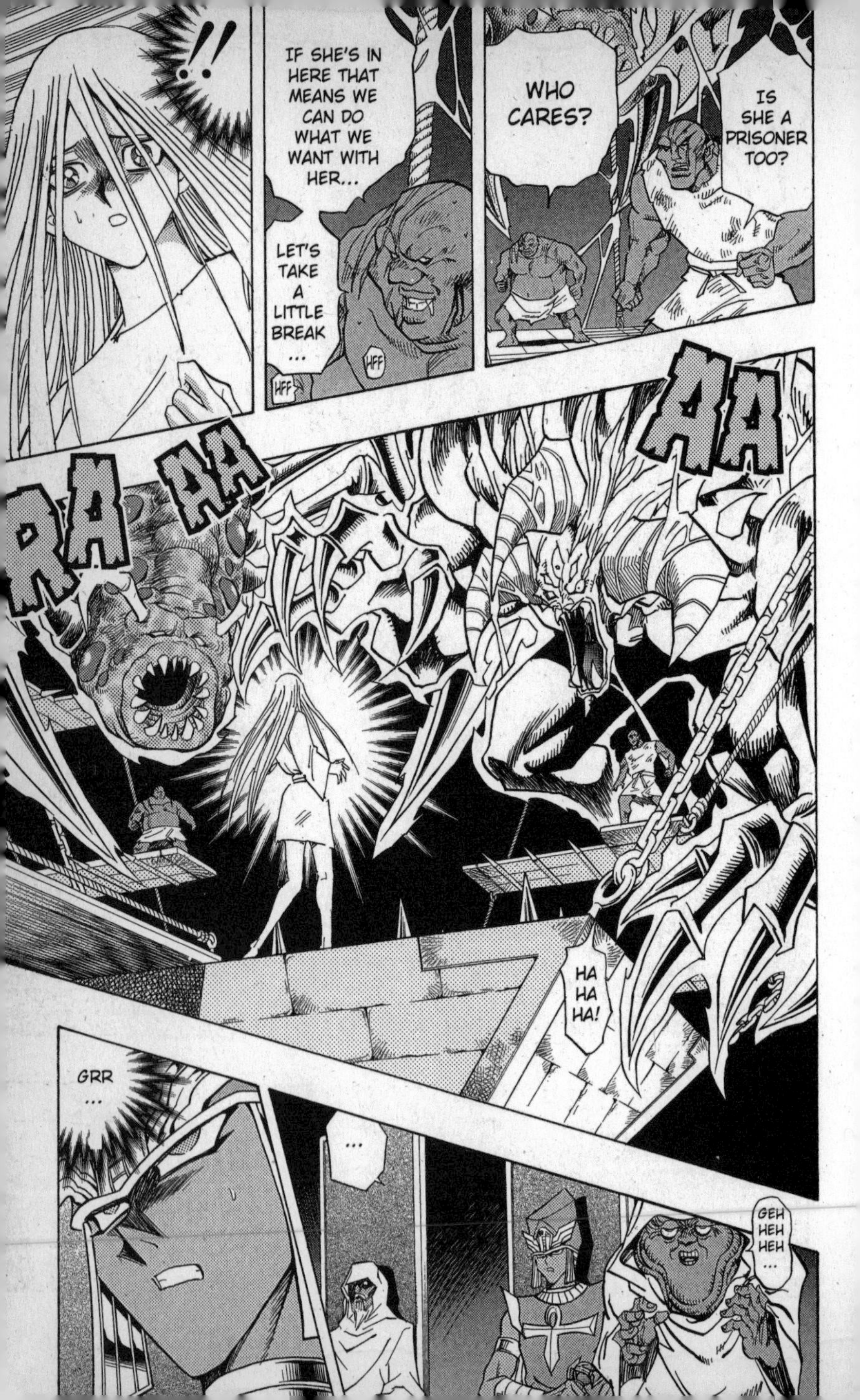
IS SHE A PRISONER TOO?
WHO CARES?
IF SHE'S IN HERE THAT MEANS WE CAN DO WHAT WE WANT WITH HER...
LET'S TAKE A LITTLE BREAK...
HFF
HFF
!!
RA AA
AA
HA HA HA HA!
GEH HEH HEH...
...
GRR...

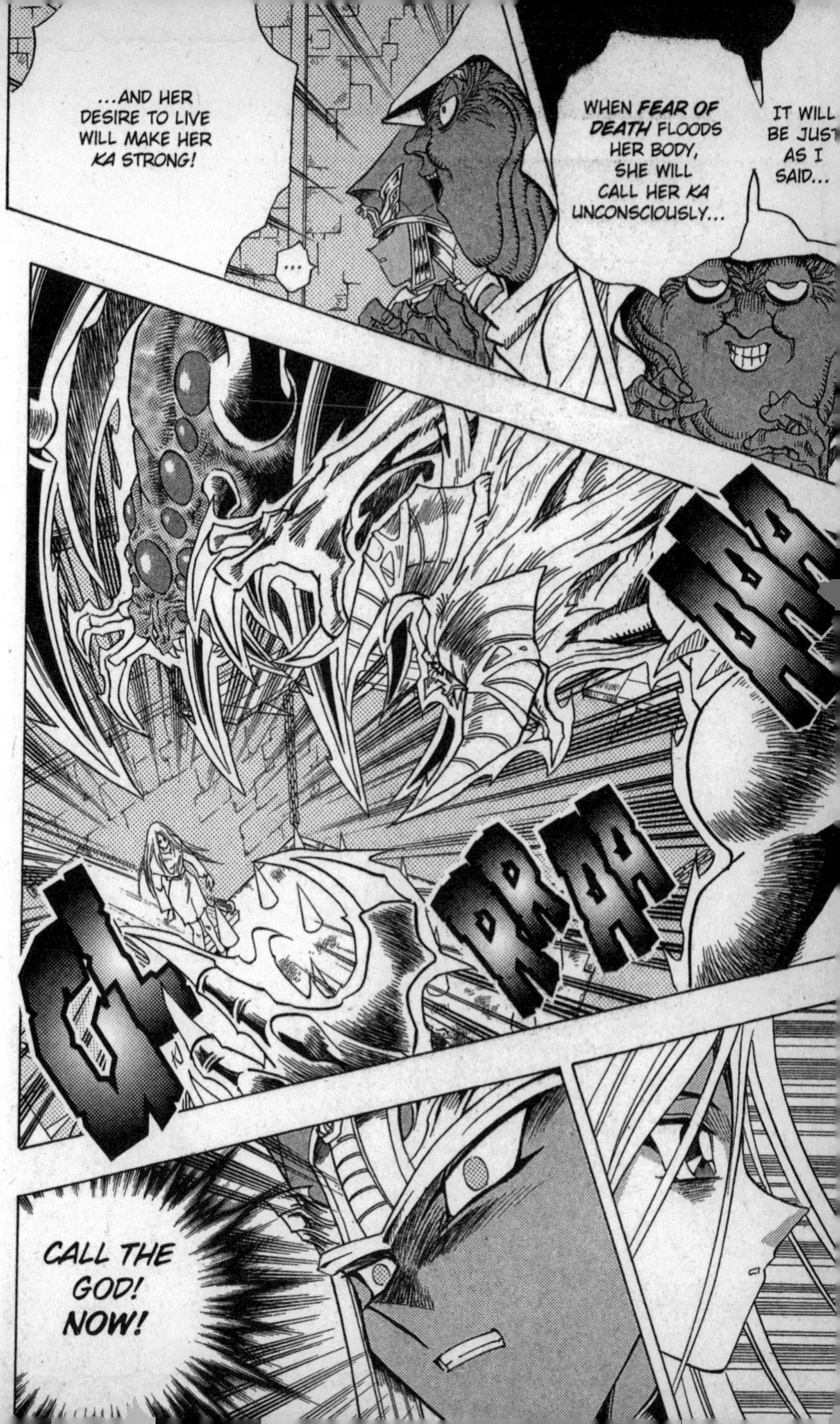
IT WILL BE JUST AS I SAID...
WHEN FEAR OF DEATH FLOODS HER BODY, SHE WILL CALL HER KA UNCONSCIOUSLY...
...AND HER DESIRE TO LIVE WILL MAKE HER KA STRONG!
...
CALL THE GOD! NOW!

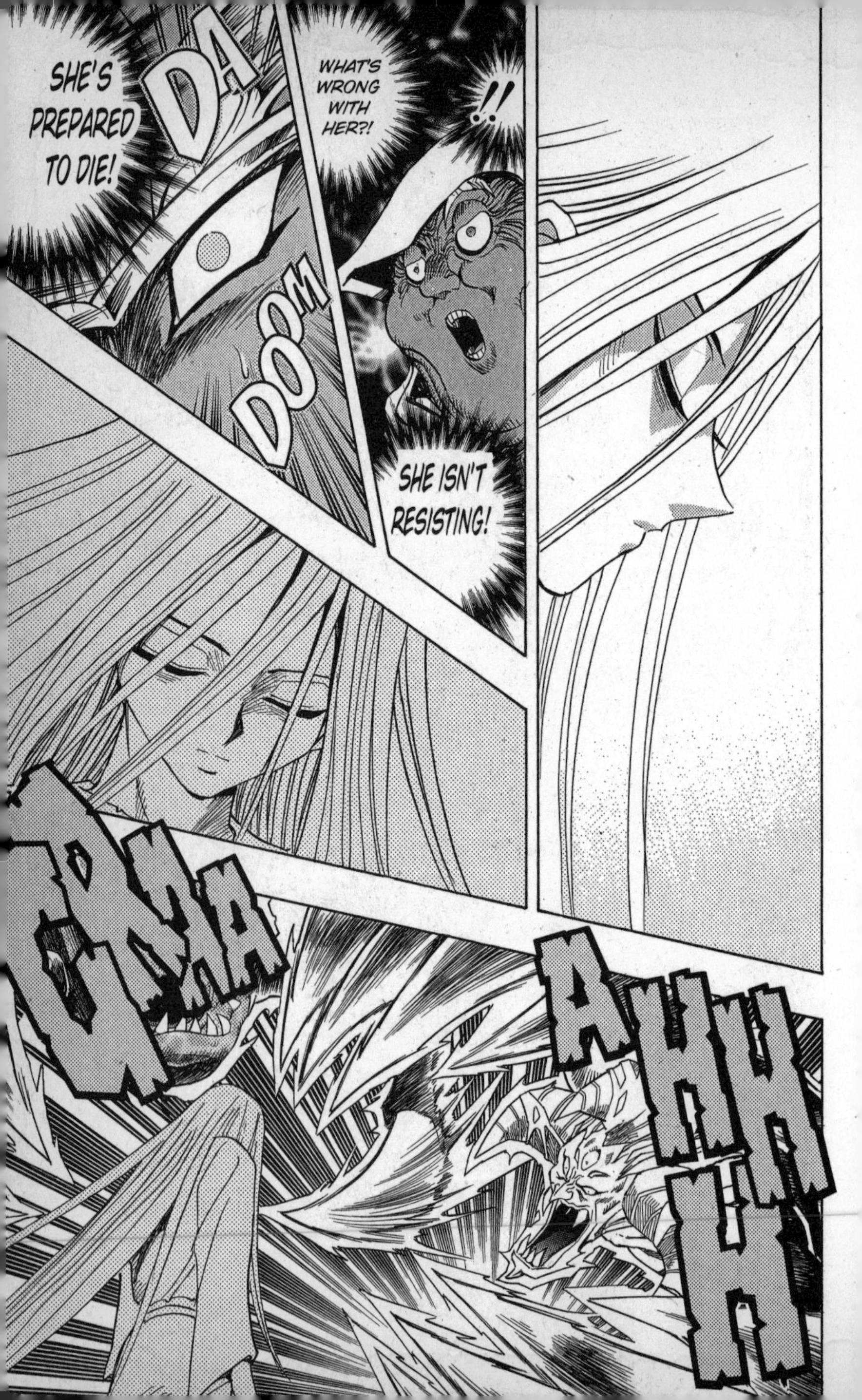
!!
WHAT'S WRONG WITH HER?!
SHE ISN'T RESISTING!
DA
SHE'S PREPARED TO DIE!
DOOM

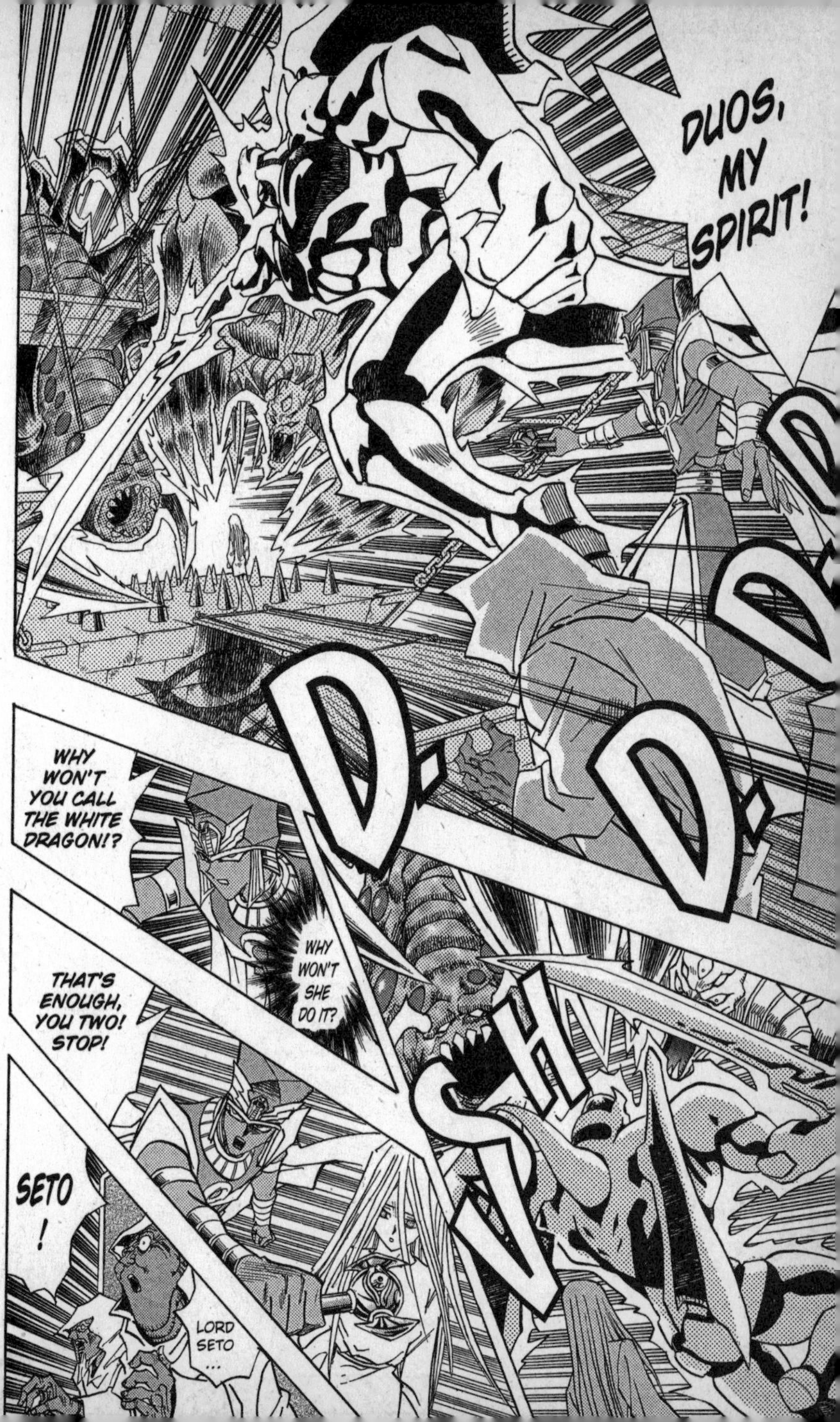
DUOS, MY SPIRIT!
WHY WON'T YOU CALL THE WHITE DRAGON!?
WHY WON'T SHE DO IT?
THAT'S ENOUGH, YOU TWO! STOP!
SETO!
LORD SETO...

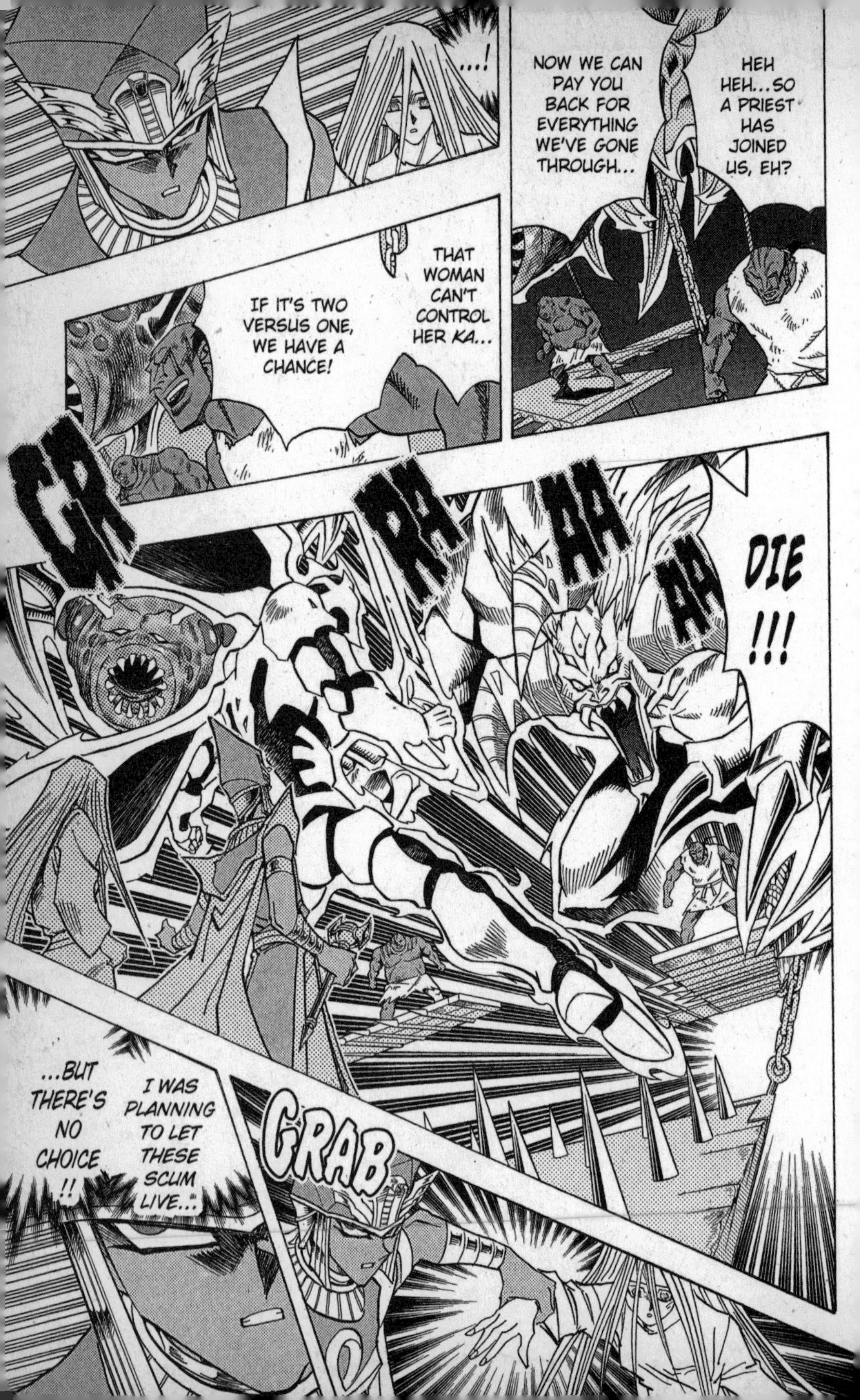
HEH HEH...SO A PRIEST HAS JOINED US, EH?
NOW WE CAN PAY YOU BACK FOR EVERYTHING WE'VE GONE THROUGH...
...!
THAT WOMAN CAN'T CONTROL HER KA...
IF IT'S TWO VERSUS ONE, WE HAVE A CHANCE!
GRRAAAAAA
DIE!!!
GRAB
I WAS PLANNING TO LET THESE SCUM LIVE...
...BUT THERE'S NO CHOICE!!

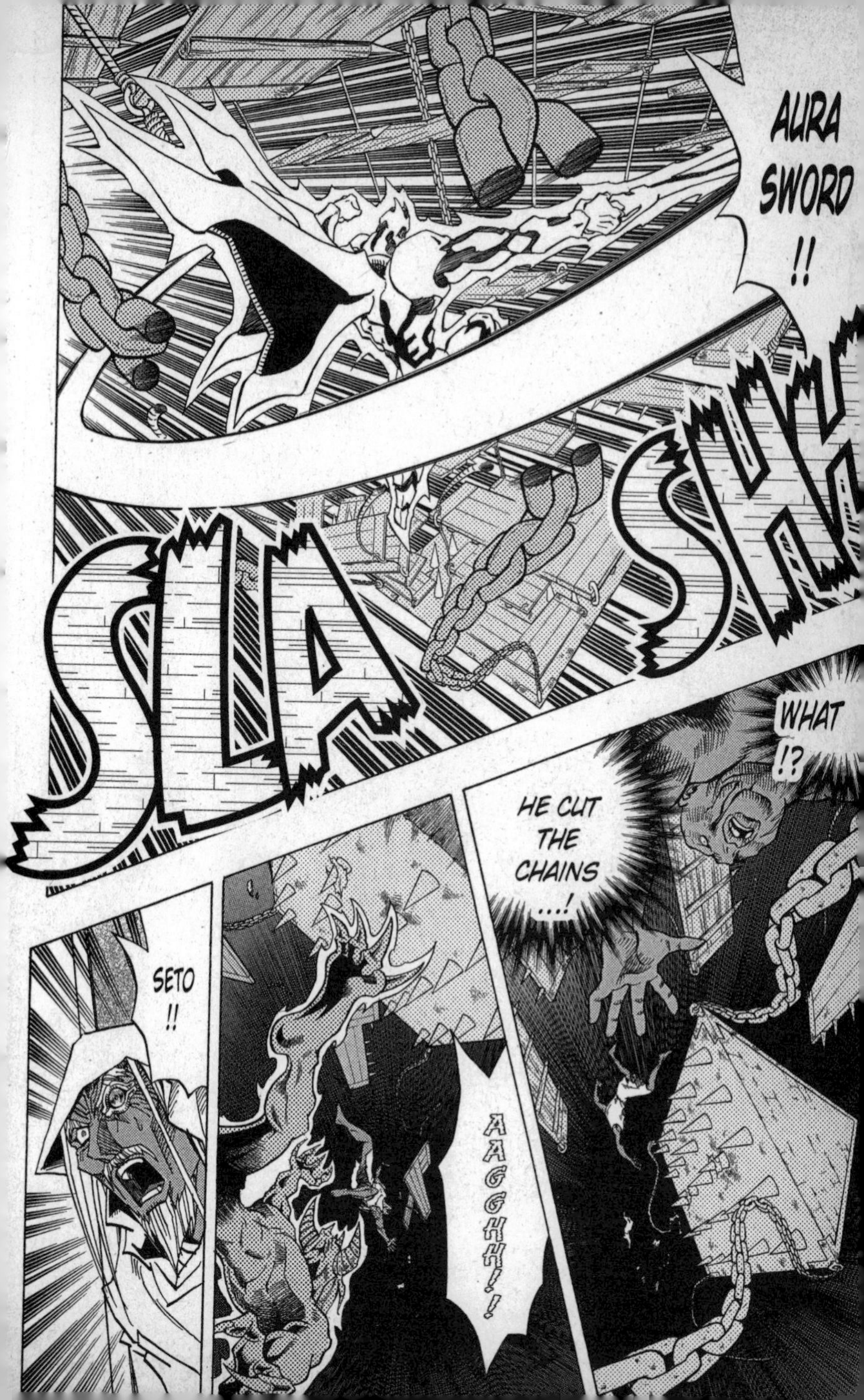
AURA SWORD!!
SLASH
WHAT!?
HE CUT THE CHAINS...!
AAGGHH!!
SETO!!

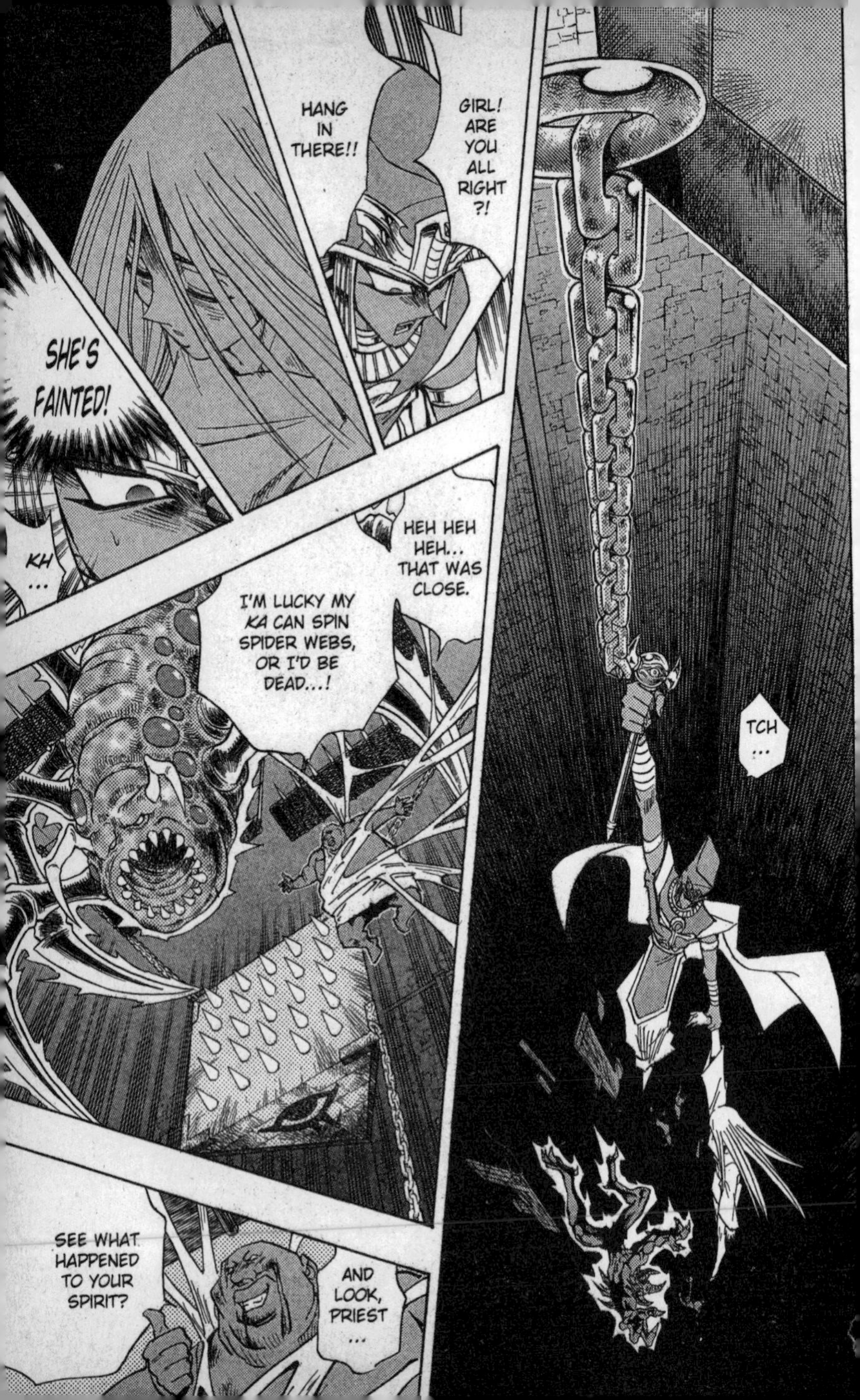
TCH...
GIRL! ARE YOU ALL RIGHT?!
HANG IN THERE!!
SHE'S FAINTED!
KH...
HEH HEH HEH... THAT WAS CLOSE.
I'M LUCKY MY KA CAN SPIN SPIDER WEBS, OR I'D BE DEAD...!
AND LOOK, PRIEST...
SEE WHAT HAPPENED TO YOUR SPIRIT?

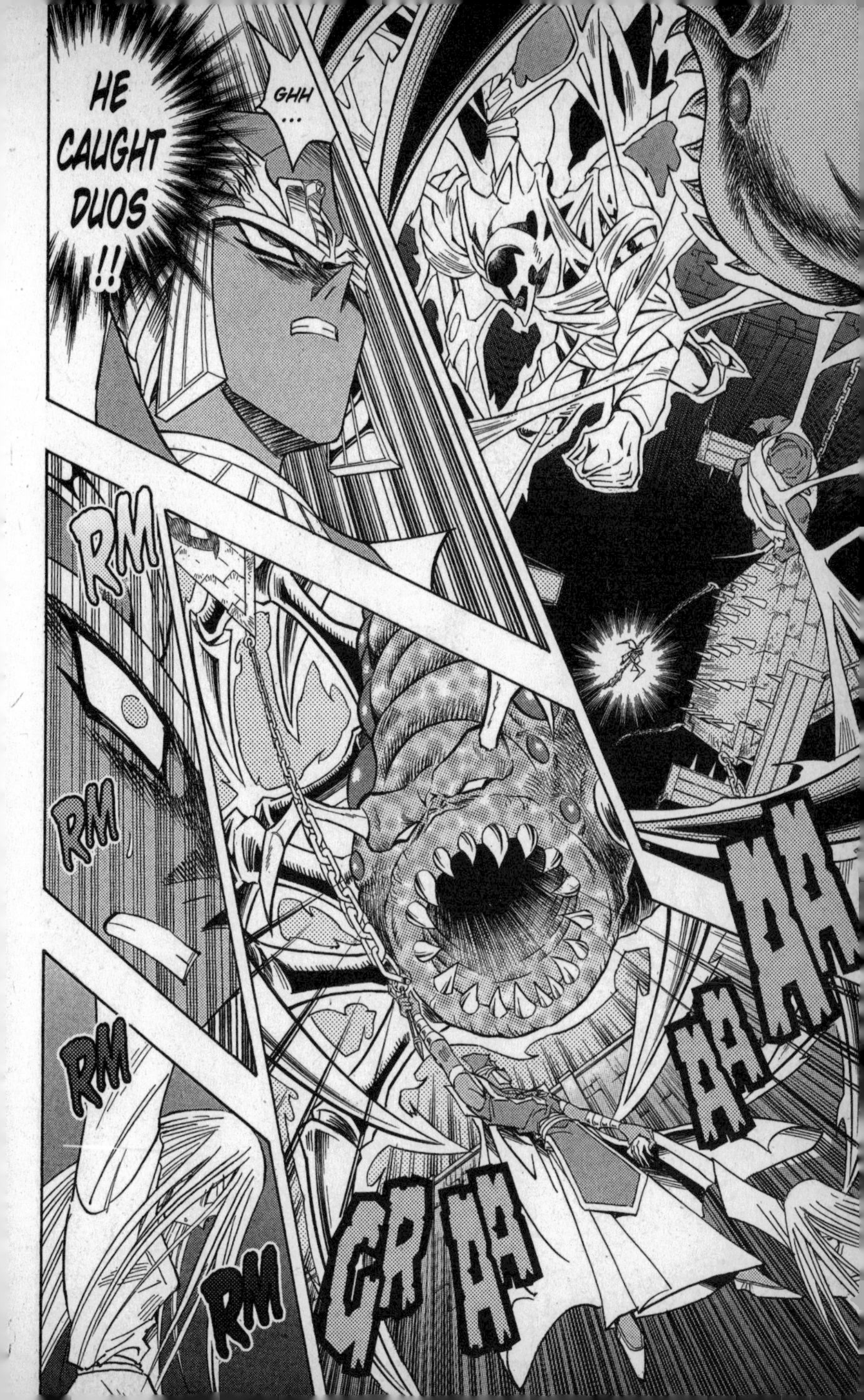

GHH...
HE CAUGHT DUOS!!
RM
RM
RM
RM
GRAA
AAAAAA

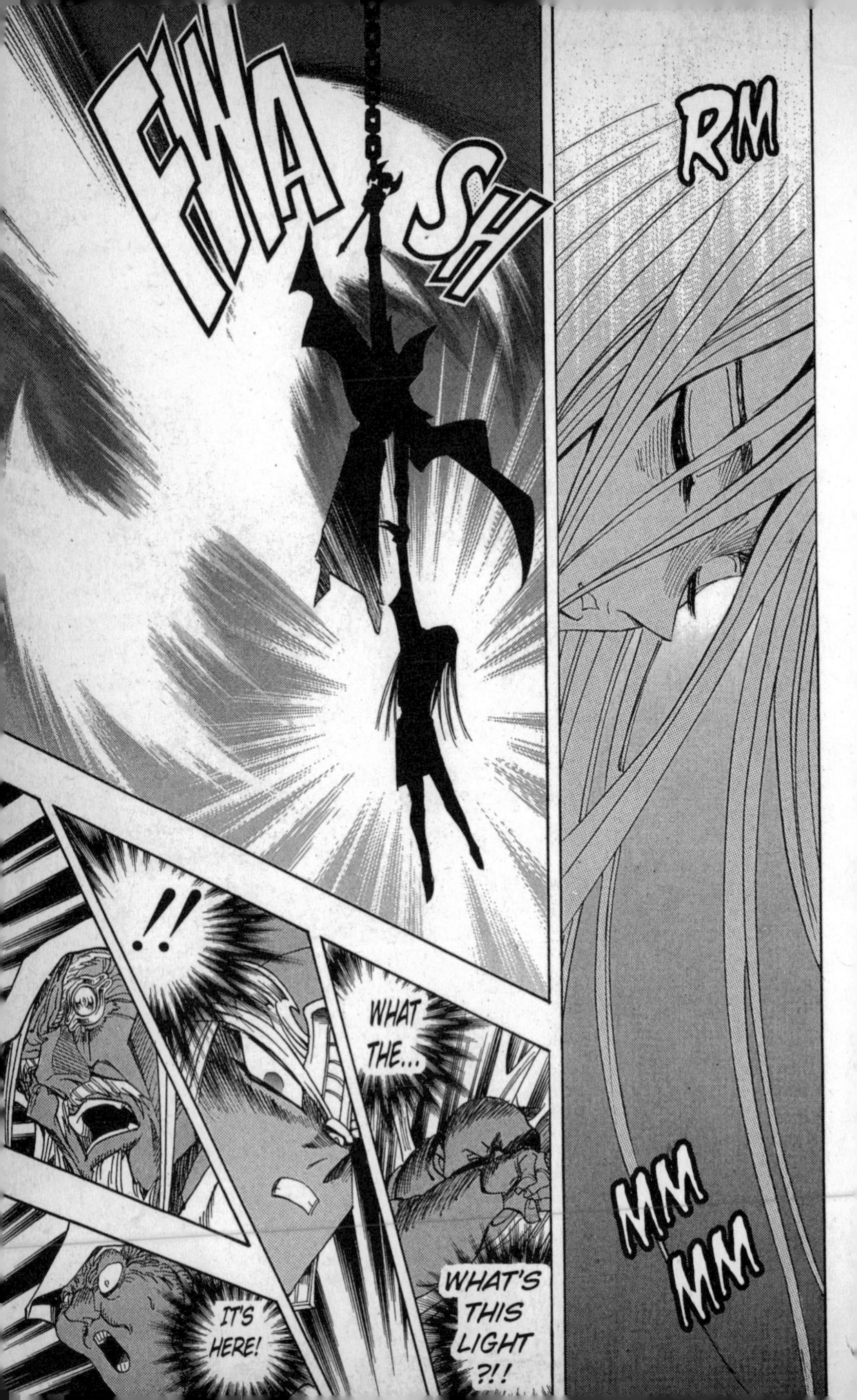
RM
MM MM
FWA SH
!!
WHAT THE...
WHAT'S THIS LIGHT ?!!
IT'S HERE!

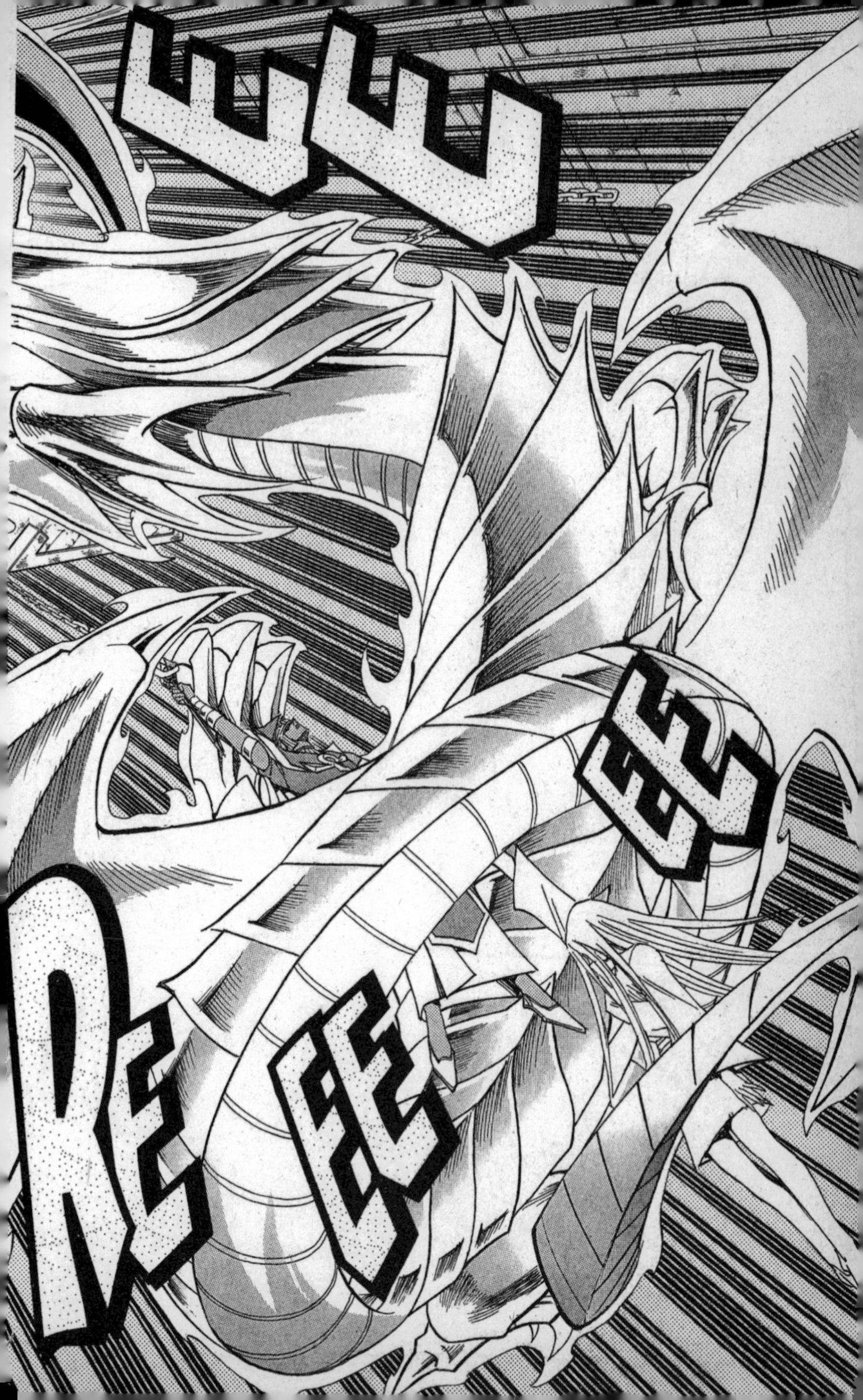

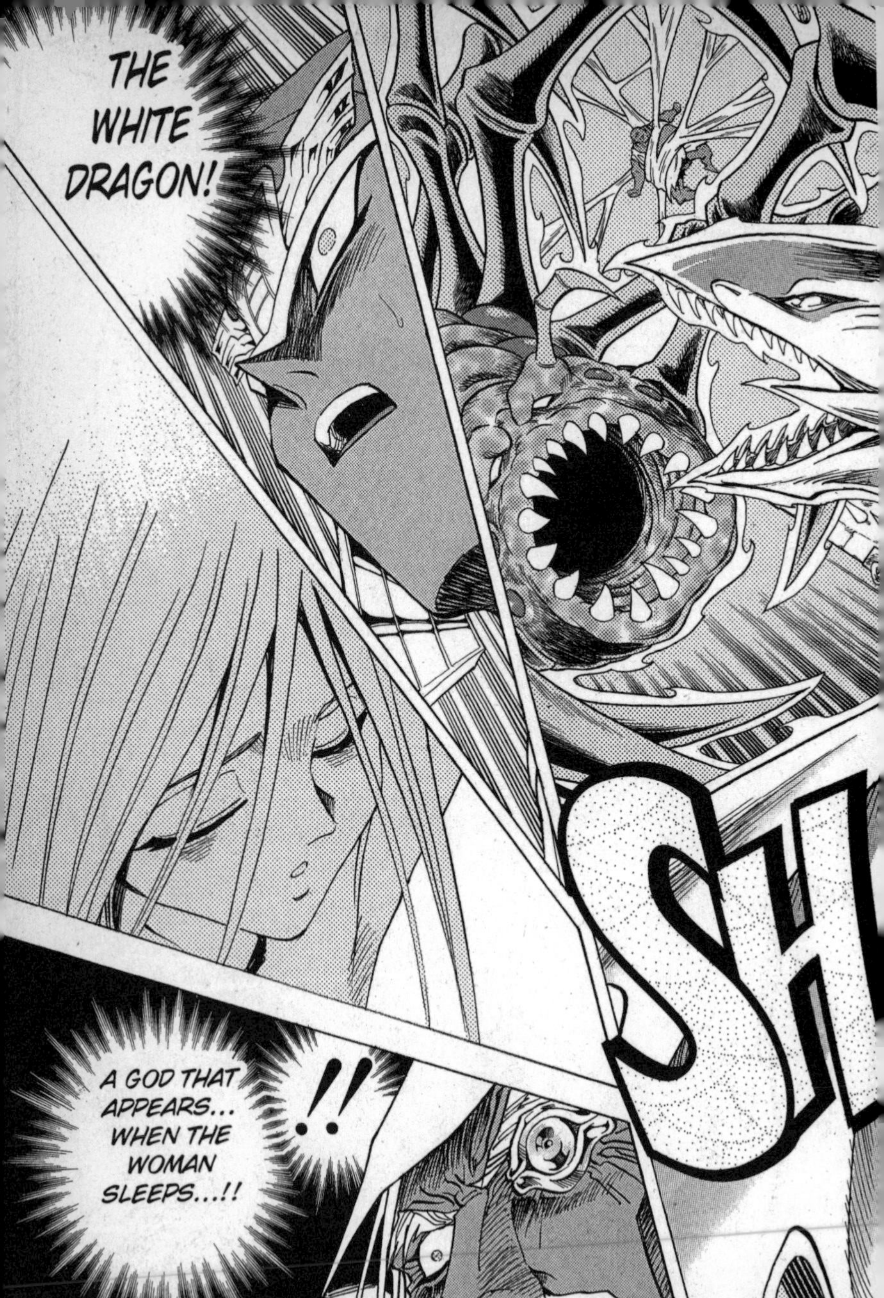
SH
THE WHITE DRAGON!
!!
A GOD THAT APPEARS... WHEN THE WOMAN SLEEPS...!!

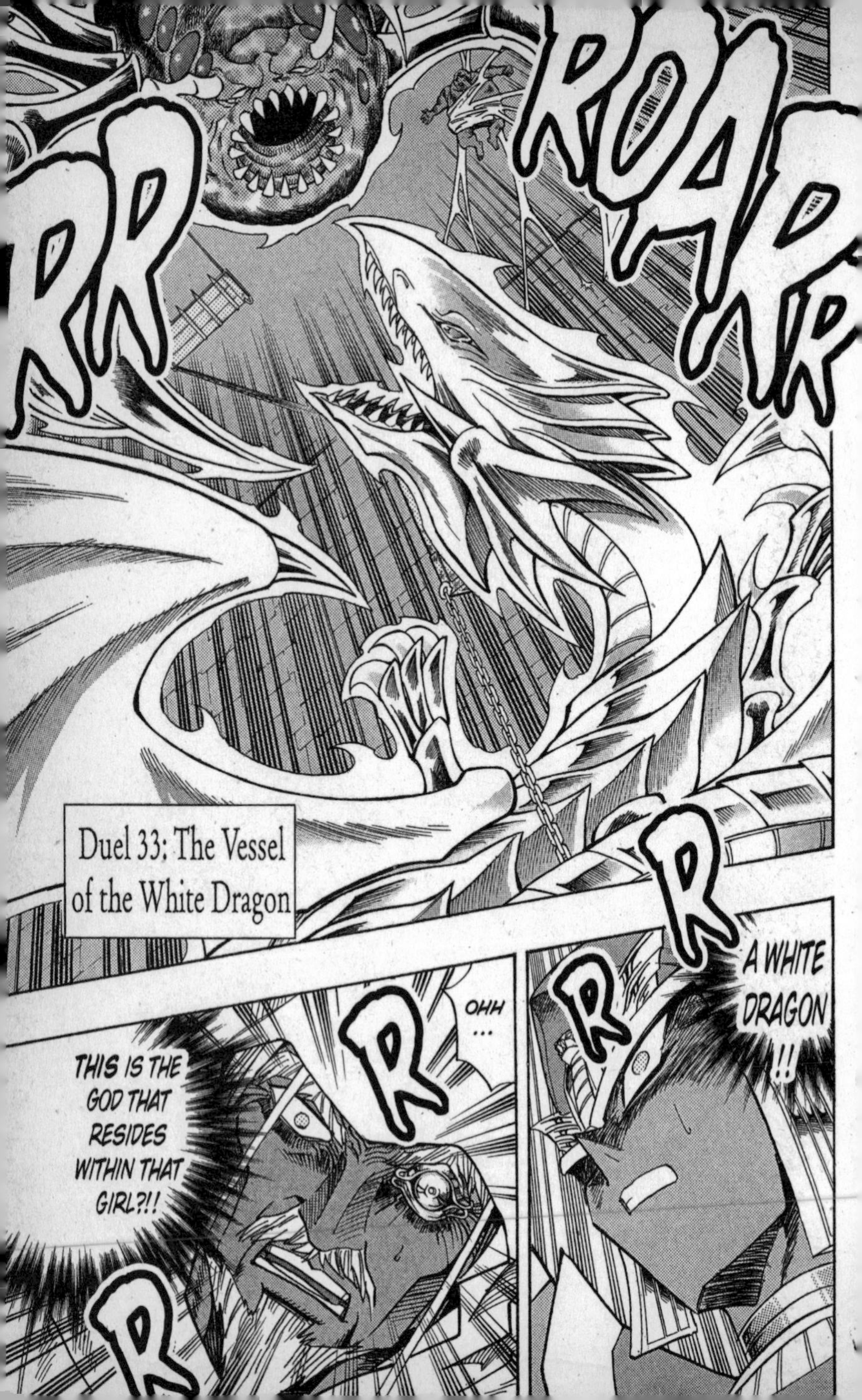
RRR
ROAR
Duel 33: The Vessel of the White Dragon
RRR
A WHITE DRAGON!!
OHH...
THIS IS THE GOD THAT RESIDES WITHIN THAT GIRL?!!
R

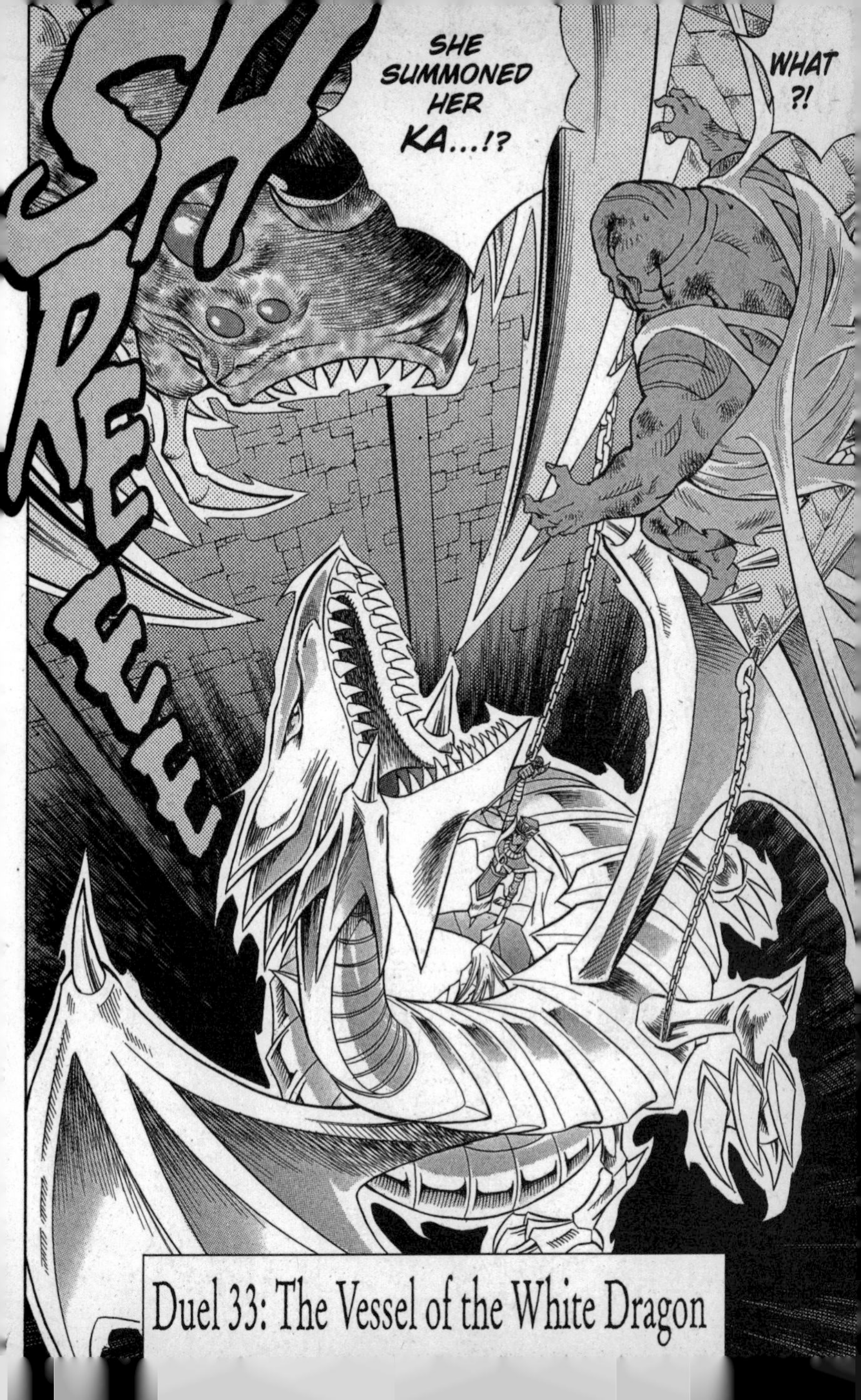
WHAT?!
SHE SUMMONED HER KA...!?

## Duel 33: The Vessel of the White Dragon

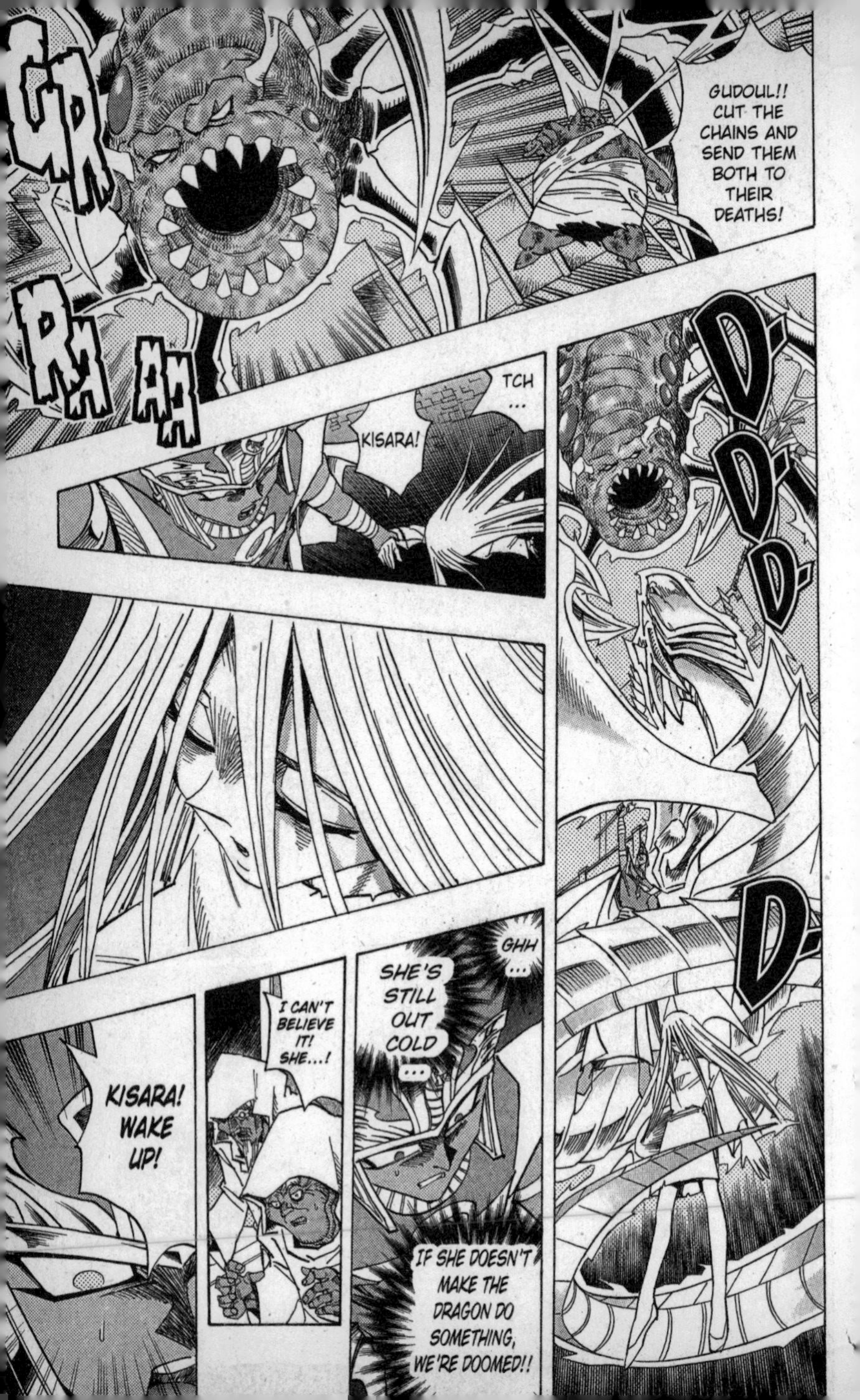
GUDOUL!! CUT THE CHAINS AND SEND THEM BOTH TO THEIR DEATHS!
GRRAAA
DDDD
D
TCH ...
KISARA!
GHH ...
SHE'S STILL OUT COLD ...
IF SHE DOESN'T MAKE THE DRAGON DO SOMETHING, WE'RE DOOMED!!
I CAN'T BELIEVE IT! SHE...!
KISARA! WAKE UP!

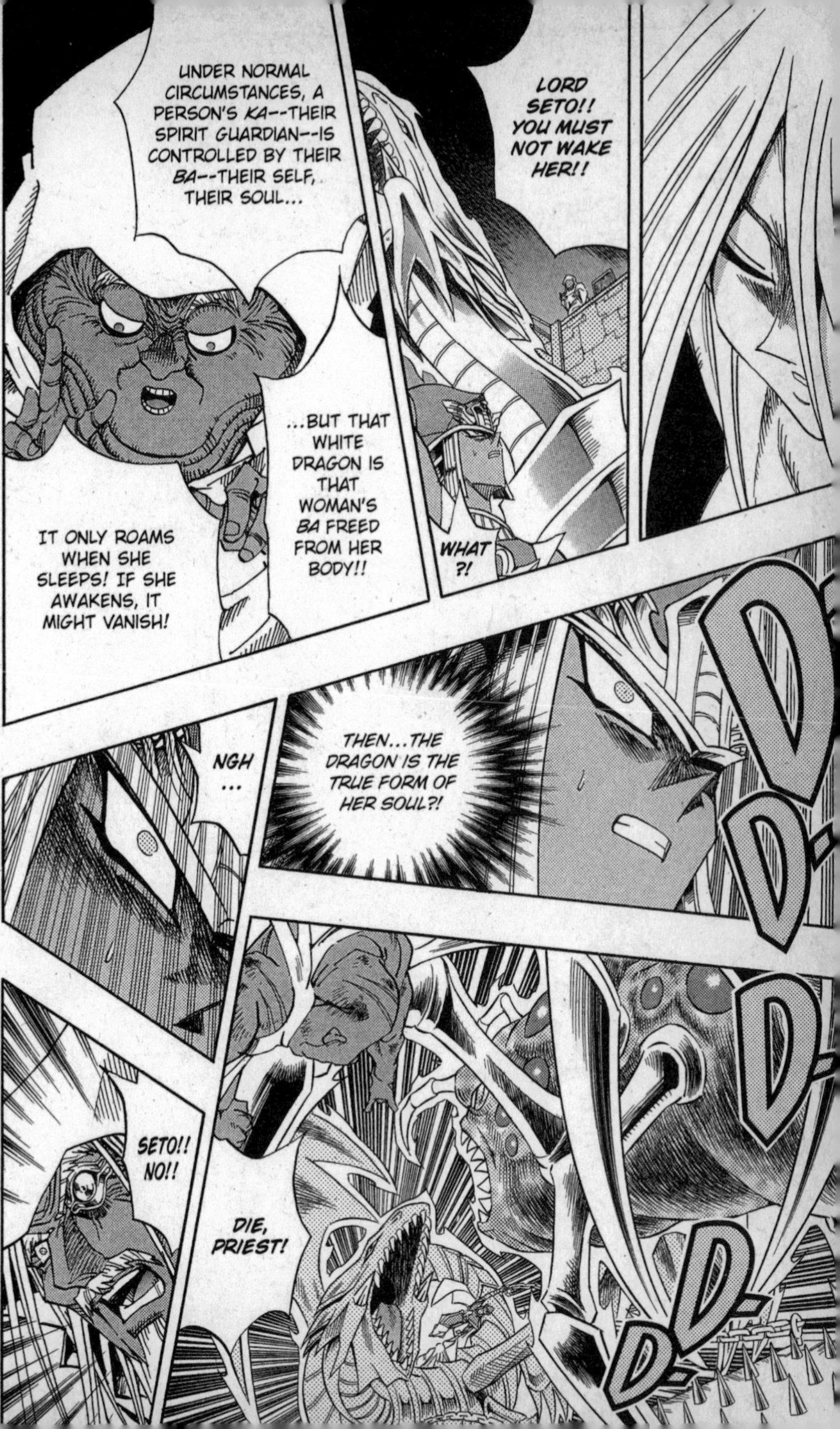
LORD SETO!! YOU MUST NOT WAKE HER!!
WHAT ?!
UNDER NORMAL CIRCUMSTANCES, A PERSON'S *KA*--THEIR SPIRIT GUARDIAN--IS CONTROLLED BY THEIR *BA*--THEIR SELF, THEIR SOUL...
...BUT THAT WHITE DRAGON IS THAT WOMAN'S *BA* FREED FROM HER BODY!!
IT ONLY ROAMS WHEN SHE SLEEPS! IF SHE AWAKENS, IT MIGHT VANISH!
D D-
THEN...THE DRAGON IS THE TRUE FORM OF HER SOUL?!
NGH ...
D- D-D-D-
DIE, PRIEST!
SETO!! NO!!

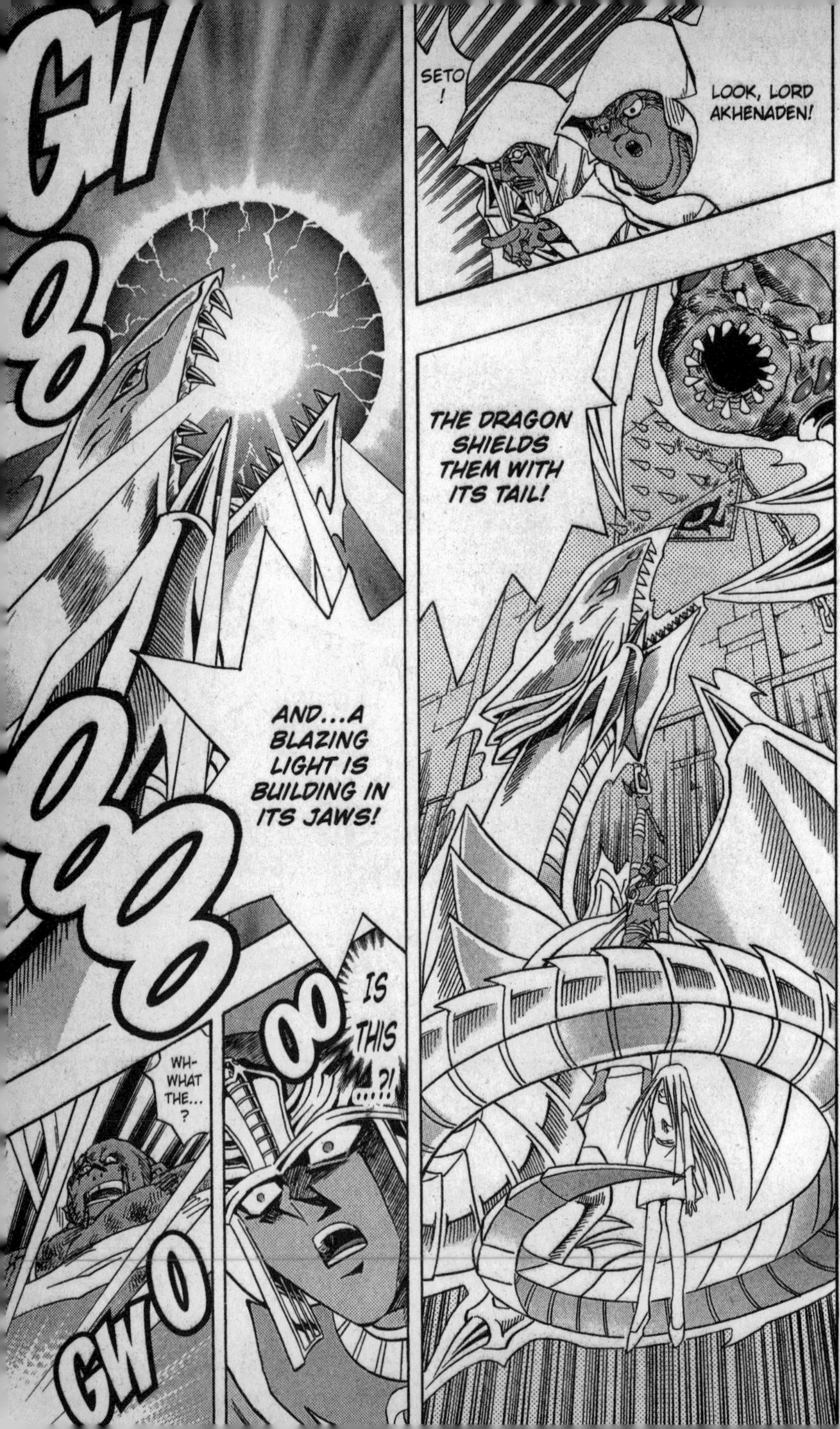
LOOK, LORD AKHENADEN!
SETO!
THE DRAGON SHIELDS THEM WITH ITS TAIL!
GWOOOO
AND...A BLAZING LIGHT IS BUILDING IN ITS JAWS!
OO
IS THIS...?!
WH- WHAT THE...?
GWO

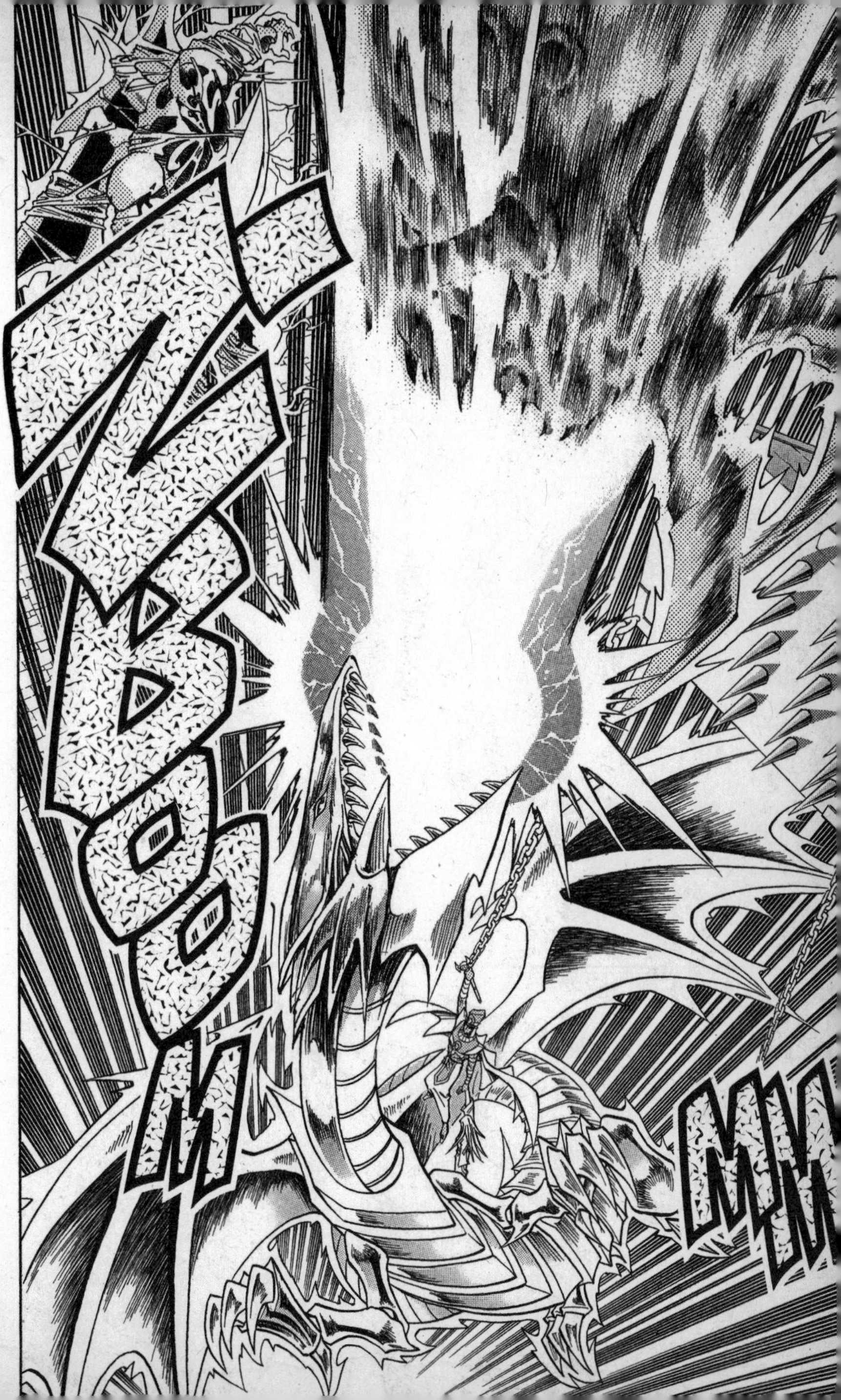

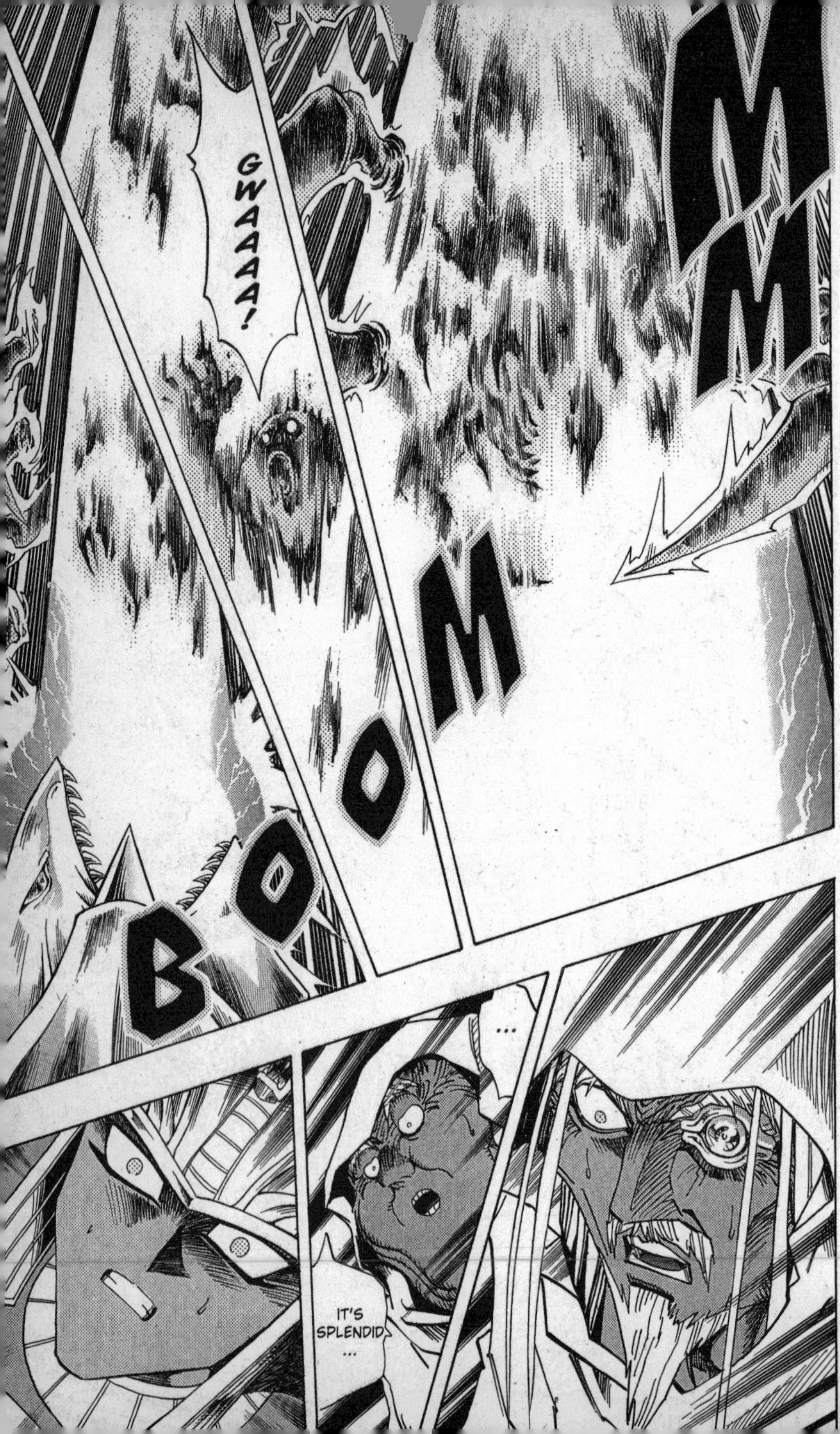
GWAAAAA!
BOOMMMM
...
IT'S SPLENDID ...

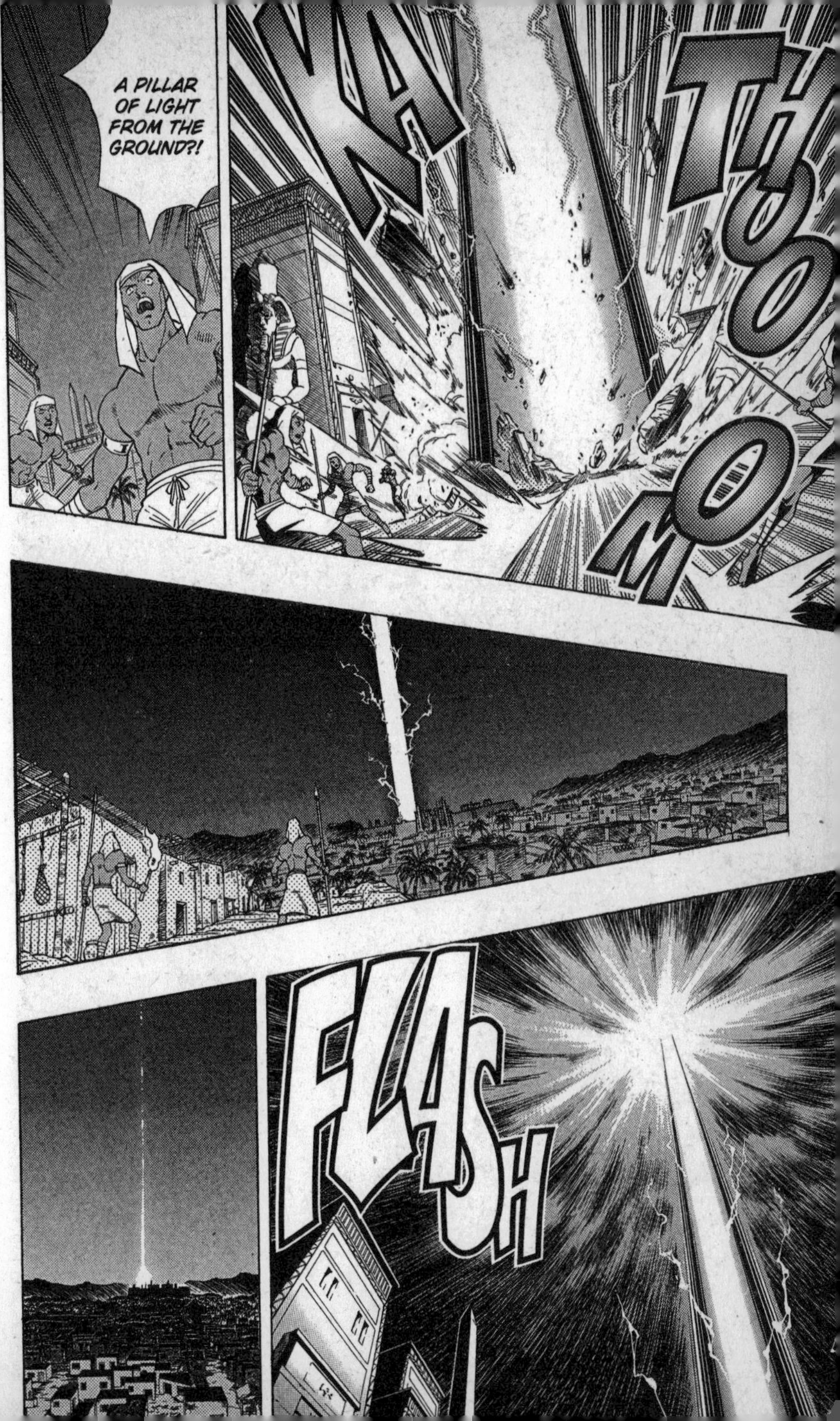
THOOOM
A PILLAR OF LIGHT FROM THE GROUND?!
FLASH

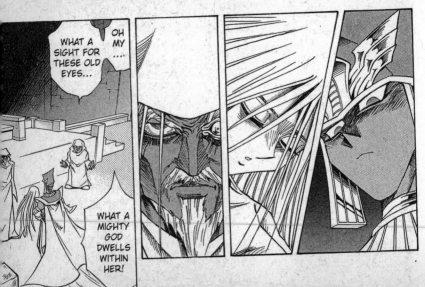

OH MY....

WHAT A SIGHT FOR THESE OLD EYES...

WHAT A MIGHTY GOD DWELLS WITHIN HER!

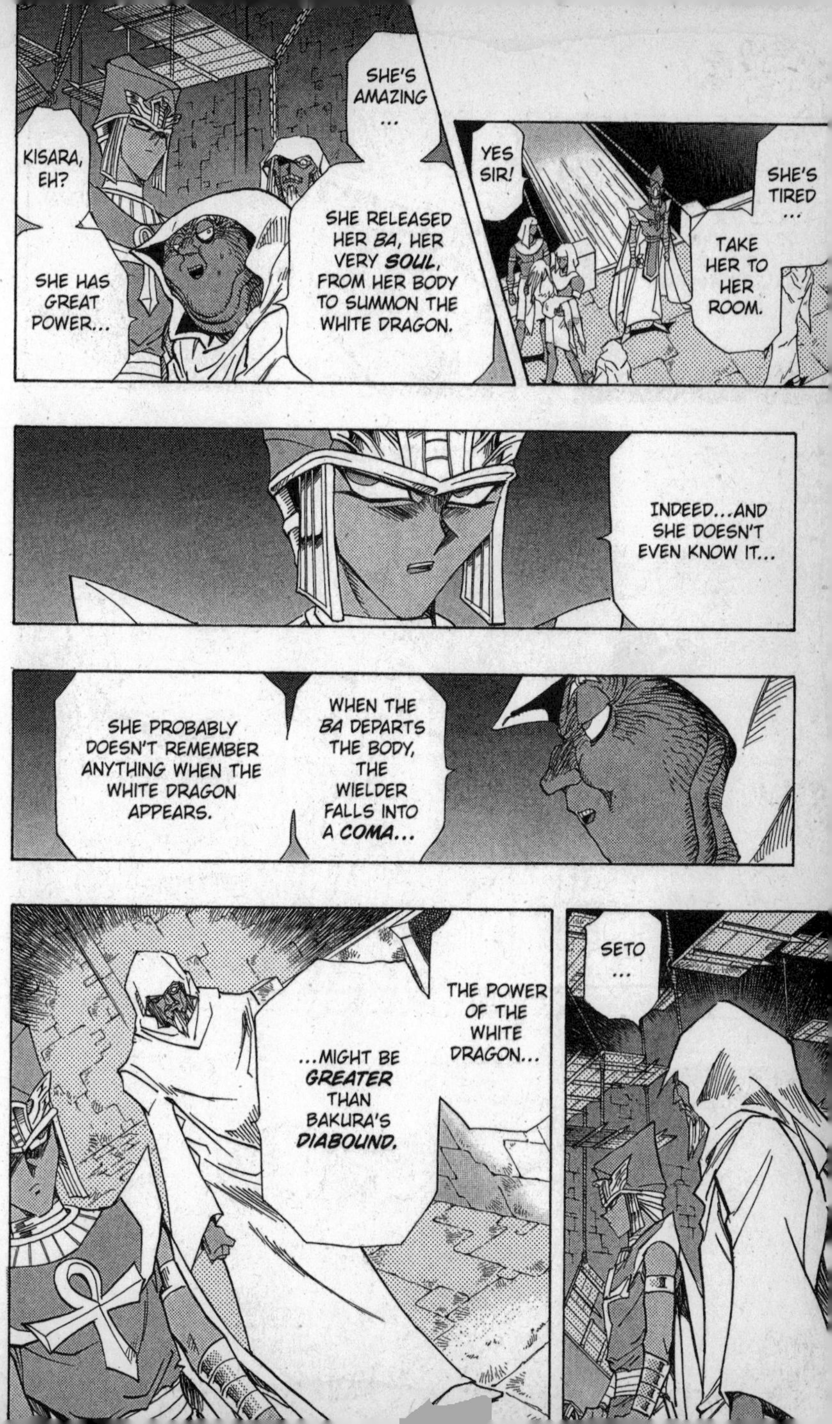
SHE'S TIRED...
TAKE HER TO HER ROOM.
YES SIR!
SHE'S AMAZING...
SHE RELEASED HER BA, HER VERY SOUL, FROM HER BODY TO SUMMON THE WHITE DRAGON.
KISARA, EH?
SHE HAS GREAT POWER...
INDEED...AND SHE DOESN'T EVEN KNOW IT...
WHEN THE BA DEPARTS THE BODY, THE WIELDER FALLS INTO A COMA...
SHE PROBABLY DOESN'T REMEMBER ANYTHING WHEN THE WHITE DRAGON APPEARS.
SETO...
THE POWER OF THE WHITE DRAGON...
...MIGHT BE GREATER THAN BAKURA'S DIABOUND.

READ THIS WAY

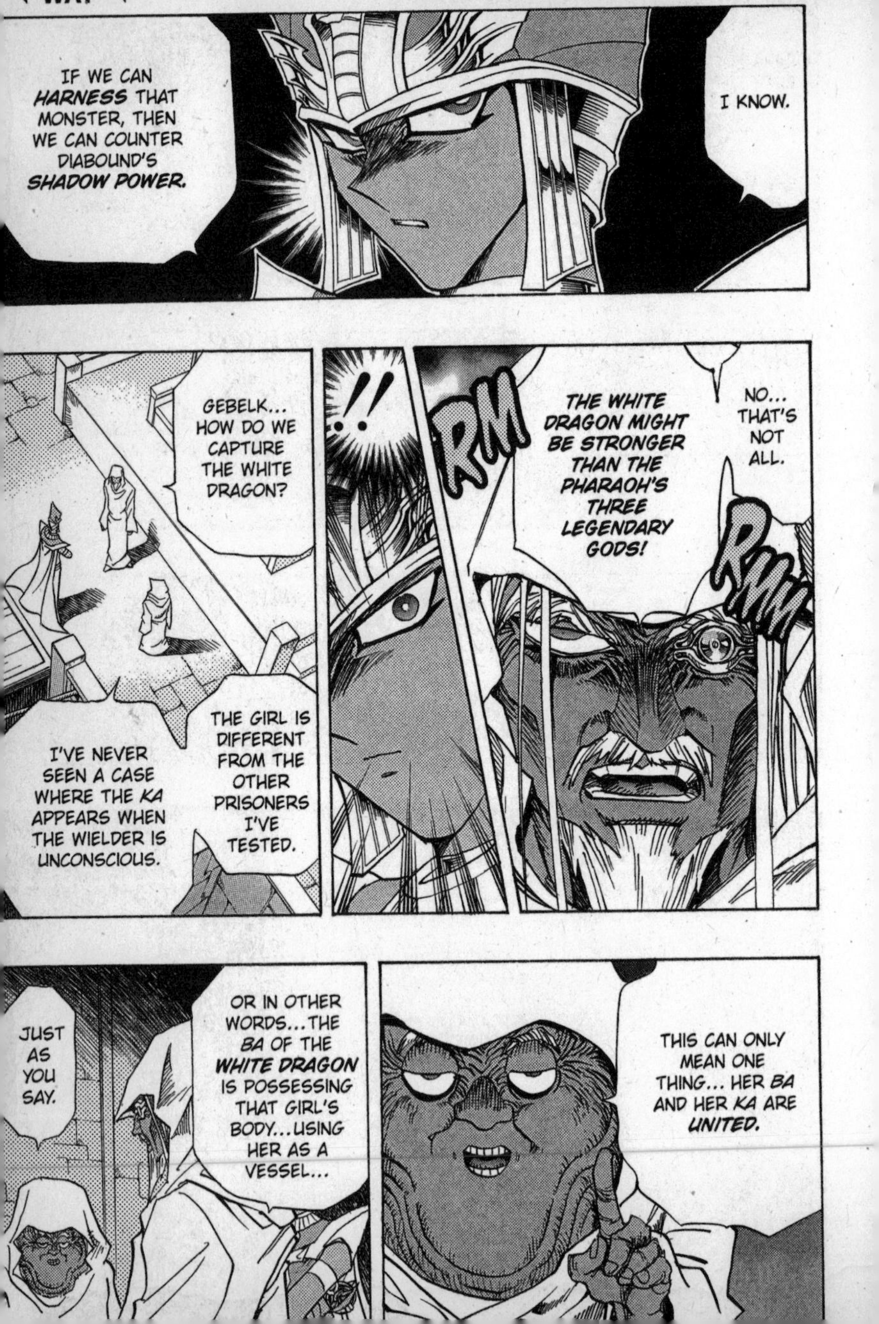
IF WE CAN *HARNESS* THAT MONSTER, THEN WE CAN COUNTER DIABOUND'S ***SHADOW POWER.***
I KNOW.
!!
RM
***THE WHITE DRAGON MIGHT BE STRONGER THAN THE PHARAOH'S THREE LEGENDARY GODS!***
NO... THAT'S NOT ALL.
RMM
GEBELK... HOW DO WE CAPTURE THE WHITE DRAGON?
THE GIRL IS DIFFERENT FROM THE OTHER PRISONERS I'VE TESTED.
I'VE NEVER SEEN A CASE WHERE THE *KA* APPEARS WHEN THE WIELDER IS UNCONSCIOUS.
THIS CAN ONLY MEAN ONE THING... HER *BA* AND HER *KA* ARE ***UNITED.***
OR IN OTHER WORDS... THE *BA* OF THE ***WHITE DRAGON*** IS POSSESSING THAT GIRL'S BODY... USING HER AS A VESSEL...
JUST AS YOU SAY.

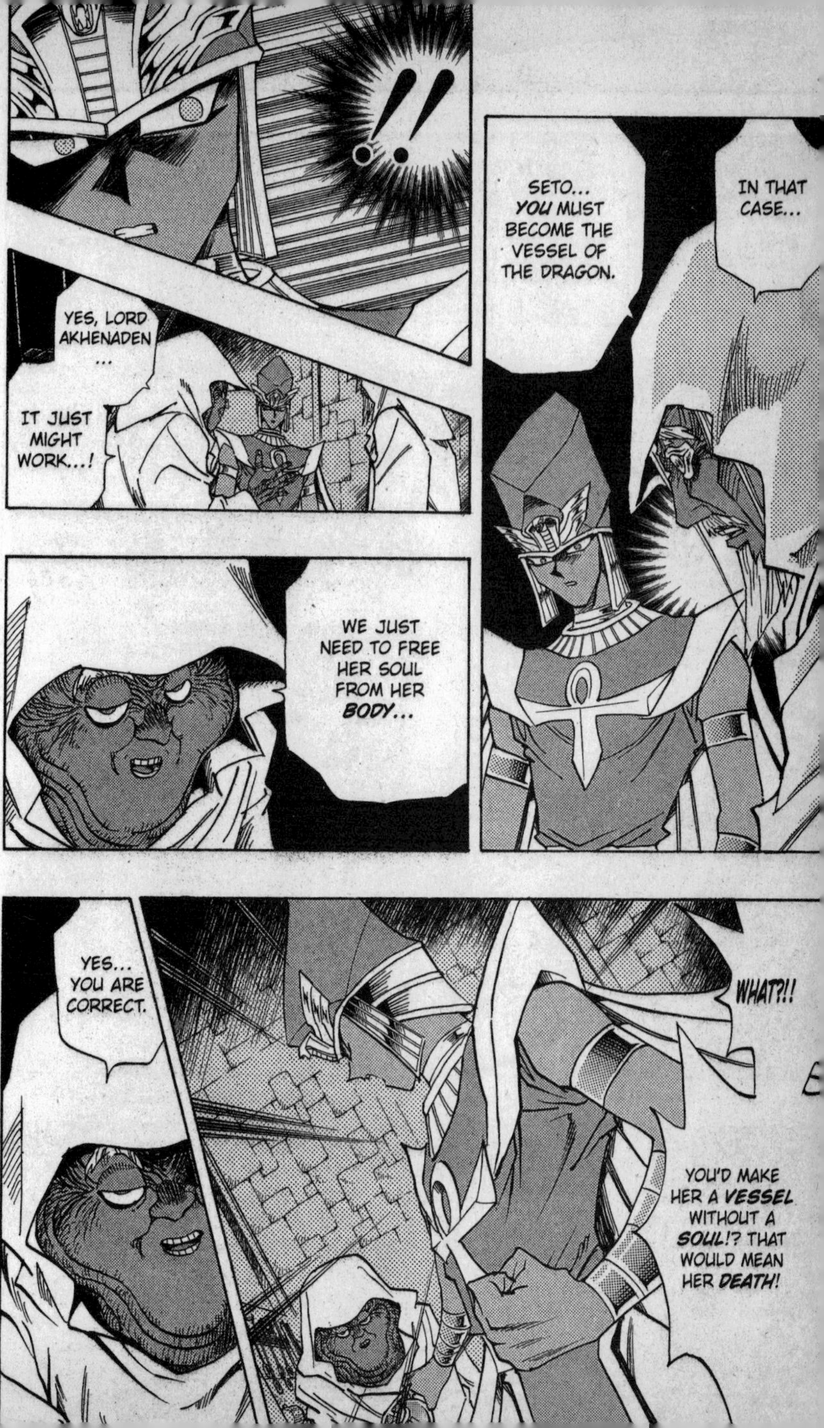
IN THAT CASE...
SETO... *YOU* MUST BECOME THE VESSEL OF THE DRAGON.
!!
YES, LORD AKHENADEN...
IT JUST MIGHT WORK...!
WE JUST NEED TO FREE HER SOUL FROM HER *BODY*...
WHAT?!!
YOU'D MAKE HER A **VESSEL** WITHOUT A **SOUL**!? THAT WOULD MEAN HER **DEATH**!
YES... YOU ARE CORRECT.

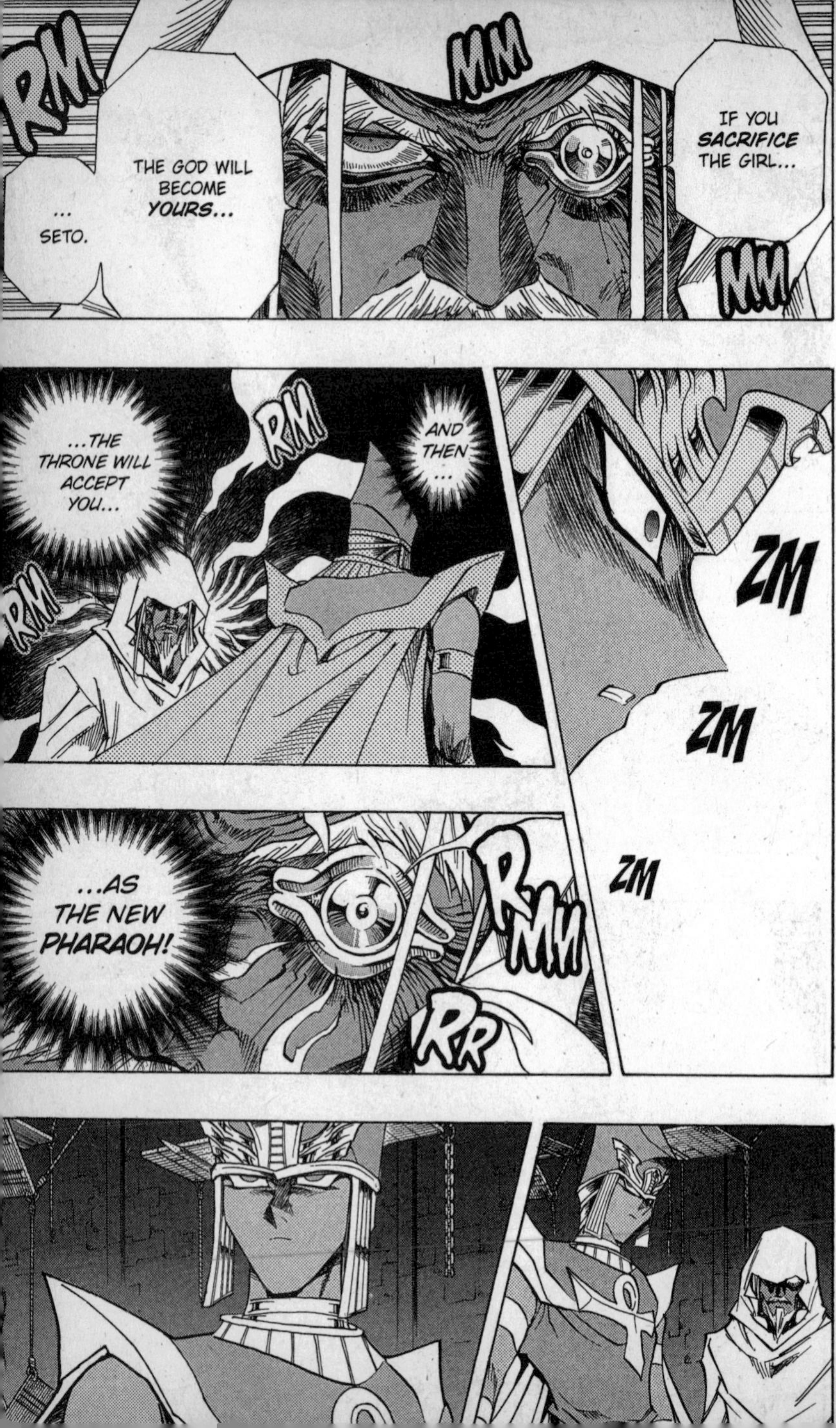
MM
IF YOU SACRIFICE THE GIRL...
MM
THE GOD WILL BECOME YOURS...
... SETO.
RM
ZM
ZM
AND THEN ...
RM
...THE THRONE WILL ACCEPT YOU...
RM
ZM
RMM
RR
...AS THE NEW PHARAOH!

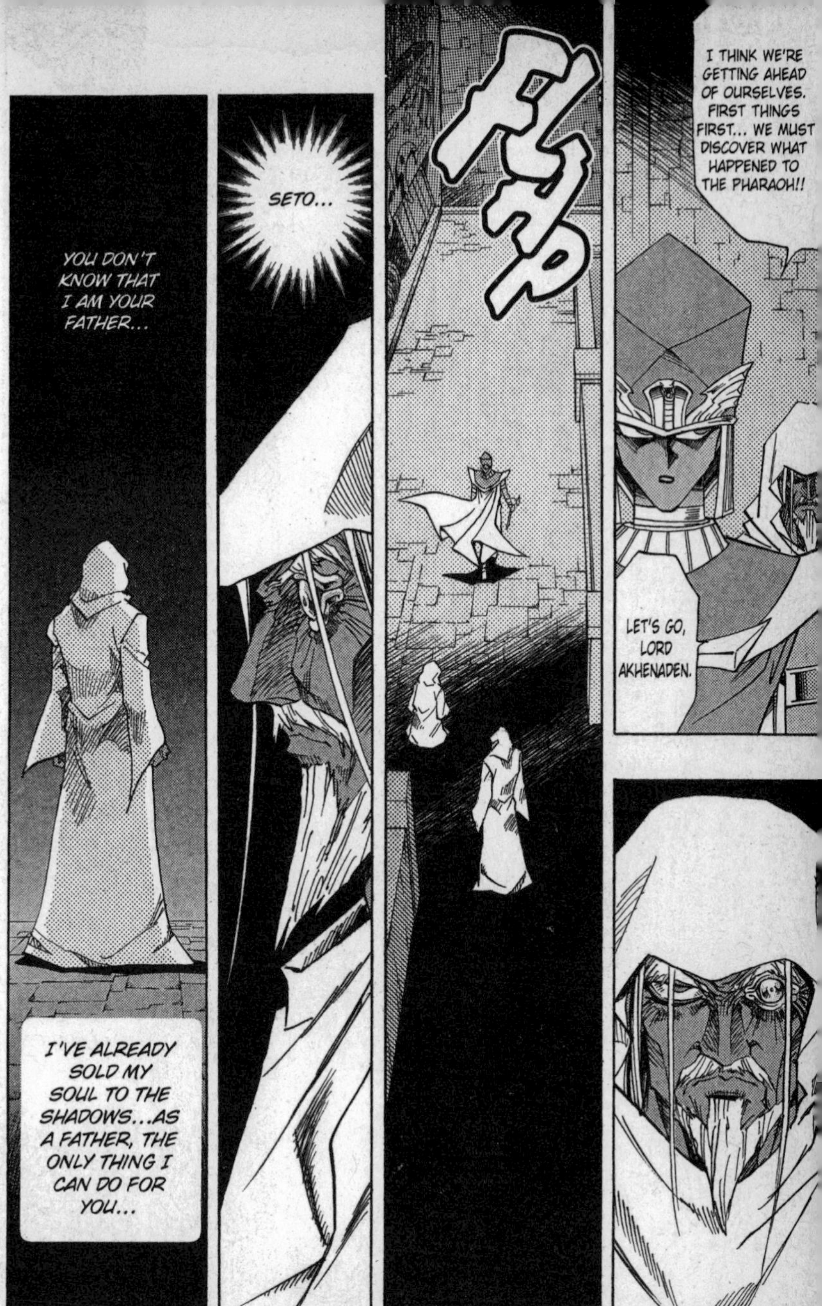
I THINK WE'RE GETTING AHEAD OF OURSELVES. FIRST THINGS FIRST... WE MUST DISCOVER WHAT HAPPENED TO THE PHARAOH!!
LET'S GO, LORD AKHENADEN.
FLAP
SETO...
YOU DON'T KNOW THAT I AM YOUR FATHER...
I'VE ALREADY SOLD MY SOUL TO THE SHADOWS...AS A FATHER, THE ONLY THING I CAN DO FOR YOU...

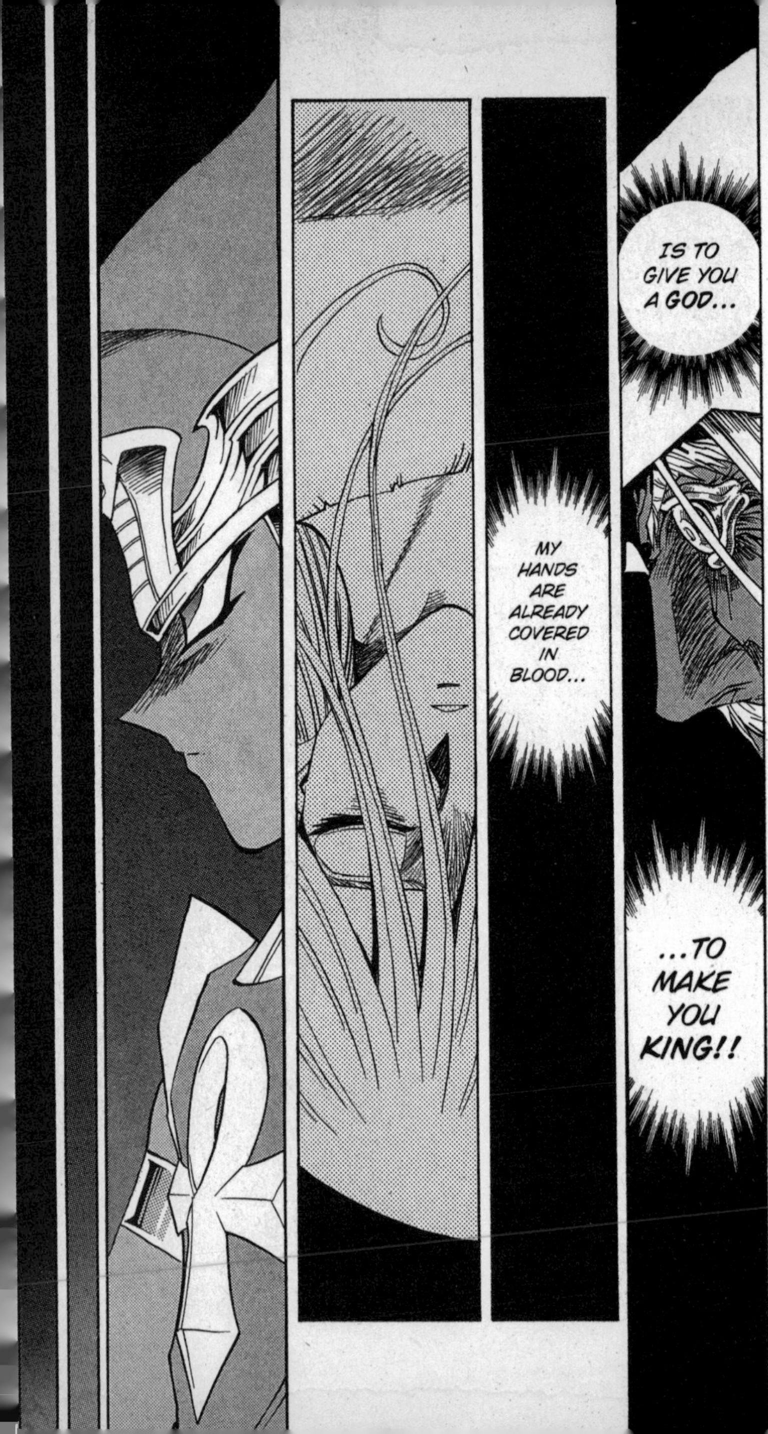
IS TO GIVE YOU A GOD...
...TO MAKE YOU KING!!
MY HANDS ARE ALREADY COVERED IN BLOOD...

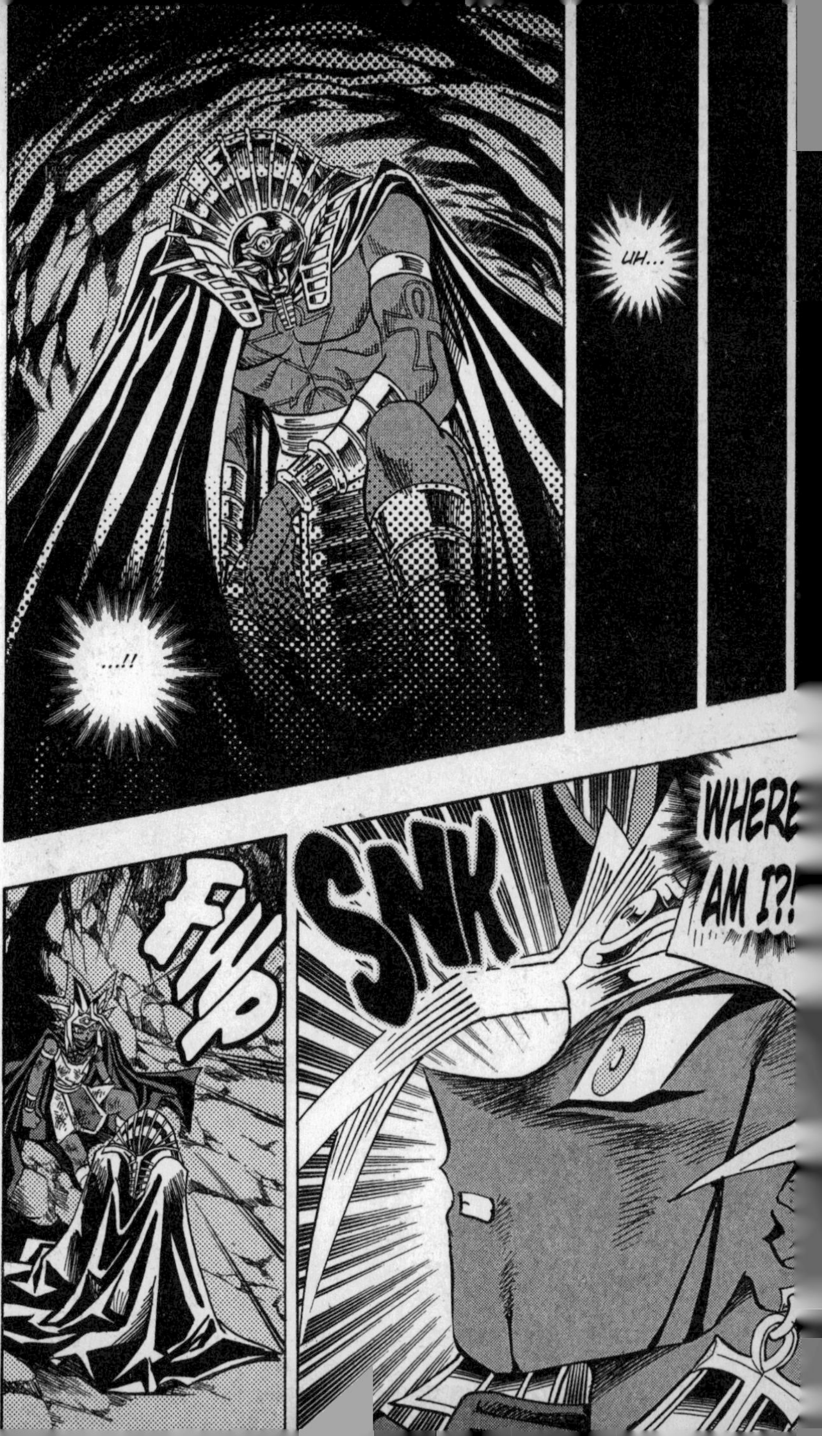
UH...
...!!
WHERE AM I?!
SNK
FWIP

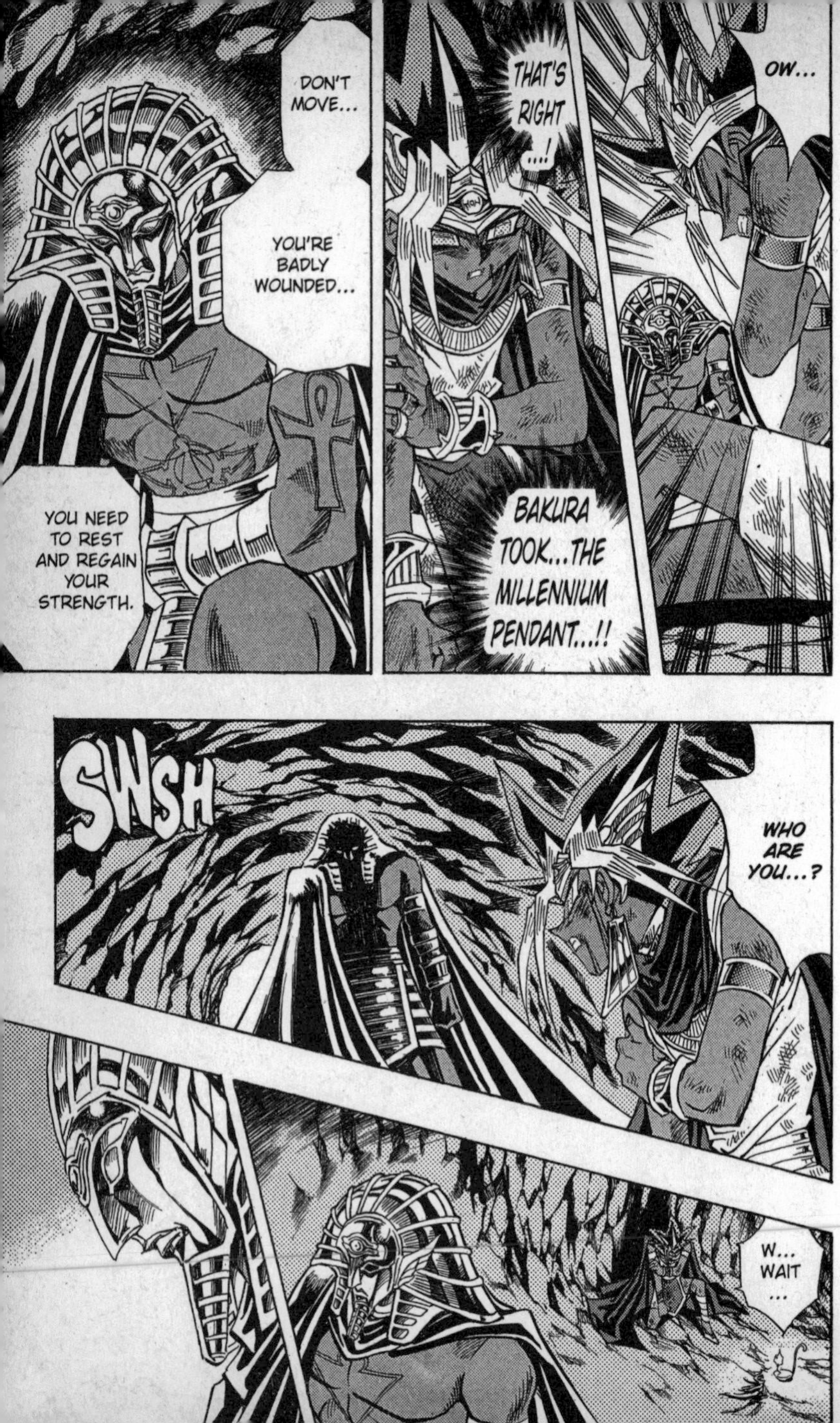
OW...
THAT'S RIGHT ...!
BAKURA TOOK...THE MILLENNIUM PENDANT...!!
DON'T MOVE...
YOU'RE BADLY WOUNDED...
YOU NEED TO REST AND REGAIN YOUR STRENGTH.
WHO ARE YOU...?
SWSH
W... WAIT ...

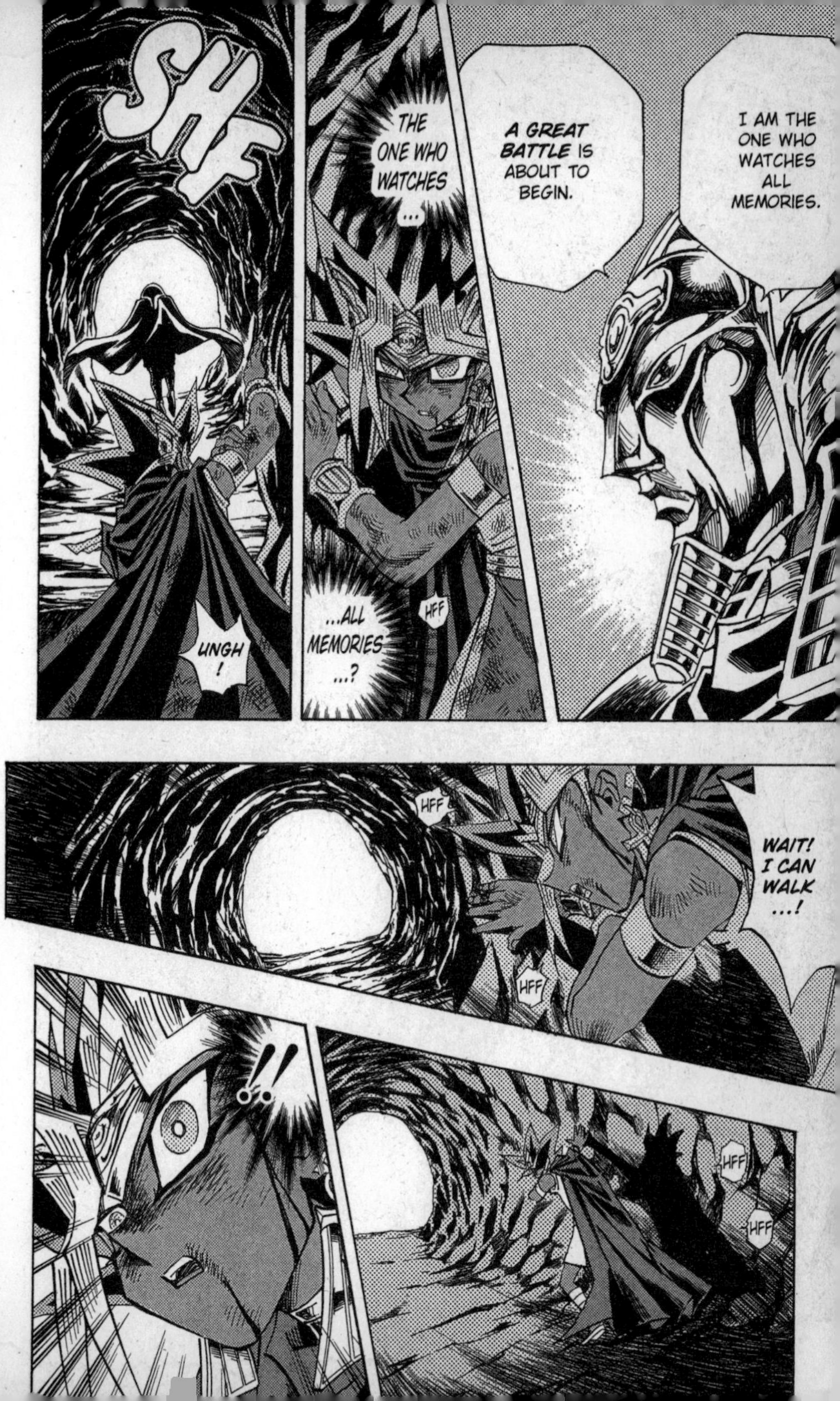
I AM THE ONE WHO WATCHES ALL MEMORIES.
A GREAT BATTLE IS ABOUT TO BEGIN.
THE ONE WHO WATCHES ...
...ALL MEMORIES ...?
HFF
SHF
UNGH!
WAIT! I CAN WALK ...!
HFF
HFF
HFF
HFF
!!

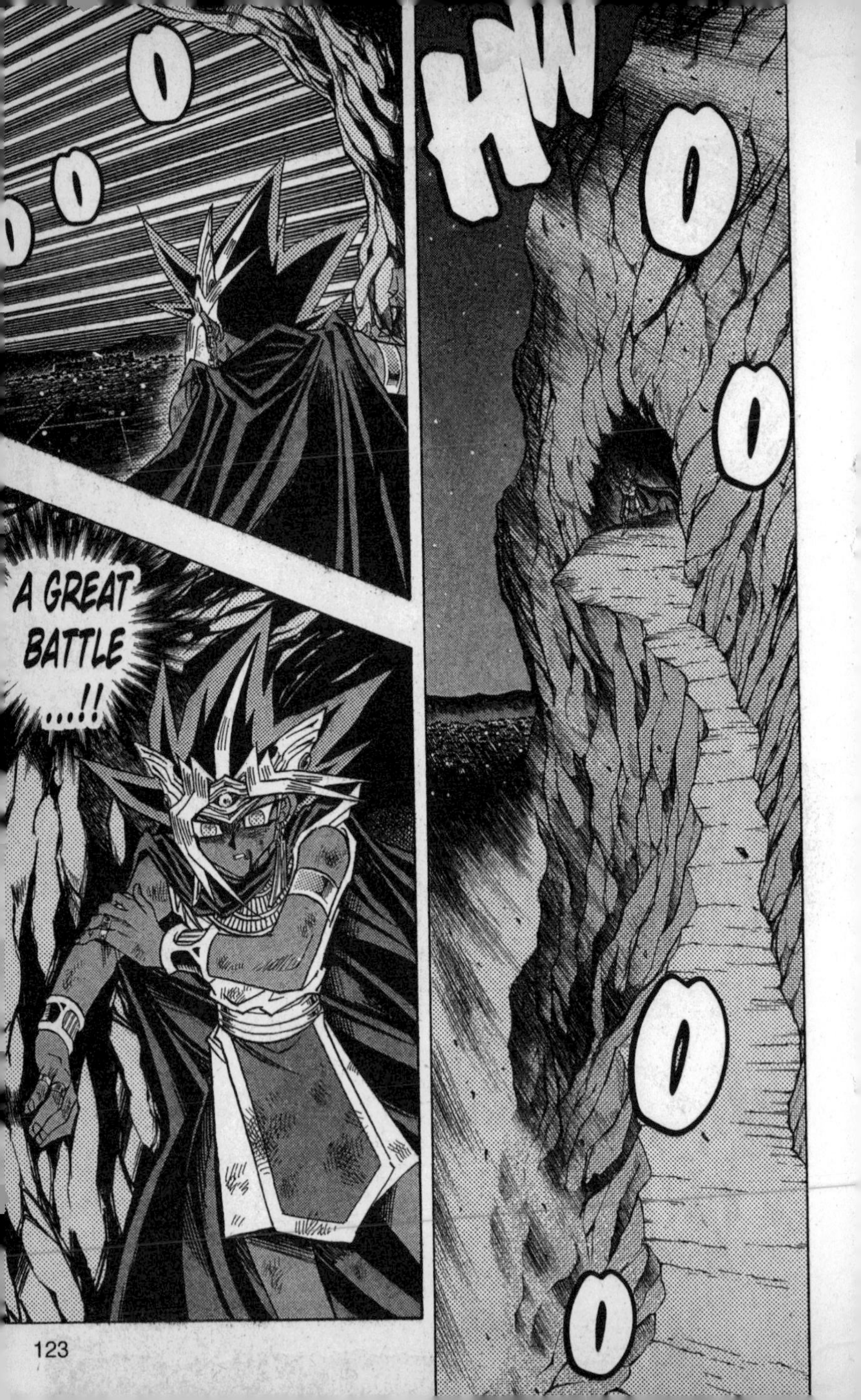
HWOOOO
OOO
A GREAT BATTLE ...!!

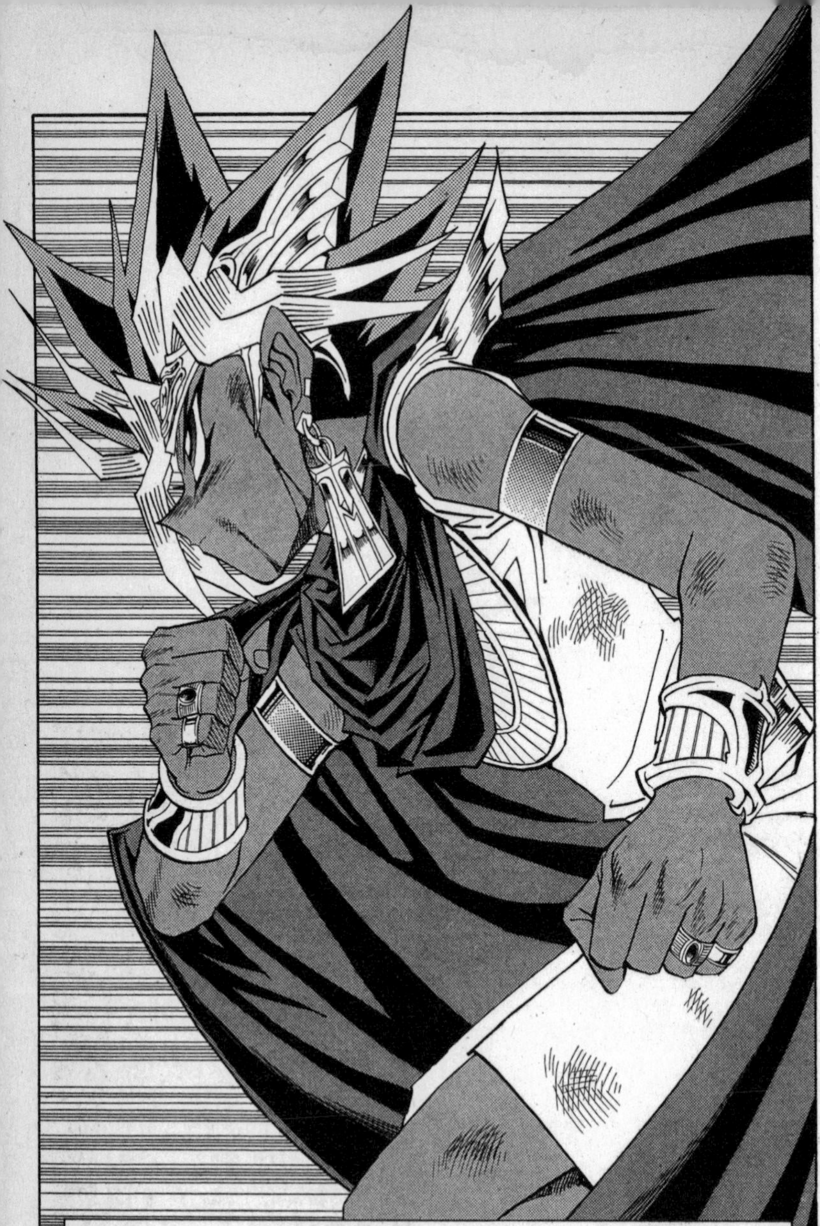

# Duel 34: The Pharaoh Returns!

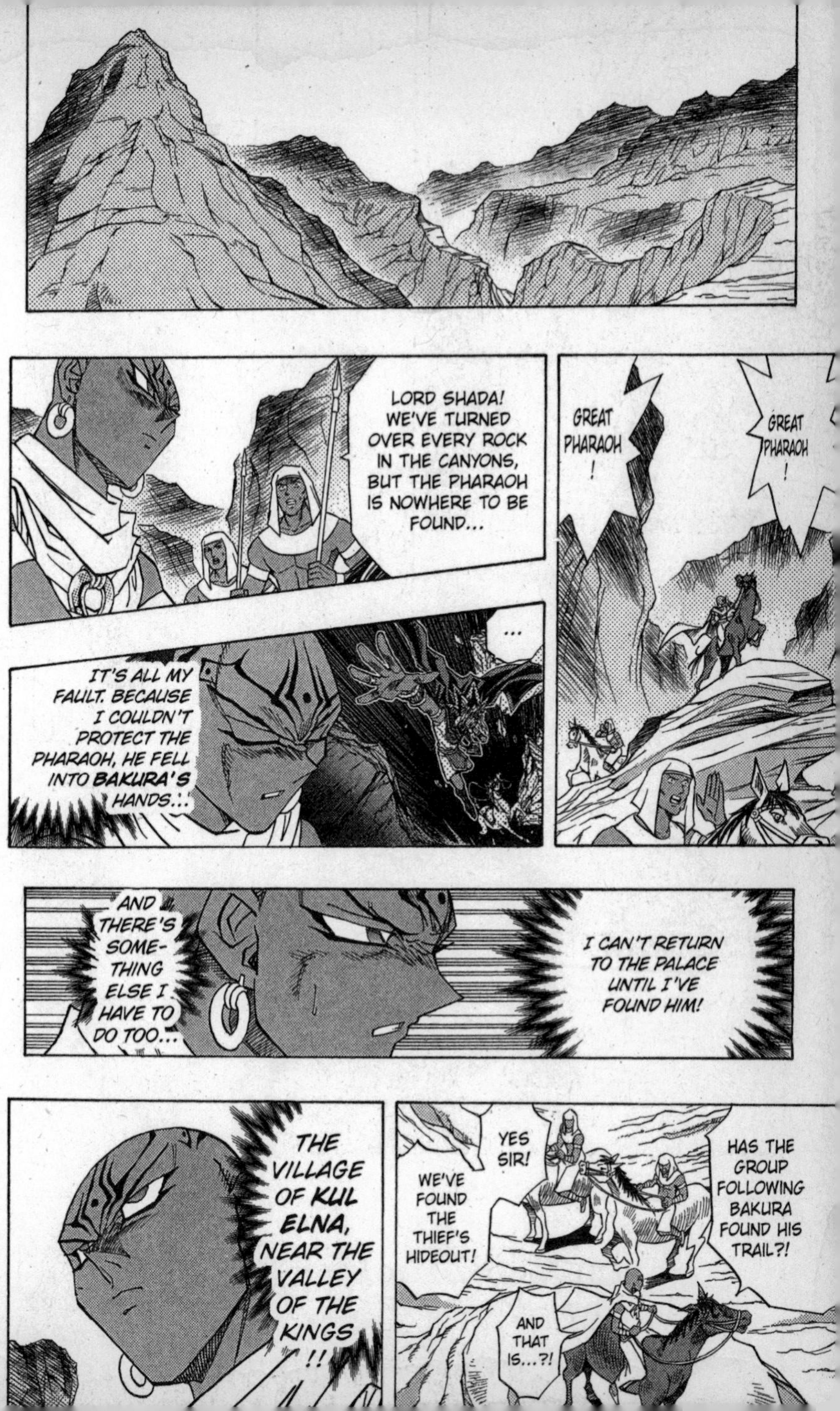
GREAT PHARAOH!
GREAT PHARAOH!
LORD SHADA! WE'VE TURNED OVER EVERY ROCK IN THE CANYONS, BUT THE PHARAOH IS NOWHERE TO BE FOUND...
...
IT'S ALL MY FAULT. BECAUSE I COULDN'T PROTECT THE PHARAOH, HE FELL INTO BAKURA'S HANDS...
I CAN'T RETURN TO THE PALACE UNTIL I'VE FOUND HIM!
AND THERE'S SOMETHING ELSE I HAVE TO DO TOO...
HAS THE GROUP FOLLOWING BAKURA FOUND HIS TRAIL?!
YES SIR!
WE'VE FOUND THE THIEF'S HIDEOUT!
AND THAT IS...?!
THE VILLAGE OF KUL ELNA, NEAR THE VALLEY OF THE KINGS!!

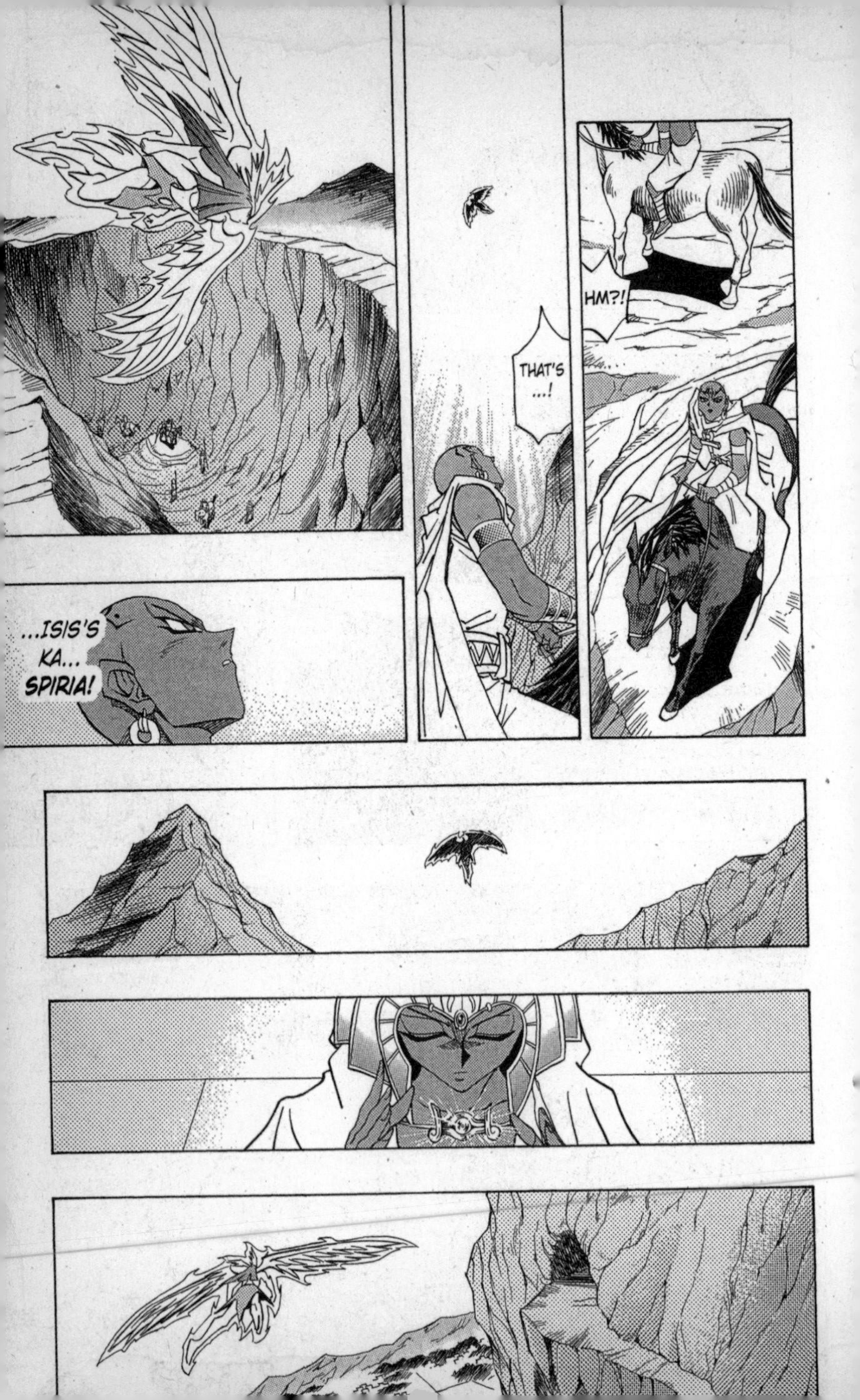
HM?!
THAT'S ...!
...ISIS'S KA... SPIRIA!

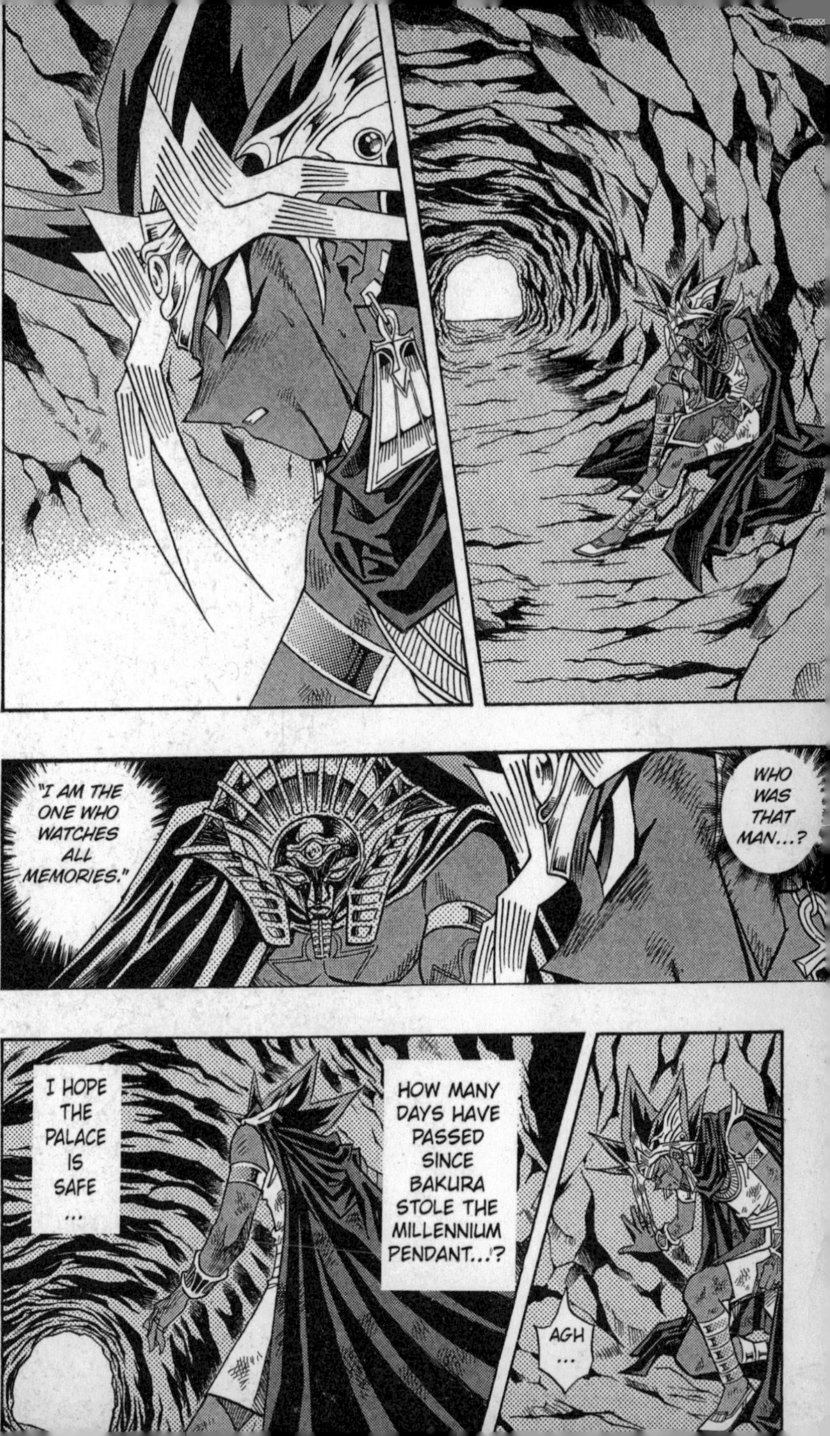
WHO WAS THAT MAN...?
"I AM THE ONE WHO WATCHES ALL MEMORIES."
AGH ...
HOW MANY DAYS HAVE PASSED SINCE BAKURA STOLE THE MILLENNIUM PENDANT...!?
I HOPE THE PALACE IS SAFE ...

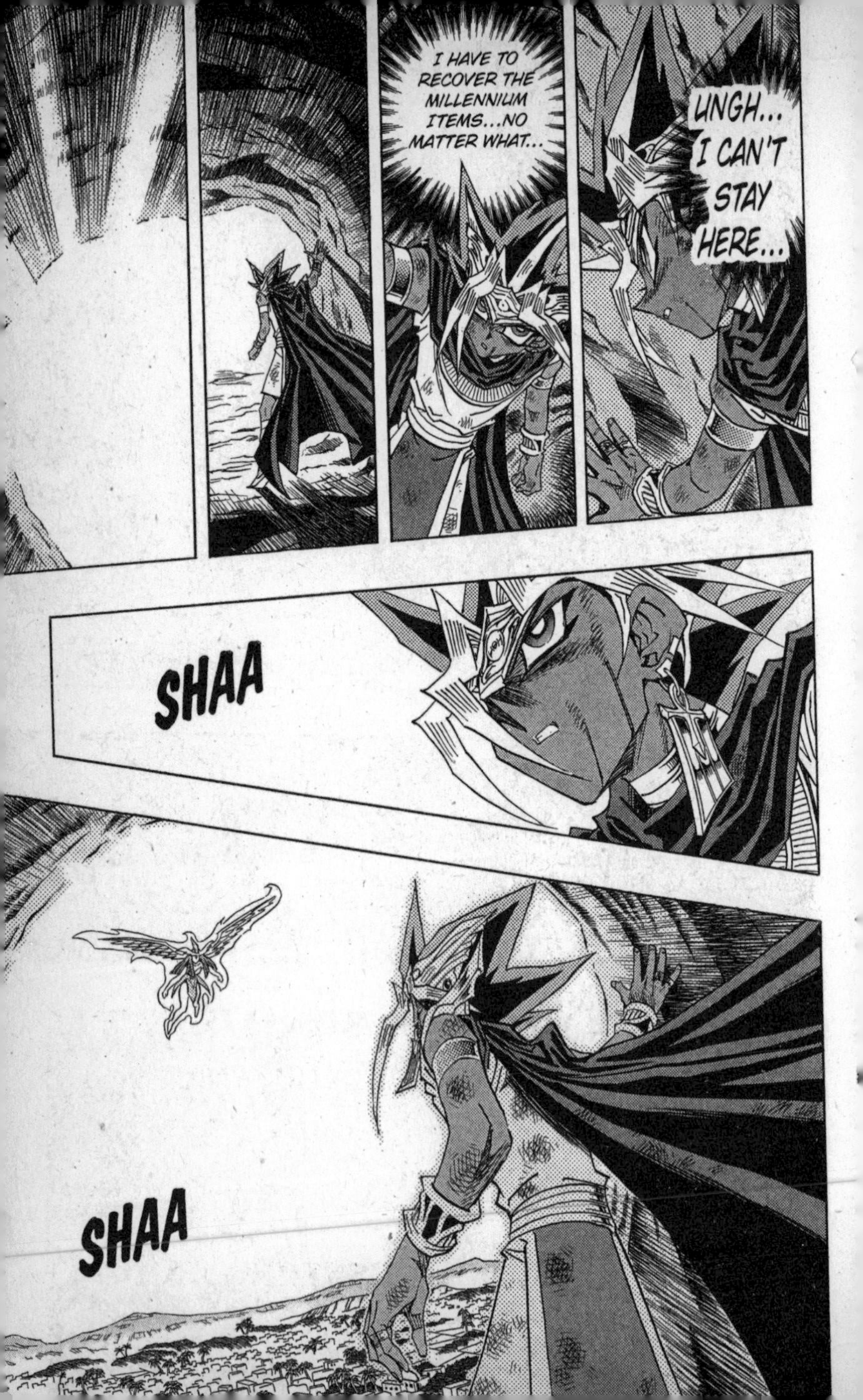
UNGH... I CAN'T STAY HERE...
I HAVE TO RECOVER THE MILLENNIUM ITEMS...NO MATTER WHAT...
SHAA
SHAA

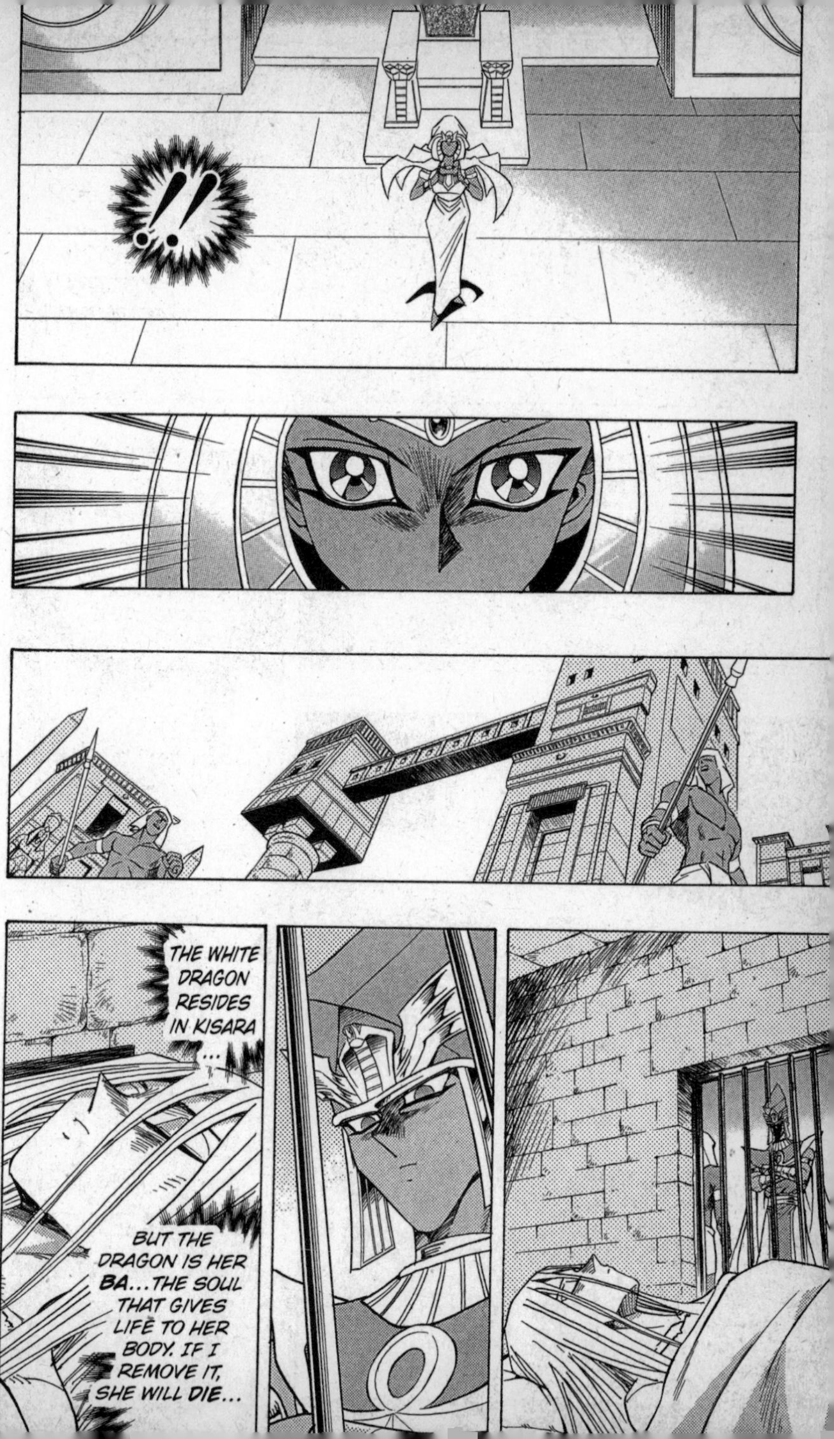
!!
THE WHITE DRAGON RESIDES IN KISARA...
BUT THE DRAGON IS HER BA...THE SOUL THAT GIVES LIFE TO HER BODY. IF I REMOVE IT, SHE WILL DIE...

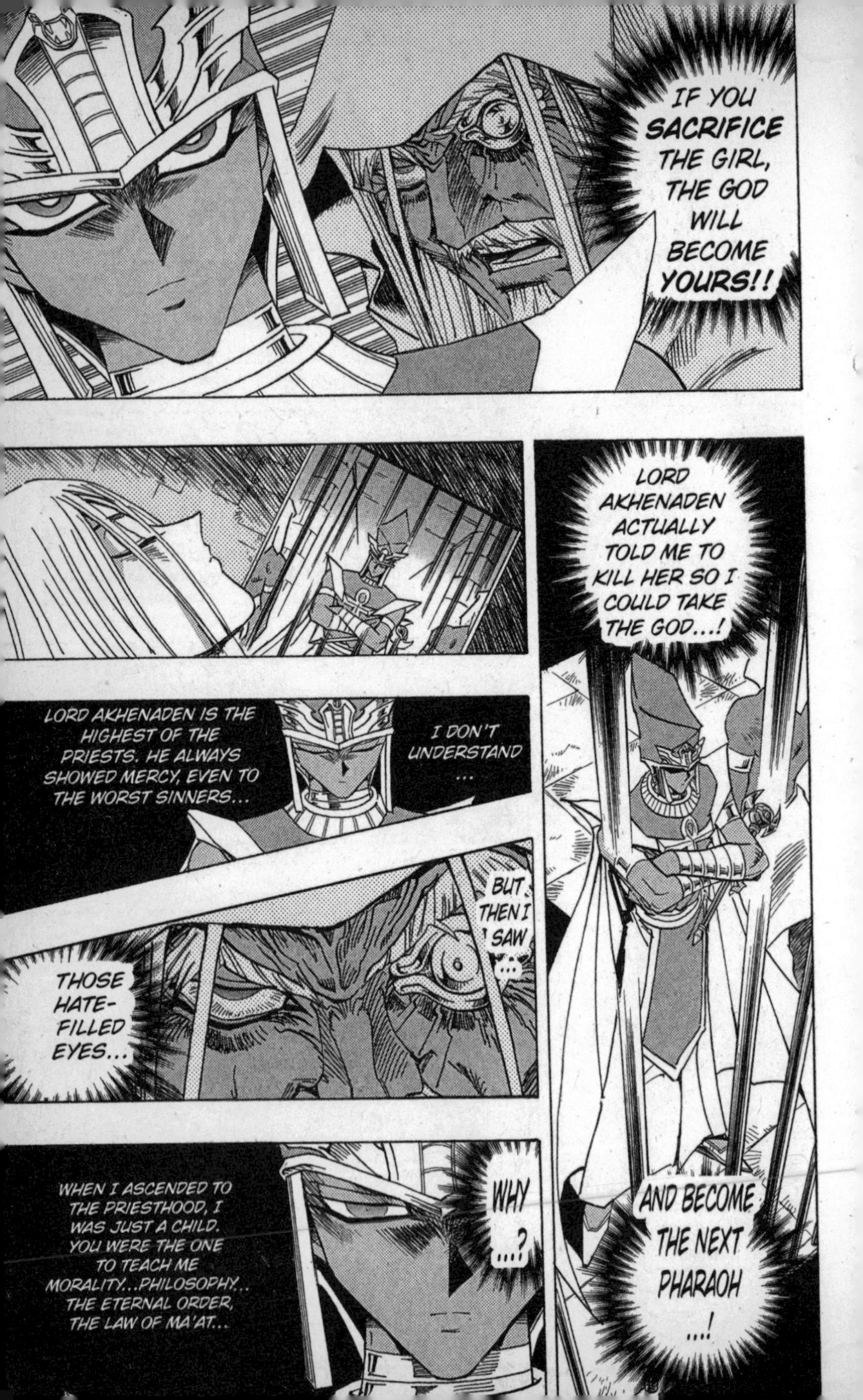

IF YOU SACRIFICE THE GIRL, THE GOD WILL BECOME YOURS!!
LORD AKHENADEN ACTUALLY TOLD ME TO KILL HER SO I COULD TAKE THE GOD...!
AND BECOME THE NEXT PHARAOH ...!
I DON'T UNDERSTAND ...
LORD AKHENADEN IS THE HIGHEST OF THE PRIESTS. HE ALWAYS SHOWED MERCY, EVEN TO THE WORST SINNERS...
BUT THEN I SAW ...
THOSE HATE-FILLED EYES...
WHY ...?
WHEN I ASCENDED TO THE PRIESTHOOD, I WAS JUST A CHILD. YOU WERE THE ONE TO TEACH ME MORALITY...PHILOSOPHY... THE ETERNAL ORDER, THE LAW OF MA'AT...

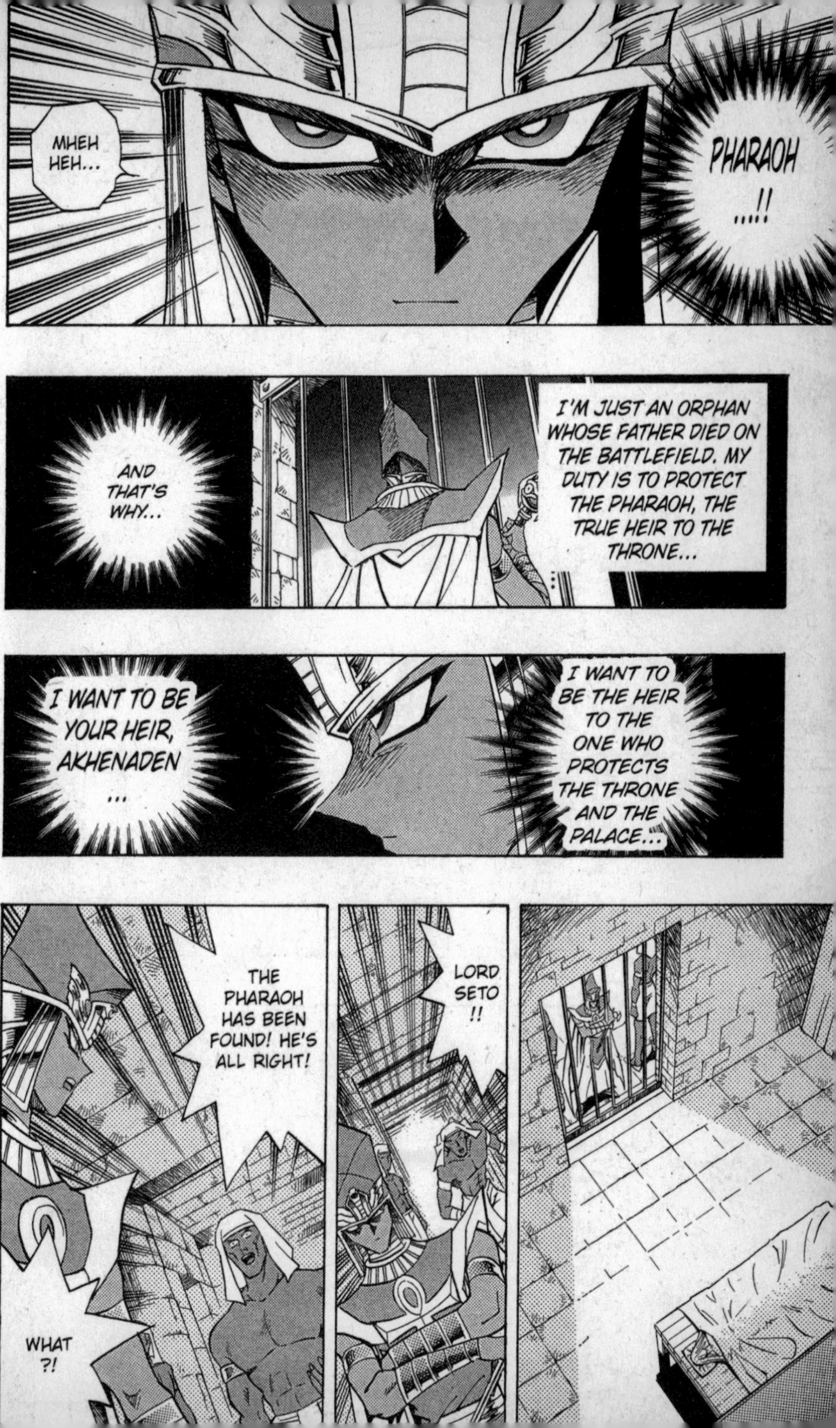
PHARAOH ...!!
MHEH HEH...
I'M JUST AN ORPHAN WHOSE FATHER DIED ON THE BATTLEFIELD. MY DUTY IS TO PROTECT THE PHARAOH, THE TRUE HEIR TO THE THRONE...
AND THAT'S WHY...
I WANT TO BE THE HEIR TO THE ONE WHO PROTECTS THE THRONE AND THE PALACE...
I WANT TO BE YOUR HEIR, AKHENADEN ...
LORD SETO !!
THE PHARAOH HAS BEEN FOUND! HE'S ALL RIGHT!
WHAT ?!

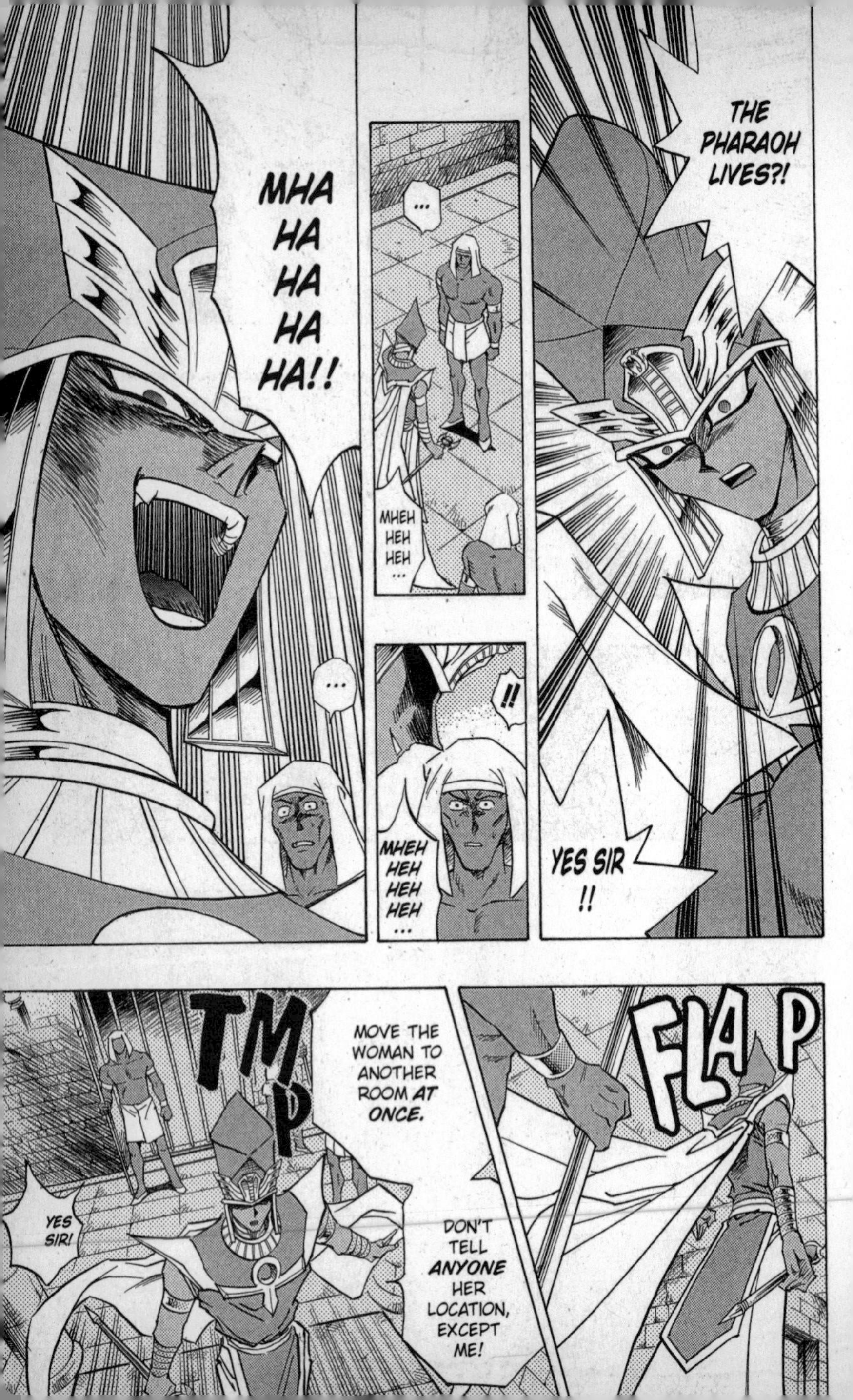
THE PHARAOH LIVES?!
YES SIR !!
...
MHEH HEH HEH ...
!!
MHEH HEH HEH HEH ...
MHA HA HA HA HA!!
...
FLAP
TMP
MOVE THE WOMAN TO ANOTHER ROOM AT ONCE.
DON'T TELL ANYONE HER LOCATION, EXCEPT ME!
YES SIR!

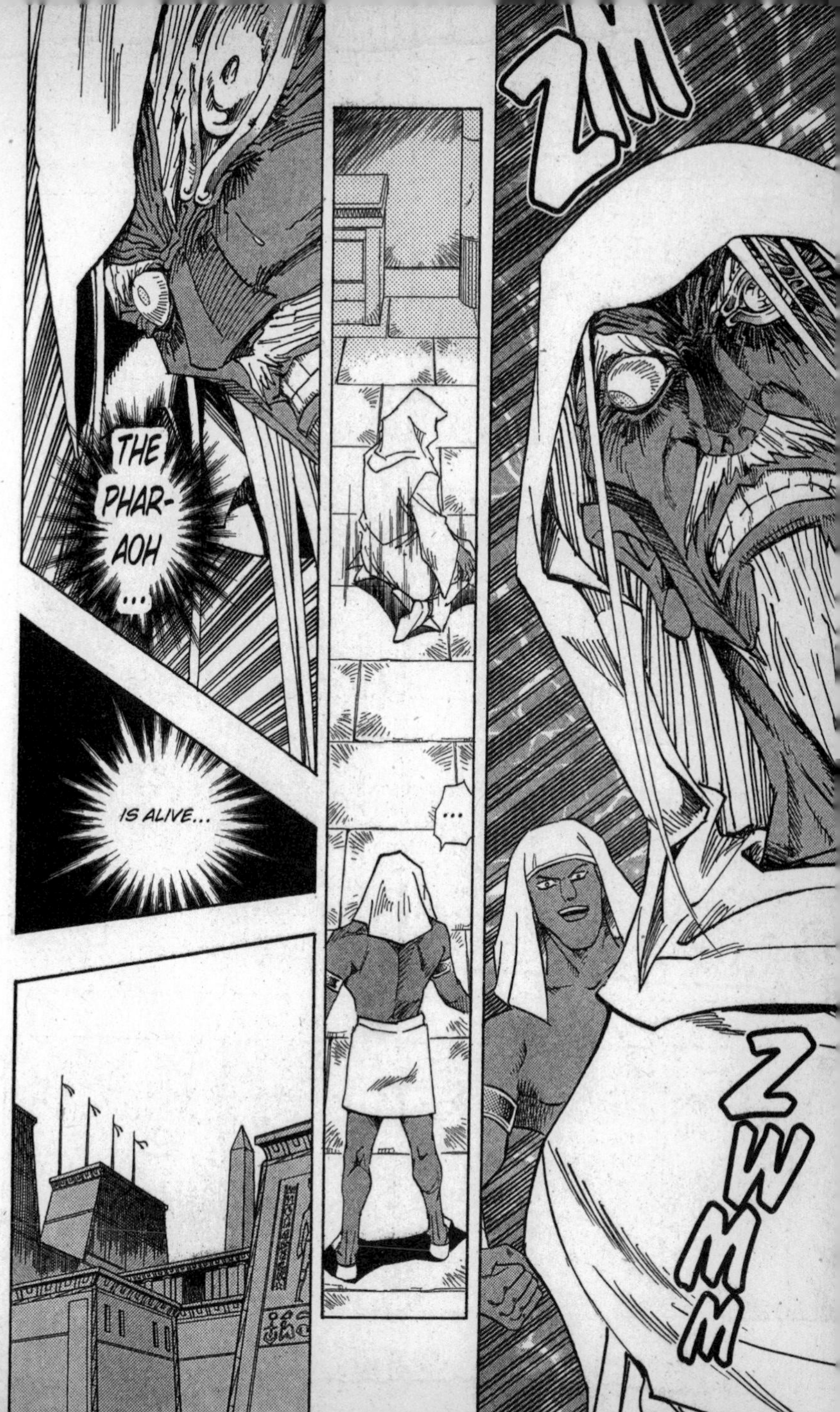

ZM
ZWWMM
...
THE PHARAOH...
IS ALIVE...

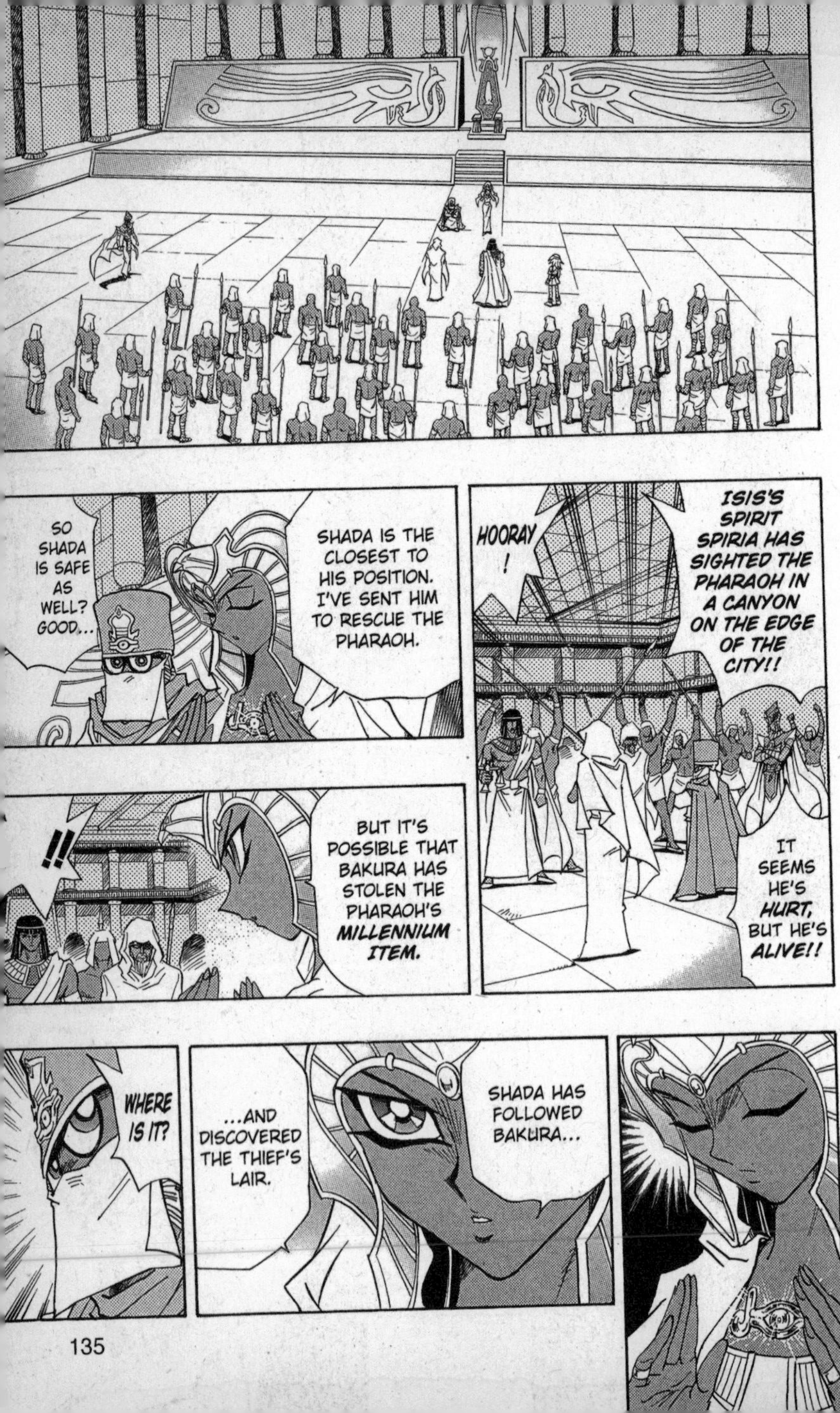
ISIS'S SPIRIT SPIRIA HAS SIGHTED THE PHARAOH IN A CANYON ON THE EDGE OF THE CITY!!
HOORAY!
IT SEEMS HE'S HURT, BUT HE'S ALIVE!!
SHADA IS THE CLOSEST TO HIS POSITION. I'VE SENT HIM TO RESCUE THE PHARAOH.
SO SHADA IS SAFE AS WELL? GOOD...
BUT IT'S POSSIBLE THAT BAKURA HAS STOLEN THE PHARAOH'S MILLENNIUM ITEM.
!!
SHADA HAS FOLLOWED BAKURA...
...AND DISCOVERED THE THIEF'S LAIR.
WHERE IS IT?

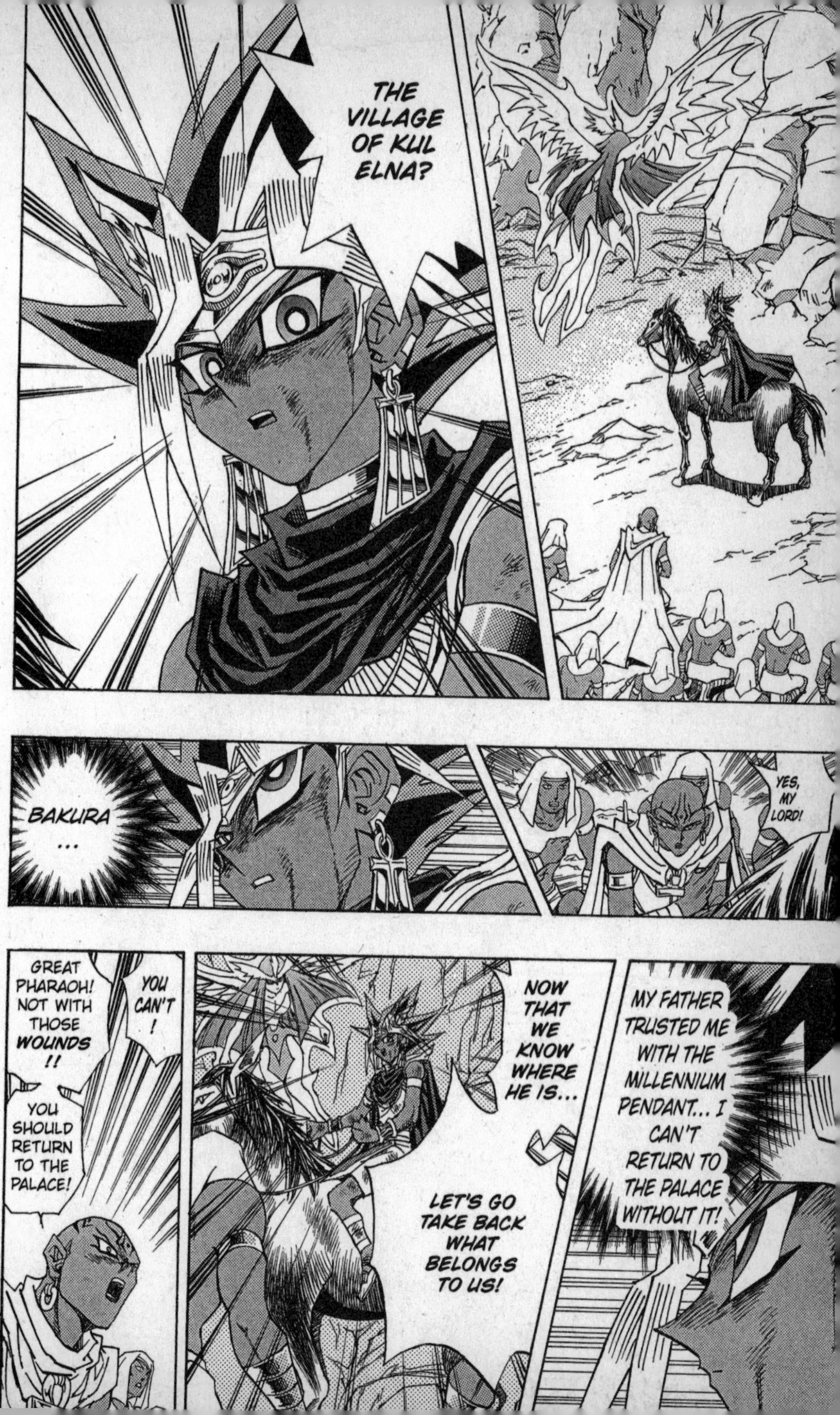
THE VILLAGE OF KUL ELNA?
YES, MY LORD!
BAKURA ...
MY FATHER TRUSTED ME WITH THE MILLENNIUM PENDANT... I CAN'T RETURN TO THE PALACE WITHOUT IT!
NOW THAT WE KNOW WHERE HE IS...
LET'S GO TAKE BACK WHAT BELONGS TO US!
YOU CAN'T!
GREAT PHARAOH! NOT WITH THOSE WOUNDS!!
YOU SHOULD RETURN TO THE PALACE!

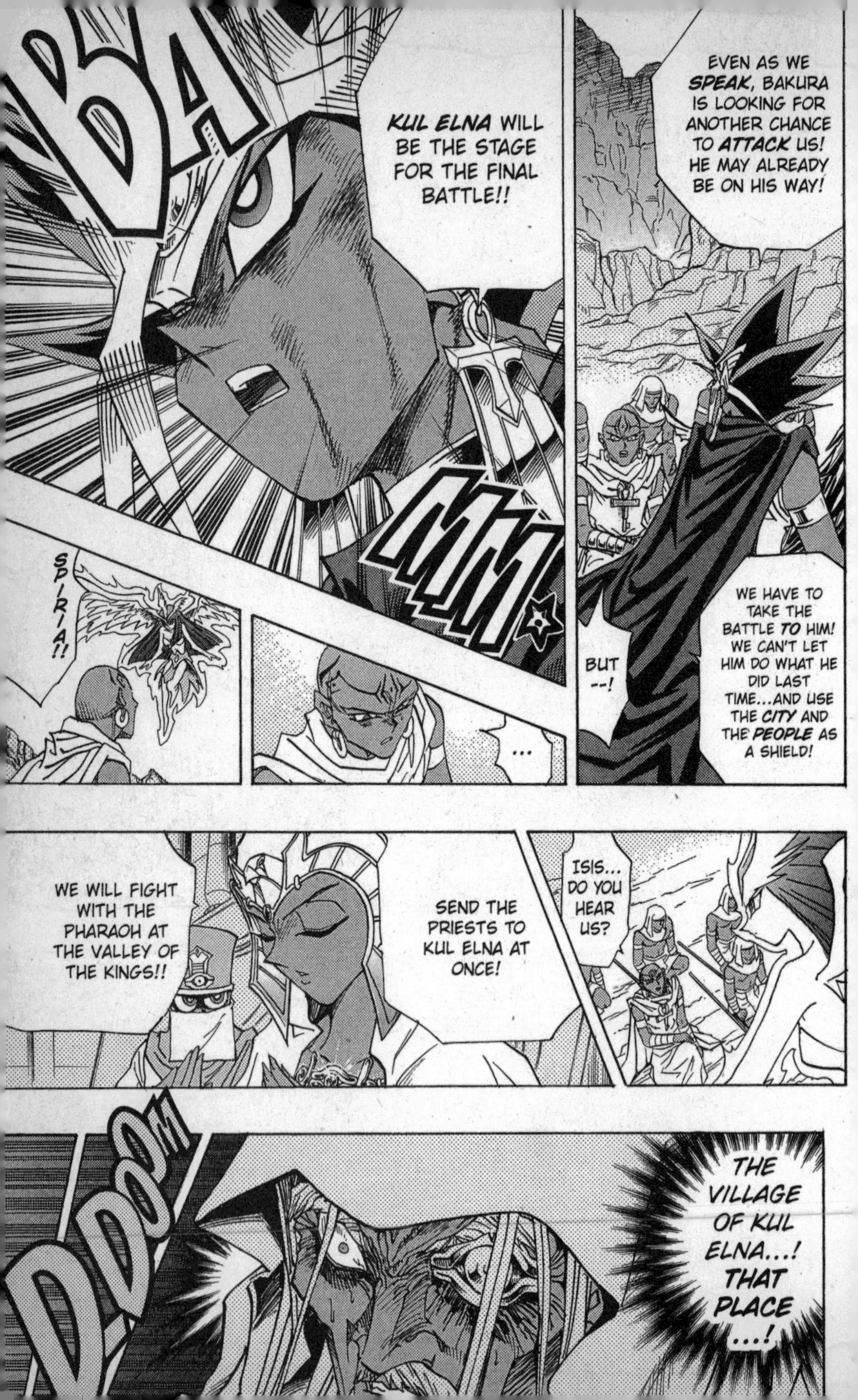
EVEN AS WE *SPEAK*, BAKURA IS LOOKING FOR ANOTHER CHANCE TO *ATTACK* US! HE MAY ALREADY BE ON HIS WAY!
WE HAVE TO TAKE THE BATTLE *TO* HIM! WE CAN'T LET HIM DO WHAT HE DID LAST TIME...AND USE THE *CITY* AND THE *PEOPLE* AS A SHIELD!
BUT --!
*KUL ELNA* WILL BE THE STAGE FOR THE FINAL BATTLE!!
DA
MM
...
SPIRIA!!
ISIS... DO YOU HEAR US?
SEND THE PRIESTS TO KUL ELNA AT ONCE!
WE WILL FIGHT WITH THE PHARAOH AT THE VALLEY OF THE KINGS!!
THE VILLAGE OF KUL ELNA...! THAT PLACE...!
DOOOM

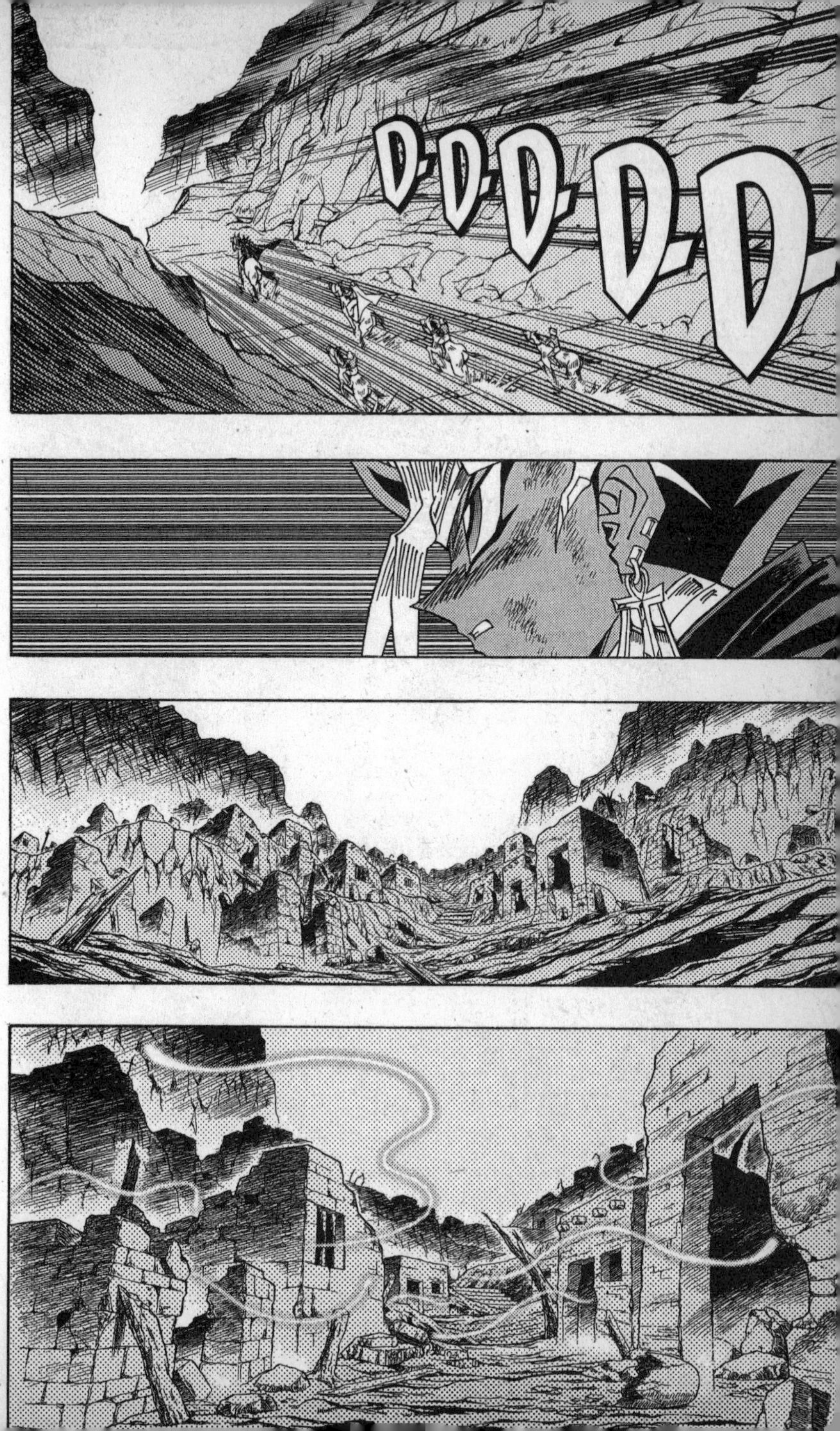
DDDDDD

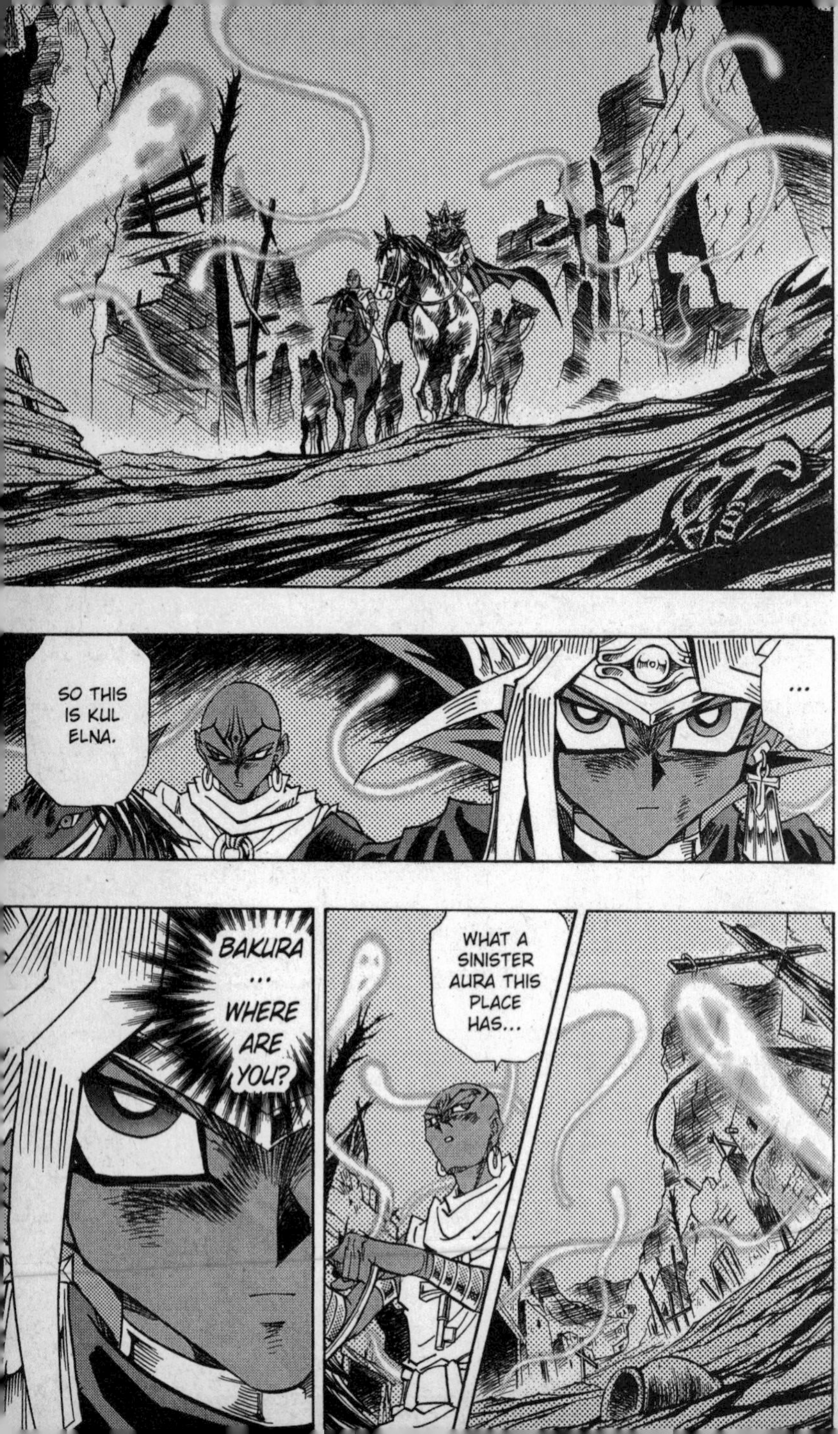
...
SO THIS IS KUL ELNA.
WHAT A SINISTER AURA THIS PLACE HAS...
BAKURA ... WHERE ARE YOU?

GWOOO
...
RM
RM
RM

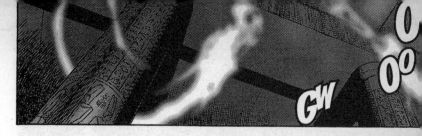

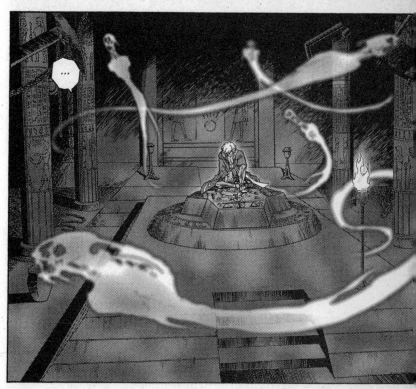

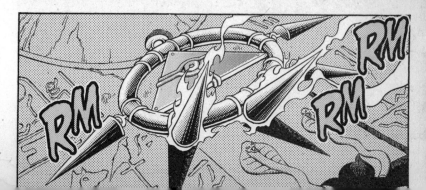

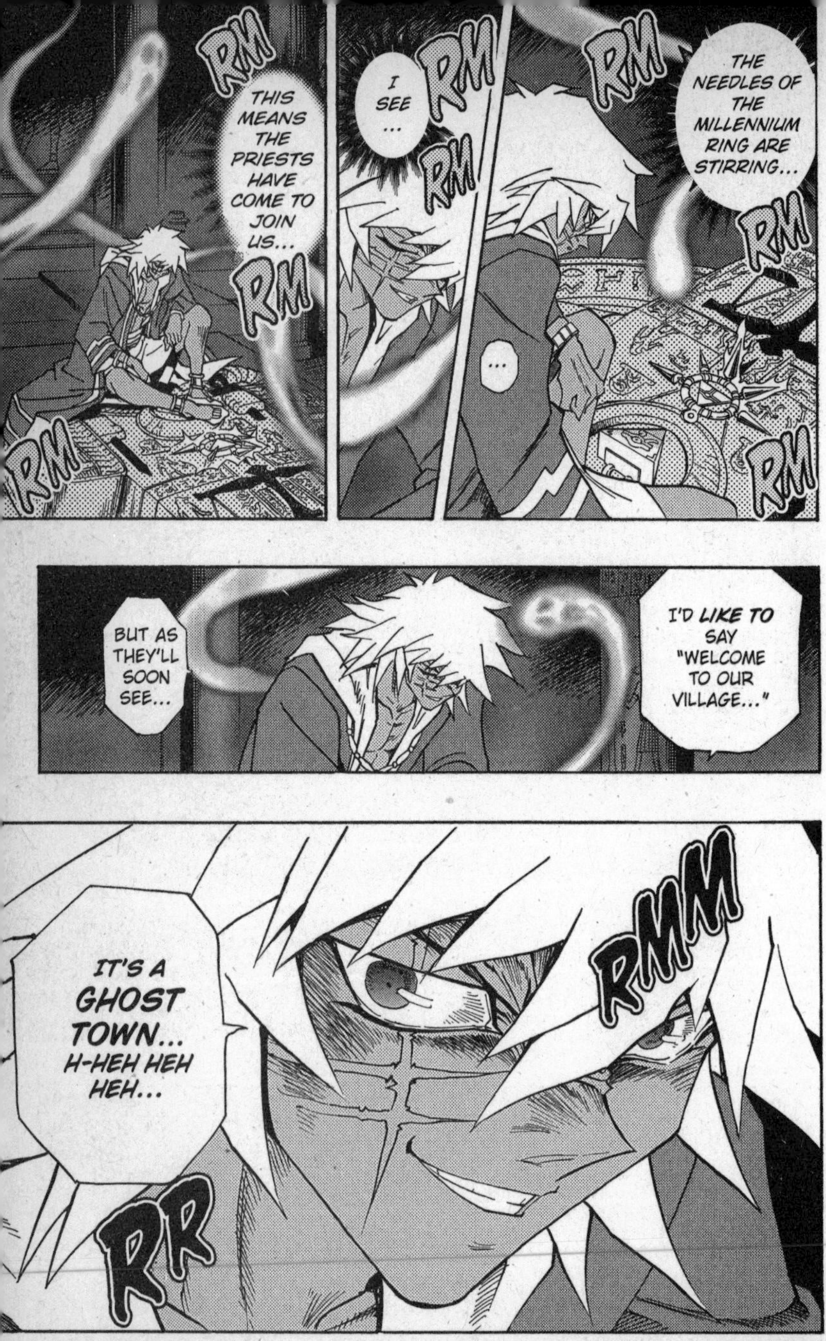
RM
THE NEEDLES OF THE MILLENNIUM RING ARE STIRRING...
RM
...
RM
RM
I SEE...
RM
RM
THIS MEANS THE PRIESTS HAVE COME TO JOIN US...
RM
RM
I'D LIKE TO SAY "WELCOME TO OUR VILLAGE..."
BUT AS THEY'LL SOON SEE...
RMM
IT'S A GHOST TOWN... H-HEH HEH HEH...
RR

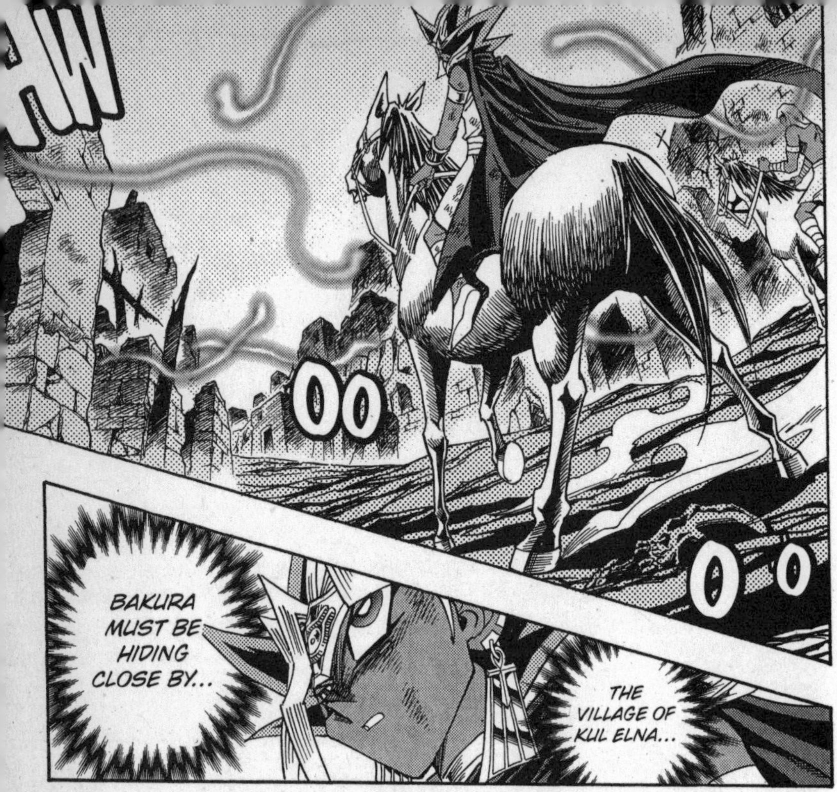
THE VILLAGE OF KUL ELNA...
BAKURA MUST BE HIDING CLOSE BY...

# Duel 35: The Village of Ghosts!!

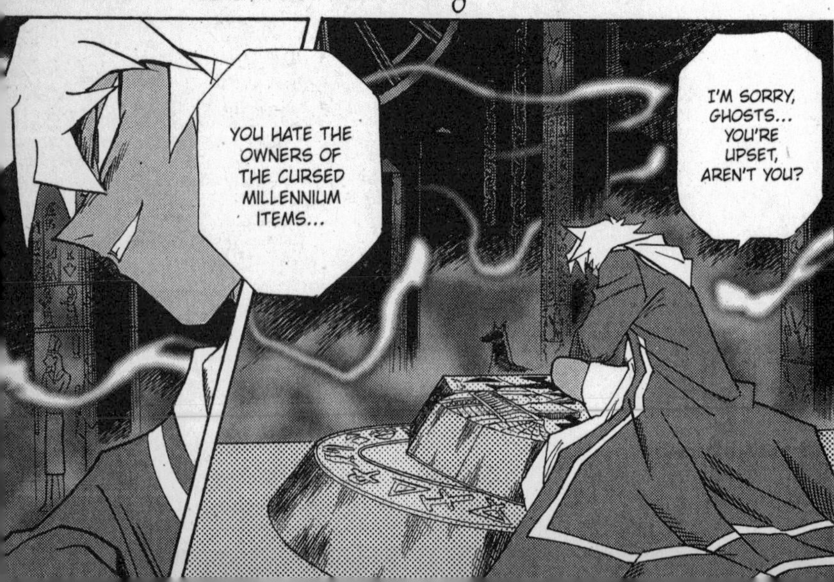
I'M SORRY, GHOSTS... YOU'RE UPSET, AREN'T YOU?
YOU HATE THE OWNERS OF THE CURSED MILLENNIUM ITEMS...

# Duel 35: The Village of Ghosts!!

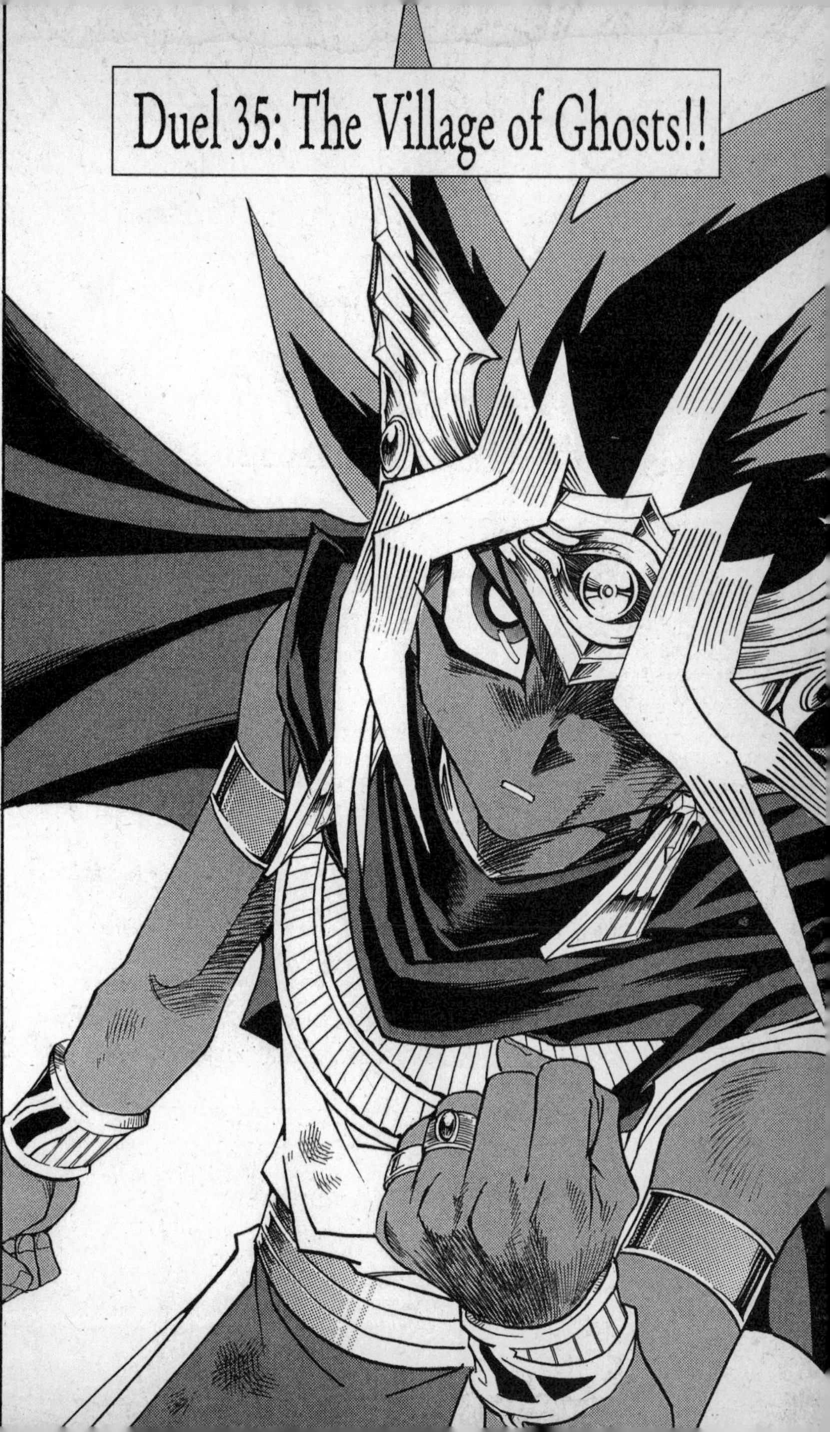

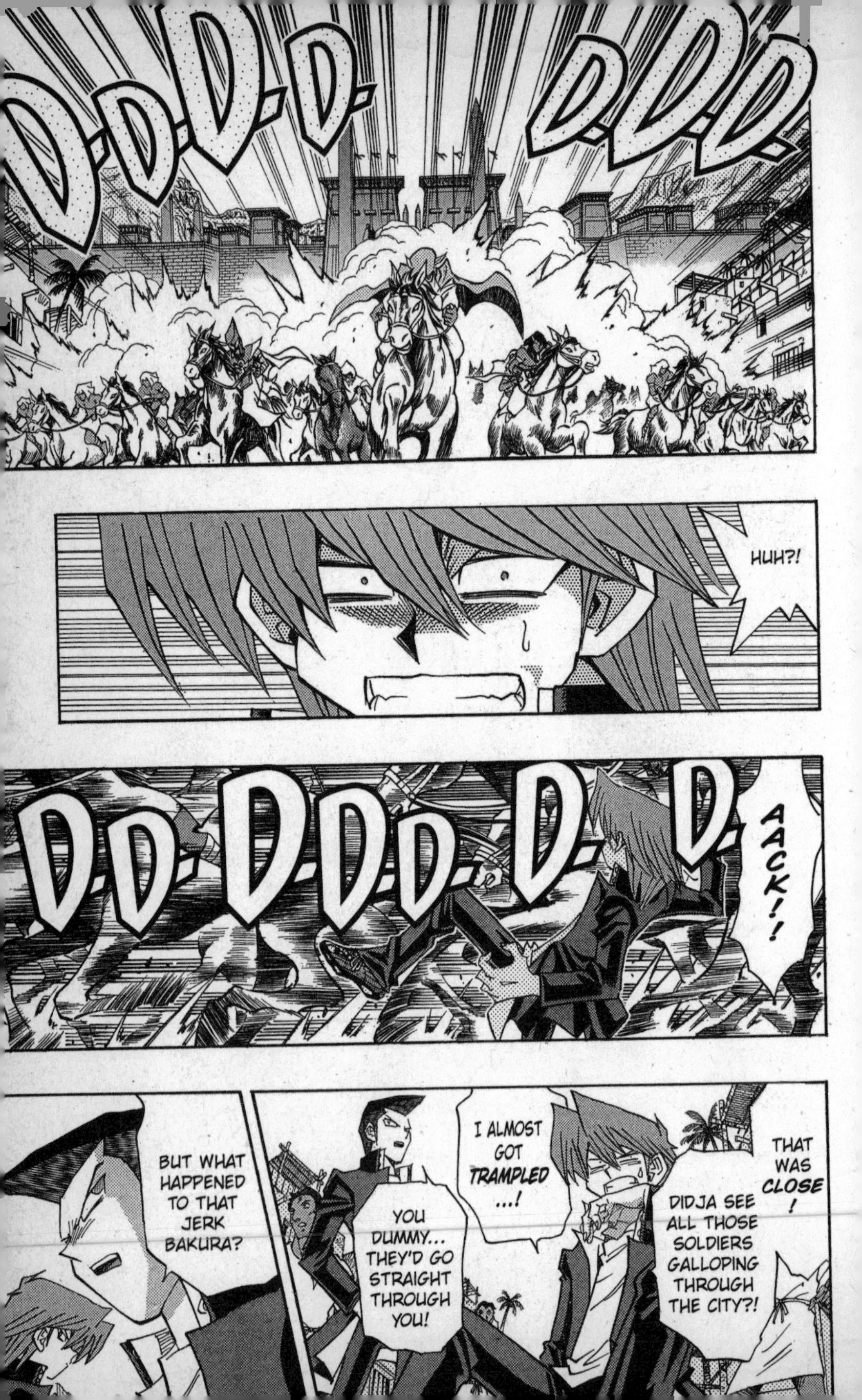
D.D.D.
D.D.D.D.
HUH?!
AACK!!
D.D.D.D.D.D.
THAT WAS CLOSE!
DIDJA SEE ALL THOSE SOLDIERS GALLOPING THROUGH THE CITY?!
I ALMOST GOT TRAMPLED...!
YOU DUMMY... THEY'D GO STRAIGHT THROUGH YOU!
BUT WHAT HAPPENED TO THAT JERK BAKURA?

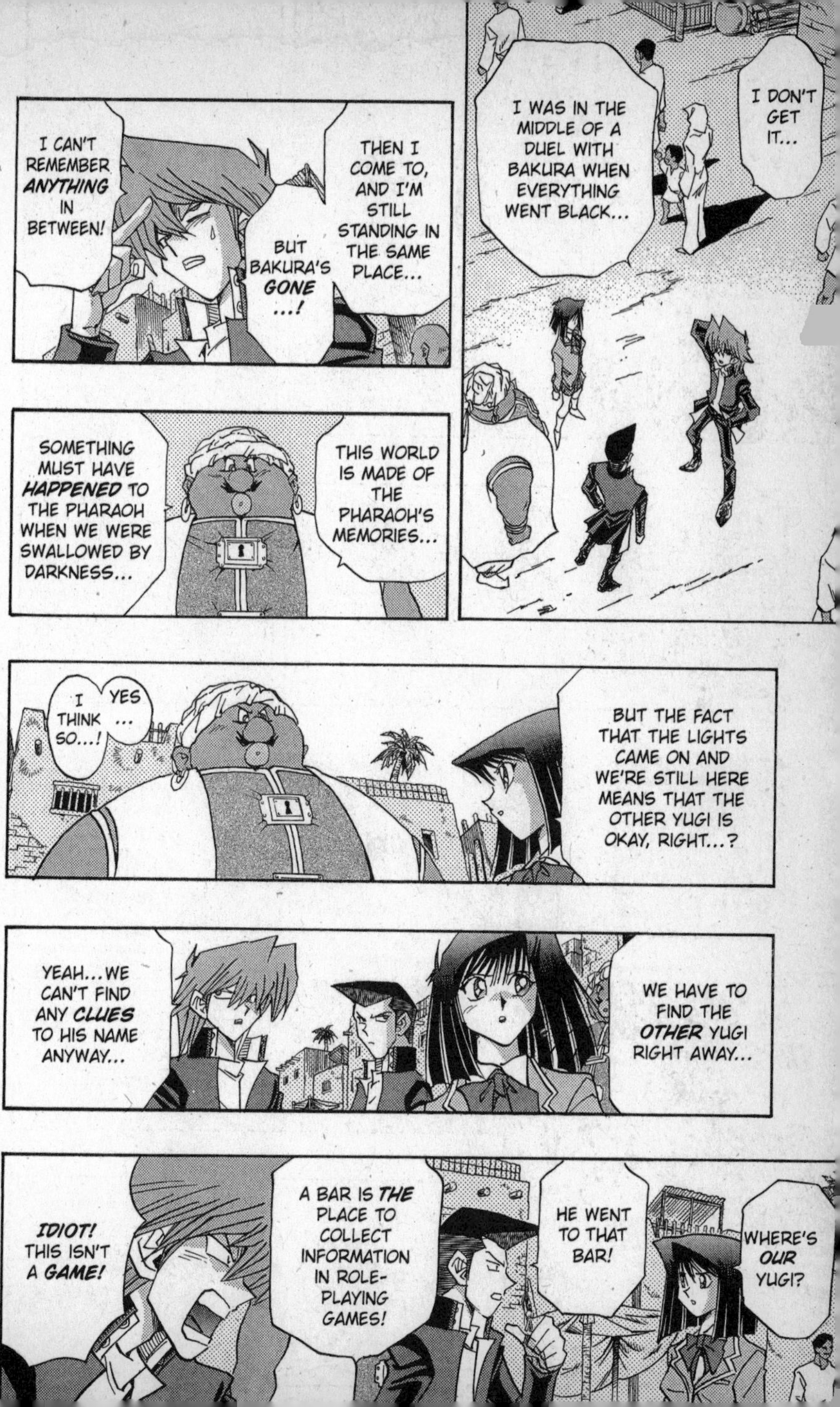
I DON'T GET IT...
I WAS IN THE MIDDLE OF A DUEL WITH BAKURA WHEN EVERYTHING WENT BLACK...
THEN I COME TO, AND I'M STILL STANDING IN THE SAME PLACE...
BUT BAKURA'S GONE ...!
I CAN'T REMEMBER ANYTHING IN BETWEEN!
THIS WORLD IS MADE OF THE PHARAOH'S MEMORIES...
SOMETHING MUST HAVE HAPPENED TO THE PHARAOH WHEN WE WERE SWALLOWED BY DARKNESS...
BUT THE FACT THAT THE LIGHTS CAME ON AND WE'RE STILL HERE MEANS THAT THE OTHER YUGI IS OKAY, RIGHT...?
YES ...
I THINK SO...!
WE HAVE TO FIND THE OTHER YUGI RIGHT AWAY...
YEAH...WE CAN'T FIND ANY CLUES TO HIS NAME ANYWAY...
WHERE'S OUR YUGI?
HE WENT TO THAT BAR!
A BAR IS THE PLACE TO COLLECT INFORMATION IN ROLE-PLAYING GAMES!
IDIOT! THIS ISN'T A GAME!

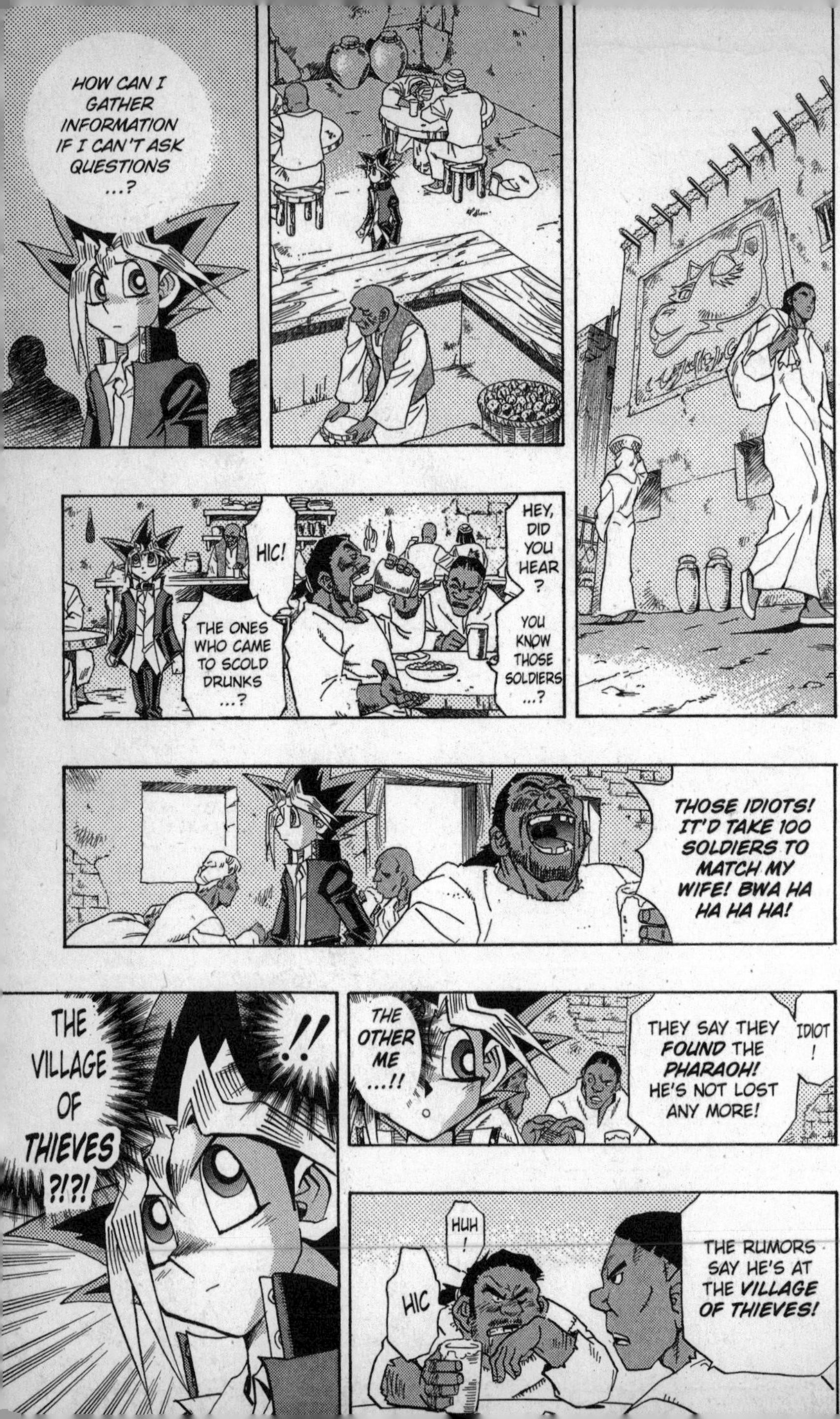
HOW CAN I GATHER INFORMATION IF I CAN'T ASK QUESTIONS ...?
HEY, DID YOU HEAR?
YOU KNOW THOSE SOLDIERS ...?
HIC!
THE ONES WHO CAME TO SCOLD DRUNKS ...?
THOSE IDIOTS! IT'D TAKE 100 SOLDIERS TO MATCH MY WIFE! BWA HA HA HA HA!
IDIOT!
THEY SAY THEY FOUND THE PHARAOH! HE'S NOT LOST ANY MORE!
THE OTHER ME ...!!
THE RUMORS SAY HE'S AT THE VILLAGE OF THIEVES!
HUH!
HIC
!!
THE VILLAGE OF THIEVES ?!?!

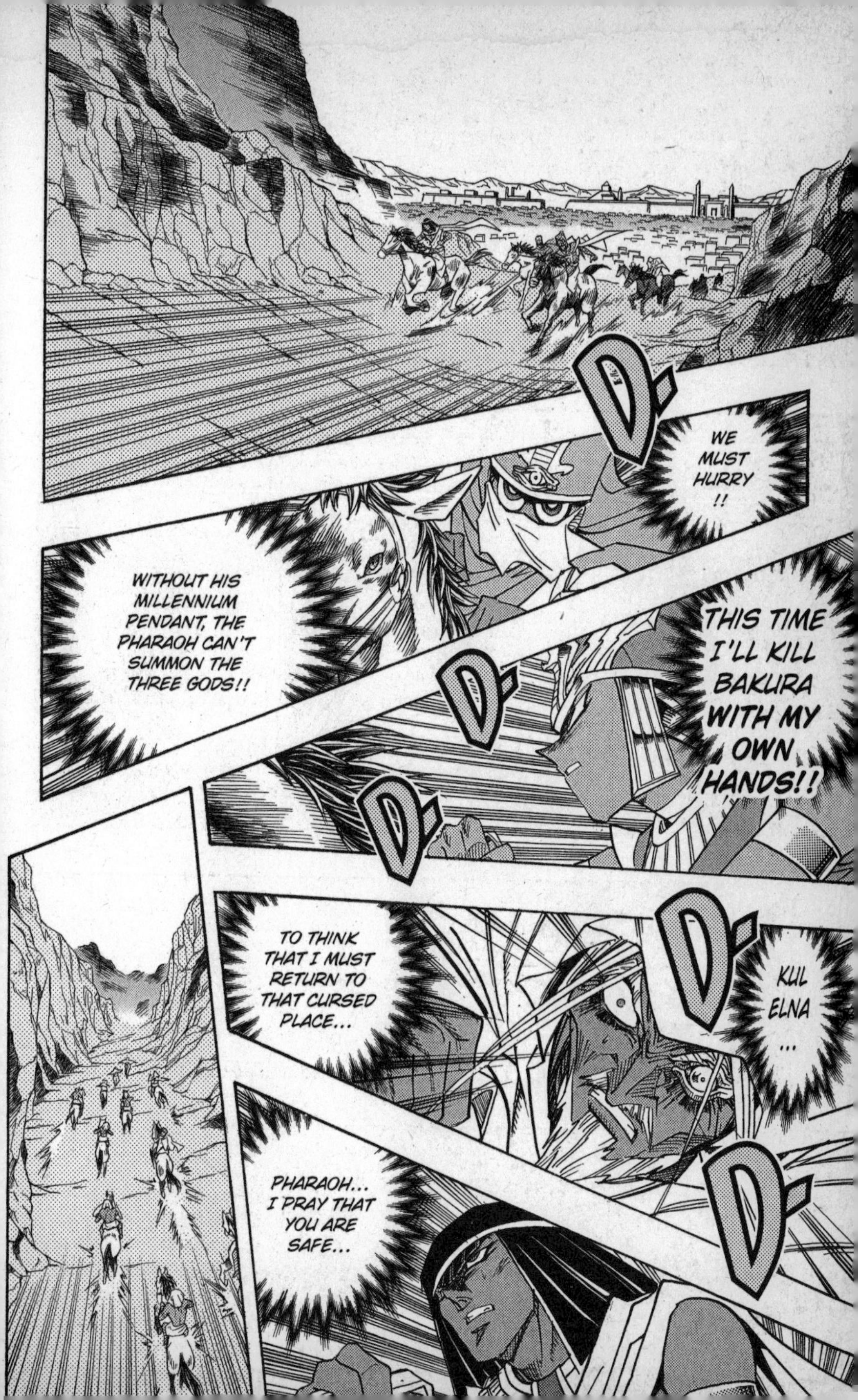

D
WE MUST HURRY!!
WITHOUT HIS MILLENNIUM PENDANT, THE PHARAOH CAN'T SUMMON THE THREE GODS!!
D
THIS TIME I'LL KILL BAKURA WITH MY OWN HANDS!!
D
D
KUL ELNA...
TO THINK THAT I MUST RETURN TO THAT CURSED PLACE...
D
PHARAOH... I PRAY THAT YOU ARE SAFE...

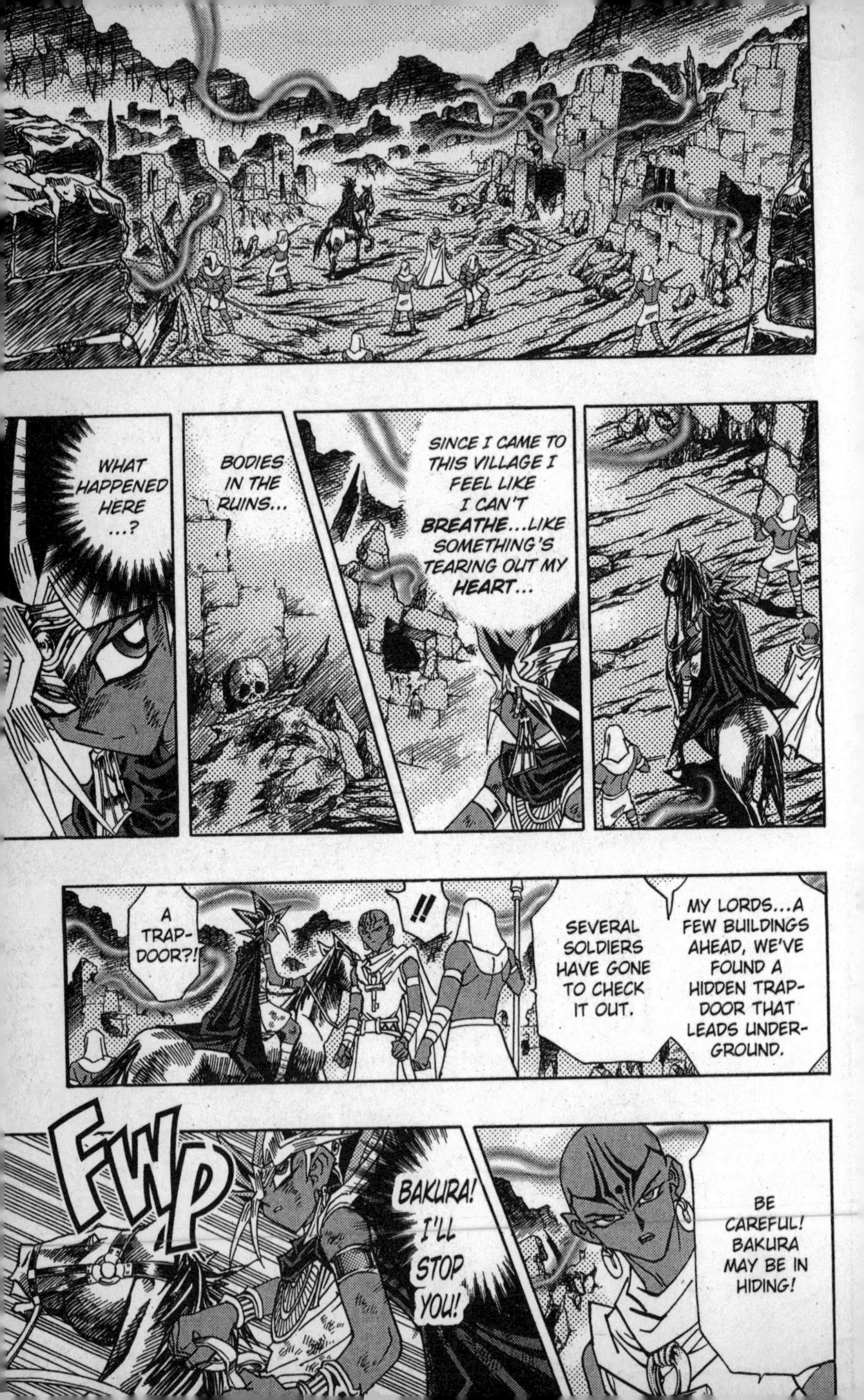
SINCE I CAME TO THIS VILLAGE I FEEL LIKE I CAN'T BREATHE...LIKE SOMETHING'S TEARING OUT MY HEART...
BODIES IN THE RUINS...
WHAT HAPPENED HERE ...?
MY LORDS...A FEW BUILDINGS AHEAD, WE'VE FOUND A HIDDEN TRAP-DOOR THAT LEADS UNDER-GROUND.
SEVERAL SOLDIERS HAVE GONE TO CHECK IT OUT.
!!
A TRAP-DOOR?!
BE CAREFUL! BAKURA MAY BE IN HIDING!
BAKURA! I'LL STOP YOU!
FWP

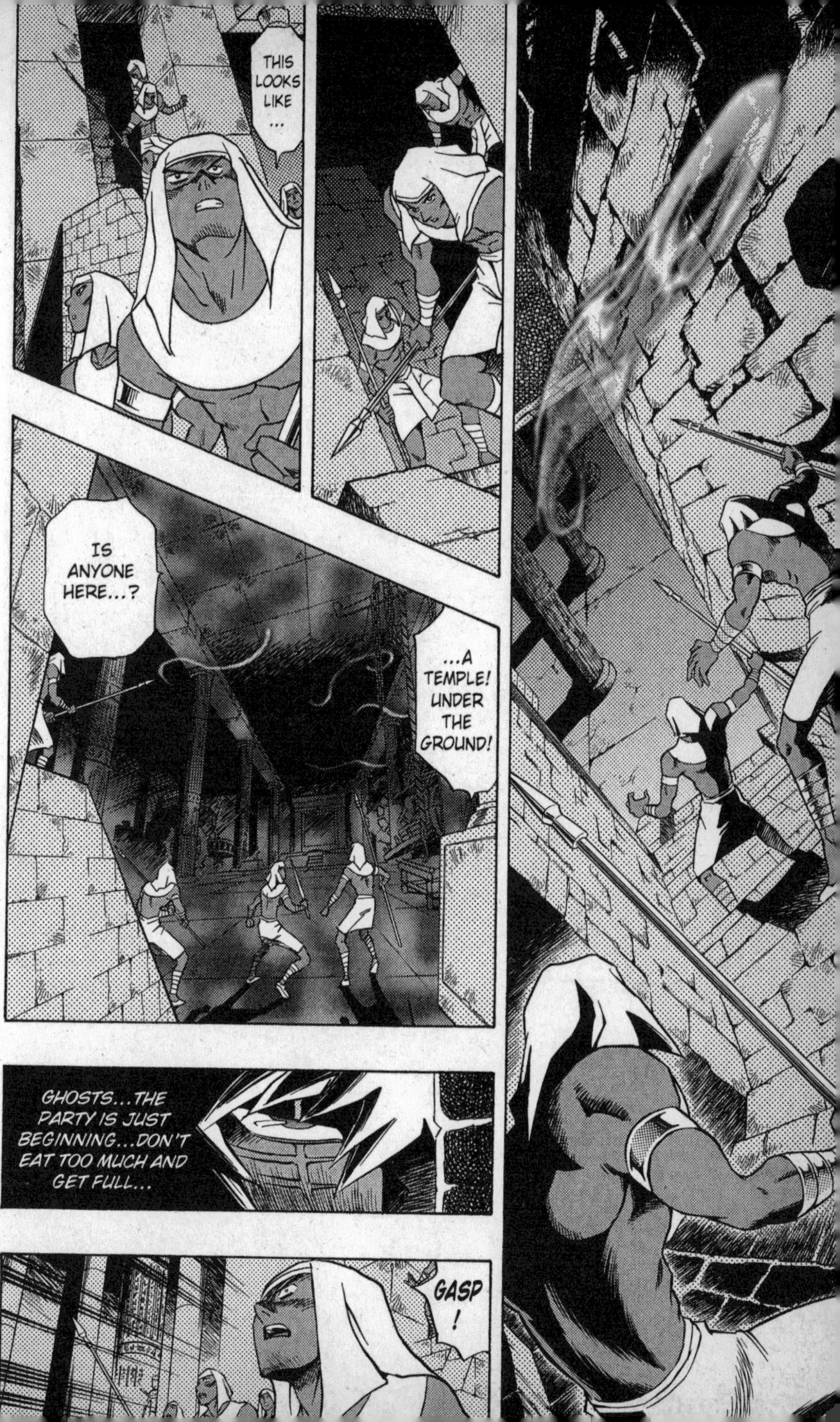
THIS LOOKS LIKE ...
...A TEMPLE! UNDER THE GROUND!
IS ANYONE HERE...?
GHOSTS...THE PARTY IS JUST BEGINNING...DON'T EAT TOO MUCH AND GET FULL...
GASP !

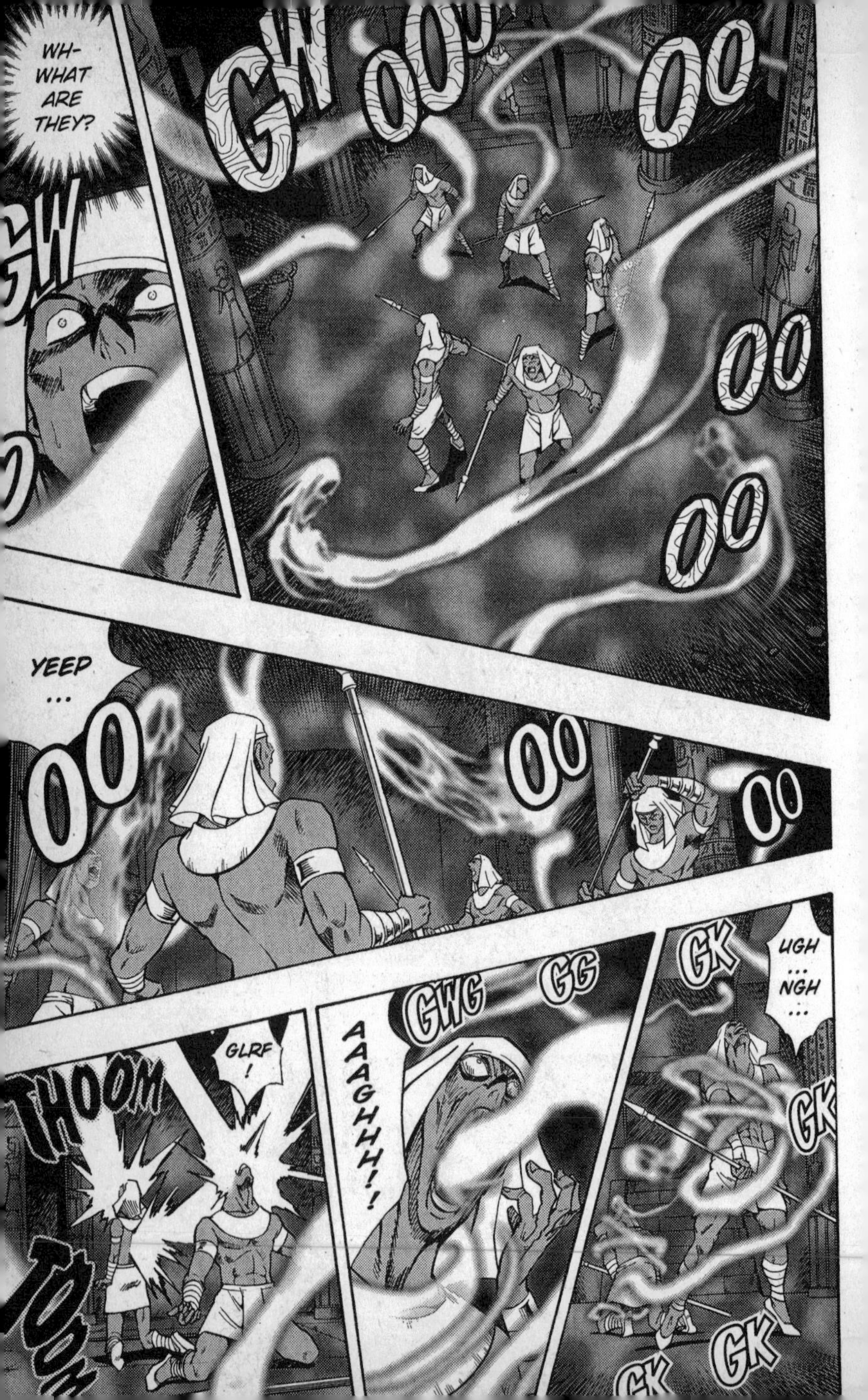
GWOOOO
OO
OO
OO
WH- WHAT ARE THEY?
GW
YEEP ...
OOO
OO
OO
GK
UGH ... NGH ...
GK
GK
GK
GWG
GG
AAAGHHH!!
GLRF!
THOOM

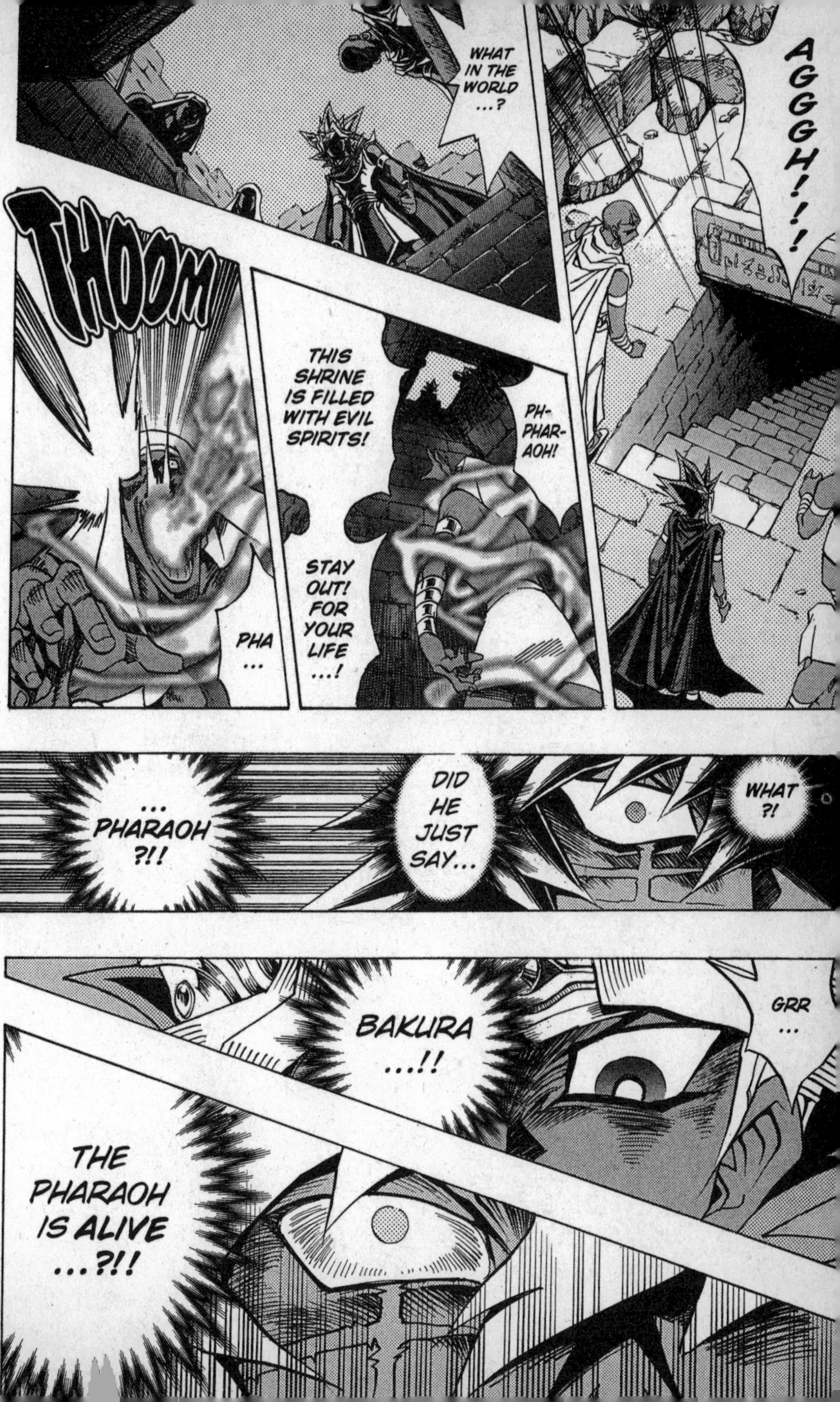

AGGGH!!!
WHAT IN THE WORLD ...?
PH-PHARAOH!
THIS SHRINE IS FILLED WITH EVIL SPIRITS!
STAY OUT! FOR YOUR LIFE ...!
THOOM
PHA ...
WHAT ?!
DID HE JUST SAY...
... PHARAOH ?!!
GRR ...
BAKURA ...!!
THE PHARAOH IS ALIVE ...?!!

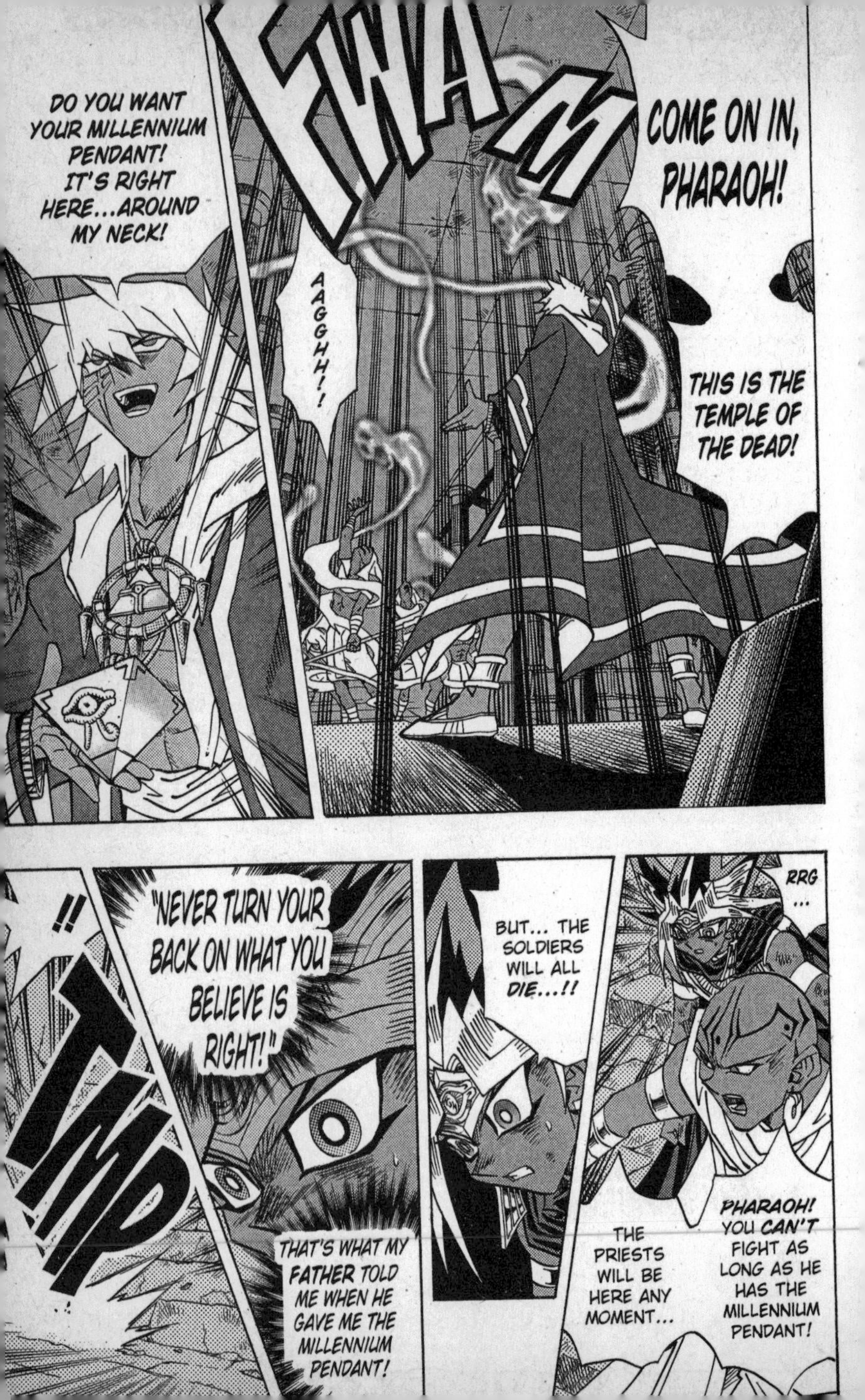
COME ON IN, PHARAOH!
WHAM
THIS IS THE TEMPLE OF THE DEAD!
AAGGHH!!
DO YOU WANT YOUR MILLENNIUM PENDANT! IT'S RIGHT HERE...AROUND MY NECK!
RRG ...
PHARAOH! YOU *CAN'T* FIGHT AS LONG AS HE HAS THE MILLENNIUM PENDANT!
THE PRIESTS WILL BE HERE ANY MOMENT...
BUT... THE SOLDIERS WILL ALL *DIE*...!!
"NEVER TURN YOUR BACK ON WHAT YOU BELIEVE IS RIGHT!"
THAT'S WHAT MY *FATHER* TOLD ME WHEN HE GAVE ME THE MILLENNIUM PENDANT!
!!
THMP

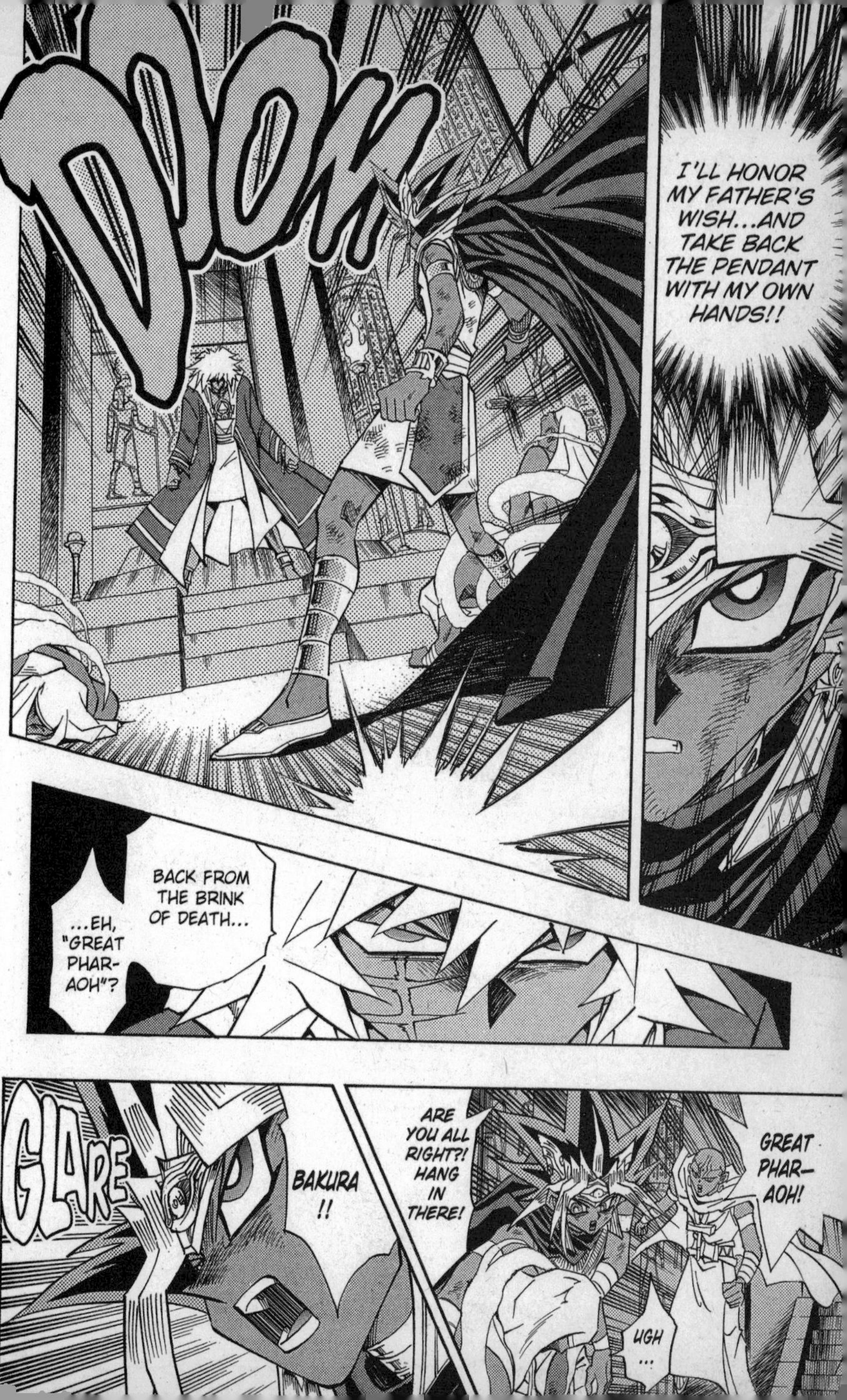
I'LL HONOR MY FATHER'S WISH...AND TAKE BACK THE PENDANT WITH MY OWN HANDS!!
DOOM
BACK FROM THE BRINK OF DEATH...
...EH, "GREAT PHAR-AOH"?
GREAT PHAR-AOH!
ARE YOU ALL RIGHT?! HANG IN THERE!
UGH ...
BAKURA !!
GLARE

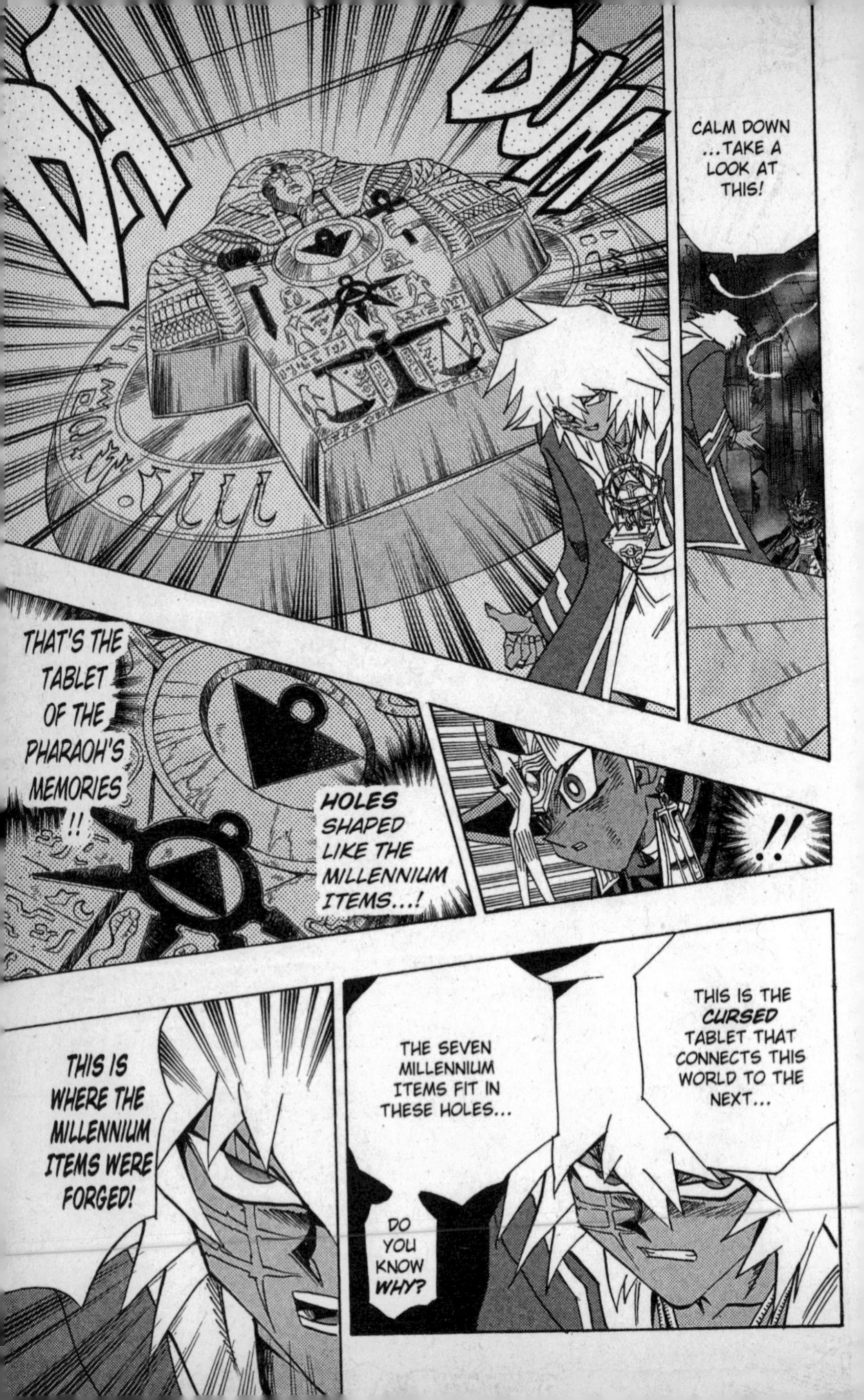
CALM DOWN ...TAKE A LOOK AT THIS!
DUM
!!
THAT'S THE TABLET OF THE PHARAOH'S MEMORIES!!
HOLES SHAPED LIKE THE MILLENNIUM ITEMS...!
THIS IS THE CURSED TABLET THAT CONNECTS THIS WORLD TO THE NEXT...
THE SEVEN MILLENNIUM ITEMS FIT IN THESE HOLES...
DO YOU KNOW WHY?
THIS IS WHERE THE MILLENNIUM ITEMS WERE FORGED!

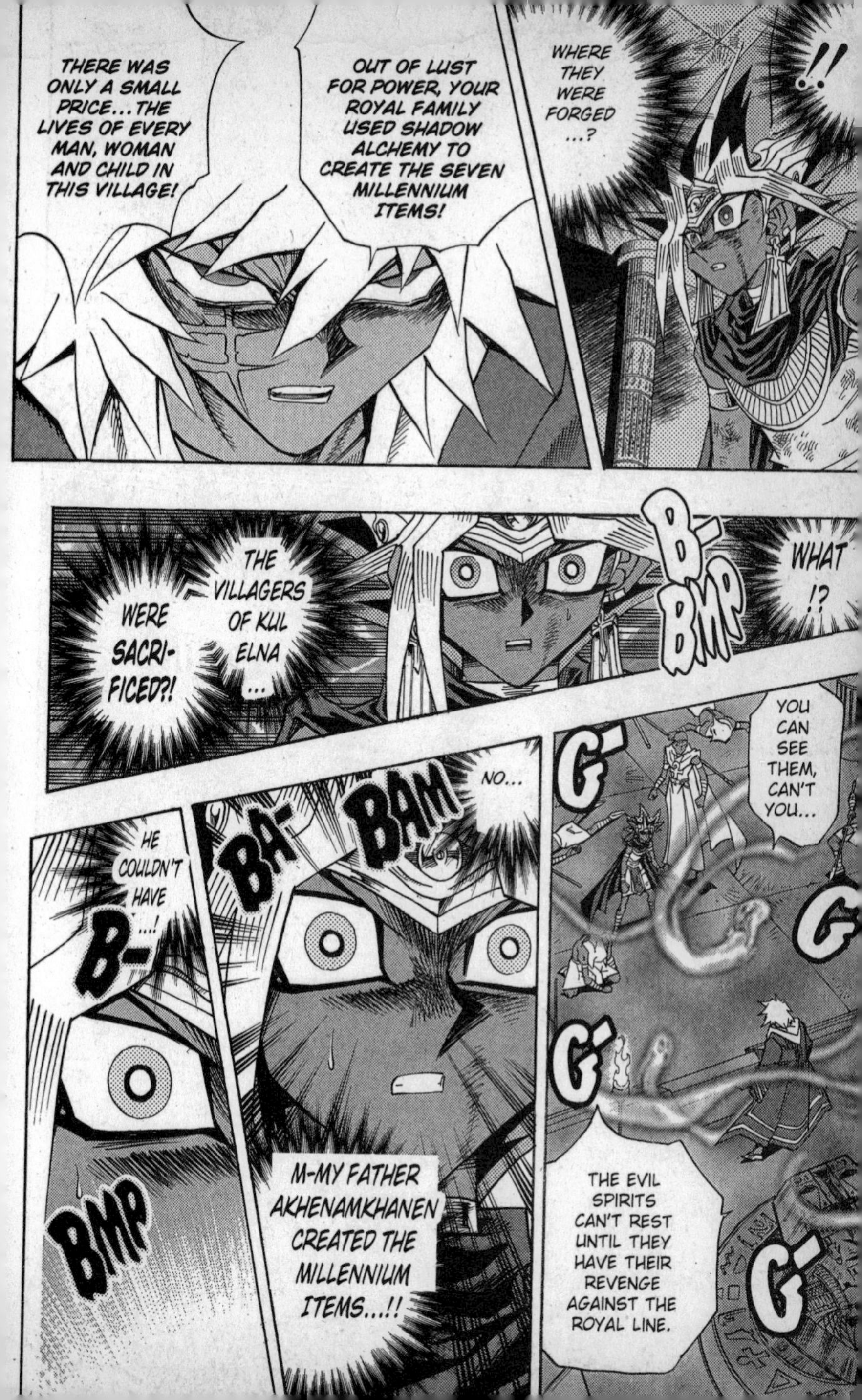

!!
WHERE THEY WERE FORGED ...?
OUT OF LUST FOR POWER, YOUR ROYAL FAMILY USED SHADOW ALCHEMY TO CREATE THE SEVEN MILLENNIUM ITEMS!
THERE WAS ONLY A SMALL PRICE...THE LIVES OF EVERY MAN, WOMAN AND CHILD IN THIS VILLAGE!
WHAT !?
B-BMP
THE VILLAGERS OF KUL ELNA ...
WERE SACRIFICED?!
YOU CAN SEE THEM, CAN'T YOU...
G-
G
G-
THE EVIL SPIRITS CAN'T REST UNTIL THEY HAVE THEIR REVENGE AGAINST THE ROYAL LINE.
G-
NO...
BA-BAM
M-MY FATHER AKHENAMKHANEN CREATED THE MILLENNIUM ITEMS...!!
HE COULDN'T HAVE ...!
B-
BMP

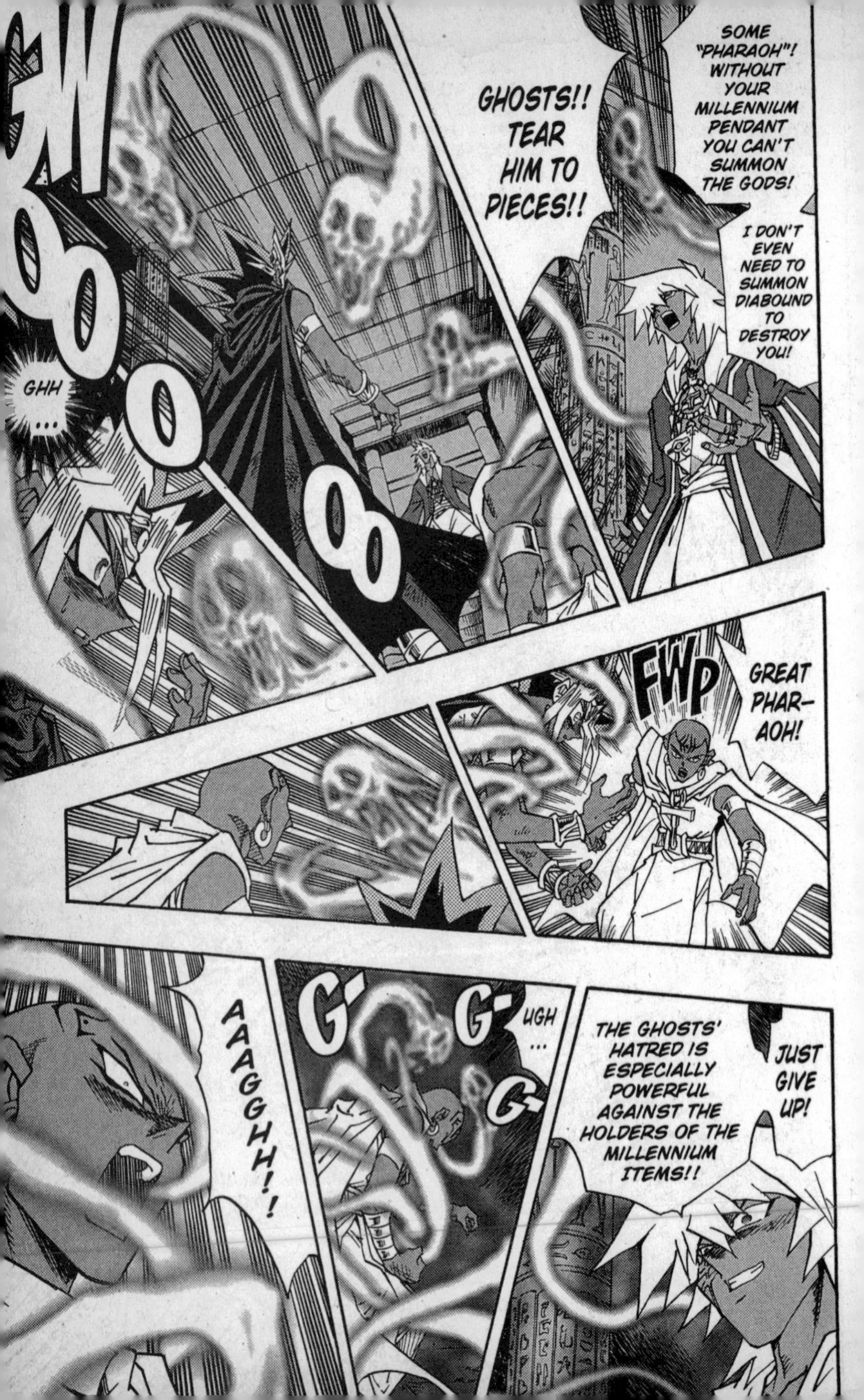
SOME "PHARAOH"! WITHOUT YOUR MILLENNIUM PENDANT YOU CAN'T SUMMON THE GODS!
I DON'T EVEN NEED TO SUMMON DIABOUND TO DESTROY YOU!
GHOSTS!! TEAR HIM TO PIECES!!
GWOOOOO
GHH ...
FWP
GREAT PHAR-AOH!
JUST GIVE UP!
THE GHOSTS' HATRED IS ESPECIALLY POWERFUL AGAINST THE HOLDERS OF THE MILLENNIUM ITEMS!!
G-G-G-
UGH ...
AAAGGHH!!

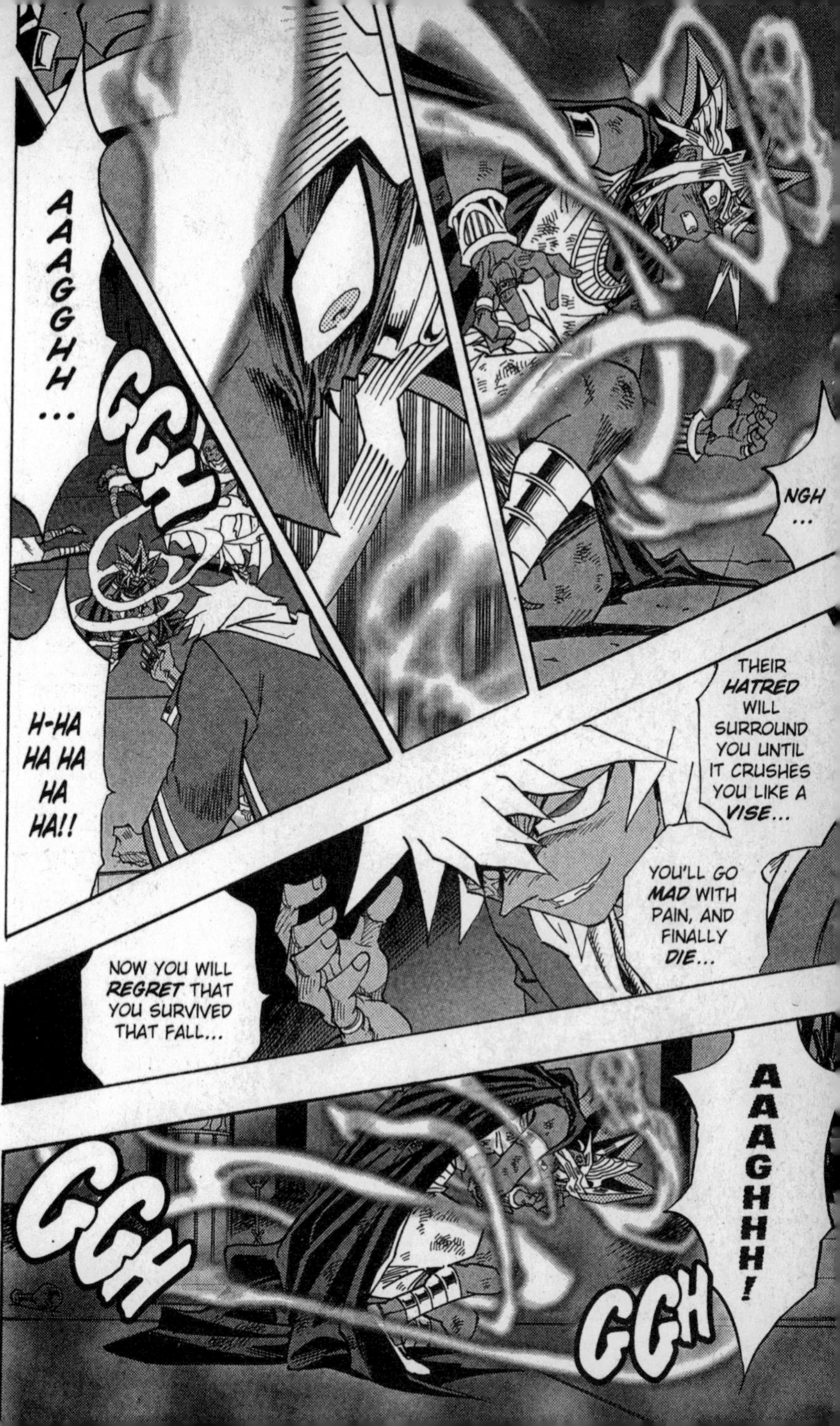

NGH...
AAAAGGHH...
GGH
H-HA HA HA HA HA!!
THEIR HATRED WILL SURROUND YOU UNTIL IT CRUSHES YOU LIKE A VISE...
YOU'LL GO MAD WITH PAIN, AND FINALLY DIE...
NOW YOU WILL REGRET THAT YOU SURVIVED THAT FALL...
AAAGHHH!
GGH
GGH

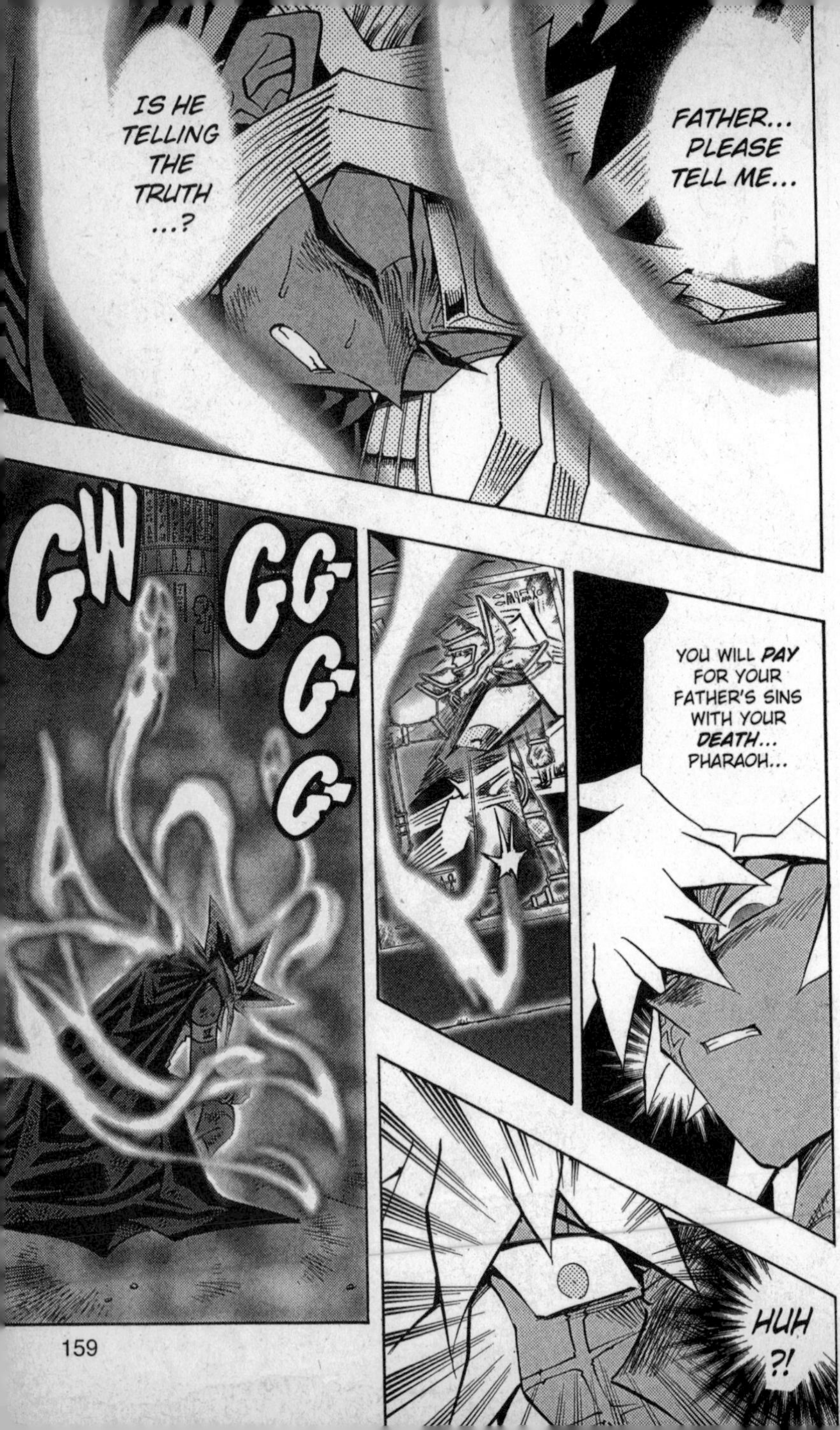
FATHER... PLEASE TELL ME...
IS HE TELLING THE TRUTH ...?
YOU WILL PAY FOR YOUR FATHER'S SINS WITH YOUR DEATH... PHARAOH...
HUH ?!
GW
GG-G-G

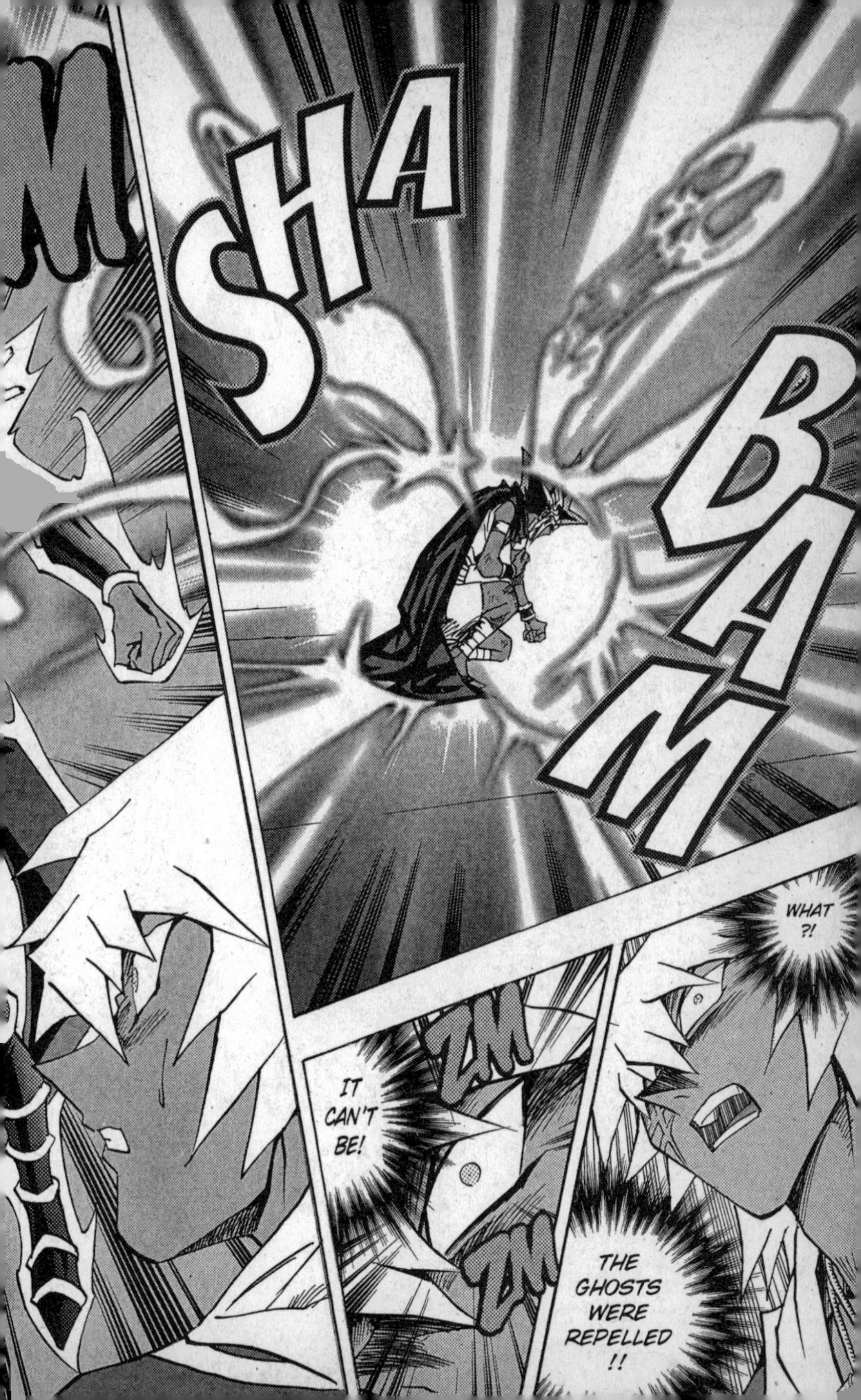
SHA
BAM
M
WHAT ?!
THE GHOSTS WERE REPELLED !!
ZM
IT CAN'T BE!

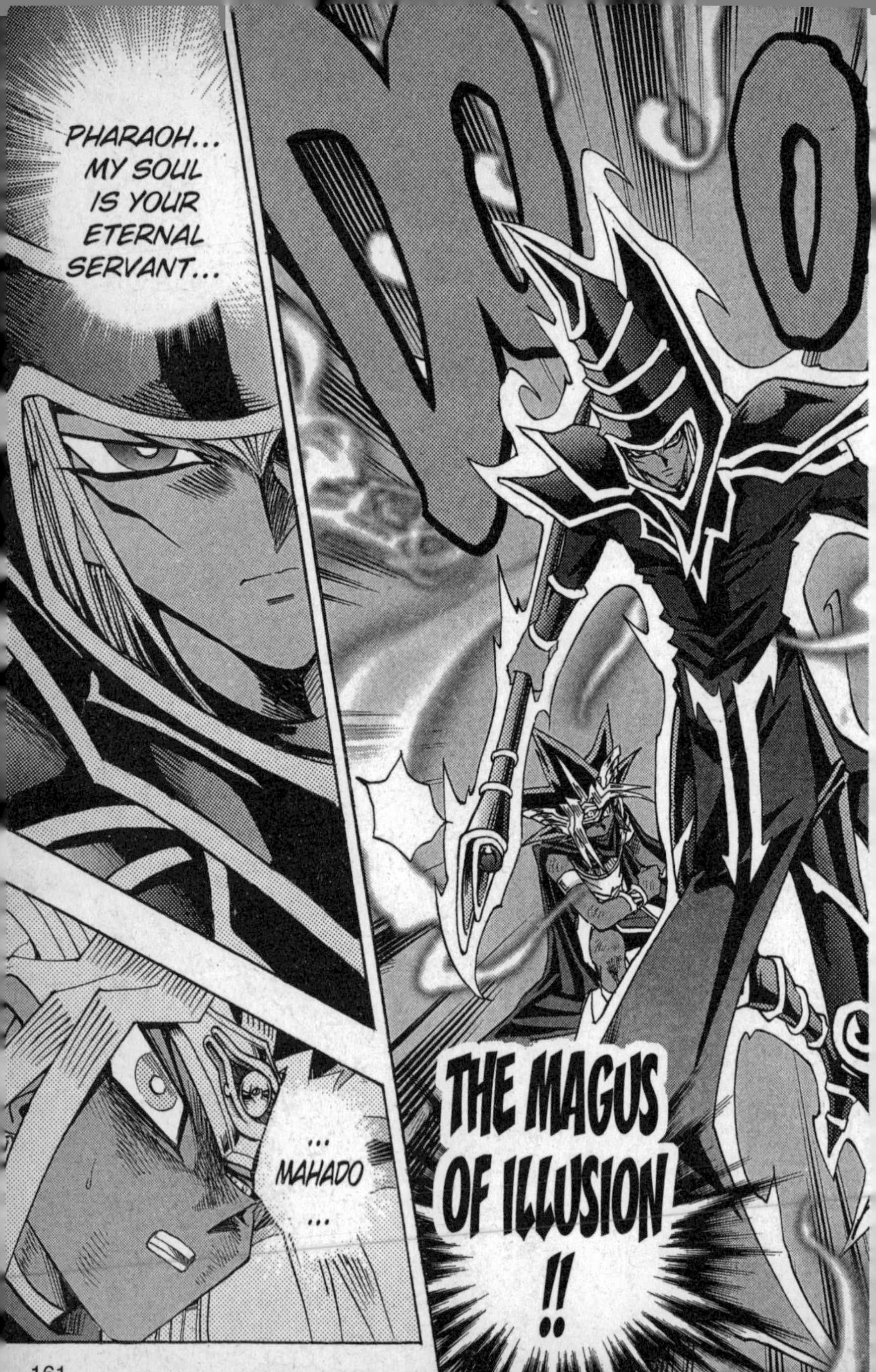
THE MAGUS OF ILLUSION !!
PHARAOH... MY SOUL IS YOUR ETERNAL SERVANT...
...MAHADO...

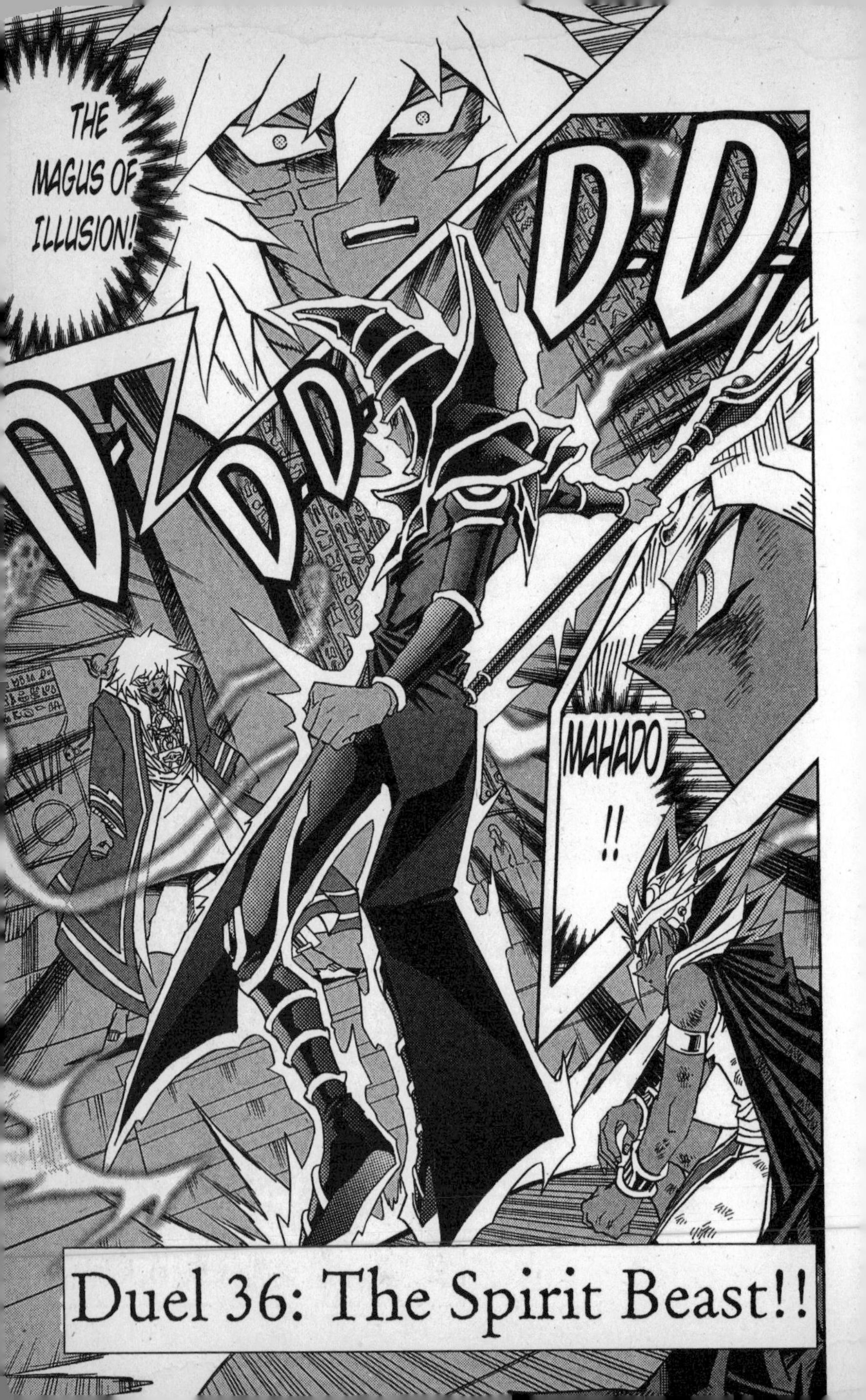
D.D.
THE MAGUS OF ILLUSION!
MAHADO !!
D.D.D.

# Duel 36: The Spirit Beast!!

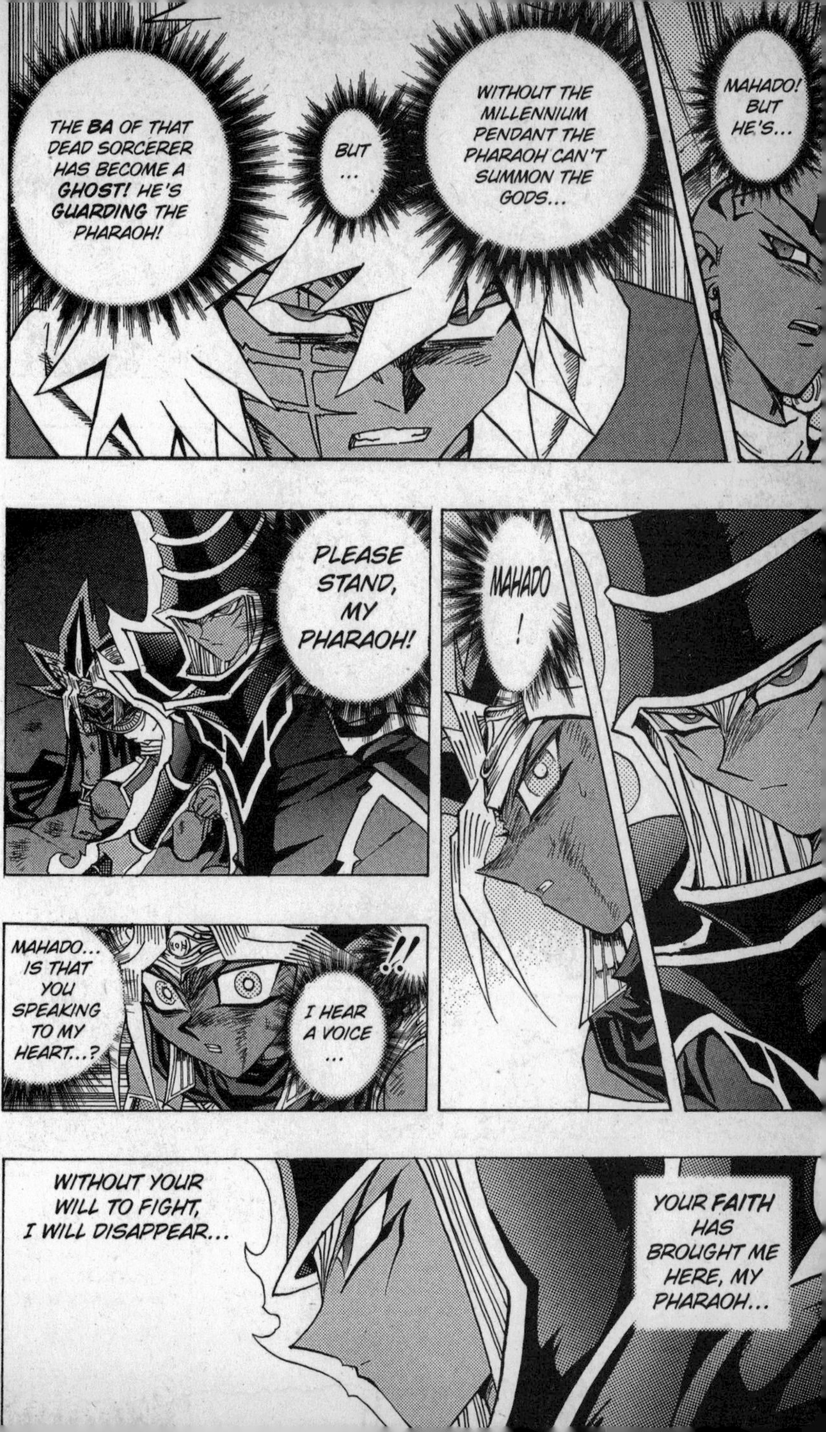
MAHADO! BUT HE'S...
WITHOUT THE MILLENNIUM PENDANT THE PHARAOH CAN'T SUMMON THE GODS...
BUT ...
THE BA OF THAT DEAD SORCERER HAS BECOME A GHOST! HE'S GUARDING THE PHARAOH!
MAHADO !
PLEASE STAND, MY PHARAOH!
!!
I HEAR A VOICE ...
MAHADO... IS THAT YOU SPEAKING TO MY HEART...?
YOUR FAITH HAS BROUGHT ME HERE, MY PHARAOH...
WITHOUT YOUR WILL TO FIGHT, I WILL DISAPPEAR...

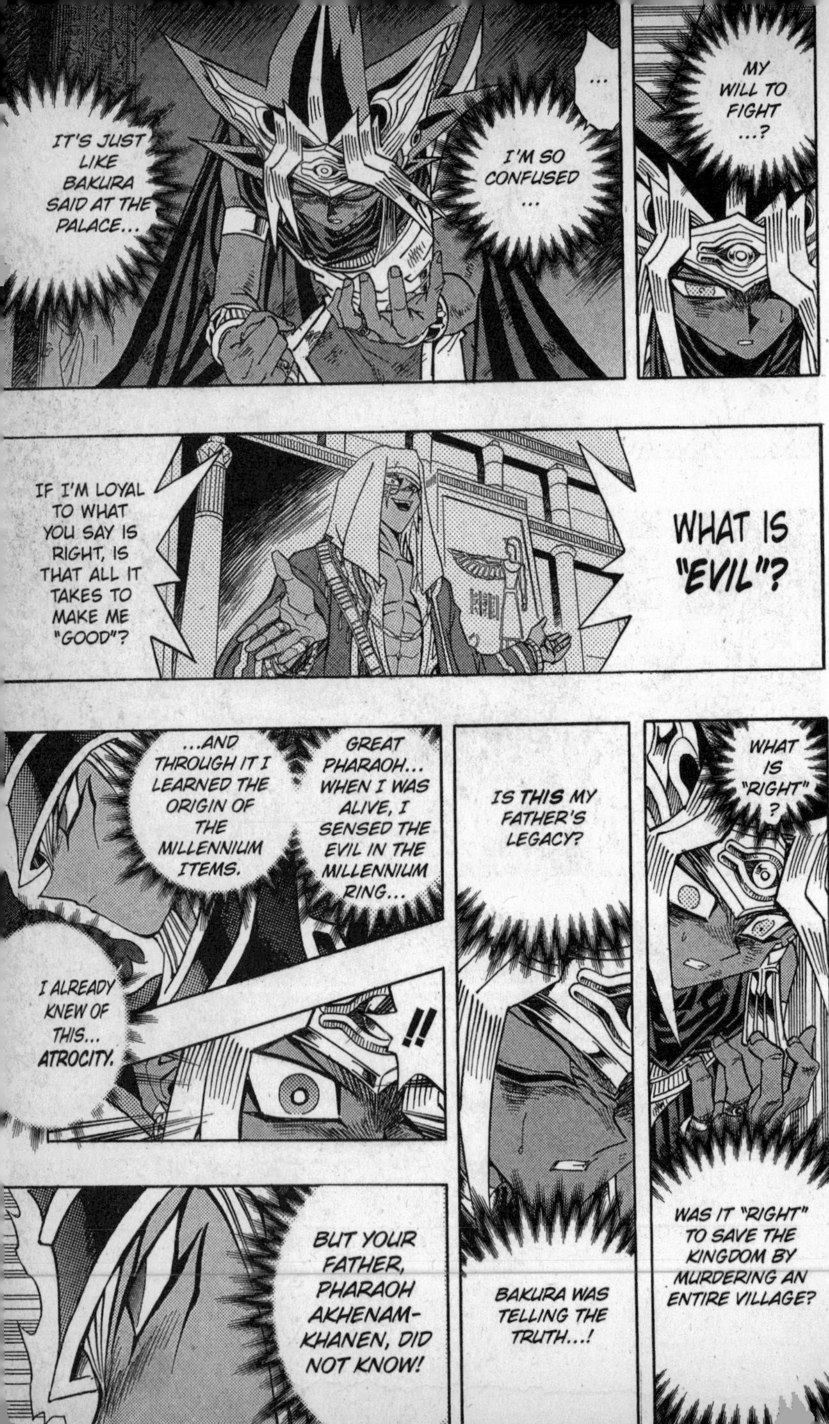
MY WILL TO FIGHT ...?
...
I'M SO CONFUSED ...
IT'S JUST LIKE BAKURA SAID AT THE PALACE...
WHAT IS "EVIL"?
IF I'M LOYAL TO WHAT YOU SAY IS RIGHT, IS THAT ALL IT TAKES TO MAKE ME "GOOD"?
WHAT IS "RIGHT" ?
WAS IT "RIGHT" TO SAVE THE KINGDOM BY MURDERING AN ENTIRE VILLAGE?
IS THIS MY FATHER'S LEGACY?
BAKURA WAS TELLING THE TRUTH...!
GREAT PHARAOH... WHEN I WAS ALIVE, I SENSED THE EVIL IN THE MILLENNIUM RING...
...AND THROUGH IT I LEARNED THE ORIGIN OF THE MILLENNIUM ITEMS.
I ALREADY KNEW OF THIS... ATROCITY.
!!
BUT YOUR FATHER, PHARAOH AKHENAM-KHANEN, DID NOT KNOW!

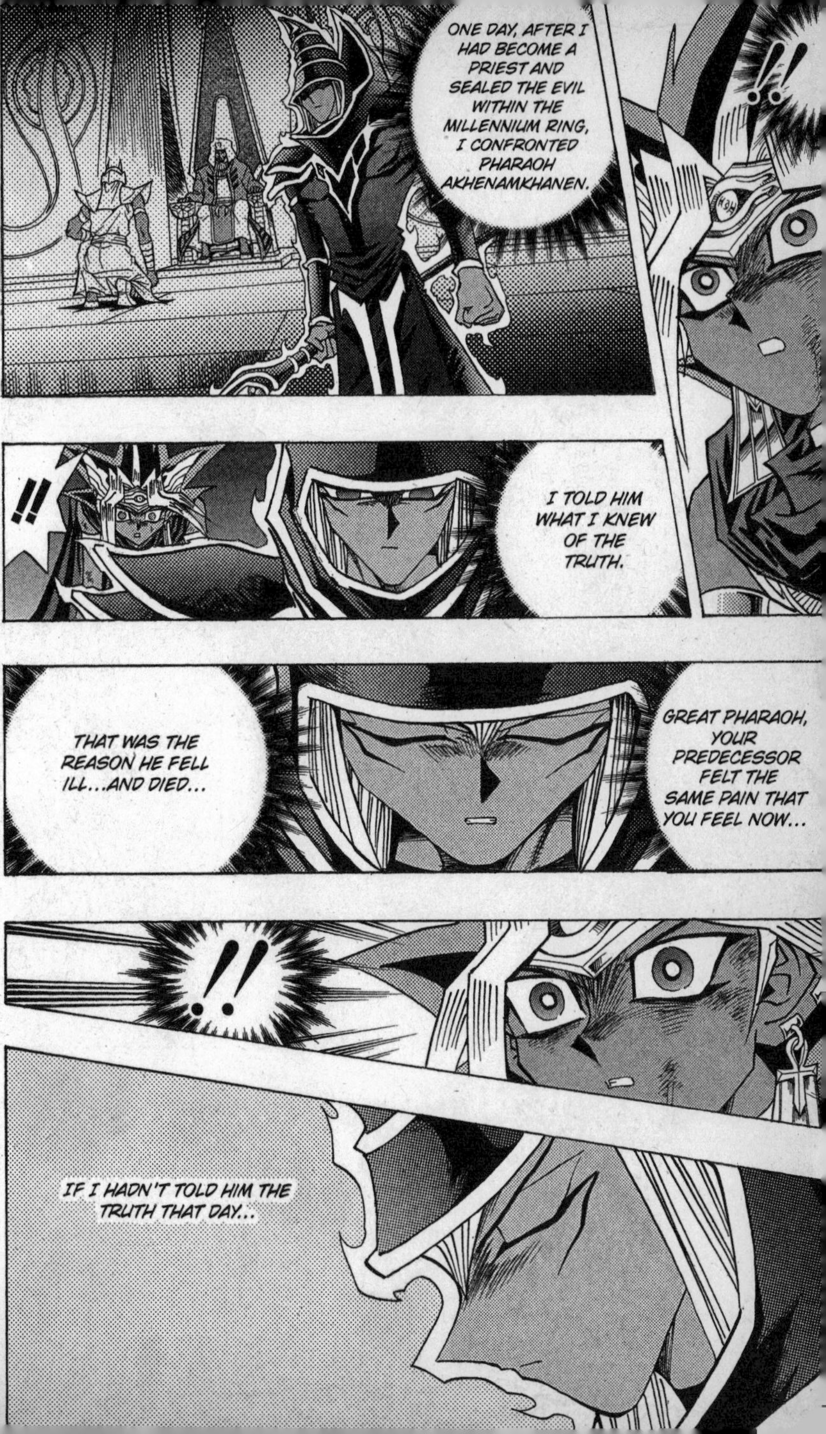
!!
ONE DAY, AFTER I HAD BECOME A PRIEST AND SEALED THE EVIL WITHIN THE MILLENNIUM RING, I CONFRONTED PHARAOH AKHENAMKHANEN.
I TOLD HIM WHAT I KNEW OF THE TRUTH.
!!
GREAT PHARAOH, YOUR PREDECESSOR FELT THE SAME PAIN THAT YOU FEEL NOW...
THAT WAS THE REASON HE FELL ILL...AND DIED...
!!
IF I HADN'T TOLD HIM THE TRUTH THAT DAY...

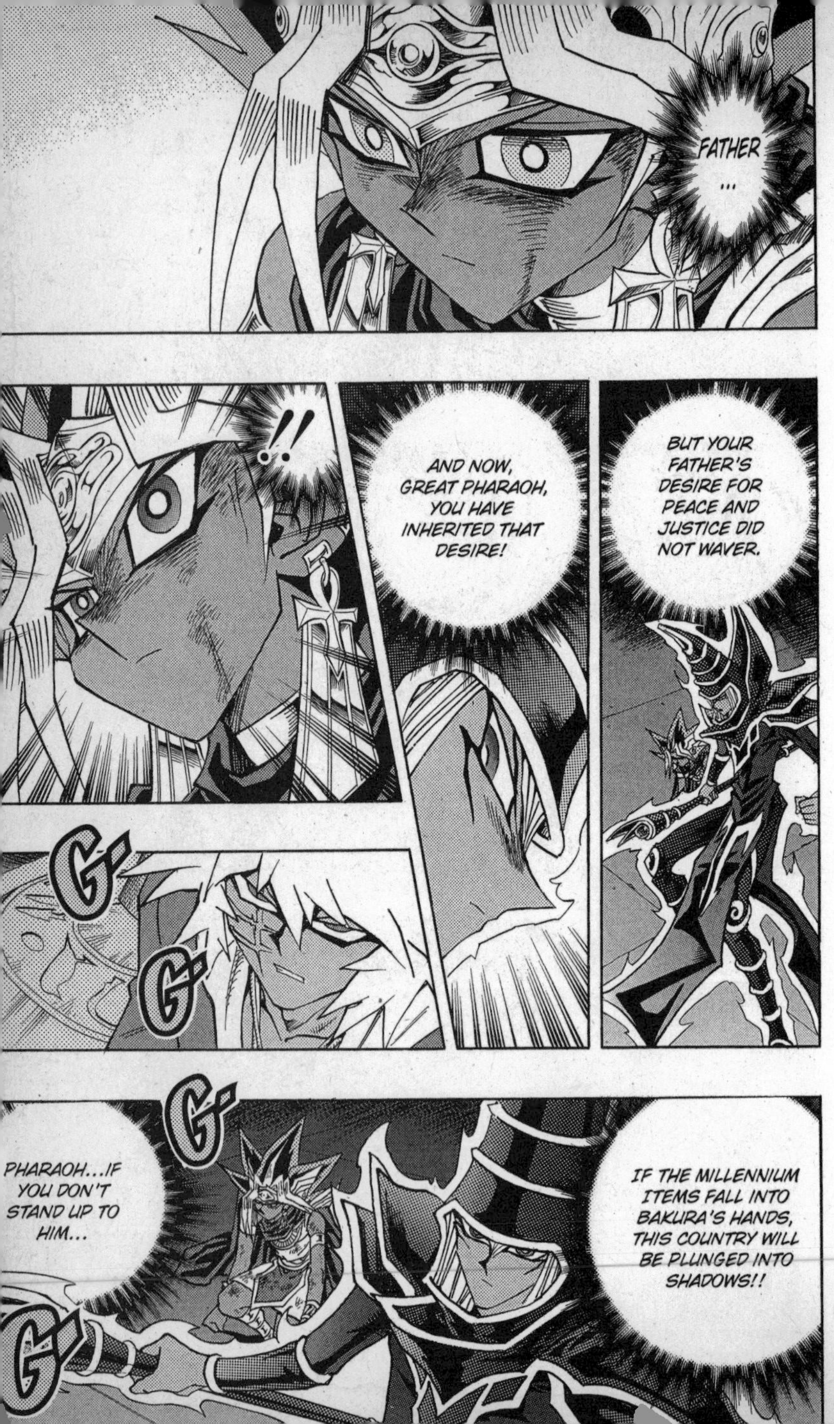
FATHER ...
BUT YOUR FATHER'S DESIRE FOR PEACE AND JUSTICE DID NOT WAVER.
AND NOW, GREAT PHARAOH, YOU HAVE INHERITED THAT DESIRE!
!!
G
G
IF THE MILLENNIUM ITEMS FALL INTO BAKURA'S HANDS, THIS COUNTRY WILL BE PLUNGED INTO SHADOWS!!
G
PHARAOH...IF YOU DON'T STAND UP TO HIM...
G

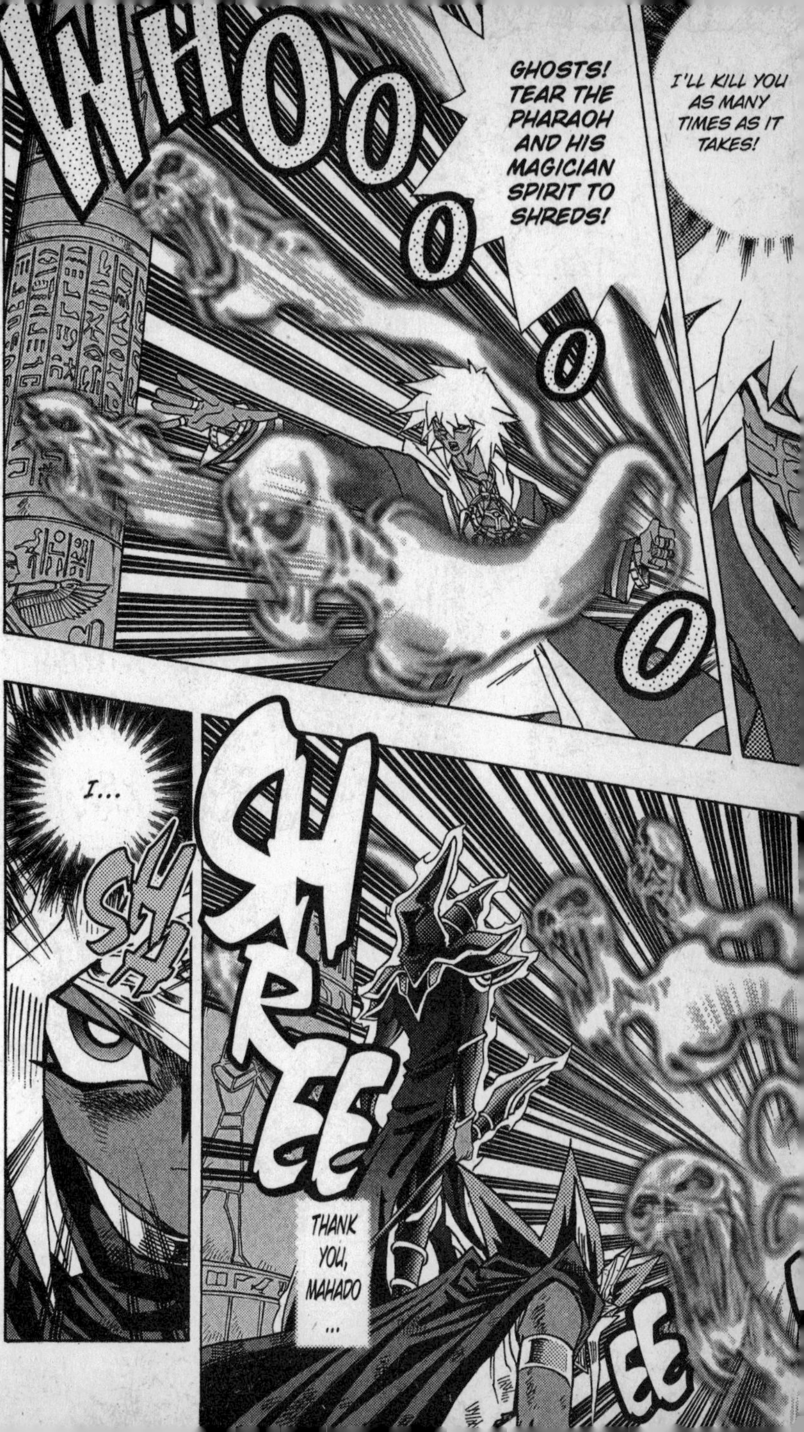
I'LL KILL YOU AS MANY TIMES AS IT TAKES!
GHOSTS! TEAR THE PHARAOH AND HIS MAGICIAN SPIRIT TO SHREDS!
WHOOOOOO
SHREE
THANK YOU, MAHADO ...
EE
I...
SHH

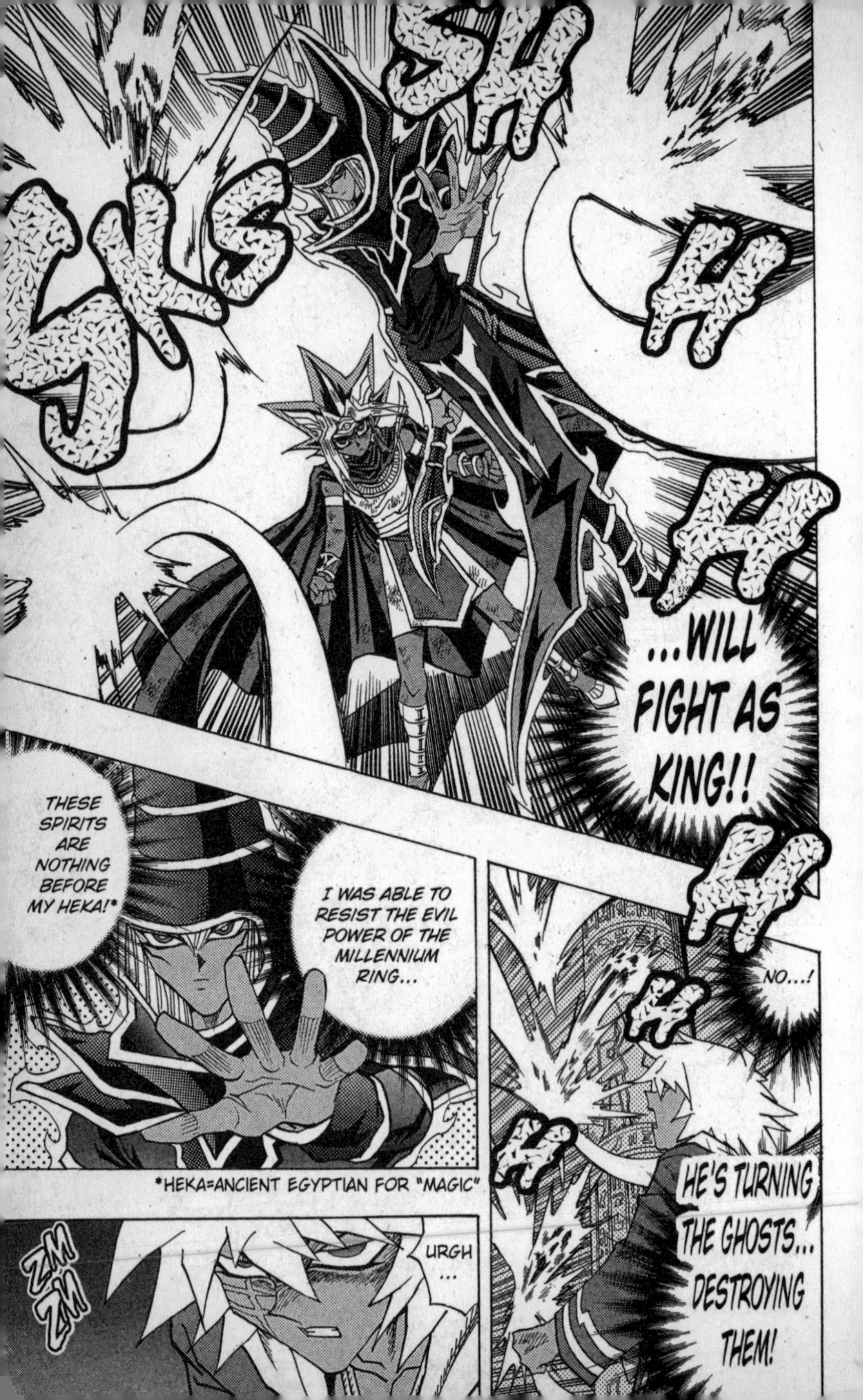
...WILL FIGHT AS KING!!
NO...!
HE'S TURNING THE GHOSTS... DESTROYING THEM!
I WAS ABLE TO RESIST THE EVIL POWER OF THE MILLENNIUM RING...
THESE SPIRITS ARE NOTHING BEFORE MY HEKA!*
*HEKA=ANCIENT EGYPTIAN FOR "MAGIC"
URGH ...
ZM ZM ZM

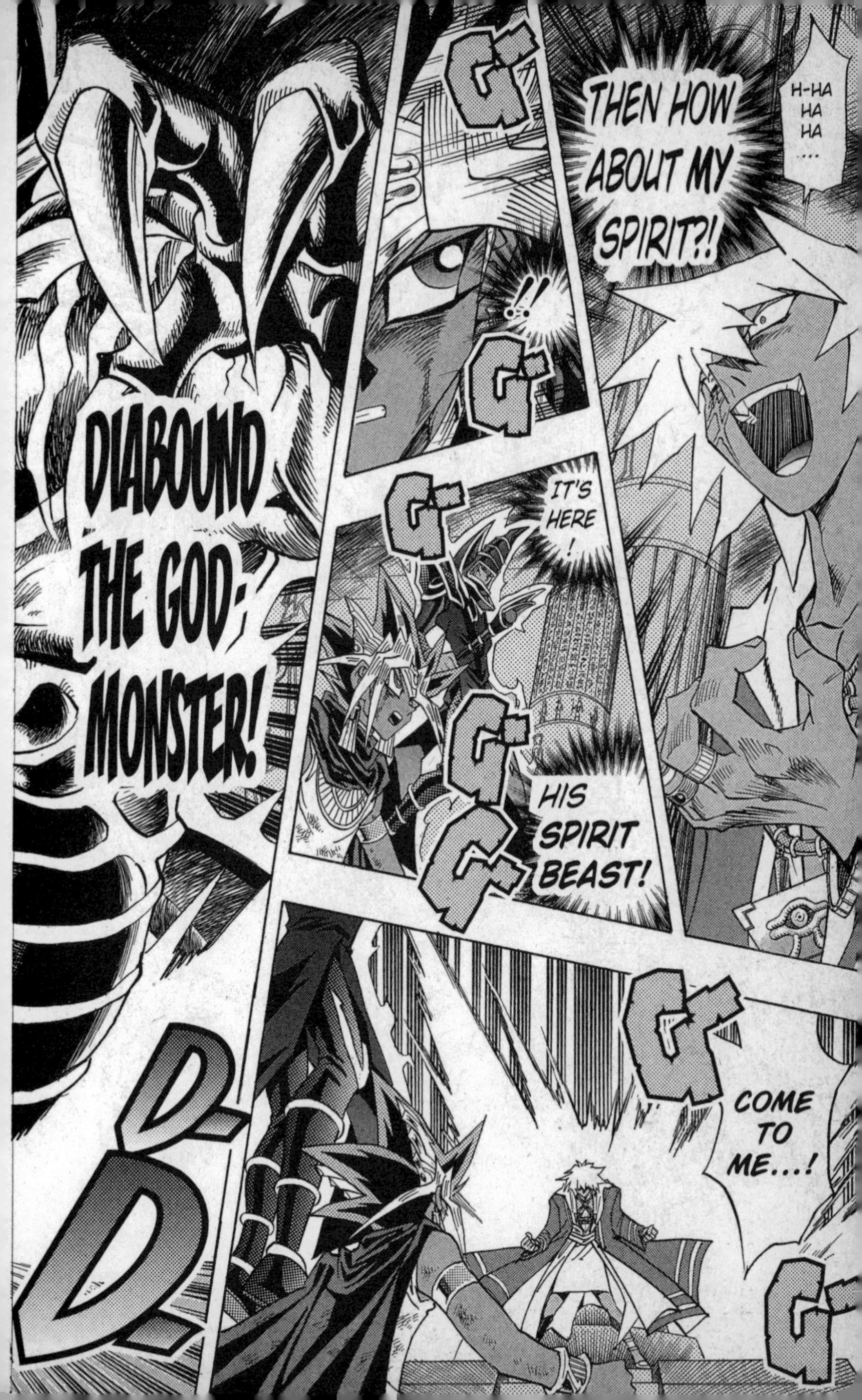
H-HA HA HA ...
THEN HOW ABOUT MY SPIRIT?!
G
!!
G
G
IT'S HERE!
G
G
HIS SPIRIT BEAST!
G
COME TO ME...!
G
DIABOUND THE GOD-MONSTER!
D
D

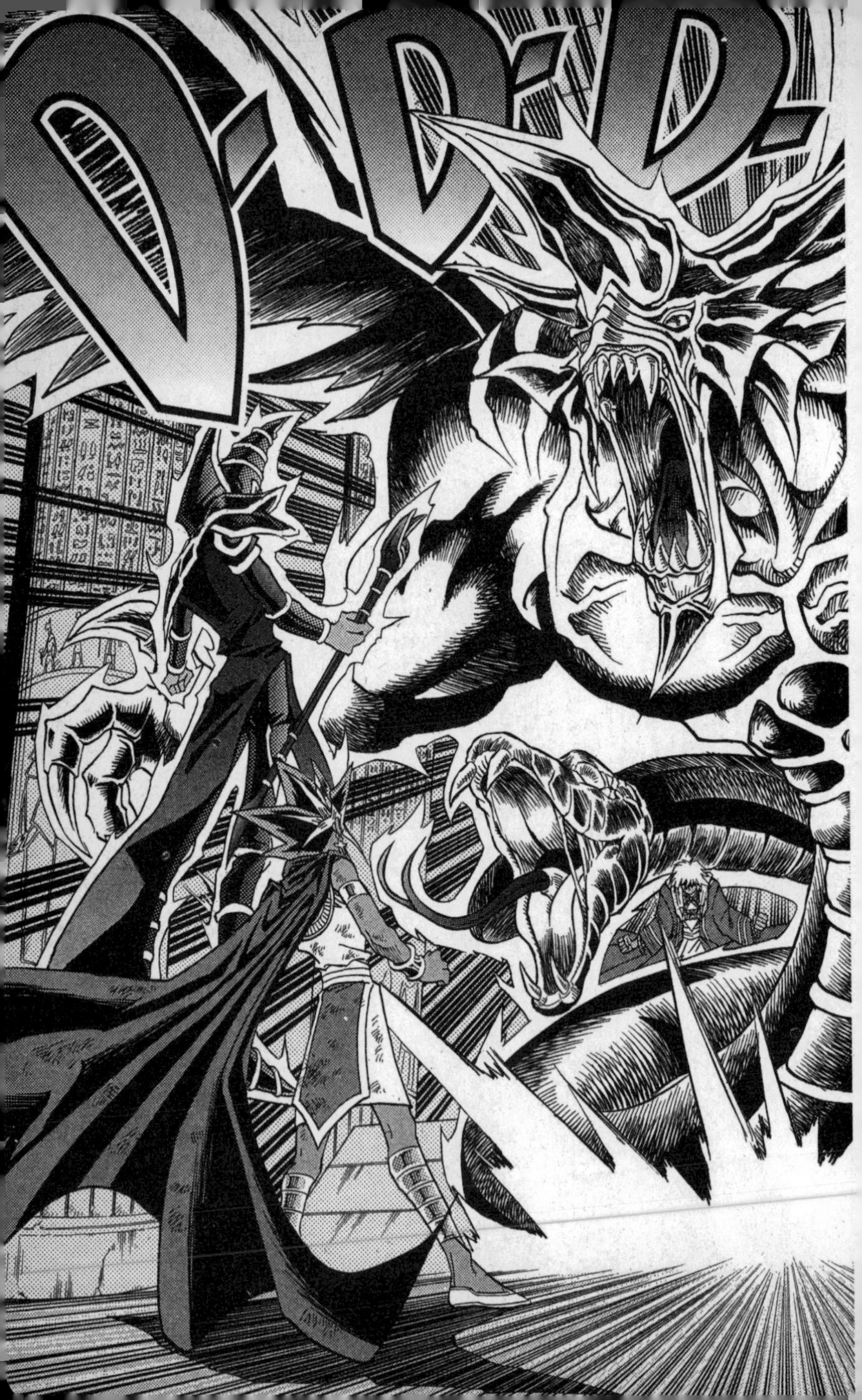

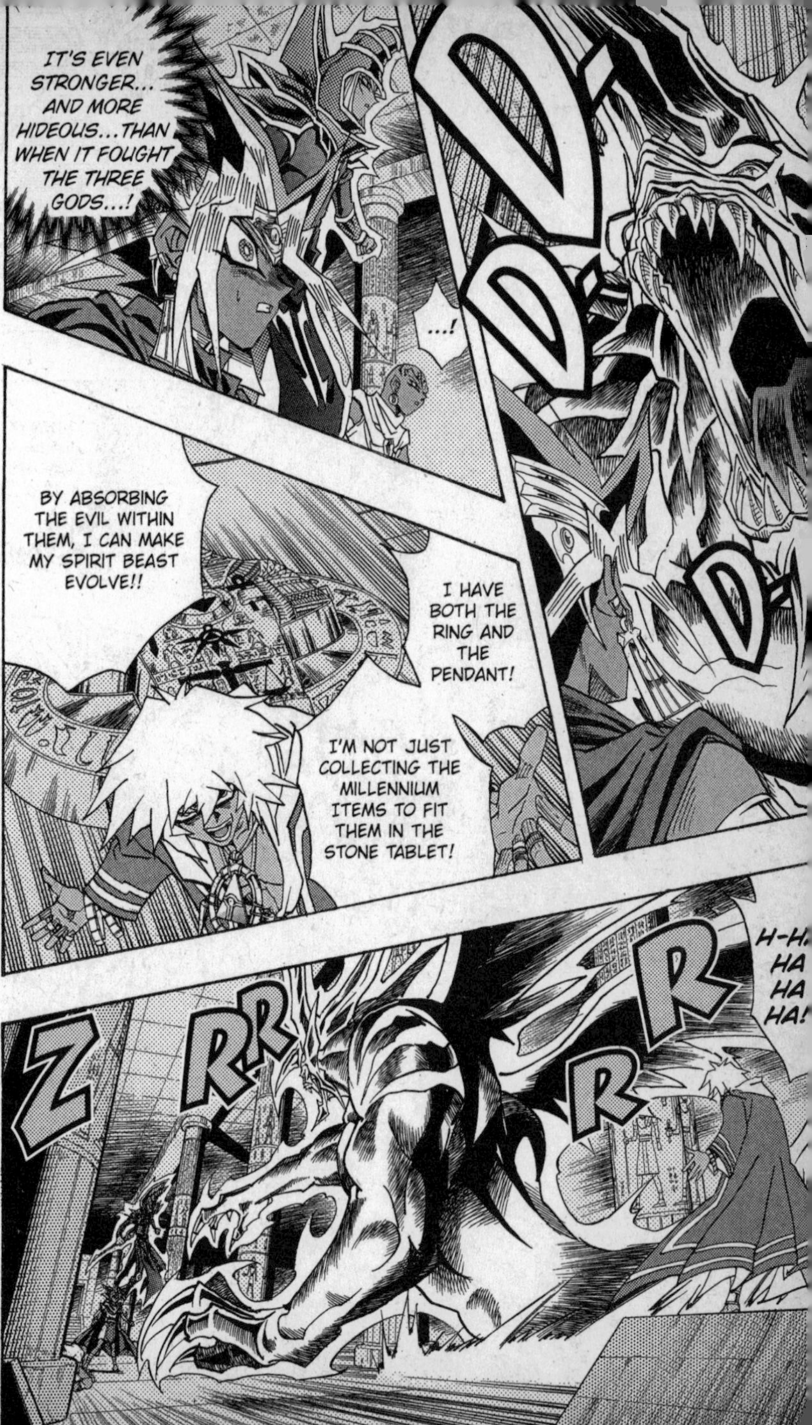
IT'S EVEN STRONGER... AND MORE HIDEOUS...THAN WHEN IT FOUGHT THE THREE GODS...!
...!
I HAVE BOTH THE RING AND THE PENDANT!
I'M NOT JUST COLLECTING THE MILLENNIUM ITEMS TO FIT THEM IN THE STONE TABLET!
BY ABSORBING THE EVIL WITHIN THEM, I CAN MAKE MY SPIRIT BEAST EVOLVE!!
H-HA HA HA HA!
ZRRRR

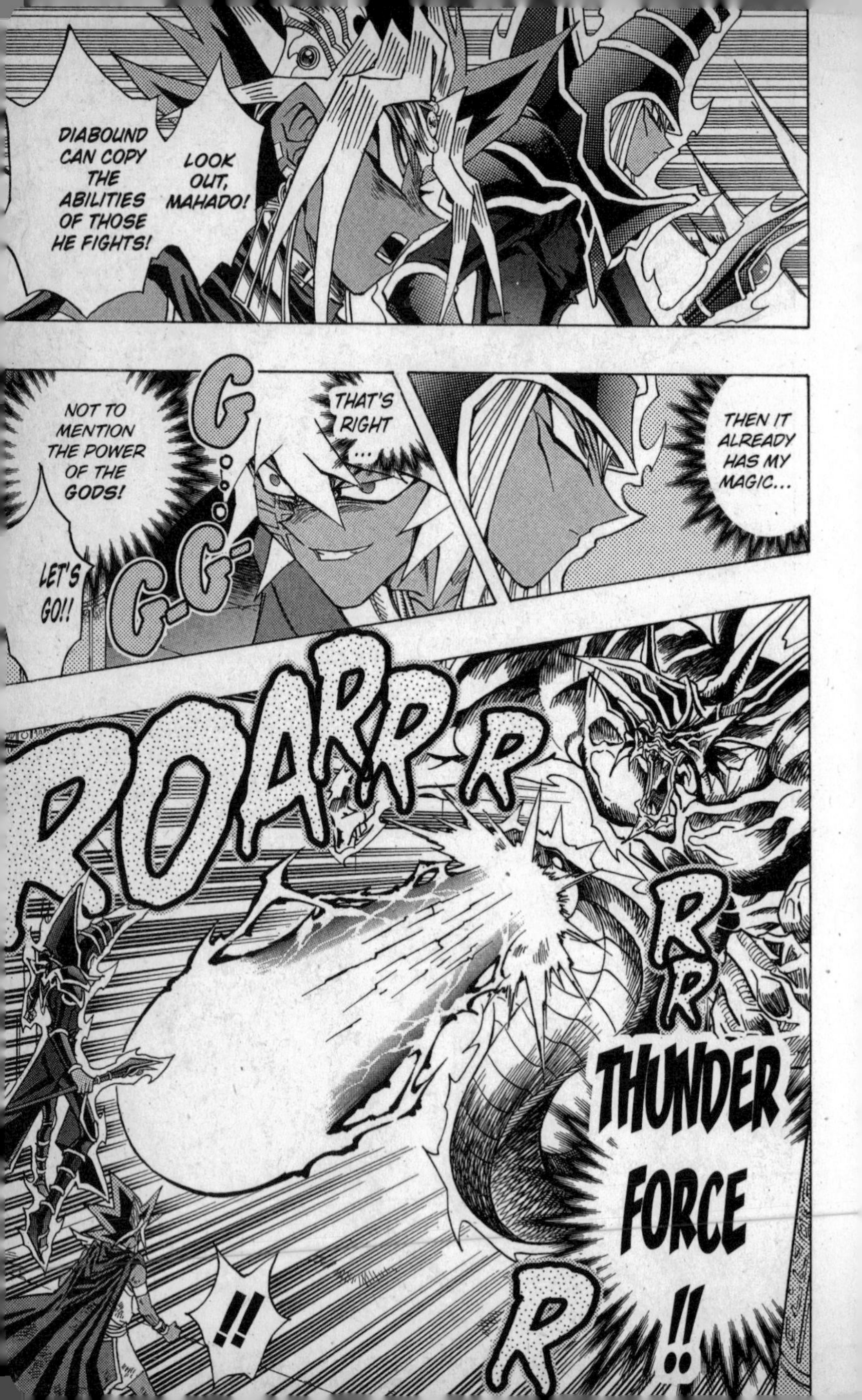
LOOK OUT, MAHADO!
DIABOUND CAN COPY THE ABILITIES OF THOSE HE FIGHTS!
THEN IT ALREADY HAS MY MAGIC...
THAT'S RIGHT...
NOT TO MENTION THE POWER OF THE GODS!
G-G-G
LET'S GO!!
ROARRRRRR
THUNDER FORCE!!
!!

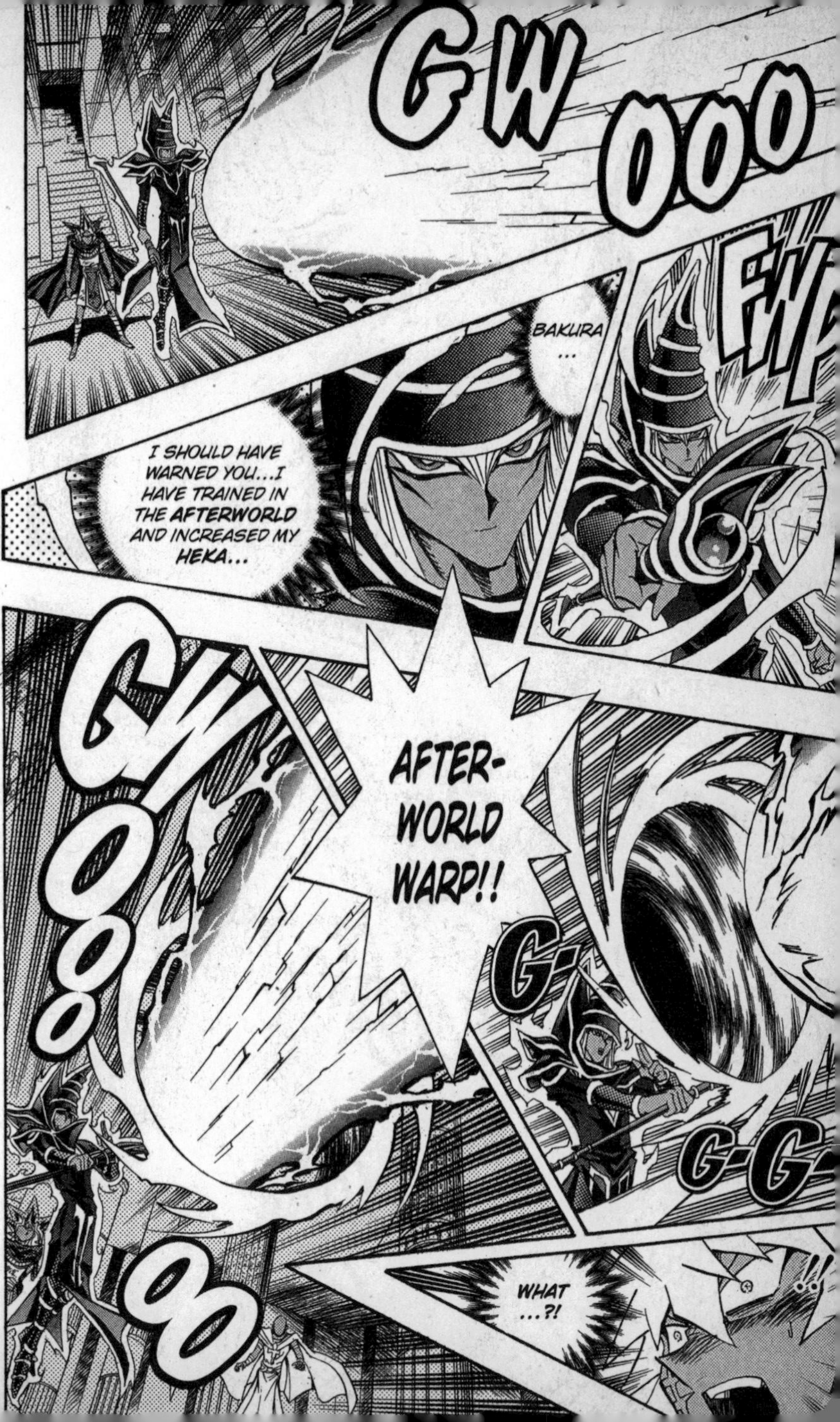
GWOOO
FW
BAKURA...
I SHOULD HAVE WARNED YOU...I HAVE TRAINED IN THE AFTERWORLD AND INCREASED MY HEKA...
AFTER-WORLD WARP!!
G-
G-G
GWOOOOOO
WHAT...?!

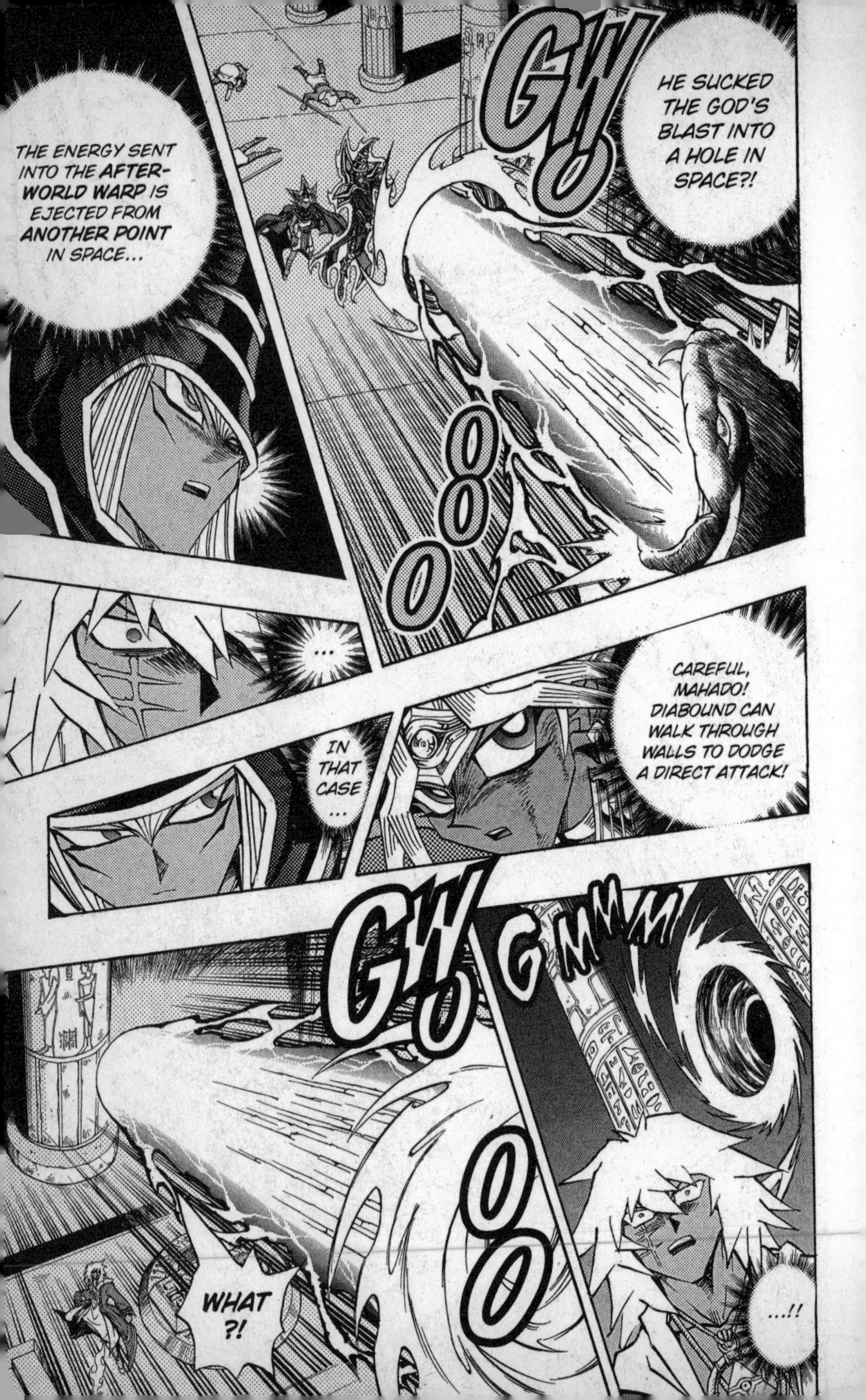
GWOOOO
HE SUCKED THE GOD'S BLAST INTO A HOLE IN SPACE?!
THE ENERGY SENT INTO THE **AFTER-WORLD WARP** IS EJECTED FROM **ANOTHER POINT** IN SPACE...
CAREFUL, MAHADO! DIABOUND CAN WALK THROUGH WALLS TO DODGE A DIRECT ATTACK!
...
IN THAT CASE ...
GMMM
...!!
GWOOOO
WHAT ?!

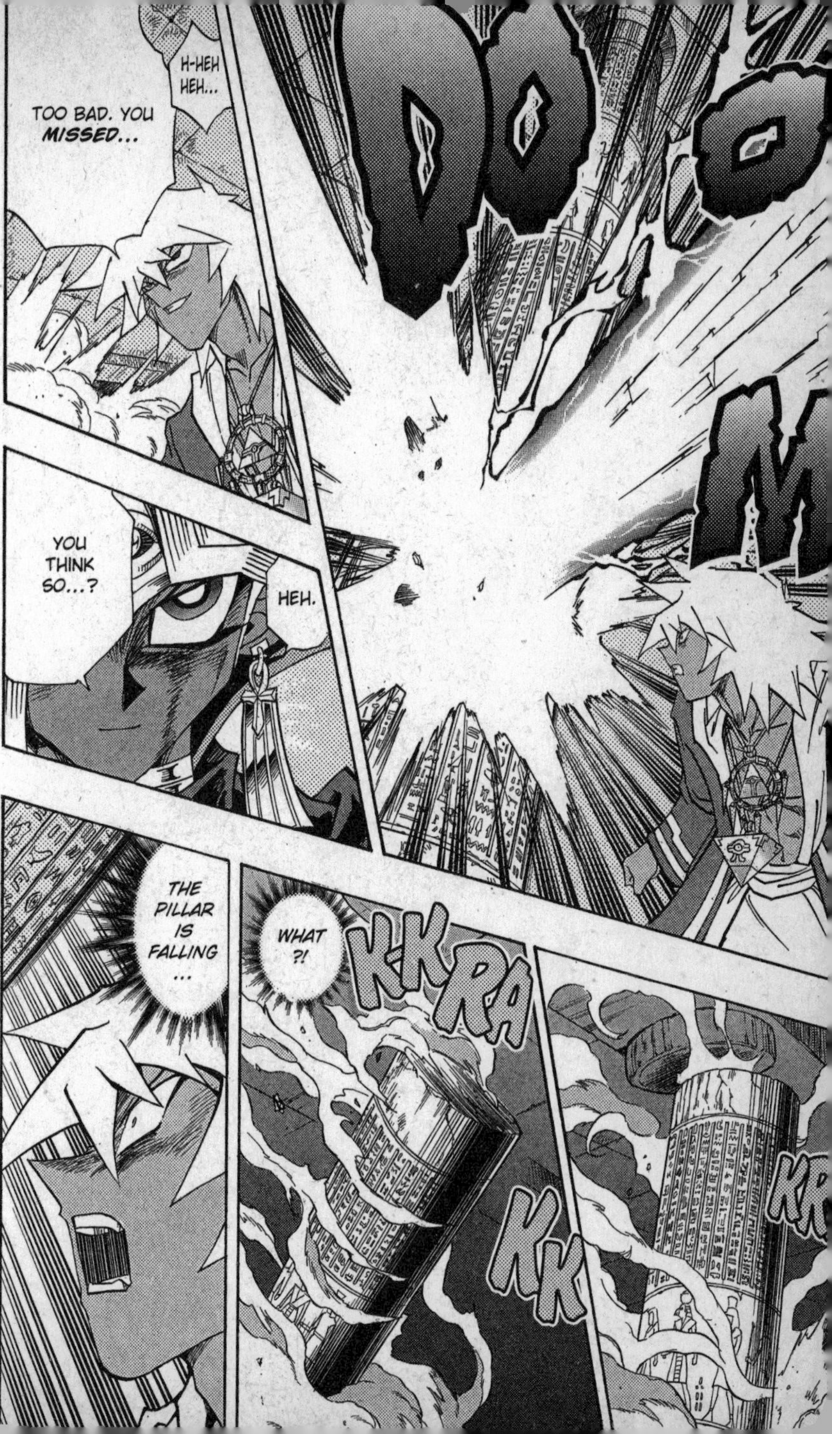
DOO
M
H-HEH HEH...
TOO BAD. YOU MISSED...
HEH.
YOU THINK SO...?
KR
K-KRA
KK
WHAT?!
THE PILLAR IS FALLING...

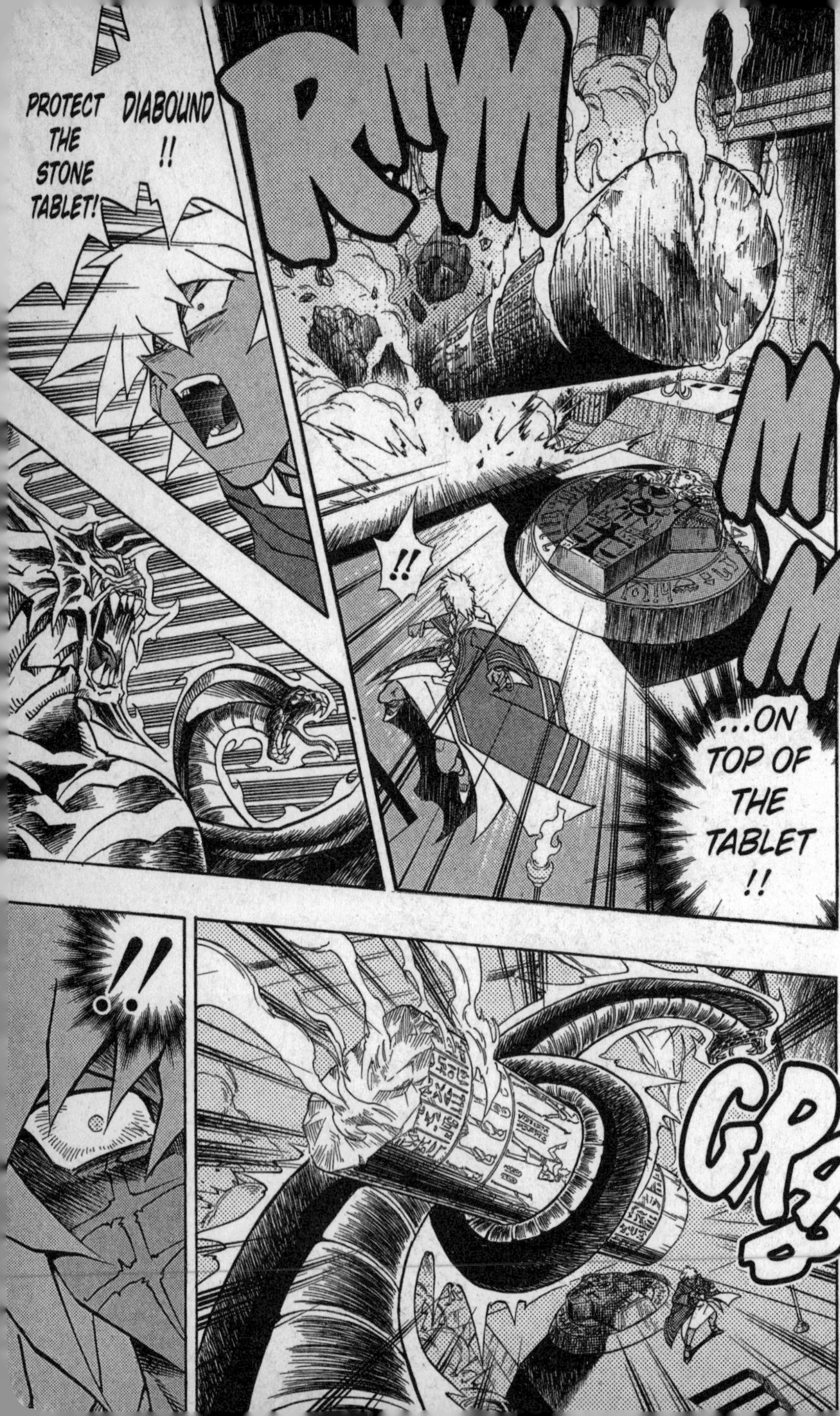
RMM
MM
!!
...ON TOP OF THE TABLET!!
DIABOUND!!
PROTECT THE STONE TABLET!
GRAB
!!

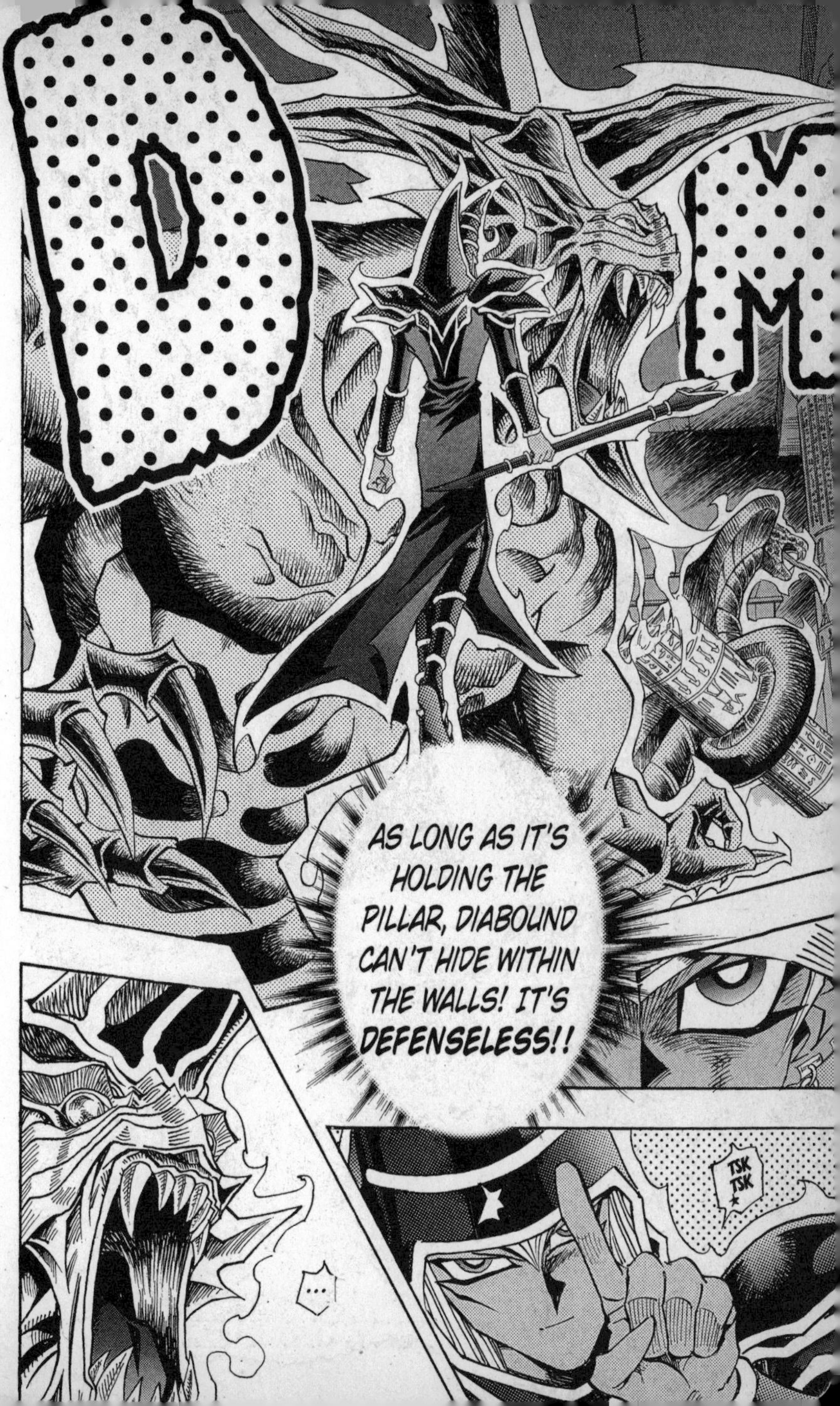
AS LONG AS IT'S HOLDING THE PILLAR, DIABOUND CAN'T HIDE WITHIN THE WALLS! IT'S DEFENSELESS!!
TSK TSK
...

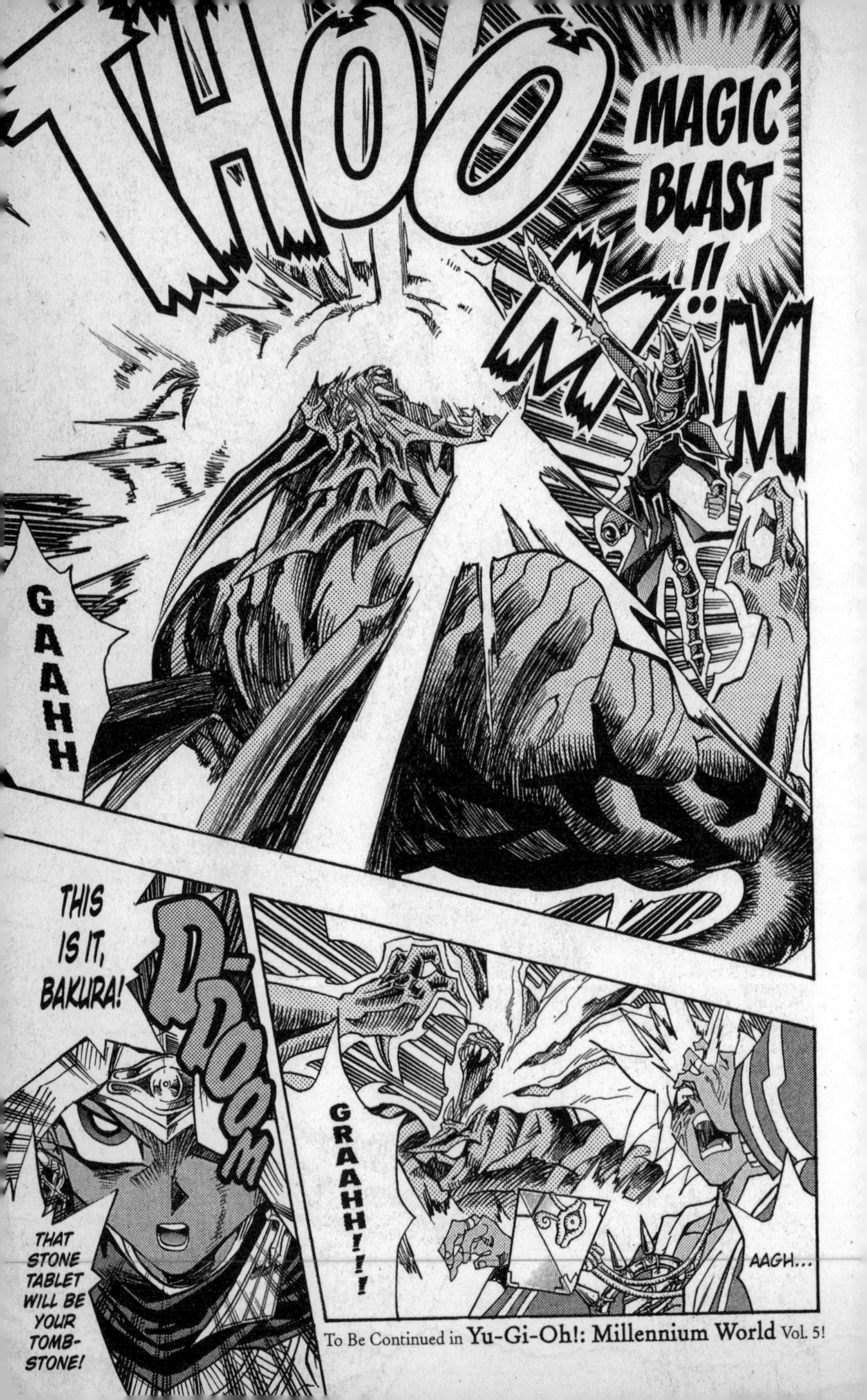
THOO
MAGIC BLAST
GAAHH
GRAAHH!!!!
AAGH...
THIS IS IT, BAKURA!
DOOOM
THAT STONE TABLET WILL BE YOUR TOMBSTONE!

To Be Continued in Yu-Gi-Oh!: Millennium World Vol. 5!

# IN THE NEXT VOLUME...

It's the end of a 3,000-year battle, as Yu-Gi-Oh and Mahado—the original Dark Magician—fight Bakura and the dreaded Diabound! Can they beat the mad tomb-robber in his underground domain, protected by the darkness and the ghosts of the restless dead? But if Yu-Gi-Oh changes the past, will the present change too? Or is something even stranger than time travel at work? The mind-blowing truth is revealed in the next volume of *Yu-Gi-Oh!: Millennium World!*

***COMING JANUARY 2007!***

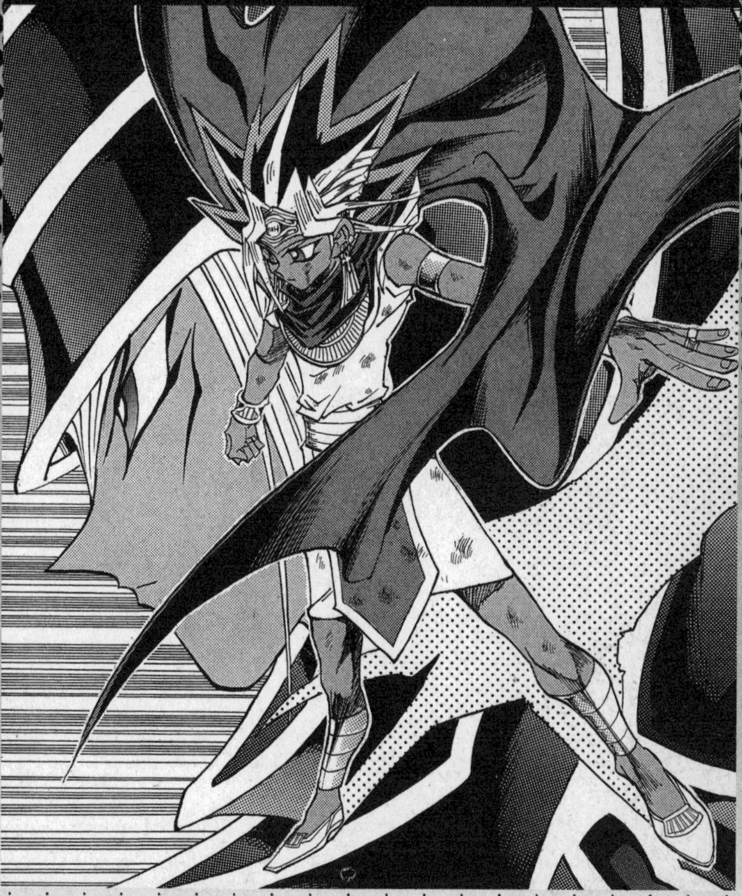

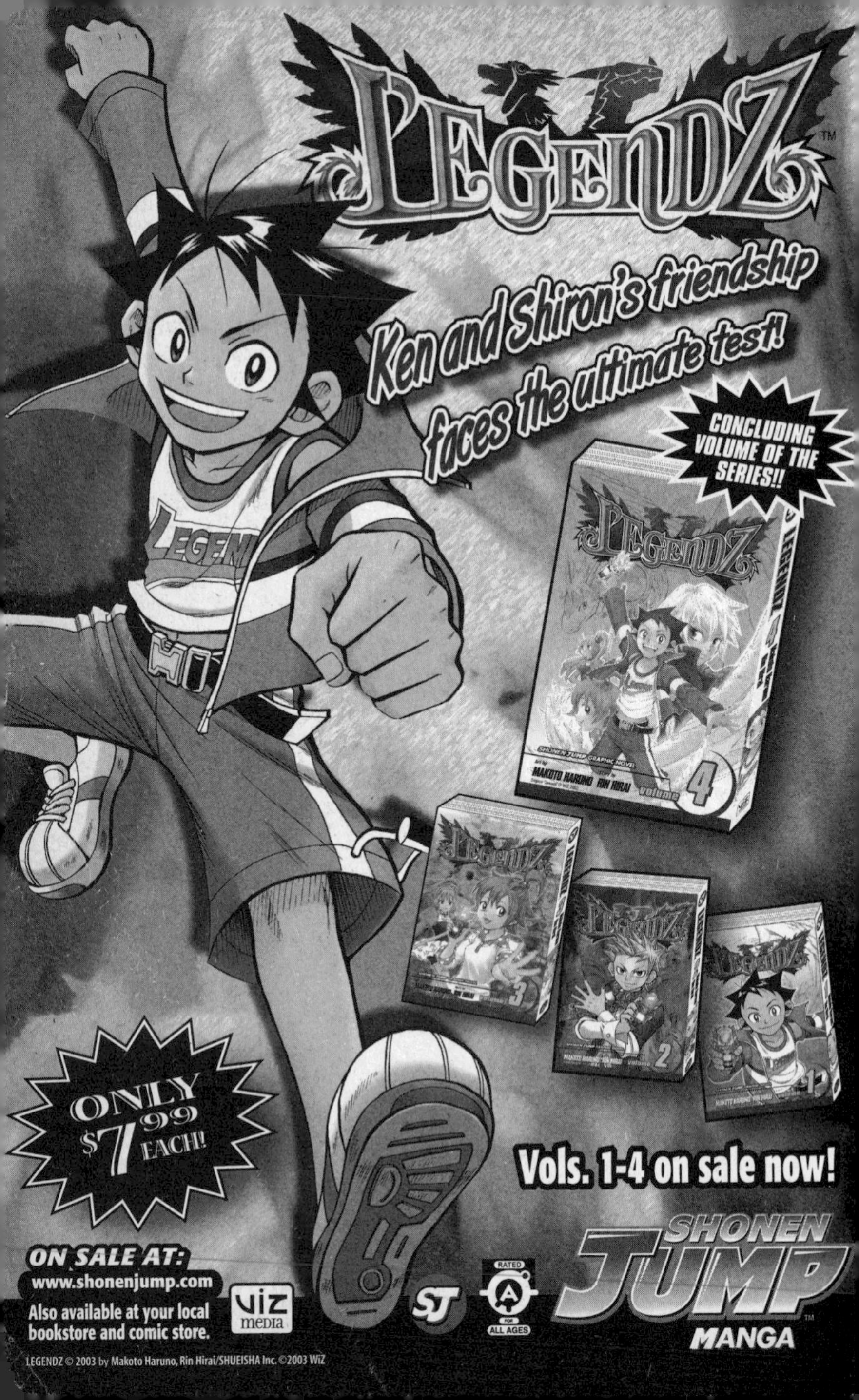
LEGENDZ™
Ken and Shiron's friendship faces the ultimate test!!
CONCLUDING VOLUME OF THE SERIES!!
ONLY $7.99 EACH!
Vols. 1-4 on sale now!
ON SALE AT:
www.shonenjump.com
Also available at your local bookstore and comic store.
viz media
SJ
RATED A FOR ALL AGES
SHONEN JUMP™ MANGA
LEGENDZ © 2003 by Makoto Haruno, Rin Hirai/SHUEISHA Inc. ©2003 WiZ

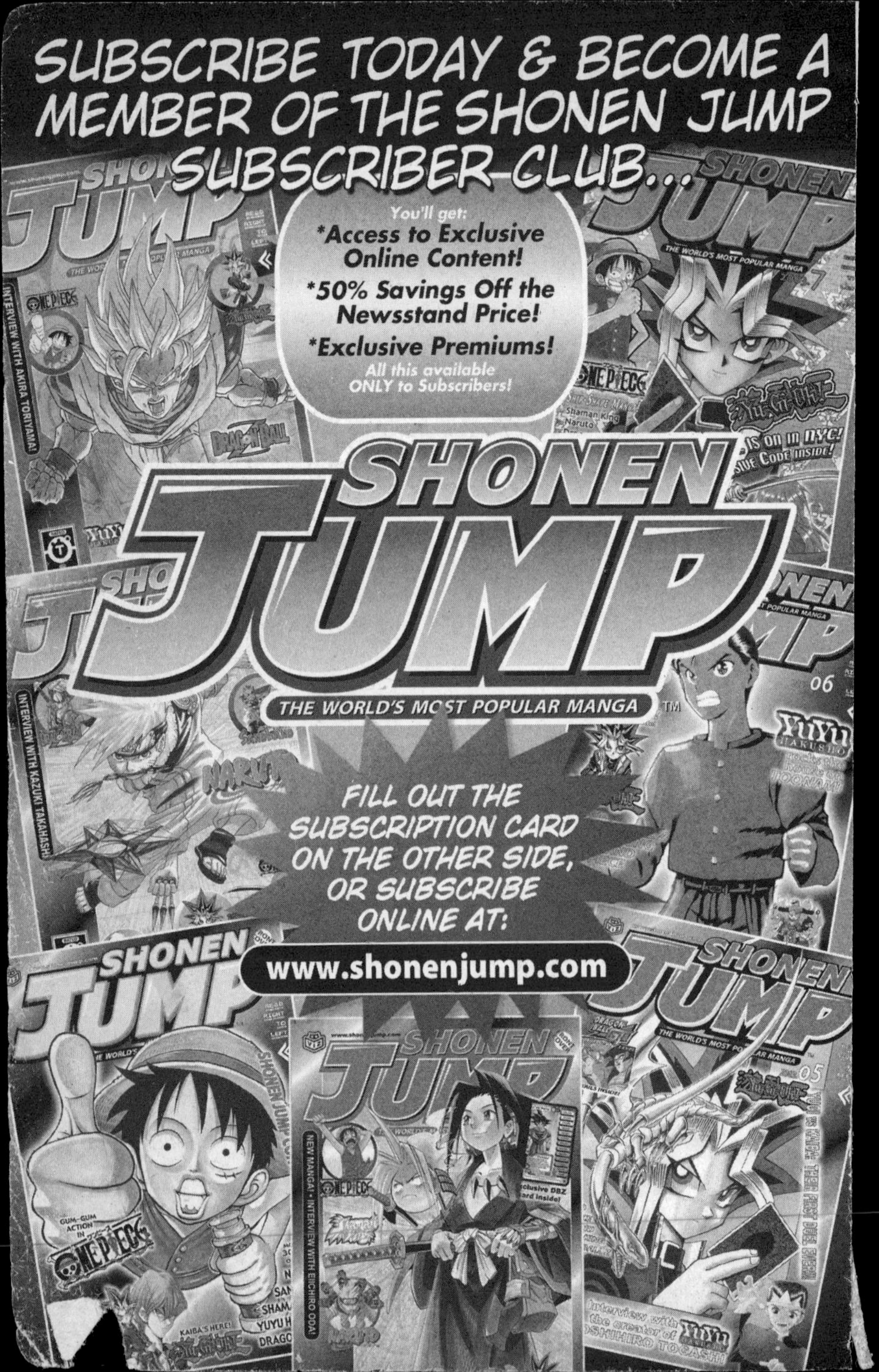
SUBSCRIBE TODAY & BECOME A MEMBER OF THE SHONEN JUMP SUBSCRIBER CLUB...
You'll get:
*Access to Exclusive Online Content!
*50% Savings Off the Newsstand Price!
*Exclusive Premiums!
All this available ONLY to Subscribers!
SHONEN JUMP
THE WORLD'S MOST POPULAR MANGA
FILL OUT THE SUBSCRIPTION CARD ON THE OTHER SIDE, OR SUBSCRIBE ONLINE AT:
www.shonenjump.com

# Save 50% off the newsstand price!

**SHONEN JUMP**

*THE WORLD'S MOST POPULAR MANGA*

SUBSCRIBE TODAY and SAVE
50% OFF the cover price PLUS
all the benefits of the S
SUBSCRIBER CLUB, exc
content & special gifts
AVAILABLE to SUBSCRIBE

**YES!** Please enter my 1 year
(12 issues) to *SHONEN JUMP* at the INCREDIBLY
LOW SUBSCRIPTION RATE of $29.95 and sign me
up for the SHONEN JUMP Subscriber Club!

Only
**$29⁹⁵!**

NAME _____

ADDRESS _____

CITY _____ STATE ___ ZIP ___

E-MAIL ADDRESS _____

☐ MY CHECK IS ENCLOSED   ☐ BILL ME LATER

CREDIT CARD:   ☐ VISA   ☐ MASTERCARD

ACCOUNT # _____ EXP. DATE _____

SIGNATURE _____

CLIP AND MAIL TO →

SHONEN JUMP
Subscriptions Service Dept.
P.O. Box 515
Mount Morris, IL 61054-0515

Make checks payable to: **SHONEN JUMP**.
Canada add US $12. No foreign orders. Allow 6-8 weeks for delivery.

**P6SJGN**   YU-GI-OH! © 1996 by Kazuki Takahashi / SHUEISHA Inc.